# ABOUT THE AUTHOR

Paul Hawkes is a lover of Greece and her beautiful countryside, in particular the magical isles with their own character and light, giving rise to the richest mythology on the planet. Paul has chosen to try to bring up to date and introduce to a much wider audience than the traditional classics perhaps our best book – certainly one of the oldest.

Paul also writes poems about the environmental crises. He came eighth in 2014 in the International Welsh Open Poetry Competition (with *TolkienWW1Thomas*) and second in 2016 (with *Shattering Earth 2016*) and again in 2022 (with *Ukraineing*). He lives in Aberteifi, by the River Teifi, near the coast of wonderfully wild south-west Wales, where the Welsh dolffins play.

Paul Hawkes

# IL-I-AD THAT LAD

AUSTIN MACAULEY PUBLISHERS™
LONDON • CAMBRIDGE • NEW YORK • SHARJAH

A CIP catalogue record for this title is available from the British Library.

ISBN 9781398462861 (Paperback)
ISBN 9781398462878 (ePub e-book)

www.austinmacauley.com

First Published 2022
Austin Macauley Publishers Ltd
1 Canada Square
Canary Wharf
London E14 5AA

*To Samantha Wynne-Rhydderch, who very kindly w(e)aved her magic wand over the tiny fragment of a poetry gene I inherited from my guardian ancestors.*

*And to the people of Ukraine, whose colours adorn the cover, along with the sea and their sandy shores.*

# ACKNOWLEDGEMENTS

E V Rieu's translation of the *Iliad* (1950), whose clear prose helped me better understand the book.

# CONTENTS

ένα

*Book 1*

# THE QUARREL

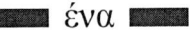

*How Achilles Agamemnon fall-out*
*at Assembly (w)hole enterprise cast(s) doubt*
*Achilles won Zeus pledge Agamemnon*
*be avenged on and army Achaean*
*Achilles self-isolates takes to heel*
*much dismay distress mates knee takes to heal*

Achilles' anger's my lasting theme | fatal flawed beach (b/r)ash t(h)rash road rage wrath meme
saying which in will of Zeus fulfilling | result Achaeans so much ill feeling
sent the gallant souls of so many no | -blemen to Hades the said Zeus' bro'
bodies as dog-meat passing birds of prey | but sing O Lady Museadonna pray
of that nasty spat King Agamemnon | and great Achilles Peleus' son
which god set a-quivering the quarrel?
'Twas angry bow-twangy son Zeus Apoll
-o Leto too who fired up the b(l)arney | when punishing King's dealings infamy
his priest Chryses deadly plague inflicting | on the army Achaeans conflicting
Chryses had come down to black Argive ships | get grips seizure daughter's hip(s)-hop-hot-lip(s)
brought along a most generous ransom | and carried with him the chaplet handsome
Archer-god on a golden staff in hand | appealed to whole Achaean boy band brand
but most of all to the host's commanders | the 'Dune' Atreides two briganders
"My lords and you Achaean warriors | hope sack Priam's town zen hen harriers
get back home in total safety | may gods Olympus grant your entreaty
only if revere Son Zeus god-Archer | by accept ransom release my daughter"
troops applauded wished see priest rewarded | respected tempting ransom accorded
but no way King Agamemnon's liking | harsh caution rudely on bike sent hiking
"Old man don't let me catch you loitering | by the ships any time their exploiting
or you may find the god's chaplet and staff | make a very poor defensive distaff
and far from my setting your daughter free | she'll see out her old age along with me
in my Argos house long way from her home | sharing my bed when not working loom comb
be off now don't provoke me any more | if for save your skin of yore shore for sure"

priest shook onomatopoeia obeyed | by wordless shore susurrating sea strayed
thinking stranger on lit(t)er-al(l) shore(ly) | littoral lateral flo(w/e) test surely
but when found self alone prayed fervently | Apollo Son Leto of Locks Lovely
"Hear me now O god of the Silver Bow | Protector of Chryse and also ho
-ly Cilla and Lord Supreme Tenedos | if ever I built you shrine Smintheus
that delighted ever burnt you fat thighs | of bull goat grant me this wish as the prize
Argives I fear even when bearing gifts | make pay with your arrows for my tear shifts"
and Phoebus Apollo now heard his prayer | flew down from Olympus fury fare fair
with bow and covered quiver on his back | and as he launched out the arrows clanged black
on the shoulder of the dart-angry god | and his descent was as in nightfall shod
sat down opposite wooden ships hollow | and with dreadful twang of his silver bow
attacked first the mules and the nimble dogs | then aimed his sharp arrows maimed lamed sea-dogs
and struck them in pain again and again | day-night fires innumerable consumed slain
nine days god's arrows rained down on the camp | on the tenth tentative troops up to ramp
at an Assembly called by Achilles | a measure of the white-armed Here's unease
prompted him in concern host Danaan | as she was witnessing its destruction
when all assembled gathering complete | great runner Achilles rises to feet
"Agamemnon my lord with plague fighting | I fear these two our strength soon benighting
that any not dead by then will be forced | give up struggle sail for home unresourced
couldn't we consult a prophet or priest | interpreter not Fr(a/e)ud of dream zeitgeist
for dreams too sent by Zeus learn from him why | Phoebus Apollo's such an angry guy?
maybe offended at some broken vow | or some failure our rites to well avow
if that's the case he might just sheep accept | or full-grown goats as savoury precept
and save us from this terrible plague-rage" | he sat down Calchas son Thestor took stage
as augur Calchas no rival in camp | past present future philatelic stamp
put on his second sight Apollo's gift | guided Troy 1,000+ ships Argive shift
loyal Argive in this spirit took floor | "Great Achilles royal lord master you're
calling me to account for Apollo | the Archer-King's wrath and I will do so
but listen to me first will you swear hence | to come forward use all your eloquence
strength to protect me? I ask this of you | well aware I'll make enemy one who
absolute authority among us | whose word is law for every Argive thus
a commoner is no match for a king | who he offends even if the said king
holds his anger in check for the moment | he'll nurse his grievance 'til anew moment
when can settle account consider then | whether my safety you guarantee then"
"Dismiss your fears now" said swift Achilles | "of any words learnt from Heaven tell these
for by Apollo Son of Zeus Calchas | in whose name you reveal oracle class
I swear that as long as I am alive | and in possession of my senses five
here by the hollow ships no Danaan | shall give you hurt not even if the man
you mean is King of Men Agamemnon | who bears the title of overlord one"
at last worthy seer plucked up courage spoke | "There's no question of any vow we broke
or shortcoming in rites the god's angry | as the King insulted his priest earthly
refusing ransom release his daughter | being reason for the present slaughter

and for that far greater one yet to come | Archer-King won't free us from scourge loathsome
until we give back the bright-eyed Lady | to holy father in no way shady
without any ransom or recompense | send holy offerings to Chryse thence
when that done we might induce him relent" | said imperial Agamemnon went
ballistic then leaping up in anger | heart seething black passion eyes flammifer
pointed first at Calchas full of menace | "Prophet evil never me word of grace
said ever ill revel in foretelling | never any prophecy fulfilling
of good just once never even made one | and now you pontificate as host's one
seer saying Archer's persecuting them | for Chryseis I refused ransom then
handsome though was and why did I refuse? | because keep her and take her home I choose
prefer her to consort Clytemnestra | quite as beautiful and no less clever
or skilful with her hands still I'm willing | give her up if seems course most fulfilling
wish to cherish my folk keep safe and sound | not perish like this but then must be found
another prize at once or left being | the sole empty-handed no proper bling
because you can see for yourselves the prize | given on way to another assize"
quick and smart Achilles leapt to his feet | "Where does your lord propose the gallant fleet
should find fresh prize for your unrivalled greed? | not heard of public fund laid by at need
the plunder we had from the towns taken | all been parcelled out all have partaken
and it is a lot more than we can ask | of the men go through all again that task
so no give girl back now as god demands | we'll quadruple compensation demands
if Zeus should ever let us enjoy ploy | gift-horse bring down the battlements of Troy"
King Agamemnon took him up at once | "A great man Achilles Prince (aside 'Ponce')
but don't think that you can trick me like that | not cajoled by mackerel catch a (s)prat
'Give up the girl'! you very boldly say | in hope of keeping your own prize safe say?
doest think I'll sit tamely by while I'm robbed? | so no if host will replace loss de-mobbed
give me fresh prize chosen to suit my taste | have no more to say if not I'll make haste
come help myself your prize or Aias' | or I will walk off with Odysseus'
and what an angry man leave behind me! | whatever let's let all that later be
for now let's run black ship down friendly sea | top crew embark creatures sacrifice see
put Chryseis of lovely cheeks on board | Councillor of ours captain of horde's hoard
Aias perhaps or Idomeneus | or that master tactician Odysseus
maybe indeed you yourself my lord thus | the most redoubtable man among us
make sacrifice win back Phoebus favour" | Achilles gave him look not of favour
"Shameless schemer profit-ability! | how can you expect the men's loyalty
in service when send raid or to battle? | what brought 'me' here Troy fight was no quarrel
they never harmed 'me' stole horses cows mine | nor ravaged any crops that deep soil mine
Phthia grows feed her men roaring seas | many dark range mounts lie between our sees
to be honest we joined up to please you | yes you you unconscionable cur you
satisfaction Menelaus and you | yet fact that's utterly ignored by you
and now comes this threat from you of all people | rob me of my hard-earned prize of battle
which was to me a tribute from the ranks | not as though ever given as much thanks
as you when the host of the Achaeans | sack some thriving city of the Trojans

heat burden of the fighting falls on me | but when comes to dealing out the booty
it's you who takes the lion's gate gape share | me return exhausted from field near bare
with something of my own however small | so now return to Phthia withal
yes that is the best thing that I can do | sail home beaked ships without further ado
see no point staying here be insulted | while pile for you luxuries exulted"
"Take to your Achilles heel's" retorted | "by all means if feeling last resorted
not begging you to stay on my account | are others with me on whom I can count
for respect Counsellor Zeus first of them | moreover of all here princely men then
you are the most disloyal to myself | sedition violence breath your life itself
though ARE top bod who made you so but God? | with your ships and men-at-arms you can sod
off home and rule only the Myrmidons | no use for your anger in cold me dons
mark my words same way Phoebus Apollo's | stealing Chryseis I now propose
to send off in my ship with my own crew | going to pay a visit to your stew
take the beautiful Briseis your prize | to make sure that you know that in your eyes
I'm the more powerful and teach others | not bandy words open defy orders
King" cut Achilles quick in shaggy breast | his heart torn between two courses which best
whether to draw his sharp sword from his side | thrust his way through the madding crowd beside
kill the King now be controlling himself | and check the impulse angry within self
so he was deep in this conflict inward | his long sword half unsheathed from its scabbard
when Athene came down to him from heaven | by the white-armed goddess Here here bidden
because she loved the two lords equally | fretting for them both at what sequel be
she stood behind seized by his golden locks | only Achilles knew no-one on locks
swung round amazed recognised her at once | so terrible brilliance eyes askonce
spoke out boldly "And why have you come here | daughter aegis-bearing Zeus? are you here
see arrogance my lord Agamemnon? | say bluntly I put no idle threat on
stands pay for this outrage with his death cries" | "I came from heaven" replies she Flashing Eyes
"in hope of bringing you to your senses | Here goddess disturbance space-time senses
sent me down both loves equally vetting | this quarrel between you for both fretting
come now give up this strife take hand from sword | sting him instead from your great word horde hoard
tell him exactly what you mean to do | and here now is a prophecy for you
day shall come gifts three times as valuable | as all that you have lost until now will
be laid at your feet payment this outrage | be advised by us hold hand in outage"
"Lady" replied Achilles great runner | "you two command must obey however
angry may be it does better for him | man listens to gods listened to by them"
with that checked his great hand on silver hilt | drove long sword back into scabbard full tilt
obeys Athene off to Olympus truce | and the palace of aegis-bearing Zeus
where she rejoined the rest of the Pantheon | not that Achilles was the appeased one
rounded on King again with bitter taunts | "Drunken sot dog-eyed courage doe's soul haunts!
never guts arm self go into battle | with the men join captains in kerfuffle
sooner die pays you better stay in camp | filching prizes of all who ramp up amp
against you flourishing at your folks' cost | as they're too feeble to resist just lost
feeble indeed or this act brigandage | would prove to be your last stand on this page

but mark my words will take a solemn oath | look at this staff cut from stem oak not loath
in hills never put out leaves twigs again | billhook stripped of bark foliage no gain
it will sprout no more moreover the men | who in name Zeus safeguard us as lawmen
Judges of nation hold in hands open | by this I swear not choose better token
day coming when Achaeans one and all | will miss me sorely to despair will fall
be powerless to help them as they fall | in their hundreds Hector killer men all
then you will tear your heart out in remorse | treat best man venture with contempt and worse"
flung down golden-studded staff with a thud | leaving Atreides stunned where he stood
on the other side at him to thunder | but Nestor now leapt up he a wonder
of courteous word clear-voiced orator | from sandy Pylos whose speech ran sweeter
than honey off his tongue already seen | two generations sacred Pylos scene
now ruled third filled benevolent concern | spoke "Enough make Achaean yearn earn urn turn
in despair! how happy Priam and sons | would be how would rejoice all the Trojans
if they were to hear of this rift between | two lead policy war Argive screen scene
you are both my juniors and what's more | mixed in past men of stature even more
than you never failed carry weight with them | finest ever seen or shall see men then
Peirithous Dryas Shepherd of People | Caenus Exadius near-immortal
Polyphemus Theseus hero's fame | strongest men to whom Earth has given name
strongest men versus strongest enemy | savage mountain tribe destroyed utterly
for those left home sandy Pylos to join | travelled far at their request them rejoin
played independent part in their campaign | all today would battle those men in vain
still they listened and followed my advice | you two must do or be trapped in a vice
won't lose by it King forget privilege | your rank don't rob him of girl civil pledge
army gave him her let him keep his prize | lord Achilles drop contentious assize
through authority from Zeus king sceptered | special claim respect be one's acceptered
you with goddess Mother may be stronger | yet he better rule of more counts longer
so be appeased my lord Atreides | I beg you relent towards Achilles
our mighty bulwark in stress of battle" | "My venerable lord no-one could cavil
at what you say but this man wants to get | whip-hand over all wants to lord it yet
play the king give each of us our orders | though I know one who won't take such orders
what if gods did make him great man of spear? | entitles use insulting language here?"
here noble Achilles broke in on King | "Pretty nincompoop craven me calling
if yield all points no matter what you say | lead the rest I've done have you to obey
and here's something else for you to ponder | not going fight you anyone yonder
with my hands for this host-gifted girl's sake | you gave her to me now back do you take
but of all have beside my good black ship | you shall not of a single thing me strip
come now and try so that the rest may see | what happens as then your blood will soon be
flowing in a dark stream right down my spear" | two stood up when war of words over here
dismissed Assembly by fleet Achaean | Achilles with Patroclus and his men
made his way back to his trim ships and huts | while King launched a fast vessel from the struts
he chose twenty top oarsmen to man her | after embarking cattle as offer
to the god fetched Chryseis lovely cheeks | put her on board where Odysseus the sleek's

the captain and when everyone was in | along the highways of sea Roda in
King made folk purify selves by bathing | and when from bodies the filth been laving
made rich sacrifice bulls goats Apollo | shore unharvested sea and to follow
odours savoury curling smoke to sky | while his men engaged on these duties high
in the camp King didn't forget quarrel | the threat he'd made at meeting to Achill
-'es called on obedient squires herald | "Go to hut son of Peleus Unchil(le)d
to take lady Briseis bring here | if nay-says come in force to enforce clear
will be all the worse for him" sent them off | stern injunction in their ears put them off
as the two men made their unwilling way | along the shore of the barren seaway
until reached the Myrmidons' camp and ships | where found prince self sitting by his black ship's
hut not pleased see them indeed well off-peed | came halt before him to address at need
to say what wished too timid and abashed | but he knew without being told and trashed
the silence "Hail heralds I welcome you | come forward for my quarrel's not with you
but who sent you fetch Briseis the King | will you the lady Patroclus out bring
my lord and hand her over to these men? | be my witnesses I shall count on them
before the happy gods before mankind | and before king himself of brutal kind
if Achaeans ever need me again | to save them from that madman's raving brain
if he had ever learnt to look ahead | be wondering now how to save the head
of his army when fighting by the ships" | Patroclus brought girl out bargain chip slip's
from hut Briseis of the cheeks lovely | gave her two men made their way girl lonely
unhappy back along line ships shot cheap's | withdrawing from his men Achilles weeps
sat down by himself on shore of grey sea | looked across the wilderness-watery
waste-land stretched out arms poured out prayers Mother | "Since you a goddess gave me life Mother
if just for while surely Olympian | owes me some kind regard but pays me none
let me be flouted by Agamemnon | stolen my prize has her with him anon"
prayed wept heard him did his Lady Mother | while sat in depths of sea with old Father
rose swiftly from grey water like a mist | came weeping son big girl's blouse well off-pis(s)te(d)
she stroked him with her hand and spoke to him | "My child why these tears? why such grieving grim?
do not keep you sorrow just to yourself | tell me so we may share as communal self"
Achilles of swift feet sighed heavily | "You know so why should I tell whole story
Thebe went tore sacred city asunder | sacked the place and brought back all our plunder
which the host shared out in the way proper | chose Chryseis lovely cheeks show-stopper
as a special gift for Atreides | Chryses priest Phoebus Archer-god comes pleads
by ships bronze-clad Achaeans for freedom | of his daughter brought generous ransom
chaplet Archer on golden staff in hand | importuned whole Argive host in his stand
but chiefly its two chiefs the Atreidae | troops showed by their applause cries of "Aye Aye"
that they wished to see the priest respected | see the tempting ransom be accepted
but this no way Agamemnon's liking | in his ears a-stern warning sent packing
about coming near the ship's rear anchor | and so the old man went home in anger
Apollo listened prayers keenly cleary | because he did love the old man dearly
let wicked arrows fly Argive army | men fell thick fast balmy army barmy
as Apollo the archer's shafts rained down | on every part of the scattered camp-town

at last a seer understood the Archer's | will explained in full the matter to us
I rose straight advised propitiate god | made King mad threatened me called me a sod
and now he has just carried out his threat | bright-eyed Argives take girl Chryse in sweat
in ship and with offerings for the god | king's heralds just left this home-from-home sod
with Briseis who army gave to me | protect your son if have power any
to Olympus if done or said made warm | heart Zeus remind him as you pray that norm
e g father's house oft heard you loudly | say how you alone among gods proudly
saved Zeus back when Darkener of the Skies | from an inglorious fate that near lies
when clique rebellious Olympian | 'twas Here Pallas Athene and Poseidon
had been plotting throw him into chains | you saved from such indignity distrains
you quickly summoned to high Olympus | monster ton arms gods call Briareus
man Aegaeon giant more power than | even his father and squatted by Son
of Cronos with such a great show of force | gods Zeus free slink-flee in terror perforce
sit by him clasp knees remind him of that | persuade if can help the Trojans so that
he flings the Achaeans back on their ships | pen in against sea slaughter amidships
would teach them to appreciate their King | Agamemnon son Atreus making
him realise just what a fool he was | insult noblest Roamer all warriors"
"My son my son! for this nursed ill-starred child? | at least ought left you carefree at ease mild
beside the ships since Fate has given you | so short life so little time great deeds do
but it seems that you are not only doomed | early death but miserable life consumed
unlucky day brought you into the world | I'll go snow-capped Olympus tale unfurled
be tell Zeus Thunderer all this myself | and see if I can just move him himself
stay by gallant ships keep up your feuding | with Argives take no part in fight brooding
yet yesterday Zeus left for Ocean Stream | worthy Ethiopians at their dream
banquet and all the gods went with him | but twelve days he'll be back Olympus limb
then you may rest assured that I shall go | to his Bronze Palace where I will then throw
myself at his feet convinced he'll hear me" | Thetis left son grieve for gentle lady
who they'd just before forced him to give up | meanwhile Odysseus and men had got up
to Chryse with the sacred offerings | brought craft into the soundings deep profferings
of the port and so they then furled the sail | stowed it in the black ship's hold dropped mast rail
into her crutch neat by down her forestays | rowed her to berth cast anchor made fast stays
hawser and then jumped out onto the beach | cattle for Archer-god brought within reach
Chryseis stepped ashore from deep-sea ship | Odysseus of nimble wits led the strip
of girl to altar gave back to father | "Noble Chryses Agamemnon order
made of me to bring you back your daughter | and to make ceremonial offer
to Phoebus on the Danaans' behalf | in hope pacify god at least by half
he who's struck their army a grievous blow" | handed lady to her father who so
joyously welcomed return his daughter | the offerings destined to do honour
to the god were then quickly set in place | around the well-built altar-piece fair space
the men then rinsed their hands and there took up | sacrificial grains Chryses lifted up
his arms prayed aloud for them "Hear me pray | God of Silver Bow Protector Chryse
and of holy Cilla and Lord Supreme | of Tenedos! must go on with this meme

my last petition found you kind indeed | and you showed your regard for me at need
struck a mighty blow at Argive army | and now grant me a second wish prithee
save the Danaans from their dreadful scourge" | thus old man prayed Phoebus heard this urge surge
when they'd made their petitions scattered grain | drew back animals' heads again again
slit throats flayed and cut pieces from the thighs | wrapped them in folds of a mighty fat size
and laid raw meat above them these pieces | burning on the faggots the old priest is
while sprinkled red wine over the flames' brim | and the young men then gathered around him
with five-pronged forks clasped firmly in their hands | when the thighs burnt up and they had laid hands
on inner parts carved rest to small pieces | and with skewers everyone there pierces
roasted them thoroughly and drew them off | their work done the feast ready for the off
they fell to on the meal with a good will | in which all of them there had shares equal
when their thirst slaked with food stuffed to the brim | stewards filled mixing-bowls wine to the brim
first pouring out a few drops in their cups | served whole company 'til up in their cups
rest of day these young Argive warriors | made music to the god as appeasers
praising the Great Archer in lovely song | and Apollo listened with delight long
and when the sun had set and darkness fell | lay down by hawsers of ship as-sleep fell
but soon as Dawn lit East with rosy hands | set sail for great Argive camp with-all hands
taking advantage of a friendly breeze | the Archer-god sent them to passage ease
they put up their mast and spread the white sail | struck full by wind swelled out beyond the pail
and a dark wave hissed loudly round her stem | as the vessel gathered pace and sped them
through the choppy seas forged ahead on course | so returned to great camp on course of course
where dragged black ship high up on mainland sands | and then underpinned her with long prop-stands
this done scattered to huts and ships several | now all this time the great runner Achill
-'es been sitting by fast ships anger nursing | not just adverse reaction reversing
to the general fighting but visiting | of the Assembly no single meeting
though at that place a man can win renown | he just stayed where he was on his own down
eats heart out sound fury fight long fasting | eleven days dawn twelfth everlasting
gods returned in full strength to Olympus | with at their head the mighty Zeus and thus
Thetis son's orders in full adorning | now from sea deeps emerged in the morning
rose into the broad sky reached Olympus | found all-seeing Zeus as wont made use thus
of seat away from rest on the topmost | of many peaks fair Olympus plays host
she sank to ground beside him put left arm | around his knees and then raised her right arm
to touch his chin and thus her petition | made then "Of Cronos Noble Royal Son
if ever served you well among the gods | by word or deed grant me wish tilt the odds
for my son already waged early death | Agamemnon insulted him to death
he's stolen his prize kept her for himself | avenge my son Olympus Judge yourself
and the upper hand give to the Trojans | 'til due respect full amends Achaeans"
Zeus the Cloud-gatherer was much perturbed | "This is a sorry business!" he averred
"because you will make me fall foul of Here | when rails at me about it if does hear
as will even as things are she scolds me | before other immortals constantly
accuses me aid Trojans in this war | you have to leave me now however or
she may notice us I'll see matter through | but first by way of reassuring you

I'll bow my head immortals recognise | no surer pledge than that from me more wise
when promise with nod be no turning back | no deceit miss mark commitment no lack"
Zeus as he finished bowed his sable brows | ambrosial locks rolled forward from browse
of the immortal head of Zeus the King | once and future affair settled parting
she swung down from glittering Olympus | into salt sea depths while palace Zeus thus
each of company arose from their chair | there in most holy deference to their
Father there was not one who dared | as he approached to keep themselves chaired
they all stood up to greet him | and Zeus sat down on his throne trim
Here's looking at him kid knew at once he | and Thetis Silver Feet Daughter of ye
Old Man of Sea had hatched plot between them | and she rounded on Zeus instantly then
"What goddess has been scheming with you now | you arch-deceiver? when my back's turned how
like you settle things own furtive way | don't own accord confide in me no way"
"Here don't think learn my every decision | you'd find that knowledge weighty prescription
though you're my Consort what's right hear for you | no god or man shall know it before you
but when choose take step without questioning | the gods don't want your cross-examining"
"Dread Son of Cronos" said the ox-eyed Queen | "what are you suggesting now? never been
my way keep pestering you with questions | always let you make your own decisions
in perfect peace but now shrewd idea | you've been talked round to an idea here
Thetis Daughter of Old Man of the Sea | sat with you this morning and clasped your knee
this makes me think you've pledged to her your word | back Achilles let host ships be slaughtered"
"Madam" said Cloud-compeller "thinks too much | I can't keep any secrets from you as such
but there's nothing you can actually DO | save turn my heart even more against you
and which will be so much the worse for you | and if the matter is as you say you
may take it that my will is being done | in heaven so sit there silent be done
or all the gods here won't be strong enough | save you from my unconquerable hands rough"
made ox-eyed Queen of Heaven tremble still | curbing self with effort of will sat still
the other immortals daunted had Zeus | hall silent 'til Hephaestus voice dared use
Artificer spoke in anxiety | for Mother white-armed Here to do his duty
"Unbearable! pretty pass coming to | spoiling for fight about mankind you two
set gods' heads turn turtle at loggerheads | how enjoy meal such awful head-to-heads?
advise Mother knows well enough what's best | to make her peace with Father Zeus as best
she can or may draw second reprimand | from him and our meal entirely unmanned
what if Olympic Lord of Lightning Flash | strongest god Heaven should feel disposed dash
us from seats? mum keep humble beg pardon | gracious to us again Olympian"
as spoke hurried up with two-handled cup | and into his Mother's hand did put up
"Mother be patient and swallow resentment | or loving son may see your rough treatment
here in front of me sorry sight to see | and yet what could I do to help you me?
Olympian hard god pit self against | once before when tried hard to save you against
him seized me by the foot hurled from threshold | Heaven flew all day as sun sank landfold
half-dead in Lemnos picked up and cared for | by Sintians" white-armed goddess therefore
smiled Here took beaker from son still smiling | went on serving rest in turn beguiling
from left with sweet nectar drew from the bowl | -mixing as watched him up and down hall bowl

bustling fit helpless laughter seized gods all | happy feast went on all day 'til sunfall
and everyone there had an equal share | all ate with zest there musical fare fair
from beautiful harp played by Apollo | Muses sang in turn delightfully so
but when the bright lamp of the sun had set | then they all went home to bed in their sep
-arate homes great lame god Hephaestus use | of his skilful hands had built for them Zeus
Olympian Lord of Lightning retired | upper room normally went when so tired
and so they then settled down for the night | Here Golden Throne beside him right rite tight

δύο

*Book 2*

# THE FORCES ARE DISPLAYED

*how Zeus by dream beguiled Agamemnon*
*and of the great Assembly Achaean*
*and marching to forth to battle Achaeans*
*names and numbers host and of the Trojans*

the other gods and all the fighting men | slept through the night but although for the men
no easeful sleep for the King of the Gods | wondering just how he could tip the odds
one way vindicate Achilles' spleen | slaughtered ships host Achaean scene keen seen
best choice King Agamemnon send False Dream | summoned ordered "Off with you Evil Dream
to Argive ships King Son of Atreus | in hut repeat exactly what say thus
"Prepare the long-haired Achaeans perchance | capture spacious city Troy has come chance
for we immortals live on Olympus | this issue does no longer divide us
as Here's pleading has brought us all round healed | so the fate of the Trojans is now sealed"
the Dream listened set forth on its errand | soon Achaean ships found down on the strand
where it sought out the King Agamemnon | found lying fast asleep in hut bed on
assumed appearance of son Neleus | Nestor King's most valued Councillor thus
the Dream from Heaven leant over his head | by his royal titles called him abed
"Asleep? not right ruler who has nation | in his charge to take a sleep vacation
listen to me carefully understand | I come from Zeus though much concerned does stand
on your behalf pities urges prepare | for battle instantly Argives long-hair
chance spacious town Troy of taking giving | for the immortals on Olympus living
are no longer divided on that issue | Here's pleading has converted them all true
Trojans' doom sealed by Zeus bear this in mind | don't let escape when wake back to your mind"
the dream went off leaving King false picture | mind future thought very day Troy capture
enraptured fool scarce knew Zeus intended | all the sufferings groans Zeus had blended
for both sides in the bitter fighting still to come | woke divine voice still rings in ears awesome
sat up on bed put on his soft tunic | lovely new over flowing mantle chic
bound stout pair sandals on his comely feet | slung silver-studded sword from shoulder neat
and then picked up the everlasting staff | sceptre of his line with his general staff
and this in his hand walked down to the ships | where his bronze-clad army lay amidships

when Heavenly Dawn reached high Olympus | announced day to gods especial Zeus thus
Argive King clear-voiced heralds instructed | summon Assembly Argives long-haired did
heralds summoned troops speedily trooped in | first of royal Council called a meet-in
by King of Sandy Pylos ship Nestor's | unfolded subtle plan to Councillors
"Friends visited in sleep Dream from Heaven | which came to me through the short night solemn
and that in its looks stature and bearing | my Lord Nestor near exactly sharing
stood beside addressed by titles royal | said 'It is not right for ruler royal
who has the nation in his charge so much | on his mind to sleep all night as you such
listen carefully to me understand | I come to you from Zeus who though does stand
far off on your behalf has grave concerns | pities you for you prepare Achaeans
of the long-hair for battle instantly | your chance of capturing spacious city
of Troy has come for the gods immortal | dwell on Olympus divided mortal
-ly no longer on that issue pleading | of Here has converted them to bleeding
doom of the Trojans so is by Zeus sealed | remember now what I have just revealed'
"With that it flew away and I woke up | so now we must take steps hasty get up
our forces to ready battle order | ensure are prepared for this new border
but first as is legitimate for me | going to test by speech the soldiery
when I shall make invitation to them | take to well-found ships and make for home then
you noble lords from your several stations | must speak out urge them stick with staycations"
he sat down Nestor King of Pylos Sandy Sh(aw)/(or)es | spoke as one of the loyal counsellors
"Friends Captains Counsellors host Achaean | if any single other countryman
gave account such dream we should have thought it | false felt aught but eagerness exploit it
but as it is the man who had the dream | our Commander-in-Chief so it would seem
right to propose that going into harm's | way take steps at once get our troops under arms"
Nestor had no sooner finished speaking | than he made a move Council end seeking
the sceptred kings cue venerable chieftain | left seats met incoming infantrymen
issued tribe on tribe ships huts by wide sea | -sands march battalions meeting-place line-bee
coming in relays buzzing swarms bees' knees | from hollow rock scatter by companies
left right clusters fall on flowers of spring | Rumour Messenger of Zeus does spring
spreads through them like an Aussie bush wildfire | driving them on 'til all gathered entire
meeting-place now became scene of turmoil | as they took their seats the earth groaned in toil
beneath them above all the noise shouting | of the nine heralds could be heard touting
wares to utmost to make them stop their din | pay attention their royal master-kin
and after much ado about nothing | seats on benches find in fear and loathing
for future and when all had been induced | settle down to zero chatter reduced
King Agamemnon rose holding a staff | which had been made before by Hephaestaff
he gave it to Zeus royal Son Cronos | Zeus to Hermes Guide and Slayer Argus
Lord Hermes presented it to Pelops | the mighty charioteer and Pelops
in his turn passed it on to Atreus | Shepherd of the People when Atreus
died left it to Thyestes rich in flocks | bequeathed to Agamemnon rich in s(t)ocks
to be held in token of his empire | of many islands all Argive lands squire
this the staff Agamemnon now leant on | as he addressed on-the-beach garrison

"I must announce to you my gallant friends | Argive troops that Zeus great Son Cronos sends
me the cruel god a truly crushing blow | he who once solemnly assured me so
that I should never sail to my home town | 'til I'd brought towers of Troy tumbling down
has changed his mind and now to my bitter | disappoint-meant retreat disgrace utter
with half my army lost and it appears | unconquerable Zeus who's downed high towers
many cities will destroy others yet | has decided in omnipotence set
scandalous tale for any descendant | of ours hears such force so large excellent
this engagement so ineffectual | no end in sight struggle unsuccessful
with a weaker enemy say weaker | as if we and the Trojans agreed truce tweat a
each side did tally enemy counting | just native Trojans Argives discounting
allies in tens so that each Argive squad | but one Trojan pour wine many a squad
would go without a wine-waiter steward | such I believe to be odds that us ward
against Trojans in the city itself | but numerous well-geared allies off-shelf
from many towns who thwart me render numb | my trying bring down great stronghold Ilium
and now nine fateful baleful years have passed | timbers of our ships rotted at the last
their frigging rigging also perishes | and our wives and our little perishers
sit at home and patiently wait for us | meanwhile the task ahead that's set for us
when we came here still now remains undone | so take your cue from me let everyone
now board the sleek beaked fast black ships I say | and back to our own home country make way!
broad-streeted Troy to us will never fall" | and his words went straight to the heart of all
save those who had attended the Council | and the whole Assembly that once been still
was then bestirred like the pure clear waters | Icarian Sea when a south-easter's
falling on them from a sky lowering | and so sets the great waves a-towering
or like the deep corn in a tumbled field | bowing its ears to onslaught wild does wield
the West Wind and they raised a mighty roar | and made a mighty dash for the oar door
dust kicked up with feet hung high overhead | shouted each other get hold of ships' head
drag down to friendly sea cleared runways out | they even started shifting the props out
from underneath every great old ship's hull | made din struck high heaven in their scramble
be off 'twas a word from Here to Athene | saved Argives unpredestined dash Mycene
"Unsleeping Daughter Zeus bearer aegis | a sorry state of affairs here is this
do we let folk run away sail home then | seas to Argos without Argive Helen?
she for so many her countrymen died | Trojan soil far motherland long denied
to be left for Trojans to boast about | Priam-airily bestir self about
put among these bronze-clad Achaeans hence | restrain them now with your crack eloquence
deal man by man and don't let them drag thee | with curved beak bleak black ships down to the sea"
and the bright-eyed goddess was nothing loath | swooped down Olympian heights effing oath
the Achaean ships quickly arriving | Odysseus godlike-wise ground hold striving
he hadn't even touched his good black ship | however was on broken-hearted trip
Athene of Flashing Eyes went up to him | "Royal son Laertes Odysseus him
of nimble wits will you take this humbling | just to run off like this with-all tumbling
aboard your galleys so keen to get home | and so leaving Helen in Priam's home
for him to boast about Argive Helen | for whom so many of her countrymen

die far from motherland on Trojan soil? | come don't loiter here and all spoil
move about among your troops use all your eloquence | to stop them deal with them man by man hence
-forth and do not perforce let them drag thee | with their curved beak ships down to the black sea"
Odysseus recognised voice goddess | set off at a run throwing off cloak dress
gathered Eurybates squire Ithacan | went straight up to the King Agamemnon
borrowed from him everlasting sceptre | House Atreus in hand went as spectre
among the ships and the bronze-clad soldiers | and when came upon any of noblers
royal birth or high rank went up to him | made courteous attempts to restrain him
"I should not think it right sir you threaten | as I would of man of standing common
but I do beg you yourself to stand fast | make your followers do same at the last
don't really know what King Agamemnon | has in mind experimented men on
and will soon feel his fist did we not all | of us hear what said at Council withal?
I'm afraid he may be very angry | with the troops may punish them as try flee
Kings are divine and so they have their pride | and by Counsellor Zeus near deified
upheld well-favoured as they always are" | with rank and file in different way would spar
when caught any of them loosing his tongue | he struck the offender for being wrong
with his staff berated him severely | "You there sit still and wait for there to be
orders officers better men than you | the coward and the weakling that is you
in battle debate counting for nothing | and we can't all of us here be a king
mob rule is a very terrible thing | let be one commander only one King
set over us by Son Cronos make use | indeed of the Crooked Ways of Lord Zeus"
restored order Odysseus brought to heel | men now all had flocking-back feel zeal seal
to the meeting-place from the ships and huts | with noise like roaring seas and the surf nuts
ride thundering upon a league-long beach | deep lifts up its voice to each within reach
all sat down quiet benches established | save one hold his tongue long disestablished
Thersites irrepressible inclined | when felt to bait his royal masters' kind
never at a loss for some vulgar quips | empty scurrilous crafted amuse ship's
company ugliest come Ilium | he was bandy-legged and had a foot dumb
rounded shoulders near met across his chest | above them sprouted egg-shaped head whose nest
flouted few short hairs none with greater hearts | loathed than Achilles Odysseus main darts
target now though noble Agamemnon | so that he raised his voice in a cannon
abuse chose very moment e-motion | troops exasperation indignation
hot against "My lord" shouted at the king | in his way loud nagging most annoying
"what's your trouble now? what more do you want? | your huts are full of bronze you do not want
and since we always give you the first pick | when a town is sacked your almighty prick
has plenty choicest women in them too | maybe you're short of a gold hoard or two
the ransom that some handsome lord Trojan | may come with from city to free a son
who's already been tied up and brought in | by myself or another of the kin?
or another girl for you to sleep with | and make your private property forthwith
though it ill becomes you as our general | through such practices army make trouble
as for you my friends the poor specimens | that you are women of the Achaeans
I can't call you men sail home by all means | so fellow left here on his spoils battens

finds how completely depends on the ranks | why just while ago he Achilles tanks
he who's a far better man than he is | he just walked off with the prize that was his
and kept her for himself but need greater | than that make Achilles lose his temper
as he's so laid back he's horizontal | or outrage left you lord horizontal"
no sooner had he launched this di(a/re)tribe | than he found Odysseus great of the tribe
and its titular head standing by him | with a look in his eye so very grim
Odysseus berated man soundly | "Thersites may be eloquence but we
have had quite enough of your drivelling | fool how dare you stand up against the King?
not for you meanest wretch my opinion | follow Atreidae to land Trojan
to hold forth with the kings' names on your tongue | slander them with eye get home before long
for nobody here knows exactly what | this business will bring triumph maybe not
all you do is sit there abuse as thief | King Agamemnon Commander-in-Chief
expostulating your way insolent | on liberality leaders gallant
show to everyone so now mark my word | I make no idle threat nor break my word
if I should catch you once again playing | the fool like this let there be a slaying
permanent of my head from my shoulders | be called no son of mine Telemachus
if don't get hold of you strip you of your | clothes cloak and tunic and all that hides your
nakedness thrash ignominiously | and then throw you out of the Assembly
to go and blubber by the hollow ships" | as finished struck him on back amidships
with well-stud(d/i)ed staff and Thersites flinched | burst into tears a bloody weal eVinced
inflicted by golden studs on the rod | swelled up stood out shoulders and back poor sod
he sat down terrified looked round helplessly | in his pain and a tear brushed away he
and disgruntled though were rest of army | at his expense they had a laugh hearty
"Good work!" cried one his neighbour's eye catching | saying what were all the feeling matching
"many fine things Odysseus' credit | what with sound schemes he's suggested edit
and his cunning leadership in battle | but not done better turn stop that prattle
from the big mouth of this windy ranter | don't think he'll be in a hurry with banter
to come to Assembly again and sling | more insults at our commander the King"
such was the verdict of the assizes | Odysseus sacker cities arises
now to address them with the staff in hand | and Athene of the Flashing Eyes took stand
beside him self disguising as herald | Assembly to order they did herald
so that the farthest benches Achaean | as well as those at the front might listen
to his words and understand their purport | Odysseus their interests heart did sport
and in this spirit he now them harangued | "My lord Agamemnon to have you hanged
out to dry Argives seem determined mind | see you their very own King undermined
an object of contempt to the whole world | breaking their promise on trip here unfurled
from Argos where the untamed horses graze | promise given in a solemn phrase phase
that you should never set sail to home come | 'til you'd brought down the towers Ilium
hear how whimper each about home-winging! | as little boys or widowed wives whingeing
not deny labours here unenlightened | enough send man off disheartened frightened
sailor in well-found ship will fret and fume | when winter gales rising seas keep the spume
from his face cooped up and kept from his wife | for even a month whereas WE in strife

and trouble have hung on here nine long years | small blame to troops moping in tears for fears
by the ships and yet what a shameful thing | it would be then to go home with nothing
after so long a time! wait patiently | my noblest friends Achaeans and country
-men and just hold out a little longer | until we may then discover whether
Calchas prophecies the truth or not you | all know exactly what I mean for you
saw the thing for yourselves though since then death | has thinned your ranks another hatch of death
occurred in Aulis not so very long | ago Achaean fleet gathering long
-ships there with its load of trouble brewing | for Priam and the Trojans a stewing
we were sacrificing to the gods on | their holy altars round a spring gushed on
sparkling under a fine plane-tree when a | momentous happening then occurred a
snake with blood-red markings on his back a | fearsome animal out from his lair a
command from Zeus himself must have driven | darted from out below altar given
head went straight for tree brood of young sparrows | on highest branch poor little all hallows
eve e'en creatures nestling under the leaves | eight birds in all or nine upon the eaves
of destruction with mother of the batch | all chirping piteously down the hatch
their mother fluttering round and wailing | for her little ones but snake availing
self ate them all also got the mother | as he coiled himself up and pounced on her
on the wing as she had come by screaming | but when finished a-live-dead streaming
of them all the god who'd the instinct formed | in him come out at that moment transformed
him he was turned into stone by the Son | Crone-os of Crooked Ways all looking on
gaping at the miracle what could be | meant by this intrusion on our holy
rites by this portentous beast? and Calchas | interpreted omen with keen skill has
then and there 'Why are you now dumbfounded | Argives of flowing locks? how plum(b)-founded
line of this prophetic scene for us did | Zeus the Thinker and we have long waited
for it and we must await the sequel | but the memory of this day die will
not there were eight young sparrows making nine | with mother all eaten by the snake nine
then is the number of years we shall have | to fight at Troy in the tenth we shall have
command and control of the broad streets that's | just what Calchas prophesied and all that's
coming true so troops Argive boy brand band | fellow-countrymen I call you to stand
your ground 'til we take Priam's spacious town" | when he finished so well his speech went down
great shout went up from army Achaean | for godlike Odysseus with a sullen
roar the ships around them echoed that shout | but Nestor the man of chariot clout
Gerenian had something to say too | to his countrymen "Upon my word you
might be little boys with no interest | in the war to judge by talk manifest
what has become of our compacts on oath? | you behave as though the warlike plans loath
now to follow together we matured | loyalties ratified in wine assured
pledged with our right hands were so much rubbish | words are the only weapons to brandish
using just them now THEY will not get us | anywhere however long we stall thus
lord Agamemnon be true as always | to your firm resolve and lead Argive-ways
into action if there are one or two | traitors among us now making plans to
sail for home before they find out whether | Zeus told us truth leave them there bad weather
rot but in any case they won't succeed | for I am convinced that he paid us heed

and the almighty Son of Cronos said | "Yes" to us the day we got aboard said
ships of war to bring death and destruction | to the Trojans there was an instruction
flash of lightning on our right his meaning | all would be well no scramble demeaning
to get home then 'til every man of you | has slept with a Trojan wife and you too
paid for the toil and groans Helen did cause | you and anyone who deserts the cause
has just to touch his good black ship to find | himself dead before the rest of his kind
and now my lord ensure that your own plans | are sound and take advice from others' plans
here's my own I'm sure on you won't be lost | your men into their tribes and clans be bossed
so clan may help clan tribes back each other | if to such dispositions troops bother
you will then see what cowards you may have | in the ranks officers and who you have
as good men for each man will be fighting | at his brothers' side and soon insighting
whether it's god's will that stands between your | goal sack Troy or the cowardice of your
soldiers and their incompetence in war" | Agamemnon complimented Nestor
on his speech "One more debate where you my | venerable lord carried all before! my!
Father Zeus Athene Apollo give me | ten counsellors such as this and dear me
King Priam's town captured and sacked by hands | Achaean would totter into the sands
but Zeus Son of Cronos WILL torment me | in fruitless broils squabbles entangles me
look at my quarrel with Achilles all | over a girl when traded insults all
though it was I who lost my temper first | if he and I see eye to eye the worst
means not be day's reprieve for the Trojans | but the first thing for all you Achaeans
is to have a meal and then to battle | sharpen all spears adjust your shield tackle
see that your good horses have their fodder | fix chariots prepare cannon-fodder
in grim pitched battle that will last all day | there'll be no respite at all 'til end day
when night parts us in our full-on fury | straps of your man-covering shields will be
well soaked with the sweat on your shaggy breast | hands will be weary of your spear haft best
and your pair of horses will be tugging | your polished chariots so be lugging
full sweating and as for any shirker | I may find disposed to be a lurker
by the curved black hollow beaked gallant ships | he's for the birds of prey dogs amid-ships"
the Argives welcomed speech Agamemnon | with great shout like thunder sea roaring on
a lofty coast when gale comes in from South | hurls the waves against a rocky cape's mouth
pla(i)ce which they are never in peace leaving | whatever way the wind is now cleaving
and so then they broke up the Assembly | at once once dispersed among ships trembly
where lit fires in their huts a meal eating | each man as made his offering meet thing
to favourite of gods everlasting | prayed through ordeal come with his life long lasting
King Agamemnon himself sacrificed | a five-year-old ox nicely fatted sufficed
mighty Son of Cronos and invited | the leading chieftains of the united
Argives attend Nestor first of all thus | of the Cretans King Idomeneus
Ajax Foam Cleanser namesake Aias thus | Diomedes of Crete son Tydeus
and for a sixth of Ithaca Odysseus | whose thoughts the very thoughts Zeus makes use thus
no need invite brother Menelaus | loud war-cry who knew the many layers
Agamemnon's burden came own accord | standing round victim they heard the word lord
as they took up the sacrificial grain | King Agamemnon pray hopes not in vain

"O most glorious and almighty Zeus | of the Black Cloud of Serious Ill Use
Cloud-gatherer and Lord of High Heaven | grant that the sun may not sigh from heaven
darkness fall before trash Priam's palace | blackened smoke send up in flames his gate-place
and rip the tunic on the breast of Hector | with my faithful bronxze spear and sword vector
and at his side let plenty of his friends | be felled bite the dust and thus meet their ends"
and so Agamemnon of prayer made use | but not prepared to grant what he wished Zeus
however accepted his offering | return doubled tribulation offing
and when they had there made their petitions | and scattered the grain drew back the ox son's
head slit its throat then arrayed and flayed it | and then from the thighs comely slices slit
wrapped them closely in great folds of fat | laid raw meat on the butty sandwich slat
these pieces burnt on faggots stripped of leaves | and put the inner parts on the spit's eaves
and then held them tightly over the flames | when thighs burnt up and they'd tasted the frames
of the entrails carved the rest small pieces | and everyone with skewers them pierces
and roasted them totally thoroughly | and drew them off very tenderly
job done now and the food fully prepared | fell to with good will on the meal well-fared
in which all had equal shares deified | when their hunger and thirst there satisfied
Gerenian charioteer Nestor | took the lead stood up stepped forward said "Your
majesty Agamemnon King of Men | let's prolong this meeting no further then
nor put off the great everlasting work | God's set our never-lasting hands to work
come let heralds Achaeans the bronze-clads | do round of ships and call out all the bronzed lads
so then each of us as a commander | inspect whole soldiery Gerry-mander
both soon work up fighting spirit in the men" | accepted his advice did King of Men
gave immediate orders to clear-voiced | heralds Argives long-haired they then clear voiced
their call to battle so cried their summons | and fell in so quickly did the commons
the royal chieftains of the King's Council | martialling the troops about did bustle
and with them of the Flashing Eyes Athene | cloaked splendid everlasting aegis screen
fadeless frieze flutter hundred gold tassels | all beautifully made each one cattle's
worth a hundred head in this resplendent | she flew through the ranks and independent
-ly urging the men forward one-to-one | she inspired in them will to carry on
fight relentlessly ere long enamoured | more with thought enemy being hammered
than with idea of flailing and failing | and in their hollow ships away sailing
to their own country and as they fell in | dazzling glitter of splendid bronze flashed in
the upper air and through to reach the sky | and so brilliant fireworks on high
as bright as the glint of flames caught in some | far spot when great forest on some fiercesome
mountain height is ravaged by fire each clan's | come out like countless flocks birds each out fans
the geese and the cranes and the long-necked swans | gather in meadows Asian avians
by the streams of Cayster and wheel about | boldly flapping their wings and flushing out
the whole meadow with harsh cries as they came | to ground full frontal advance so came same
clan after clan pouring from the ships' stand | and huts out onto the plain of Scamand
-er and the earth resounded sullenly | to the heavy tramp feet marching many
and horses' hooves as they found their place time | in full flowery meadows riverine
innumerable as the leaves and blossom | in their season so the youthful blossom

long-haired Achaea there drawn up on plain | facing the Trojans with in their hearts plain
slaughter as many then and as restless | as the flies unnumbered doubtless countless
that swarm around the cowsheds in the spring | when the pails full milk of kindness does spring
and now with their practised ease the goatherds | sort out their lost wandering flocks like pot-sherds
been scattered over the past years' pastures | captains to war-order brought their treasures
in among them moved Agamemnon King | Zeus the Thunderer head eyes like looking
waist like War-god's breast like Poseidon's brand's | as from cattle in herd the bull out stands
conspicuous among the grazing cows | Zeus made the son of house Atreus house
in self stand-out grandeur from idle crowd | eclipse his fellow kings then thus allowed
now tell me you Muses Olympus tress | living since you're goddesses and witness
to all that happens while we men know nowt | we're not told so now be me telling out
who were captains chieftains Danaan tanks | I could not name nor even count the ranks
and files came to Ilium not if I | had ten tongues ten mouths voice that could not tie
up heart of bronze unless you Muses of | Olympus aegis-bearer Zeus Daughters of
would serve me remembrance time past here then | the ships from first to last and each captain
of the fleet first the Boeotians Leitus | and Peneleos with Archesilaus
Prothoenor and Clonius in command | came from Hyrie and Stony Aulis stand
from Schoenus and Scolus Etoneus | where the hills run high and Mycalessus
of the spreading lawns and from Graia | Thespeia with them those from Harma
Eilesion Erythrae Eleon | and Hyle also sent their men Peteon
so did Ocalea and the stronghold | of Medeon Copae Eutresis bold
Thisbe rich in doves and Coronea | too grassy Haliartus Plataea
Glisas and the strong town of Lower Thebes | holy Onchestus with the sacred eaves
of Poseidon's wood and from Arne where free | grapes hang thick Mideia and holy
Nisa Anthedon borders of beyond | all these in fifty ships hundred beyond
twenty young Boetians stowed in each one | men from Minyaeon Orchomenus Aspledon
also came men led by Ascalaphus | and another son Ares Ialmenus
Astyoche conceived in Actor son | Azeus' palace gentle maiden
went in secret to an upper room slept | with the mighty War-god in they had swept
with good thirty-hollow-ship-worth squadron's | Schedius and Epistrophus the sons
of the magnanimous Iphitus son | Naubolus commander disposition
from Phocis who lived in Cyparissus | and Rocky Pytho in Panopeus
in Daulis and in sacred Crisa round | Anemoreia Hyampolis sound
with the lovely waters of Cephisus | and Lilaea rises Cephisus
there forty black ships travelled with these two | under whose command Phocians came too
took up when fallen in battle stations | on left by the side of the Boeotians
leading the Locrians fleet-footed son | Oileus lesser Aias not a one
indeed like Aias Telamonian | far inferior short corslet linen
wore but not Hellene or an Achaean | his equal in kill skill of a spearman
and his following had come from Opus | number 1 Cynus and Calliarus
from Bessa beautiful Augeiae | from Scarphe and Tarphe a lovely high
Thornion and the banks of the River | Boagrius forty black ships under

him had set out the Locrians spanning | the straits holy Euboea there manning
Euboeia itself sent Abantes fiery | men of Chalcis Eiretria Histi
-aea rich in vines of Cerinthus | by the seaside high fortress of Dius
and those who had their homes at Carystus | and Strya and these were all captained thus
by Elephenor of War-god offshoot | son of Chalcodon of the resolute
Abantes the chieftain his followers | swift on feet wore hair lock-fettered feathers
at the back they carried the ashen spear | were desirous of nothing better here
than to lunge with them and tear the corselet | corsets Amazon enemy's breast get
and forty black ships came under command | Elephenor next from Athens of grand
citadel in the realm magnanimous | child of fruitful Earth Erechtheus
who brought up by Daughter of Zeus Athene | established Athens in own rich shrine scene
where bulls and rams offered in due season | annually by youth Athenian
these commanded by Menestheus son | of Peteos living rival had none
in art of horse and infantry top man | except Nestor who was the older man
had come across with him fifty black ships | from Salamis Aias had brought twelve ships
beached where were stationed the Athenians | the citizens of Argos and Tyryns
of the Great Walls men of Hermione | and Asine towns embrace deep gulf sea
and those from Eionae and from Troezen | vine-clad Epidauraus Athenian
youth with of Aegina and too Mases | they were commanded by Diomedes
of the loud war-cry and by Sthenelus | the son of the far-famed Capaneus
highborn Euryalus Mecisteus | King son of and in turn son of Talaus
had come with them too as third in command | but warlike Diomedes in command
overall and eighty black ships set sail | the troops that from that great stronghold did hail
of Mycenae wealthy Corinth good town | of Cleonae and the men who lived down
in the fine old town great Orneiae | and in lovely Araethyrea high
the Argentine where Aguero reigned in | early years in steep Gonoessa in
Hyperesie around Aegion in | Pellene and all the length of the coast in
the broad lands of Helice in ships hundred | King Agamemnon son Atreus led
dread following was by far the finest | and also in pure numbers the greatest
he was a proud man as he took his stand | among his people gleaming bronze in hand
greatest captain of them all by virtue | his rank and chief of largest force on view
men from rolling lands Lacedaemon deep | in the hills Pharis Sparta Messe deep
in doves love Briseis Bryseiae | and from the beautiful Augeiae
Amyclae and the seaside fort Helos | the villagers of Laas and Oetylus
and all these came under the King's brother | Menelaus loud war-cry another
sixty ships had their own separate station | Menelaus strode among them full-on
in all confidence of own gallantry | and urged them to battle as nobody
more eager avenge self toil groans Helen | had caused him next the sandy Pylos men
and from lovely Arene and from Thyron | a spot where the Alpheus can ford one
handsome Aepy and Cyparisseis | Amphigenia and Pteleus
Helos and Dorion where Muses met | Thamyris the Thracian as he was set
on way from Oechalia and the home | Oechalian Eurytus pride genome

caused Thamyris to boast he'd win singing | -match Muses selves Daughters aegis-bearing
Zeus angered them and so they struck him blind | of the divine gift of song robbed him blind
also caused him to forget his harping | then Gerenian Nestor on harping
about leading ninety black ships squadron | then came the great army Arcadian
from the lands where Mount Cyllene lifts its peak | Aepytus buried where men trained to peak
in hand-to-hand fighting from Pheneus | and from the rich-in-sheep Orchomenus
from Rhype Stratie and from Tegea | windy Enispe town Mantinea
pleasant Stymphelus Parrhasie led by | King Agapenor son Ancaeus ply
sixty ships each one with its full complement | trained Arcadian warriors hell bent
Agamemnon King of Men had given | Agapenor well-found black ships driven
then to cross the wine-dark sea there being | no knowledge Arcadia sea-faring
the men of Bupraison and as much as | that part of kindly land of Elis as
lies between Hermine and Myrsinus | the Marches Olenian Rock Alis
-ion all came under four commanders | each with squadron ten fast ships filled troopers
Epean and two of their companies | were led firstly by Amphimachus he's
son of Cteatus and Thalpius | son of Eurytus House Actor each plus
a third by son of Amarynceus | stalwart Diores Prince Polyxeinus
fourth by the son of King Agasthenes | Augeas' son from across the seas
from Elis those from Dulichium be | Echinean Isles led by he
Meges warrior son Phyleus use | -ful charioteer who'd been loved by Zeus
who'd parted from his father once upon | his time in anger and made migration
Dulichium forty ships company | made up and the next up Odysseus he
proud Cephallenians leading crafters | of Ithaca and wooded peak masters
windswept Neriton Crocyleia | from and rugged Aegilips and from Za
-cynthus forested and from Samos strand | the mainland opposite the string island
these were forces to Odysseus of use | whose wisdom rivalled even that of Zeus
twelve ships with him with bows crimson-painted | and Thoas Andraemon's son captain did
Aetolians from Pylene Pleuron | Olenus Chalcis-on-sea Calydon
the rocky as the sons of Oeneus | the Magnificent no more Oeneus
himself was dead and Meleager red-topped | on whom the kingship in turn had been dropped
over all Aetolians Thoas | forty hollow black ships under oars has
the renowned spearman Idomeneus | led Cretans bullish men from Knossos
from Gortyn of the Great Walls from Phaestos | Lyctus Miletus chalky Lycastus
Rhytion fine cities all from hometowns | other troops of Crete of the Hundred Towns
Idomeneus led the great spearman | and Meriones compeer of the man
-destroying War-god eighty black ships these | and now Tlepolemus of Heracles
the tall and handsome son had brought from Rhodes | nine beaked shiploads of lordly sea roads Rhodes
-eslans whose three tribes own Ridder-mark | made separate Cameirus on chalk mark
Ielysus and Lindos these the forces | Tlepolemus spearman famed of course is
and the son by Astyocheia | of Heracles who took from Ephyre – a
prize – River Selleis sack strongholding | many a warrior-chief been holding
when Tlepolemus had grown to manhood | in palace own father's uncle a hood

killed Licymnius offshoot of War-god | who was an old man by then so the bod
quickly built some ships gathered following | large overseas fast ships off hollow wing
menaced as he was by the other sons | of the mighty Heracles and grandsons
thus fugitive after many hardships | to Rhod-esia came squadron of ships
where his people settled in three districts | according to their own tribal prescripts
enjoyed the smiles of Son of Cronos Zeus | King of gods and men who gave them profuse
treasures of wealth untold and next Nireus | with three trim ships from Syme Nireus
son Aglaia and King Charopus | handsomest Danaan Troy Nireus
save only flawless son of Peleus | yet was a weakling and following thus
small men from Nisyrus also Kos | – from Casus and Crapathos/Karpathus
Calydnian Isles – of Eurypylus | city led Antiphus Pheidippus
the two sons of King Thessalus a son | of Heracles thirty black ships squadron
we come now to Pelasgian Argos | in Trachis in Alope and Alus
Phthia and Hellas land of women | lovely bearing names Hellene Achaean
and Myrmidon in fifty ships set sail | under command the great Achilles hail
but now sound war did not them concern | at all no-one in battle order stern
to draw them up as the great Achilles | lay by ships heartsick for Briseis he's
gentle girl he had won from Lyrnessus | by sweat of his brow when he sacked town thus
he stormed the walls of Thebe brought down then | Mynes Epistrophus sturdy spearmen
the sons King Euenus son of Selepus | this was the girl he grieved for as lay thus
save to lie idle long he not destined | list goes on live in history destined
Phylace and Pyrasus the flowery | Demeter's sanctuary Iton mummy
of the bleating sheep and down in Antron | by the sea Pteleus deep deep green
grass-ho(l)me led by Protesilaus warlike | while he lived but now did the black earth like
received him in her bosom had been first | of Argives to leap ashore but fate worst
fell full flow then to Dardanian foe | left wife Phylace lacerated cheeks woe
house only half-built so followers stress | grieved for leader but not left leaderless
led by Podarces offshoot of War-god | son Phylacus' son Iphiclus lord
of many sheep Podarces a brother | great-hearted Protesilaus' brother
younger noble Boromir-like warlike | being older than Faramir alike
the stronger so troops did not lack leader | though mourned the gallant dead and came under
his command forty black ships hollow beaked | next again the men who in Pherae peaked
by Boebeian Lake Boebe | and Glaphyrae and Iolcus lovely
eleven ships led by Admetus' | son Eumelus she who Pelias'
most beautiful daughter the most queenly | Alcestis bore Admetus serenely
Methone Meliboea Thaumacie | harsh Olizon brought keenly serenely
great archer Philoctetes in seven | ships with each one manned by fifty oarsmen
trained to go into battle with the bow | but their captain in agony laid low
on lovely isle of Lemnos where Argive | army had left him just barely alive
suffering there from the bite poisonous | of a malignant water-snake and thus
lay there pining though the Argives by their | ships destined before long think once more there
of King Philoctetes but meanwhile though | his followers missed their leader in no

way left without a chief led by Medon | of renowned Oileus the bastard son
who Rhene bore to Oileus sacker | of towns and these the men not play slacker
from Tricce and terraced-hilled Ithome | and then too from Oechalia city
of Oechalian Eurytus were led | two sons of Asclepius they the med
-ics Machaon and Podleirius | fifty black ships the doctors' orders us
then those from Ormenion and the spring | Hypereia along with hailing
Asterion white towers Titanus | who were commanded by Eurypylus
Eumaeon's high-born son forty black ships | under him of those who dwelt on the hips
of Argissa's lips Gyrtone Orthe | Helone and white town Olooson see
dauntless Polypoetes the lead one | and he was a son of Peirithous son
immortal Zeus Hippodameia | far-famed for Perithous conceived on a
day when he took his revenge on shaggy | folk of the wilds expelled Centaury
Pelion drove into hands Aethices | Polypoetes was not alone he's
sharing his command with Leonteus | War-god offshoot son viral Coronus
son Caeneus squadron forty black ships | Gouneus from Cyphus twenty-two ships
led the Enienes and the dauntless | Peraebians who'd pitched their houses' press
round wintry Dodona tilled fields able | by Titaresius delectable
pours lovely stream into the Peneus | mingles not silver eddies Peneus
though but floats along on their top like oil | being part of the most formidaboil
waters of the Styx river of the oath | next again the son of Tenthredon Proth
-ous led Magnetes lived by Peneus | and Mount Pelion of leaves timorous
trembling these the men dashing Prothous led | forty more black ships were then in there fed
these then were each commander and captain | Danaan now tell me Muse of all men
horses that crossed with the Atreidae | which ones were the first and foremost and why?
of all the horses those of Admetus | the best by far which his son Eumalus
drove swift as birds alike in coat and age | matched to a plumb-line along their backs sage
both mares been raised in Peraea by | Apollo of the Silver Bow fly cry
panic through the ranks Telamonian | Aias best man by far while in dudgeon
Achilles only since he the peerless | finest man of all son of Peleus
drove the finest horses but lies cursing | now by his beaked sea-going ships nursing
his quarrel C-in-C Agamemnon | the son of Atreus and meanwhile on
the sea beach his people passed the time in | archery and casting the javelin
and throwing discs the horses idle be | each by its own chariot and idly
munching from the marsh parsley and clover | masters' chariots lay under cover
in the huts and the men themselves who missed | their battle-loving chief aimlessly pissed
about the camp and they did no fighting | rest host away marching fighting plighting
selves on the whole plain seemed be so consumed | fire whole earth beneath groaned burden assumed
resumed as does for Zeus Thunderer sound | in his anger when he lashes the ground
above Typhoeus in the Mountain | Arimean where Typhoeus lain
there abed thus earth reverberated | to marching feet as perambulated
swiftly on across the plain meanwhile fleet | Iris was sent out of the Whirling Feet
to the Trojans by aegis-bearing Zeus | bring to them the news of portentous use

young and old alike they'd all foregathered | at Priam's doors where were to have blathered
Iris of the Nimble Feet came to them | and spoke in a voice like that of Priam
-'s son posted as lookout Polites | for Troy on top of old Aesyetes
-'s tomb ready to dash home at first sign | of sortie from ships Achaean fine line
Iris looked now exactly like this man | as she addressed herself then to Priam
"Sire" she said "I see that you are still as | fond of interminable talk now as
you were in peace-time though the death-struggle | is on us been part many a battle
but have never seen so formidable | a force rolling over plain well able
wall of city to fight at like the leaves | of the forest or the sands of the seas
Hector I hector you above all to | do as I say in this great city too
Priam has many allies and yet this | bunch foreigners talk different languages
let their own captains in each case take charge | draw them up and to battle lead the charge"
and Hector did not fail to recognise | goddess' voice in a trice no surprise
dismissed the meeting they then rushed to arms | the gates were all thrown open and all arms
infantry horse poured out with a great din | outside town some way off in plain set in
there is a high mound which has ground open | every side which is called Thorn Hill by men
but as the tomb of dancing Myrine known | to the immortals host and Trojan's own
allies here now formed up battle order | Priam's flashing helmet son great Hector
led the Trojans and with him marched by far | finest and most numerous force keen sp(e)a(r)
-men all the Dardanians were led by | Anchises' admirable son by
Aphrodite when she clasped Anchises | to conceive in her divine embrace he's
on the slopes of Mount Ida Aeneas | the son not in sole soul command but as
support Antenor's two sons Acamas | and Archelocus and each other as
experienced in all kinds of fighting | men in Zeleia lives delighting
under the lowest spurs of Ida drank | the dark water of Aesepus clan thank
-fully prosperous Trojan were led by | Pandarus the son of repute of Ly
-caon owed bow skill Apollo himself | those from Adresteia and the shelf
-land Apaesus from Pityeia | and from the steep slopes of Tereia
led by Adrestus later addressed us | and in his linen corslet Amphius
the two sons of Merops of Percote yet | who was of surpassing skill as prophet
and had done his best to dissuade his sons | from hazarding their lives in war of sons
but they would not listen to him black Death | enticed them to a plagued fate worse than Death
and the men from Percote and Practius | holy Arisbe Sestus Abydus
led by Asius son of Hyrtacus | great glossy horses lordly Asius
brought from Arisbe River Selleis | and the next along is Hippothous his
the command tribes Pelasgian spearmen | who lived in deep-soiled Larissa these men
followed both Hippothous and Pylaeus | Ares offshoot the two sons of Lethus
Pelasgian the son of Teutamus | now Acamas and the noble Peiros
commanded the fearsome Thracians whose land | by the swift-flowing Hellespont bound band
while Euphemism son King Troezenus | of Ceas led warlike Cicones thus
and Pyraechmes led the Paionians | with their curving bows and from Amydon's
their coming banks broad river Axius | most beautiful waters the Axius

that flow over the earth Pylaemenes | of the very shaggy breast Paulman he's
led Paphlagonians from Eneti | where the wild mules became an entity
and they all lived together in Cytorus | round Sesamon River Parthenius
in pleasant homesteads in Aegialus | Cromna high Erythini Odius
Epistrophus led the Alizones | from the distant Alybe native zone's
silver of the Mysians Ennomus | Chromis were in command Ennomus
an augur save all his bird-lore did not | save him from the black hand of the Death plot
fell victim another fell Achilles | great runner in the river-bed when he's
made havoc of the Trojans and allies | Phorcys and Prince Ascanius (s)allies
led the Phrygians eager for battle | from the far distant land of the castle
Ascania Maionians Mesthes | led Antiphus sons of Talaemenes
whose mother was the Gygaean Lake | these two the Maionians did then take
under their far-seeing and wise command | under Tmolus there their native land
Nastes led Carians men of uncouth | speech who possessed Miletus in its youth
Mount Phthires of the myriad leaves | ox-bowed Maeander's wandering streams' eaves
and the steep crest of Mycale and was these | men brought by Amphimacus and Nastes
the noble sons of Nomion what a | fool Amphimacus! to battle like a
girl decked in gold not that saved him from a | dreadful end fell to Achilles runner
the great right there in the river-bed bold | Olympian Achilles took the gold
last Sarpedon and the peerless Glaucus | led Lycians from swirling-streamed Xanthus

τρία

*Book 3*

# A TRUCE AND A DUEL

*single combat Menelaus Paris*
*and how Aphrodite rescued Paris*
*and of how from the walls of Troy Helen*
*and Priam beheld the host Achaean*

when all were drawn up with each company | under own commander organically
Trojans advanced with a din and shouting | as birds air flouting with clamour clouting
and like from the onset of winter cranes | are flying also from the sudden rains
and make for Ocean Stream with cries raucous | bring death and destruction Pigmy caucus
launching their wicked onslaught from the sky | morning but the Achaeans without cry
moved forward breathing valour with resolve | filled to stand by one another and solve
the battle puzzle in their swift advance | across the plain their marching feet did enhance
the dust raised into a cloud dense as mists | the South Wind wraps around the mountain-trysts
when a man can see no farther than can | heave a rock shepherds grumble to a man
while the thief he who finds it better than | the night rejoices two forces on ran
collision course when the godlike Paris | out from the ranks of the Trojans sallies
offers single combat a panther's skin | on his back curved bow and sword slung swingin'
from his shoulders a couple brandishing | of bronze-headed spears then not languishing
challenge an Argive champion meet him | and man to man to fight it out with him
when veteran Menelaus saw him | in front of the crowd striding towards him
was as happy as a hungry lion | when he finds the massive carcase lyin'
of an antlered stag or wild goat devours | greedily despite all hunters' powers
sturdy nimble hounds to drive him away | so Menelaus rejoiced when saw way
-ward Prince Paris thought chance fate come paying | out the man who'd him been away playing
leapt down at once from chariot to ground | with all his arms when royal Paris found
Menelaus taken up the challenge | heart failed him completely and with a lunge
slipped back into friendly ranks in terror | for his life like one who comes on horror
of a snake in a deep wooded ravine | recoils goes back way entered into scene
with pale cheeks and trembling limbs so royal | Paris slunk back among lordly loyal
Trojans in terror of Atreides | Hector saw his brother had betrayed these

fell out with him at once shouted "Paris" | towards him "you pretty boy you limp-wris
-ted woman-struck seducer what was your | point being born? why not killed before your
wedding day? yes I could wish it so far | better than be a disgrace as you are
to the rest of us and too of contempt | object the long-haired Achaeans you tempt
to laughter see us try make champion | of a prince because he looks champion
forgetting that he has no strength of mind | no courage when I look at you now mind
can YOU be the man I ask picked yourself | a crew of friends sailed off over sea-shelf
in your much-travelled ships where you hobnobbed | with foreigners one of whom you slobbed fobbed
off and carried away a beautiful | woman from distant land familial
warlike to be a curse to your father | to the city the whole people rather
and to cause our enemies to rejoice | and you to hang your head in shameful choice?
and now are you too cowardly to stand | up to the brave man you've wronged out of hand?
you would soon find out the kind of fighter | he is whose lovely wife you made lighter
of your lyre liar get no help at all | nor would the gifts of Aphrodite all
those curly locks of yours your soft good looks | when he'd swiftly left you on tenterhooks
Trojans too soft or you would have been stoned | to death long since for the evil you've honed"
"Hector" the noble Paris then replied | "your bitter taunts are fully justified
you've not said a word too much how like your | indomitable spirit! and now your
tireless energy has put me in mind | of an axe held in a carpenter's bind
through a sturdy log its strong way hacking | power to shape ship's timbers not lacking
but there's something you must not me reproach | Golden Aphrodite's great gifts don't broach
precious gifts the gods unasked lavish wise | lovely on a man one should not despise
even though he might not choose them if he | had the chance but if you insist on me
undertaking this duel make all the troops | sit down and between the two army groups
I'll meet Menelaus formidable | fight for Helen and her wealth biddable
he who wins proves himself the better man | carry off the lady to own house can
goods and all while rest make a peace treaty | by which we stay deep-soiled Troy entreaty
and the enemy sail home to Argos | Achaea of top gals and grazing horse"
this delighted Hector new hope clasping | stepped into no-man's-land spear-gun grasping
by the middle thrust back the Trojans' line | all sat down but long-haired Achaean line
kept up their archery Hector making | target for their arrows John Stones making
King Agamemnon intervene shouting | "Argives enough! men you must cease shooting
Hector of the flashing helmet trying | to make himself heard" the troops ceased firing
and silence was then established promptly | and now Hector spoke between each army
"Trojans and Achaean men-at-arms hear | from me what Paris now proposes here
he who began this trouble now suggests | that each army its weaponry now rests
while he and warrior Menelaus | between two hosts fight duel many layers
he who wins proves himself the better man | carry off the lady to own home can
goods and all while the rest make peace treaty" | Hector's speech greeted silence completely
at last Menelaus of loud war-cry | spoke up "Listen now to me because I
am the chief sufferer here and thus I've | thought that the armies Trojan and Argive
can now part in peace quite enough brooding | death had to bear result of this feuding

between myself and Paris who embarked | barney one of us must die Fate has marked
him out for death already and then rest | of you will soon be reconciled invest
a couple of sheep white ram and black ewe | for Earth and the Sun and we will bring ewe
for Zeus and let King Priam be fetch-ed | so take the oaths himself for sons wretched
arrogant and unscrupulous and we | don't want solemn treaty wrecked treachery
lying young men for most part unstable | whereas old man tends lend a hand able
in such affairs considers the future | as well as past and to avoid suture
for both parties he does the very best" | Menelaus' pronouncement was best
welcomed by Trojans Achaeans alike | reprieve painful business fight pike-hike spike
charioteers fell back on infantry | got down from chariots made themselves free
of their equipment laid on the ground all's | in separate heaps at close intervals
Hector sent two messengers at all speed | to city fetch sheep make Priam take heed
King Agamemnon sent Talthybius | bring a lamb from the stealthy Sheep-B-Us
Talthybius hastened to carry out | sovereign's orders meanwhile Iris about
give news to white-armed Helen disguising | self Helen's sister-in-law high-prizing
Laodice as the most beautiful | Priam's daughters married to worshipful
Helicaon Antenor's son Helen | found her palace great purple web works on
double width in which weaving battles key | of many between the horse-loverly
Trojans bronze-clad Achaeans in the war | been forced on them all for her sake come far
Iris of the Nimble Feat went to her | made address "Come and see my dear sister
how Trojan Achaean troops behaving | strange little while ago they were braving
each other terrible battle on plain | looked as though meant fight to the death in p(l)ain
but battle now off and they are gleaning | peace quite quiet thereon their shields leaning
the long javelins stuck on end beside | Menelaus redoubtable betide
woe Paris are to fight a duel for you | with their great spears the winner to claim you
as his wife" news from the goddess burning | Helen's wayward heart with tender yearning
for her former husband and her parents | city she'd left memories fine remnants
wrapped veil of white linen around her head | tear-drops running down her cheeks left her bed
-room attended by two waiting-women | Aethre daughter of Pittheus then
ox-eyed lady Clymene sooner than late | reached the neighbourhood of the Scaean Gate
where Priam was sitting in conference | with the Elders of city Panthous hence
Thymoetes Lampus and Clytius | Hicateon offshoot of War-god plus
his two wise counsellors Ucalegon | Antenor for old age had brought to one
and all an end to their days of fighting | but they were excelling at words plighting
Trojan Elders on tower in chipping | like cicadas delightfully chirping
perched on a tree in the woods when they saw | Helen coming their voices lower saw
"Who on earth" asked one another "could blame | Achaean Trojan troops ready go lame
for such a woman'? indeed does possess | very image of immortal goddess
all the same lovely as she is let her | sail off home not stay here not vex us her
nor our children after us" in meanwhile | Priam to his side did Helen beguile
"Dear child come here and sit in front of me | so that your former husband you may see
and your relatives and friends bear no ill | will blame the gods who brought this terrible

Achaean war upon me and now you | can name me that giant over there who
is that tall and most handsome Achaean? | there are others taller by a head than
but I have never set eyes on a man | of such good looks and such majesty man
every inch a king" "I pay you homage | reverence my dear father-in-law sage"
gracious she "I wish I'd chosen to die | in misery before here I came nigh
your son bridal chamber self from hurling | and my kinsfolk and my daughter darling
dear friends with whom there I had long grown up | but things did not fall out so in my cup
to my unending sorrow however | must tell you what you wished to know ever
imperial Agamemnon the son | Atreus good king mighty spearman one
too who you pointed out brother-in-law | once – shameless creature I am now out-law
unless 'twas all a dream" when heard this thus | old man with admiration obvious
gazed at Agamemnon "Ah lucky son | of Atreus" exclaimed "child of fortune one
blessed by the gods! so it is you the man | all these thousands serve in host Achaean!
I went to Phrygia once land of vines | and galloping horses and learnt betimes
how numerous the Phrygians are when | saw armies Otreus King Migdon then
encamped by the River Sangarius | I was their ally bivouacked with them thus
the time the Amazons who fight like men | came up to the assault but they even
were not as many as host Achaean | with the flashing eyes" and then the old man
noticing Odysseus next "Tell me dear | child now who is he by head shorter here
than King Agamemnon but is broader | in the chest and in area shoulder
on the ground left his armour rejecting | now goes like a bellwether inspecting
the ranks recalls a fleecy ram ringing | a great flock of white sheep to heel bringing"
"That child of Zeus is Laertes' son | Odysseus of the nimble wits raised on
Ithaca poor rocky land but is a | tactics intrigue and stratagem master"
then the wise Antenor added new thing | to Helen's Odysseus's viewing
"Madam your words I endorse Odysseus | has been here he came with Menelaus
on an embassy on your behalf I | was their host in my own house did I
entertain them I know not only what | they look like but also what way is that
in which they think and in conference when | with the Trojans they were all standing then
broad-shouldered Menelaus over-topped | whole company but when both seated cropped
Odysseus the more imposing when their | turn came round to express in public their
views Menelaus then spoke fluently | not at much great length but apparently
a man of few words who kept to the point | though the younger one but in counter-point
when nimble-witted Odysseus took floor | he stood there bent firmly down his head bore
with browsing glances from under his brows | so swinging the staff also not allows
front or back but held it stiffly as though | he had never handled one before so
you'd have taken him for sulky fellow | no better than fool but when great bellow
of a voice came booming from his chest words | poured from lips like winter snow in flood fjords
there was no man alive who could compete | with him and with that knowledge then replete
no longer misled by appearances | third old king noticed stature Aias'
"Who is that other fine and upstanding | Achaean taller than the rest standing
by head and shoulders?" the gracious lady | Helen of the long robe "That's the mighty

huge Aiax foaming cleanser Achaean | Idomeneus other side Cretan
was standing out among them like a god | Cretan captains gathered round local bod
my lord Menelaus oft entertained | in our house when from Crete visit entrained
now I've picked out all the Achaeans who | can name and recognise save chieftains two
I cannot find Castor the horse-tamer | Polydeuces great boxer fame not err
my own brothers born of the same mother | as myself did not join army either
from lovely Lacedaemon or if they | crossed the seas and came here with the rest they
are unwilling parties in the fighting | on account of the scandal alighting
on my name and the insults they may hear" | she did not know when she said this in dear
lap fruitful earth them enclosed already | Lacedaemon land loved ready dead be
heady heralds bringing through town meanwhile | for treaty of peace the wherewithal style
the two sheep and a goatskin bottle filled | mellow wine fruit of the soil the herald
Idaeus who carried a bowl gleaming | golden cups came up to the old king meaning
to rouse him to action "Up my lord the chiefs | of the Trojan and Achaean force-fiefs
call for you to come down onto the plain | make truce as for Helen plainly plain pain
Paris and warrior Menelaus | fight with long spears those of many layers
winner to have the lady goods and all | the rest make a treaty of peace withal
by which we can stay here in deep-soiled Troy | while sail home to Argos enemy boy
to where horses graze and to Achaea | land of lovely women" when to his ear
news penetrated the old man shuddered | told his men to get his horses ruddered
to his chariot they promptly obeyed | into the chariot Priam essayed
and drew back the reins then Antenor got | in beside in the splendid chariot
and they drove their fast horses speedily | through Scaean Gate into open country
and when they reach each assembled army | stepped down from chariot onto bounty
of the good earth walked to mid-spot between | the forces Trojan and Achaean scene
King Agamemnon and the resourceful | Odysseus rose at once and heralds full
stately brought the victims for sacrifice | together mixed wine in bowl to suffice
and poured some water on the king's hands then | drew knife ever carried Agamemnon
beside the great scabbard of his sword hair | from the lamb's head cut and some of it there
fair distributed among the Trojan | Achaean captains then Agamemnon
lifted his hands prayed aloud so that all | heard "Father Zeus you the One rules all
from Mount Ida most glorious and great | and you the Sun whose eye and ear of fate
missing nothing in the world you Rivers | and you Earth of world below you Powers
make souls of dead men pay for perjury | call on you all to our oaths be jury
judge fair they are kept if Paris does kill | Menelaus he'll keep Helen we will
sail away in our swift ships seagoing | but if red-haired Menelaus going
gets kill Paris Trojans must surrender | Helen all possessions accounted her
and compensate the Argives suitably | scale generations future shall surely
remember and if in the event death | Paris Priam and sons refuse give breath
of life to payment I'll stay here fight for | the indemnity 'til finished the war"
Agamemnon slit lambs' throats with the bronze | relentless dropped gasping on ground where one's
life-force ebbed left them for knife done its work | then they drew wine from the bowl in the work

-ing cups and as they poured it on the ground | made petitions to the gods been around
since time began and the watching Trojans | did pray as also did the Achaeans
same prayer served them both "Zeus most glorious | great and you other gods victorious
over time may the brains of whichever | party breaks this treaty be poured ever
on the ground and poured out not only theirs | but their children also and may their heirs
be from foreigners possessing their wives" | and such were their hopes then for peaceful lives
but Zeus no intention yet peace-making | and now Dardanian Priam making
himself heard "Trojan and Achaean men | -at-arms attend to me going back then
windy Ilium since bear look not able | while my own son fighting formidable
Menelaus all can think is that Zeus | rest immortal gods must of suss made use
already which of two goes to his doom" | the venerable king with these words of gloom
put the lambs in the car himself got in | drew back the reins Antenor leapt hot in
at his side in his splendid chariot | and drove back to their Ilium hotspot
Priam's son Hector the admirable | Odysseus paced ground footy match table
subbuteo lots from metal helmet | cast see which one might be with all hell met
with the casting of the first spear the two | watching armies prayed with their hands raised to
the gods the same prayer served them both "Father | Zeus most glorious great from Mount Ida
rule let the man who brought these troubles on | both peoples' houses be killed and go on
down to House of Hades and let peace be | established between us prayers offered be"
great Hector of flashing helm shook them lots | turning his eyes aside one of the lots
leapt out at once it was that of Paris | the troops sat down in rows each man by his
high-stepping horse where his ornate arms piled | Prince Paris husband Helen lovely-piled
hair put on his beautiful armour there | began by tying round his legs a pair
of splendid greaves fitted with silver clips | for the ankles and next put cuirass grips
on his breast belonging to his brother | Lycaon and had to adjust over
his shoulder slung bronze sword silver-studded | hilt and then a great thick shield well-blood(i)ed
on his sturdy head set well-made helmet | which had a horse-hair crest with fine plume set
nodded grimly from top-knot last took up | powerful spear fitted to his grip-cup
battle-loving Menelaus equipped | self in same when both were fully agripped
each behind his own front line was striding | hosts look took so terrible a hiding
the spectators were spellbound horse-taming | Trojans Achaeans alike men gaming
-stations the two took to not far from one | another on the measured piece ground one
-two mutual fury weapons brandished | Paris first his long-shadowed spear banished
landed on Menelaus' round shield | bronze no breakthrough point bent back shield not yield
stout Menelaus son Atreus spear | brought to play-ing field Eton with prayer queer
-y Father Zeus "Grant me revenge King Zeus | on Paris man wronged me at start make use
my hands to bring him down so our children's | children might shudder thought be one offends
a host who has once received them kindly" | balanced his long-shadowed spear hurled heavy
weapon struck the son of Priam's round shield | piercing the thick great glittering shield's yield
forcing its way through the ornate cuirass | pressed straight on tore tunic and scared the ass
off Paris' flank swerved avoided death | thus Menelaus drew from sheath of death
his silver-mounted sword swung it back brought | down on ridge enemy's helmet well-wrought

sword broke on helm into half a dozen | pieces and dropped from his hand gave groan then
and he looked up into the vast broad sky | "Father Zeus is there a god" he did cry
"more spiteful than yourself? thought had paid out | Paris' infamy now sword gives out
in my hand when already cast a spear | for naught never touched man anywhere near!"
then hurled himself at Paris and seized him | by the horsehair crest and then swinging him
round began to drag him into the line | Achaean Paris was choked pressure fine
tender throat of embroidered helmet-strap | which he'd fitted tightly as a chin-strap
Manos then would have reel-y hauled him in | and thus with glory covered himself in
but for the quickness of Aphrodite | Daughter of Zeus who saw his plight mighty
broke strap for Paris though made of leather | of slaughtered ox helm came off however
in great hand of noble Menelaus | with a full swing he then did it toss thus
into Achaean lines where picked up by | retainers flung self at enemy nigh
again in the hope of despatching him | with bronze-pointed spear Aphrodited him
again with her powers by hiding him | in a dense mist there and then whisking him
off easy feat for the goddess put him | down in own perfumed fragrant bedroom trim
then she went herself to summon Helen | on the high tower she found her then
surrounded by Trojan women and looked | out her hand at her sweet-scented robe plucked
spoke to her in guise of an old woman | she was very fond of Lacedaemon
when she had lived there met a wool-worker | who used to make beautiful wool for her
"Come!" said goddess this woman mimicking | "Paris wants you home to him love p(r)icking
he's there in his room on the bed inlaid | radiant beauty lovely clothes out-laid
you'd never believe just come from a duel | you would think that he was a bright jewel
going to a dance or just stopped dancing | sat down to rest" Helen perturbed glancing
at the goddess with the beauty darkling | of her neck her lovely breasts eyes sparkling
struck with awe but made no pretence being | deceived "Lady of mysteries being
what's the object of this mummery now | Menelaus beaten Paris is now
willing take back home wife a lost plot thing | and now I suppose that you are plotting
carry me off to some other city | more distant still Phrygia or lovely
Maeonia a favourite he maybe | of yours then O mighty Aphrodite
who might just around those parts be living? | so you begin by coming here giving
incentive return Paris no go sit | with him yourself you goddess forget it
never set foot again in Olympus | devote yourself wholly to Paris plus
pamper him well and one day may be his | wife or indeed slave to go and share his
bed again would never hear end of it | not a woman Troy speech would not end it
without a curse on me if I did so | I have enough to bear already though"
Lady Aphrodite rounds fury high | on "Obstinate wretch! do not "she did cry
provoke me or might desert you in my | anger and then hate you as hearty high
as I have loved you up 'til now rousing | Trojans Achaeans bitter carousing
as would bring YOU to a miserable end" | and a child of Zeus though she was Hell-end
-ed cowed wrapped self up in glossy robe she | went off without a sound like Niobe
not one of the Trojan women saw her | go for she had a goddess to guide her
when reached the house of Paris beautiful | maids attendant took up tasks dutiful

at once great lady Helen to lofty | bedroom laughter-loving Aphrodite
goddess herself picked up chair carried it | across the room before Paris set it
daughter of aegis-bearing Zeus sat there | began by scolding lover from chair there
eyes turned aside "So back from battlefield | and I was hoping that back from that field
you would not come fallen there to the great | soldier who was my husband of not late!
you used to boast that you were a better | man than mighty Menelaus better
spearman stronger in the arm then why not | go at once challenge him again? or not
for should I warn you to think twice before | red-haired Menelaus offer once more
single-combat? do nothing rash may end | up yourself falling to his great spear-end!"
Paris had his answer ready "My dear | chide not my soul cruel taunts bitter cheer sear
indeed Menelaus has victory | with Athene's aid and yet the victory
on another day may indeed be mine | as on our side too we have gods divine
but come now let us have the joy of love | upon our couch for never yet has love
so enwrapped my heart not even then when | first snatched thee from lovely Lakedaimon
and sailed with thee on my seafaring ship | and on the isle of Kranae come to grip
with thee lying upon thy couch in love | as indeed now how much I do thee love
sweet desire has taken hold upon me" | and so saying he then led the lady
who followed to not-yet-Peter( ed)-out C(r)ouch | on that well-fretted bed much crutch did couch
Menelaus meanwhile throughout the host | strode boldly like unto beast wild the most
if anywhere in area set eyes | godlike Paris but no Trojans allies
could any way reveal Alexandros | to the dear-to-Ares Menelaus
not for love would any have hidden him | for even as black death all hated him
and so Agamemnon the King of Men | spoke among them right there and then "Hearken
to me Trojans Dardanians allies | win called Menelaus dear Ares lies
give back Helen of Argos possessions | with her as seemly compensations
may live on even among men to come" | all Achaeans gave their assent welcome

τέσσαρα

*Book 4*

# PANDARUS BREAKS THE TRUCE

*how Pandaros wounded by treachery*
*Menelaos King urged on captains key*

Zeus called gods confer Hall of Golden Floor | in their midst the lady Hebe did pour
their nectar with golden goblets pledged one | another gazed on city Trojan Son
of Cronos tried to provoke Here with key | vexing words he thus spoke maliciously
"Goddesses to aid Menelaus twain | Here Argos Alalkomenean strain
Athene yet these sit apart beholding | by Paris stands laughter-loving holding
fate ever Aphrodite wards off him | as he thought to perish she did save him
but victory is to Menelaus | who is dear to Ares and thus let us
take thought exactly how these things shall be | whether once more ill war arouse shall we
and the dread battle-din or make between | those enemies some sort of friendship scene
if this be welcome to all and pleasing | may the city of Troy not be ceasing
now as a place of habitation | Menelaus take Helen home station"
this speech drew muttered protests from Athene | Here sitting together plotting mean gene
evil for the Trojans and yet Athene | bit her lip for all the annoying scene
seen with father Zeus made no rejoinder | but Here could not here contain her anger
burst into speech "O dread Son of Cronos | what you are proposing here is monstrous!
how can you think of making all the dull | pains that I took and all my labour null
and void with all the sweat that poured from me | while my horses were toiling around me
as I was gathering the clans to make | trouble for Priam not just his sons' sake?
do as you please but do not imagine | that all the rest of us this image in"
Zeus the Cloud-gatherer this then fiercely | resented "Madam just what injury
can Priam and sons have done to you to | spark the vehemence of your desire to
sack the lovely Troy town? will no norm thing | satisfy your malice but the storming
of the gates and long walls the eating up | raw Priam sons folk yoke sunny side up?
do your own thing don't wish this difference | of ours grow into serious offence
but one condition I make recall it | when the downfall of a town MY turn it
is to desire and I choose one where friends | of yours live don't try to hamper my ends
let ME do My own thing since I've given | way now much against my inclination

for of all the cities that men live in | under the sun starry sky the most in
my heart holy Ilium with Priam | and of good ashen spear folk of Priam
never at their banquets did my altar | go without wine and fat its share proper
those offerings that we claim as our own" | then the ox-eyed Queen of Heaven "MY own
three towns I love best are Argos Sparta | Broad-Streets Mycenae sack those if ever
they wind you up good and proper I shan't | hold it against you their destruction shan't
stick my nose in on their behalf even | if do object meddle with your plan un
-likely make progress far too strong for me | you are and yet you ought not to thwart me
my enterprises any more than yours | should be for shared parentage mine and yours
as I too divine of all the children | of Cronos of the Crooked Ways I then
precedence by birth-right and as Consort | you're King overall with all gods consort
however by all means in this matter | let us yield now to each other flatter
I to you and you to me and the rest | immortal gods take vital viral test
will follow us and all that I ask you | to do just now is to tell Athene to
visit the front arrange for the Trojans | to break the truce by acting aggression's
part against the triumphant Achaeans" | not demurring Father of gods and men's
at once made his wishes clear to Athene | "Be off to the front of the battle scene
visit the armies and contrive to make | the Trojans there and then the truce to break
attacking Achaeans in their triumph" | with this encouragement as a triumph
Athene who had already set her heart | on action then down made a speedy start
from high Olympus like a meteor | discharged by Zeus as a warning sailor
or some great army on the land blazing | through the sky countless sparks them tasering
so Pallas Athene flashed down to earth leapt | into Trojan and Achaean midst swept
through horse-tamers and men-at-arms awestruck | and each man at his neighbour struck look stuck
question on lips "Does this mean we in shtuck | again bloody muck and bullets no luck?
or is Zeus our arbiter in battle | making peace between us end death-rattle?"
while Achaeans and Trojans were asking | each other just what on earth next tasking
Athene now disguised herself as a man | and inserted self into ranks Trojan
in the likeness of a spearman sturdy | Laodocus Antenor son worthy
trying find stalwart and admirable | Pandarus Lycaon's son if able
found there Prince Pandarus standing aside | a powerful shield-bearing force beside
at his command from river Aesepus | went up to him and made clear her purpose
"Pandarus lord will wits into use bring | and take a tip from me? if you could bring
yourself to shoot Menelaus with an | arrow cover self in glory Trojan
host all in your debt and Prince Paris most | of all he would be very first of host
to come forward then with a handsome gift | if saw great Son of Atreus adrift
Menelaus struck down by a shot from | you laid out on a funeral pyre come
shoot at Menelaus in his glory | to Archer-King Apollo pray (w)ho(l)ly
your own Lycian god promise splendid | sacrifice firstling lambs when your sacred
city of Zeleia you regain" | Athene's eloquence prevailed once again
fool then and there unsheathed his bow polished | made from horns ibex he'd self off polished
with a shot in the breast had lain in wait | for the beast caught on the breast-no-plate late

as it was exiting from a rock's cleft | so tumbled back into the cleft bereft
horns on head measured across sixteen hands | worked up then by a horn-y craftsman's hands
who fitted them together made all smooth | put a golden tip on the end forsooth
Pandarus slung the bow slanting against | ground laid careful down whilst his men against
attack by the fierce Achaeans made shield | -wall before to protect him in the field
'til he'd shot Menelaus the battle | -loving son Atreus lid off quarrel
-carrier picked out an arrow feathered | unused until now and so well tethered
its bearing now so fraught with agony | sharp arrow to string fitted most gainly
offered up prayer Apollo Archer-King | own Lycian god promise forthcoming
a most splendid sacrifice firstling lambs | when home return then kicking out the jambs
own town sacred Zeleia gripping | notched end ox-gut string grip waiting go ping
when had bent the bow to circle went twang | the taut string a-quivering out then sang
and the sharp quarrel leapt into the air | eager winged way into oppo ranks there
ah but the happy gods that never die | not leave you Menelaus high and dry
Athene above all the Fighting Daughter | of Zeus made her stand against his slaughter
before warding off then the piercing dart | turning just a little from fleshy part
like a mother a fly away sweeping | from her child who lies there gently sleeping
with her own hand guided to where golden | buckles of belt fixed and corslet folden
over so sharp arrow struck fastened belt | and drove on through fine decorated felt
pressed on again through the cuirass ornate | and through apron Menelaus by fate
wore at last protection against raving | weapons this more than all rest him saving
yet arrow went through metal apron though | in the end made a shallow wound also
at once dark blood from cut came swift draining | it was like the purple dye for staining
Carian or Maeonion woman | makes cheek-piece for a horse uses on an
ivory ornament lovely laid in store | though each driver would rather see it more
on his horse 'til one day takes fancy king | who buys it to adorn his horse thinking
badge of honour for his charioteer | thus Menelaus blood-stained tour come-here
thighs and legs down to your shapely ankles | Agamemnon shudders 'til it rankles
when saw the dark blood streaming from the cut | indeed veteran Menelaus cut
up aghast but when binding barbs observed | arrow-head not sunk in got back reserved
composure but Agamemnon deep groan | seized him by hand while consternation own
their his men expressed there "My dear brother!" | cried Agamemnon "'twas yours not other
death then I swore to when I made the truce | to fight alone for us sent out make use
against the Trojans who now you have shot | trampled all over their solemn pact plot
yet a pact ratified by our right hands | sanctified special grand cru wine bond brands
in blood of lambs not easily annulled | the Olympian may stay those be culled
but awards the penalty in the end | transgressors pay heavy price dividend
they pay with their lives and with their women | even with lives of their little children
day will come I know in my heart of hearts | holy Ilium dissected corpse parts
along with Priam people of Priam | of the good ashen spear and sure I am
Zeus the Son of Cronos from his high seat | in Heaven will wave sombre aegis feat
over them all in his anger at this | perjury of theirs without fail all this

will happen yet Menelaus if you | die and if your end really comes to you
how bitterly then I shall lament you | and what a sorry figure I'll cut too
my return thirsty Argos expectant | as Achaeans will be full on intent
of getting home at once be under force | leave Achaean Helen Troy boast perforce
while the earth would rot your bones as you lay | Troyland task undone already hear say
Trojan braggart as he stomps on your tomb | illustrious Menelaus "Grand doom!
and may every single quarrel picked by | Agamemnon prove futile empty-sigh
-ships retreat and 'heem Sterling Menelaus | left behind! that is how they will talk plus
I shall pray too for earth to swallow me" | but red-haired Menelaus able free
-ly comfort him "Courage! say nothing to | dispirit the men arrow not reach to
a vital spot before it got so far | it was stopped by the metal avatar
of my belt corslet beneath apronly | with the bronze they put on it" "If only
you're right my dear Menelaus!" exclaimed | King "but wound shall be examined reclaimed
by a physician and ointments applied | ease pain" to noble squire order applied
"Talthybius go as fast as you can | fetch Machaon I'm sure you know the man
son Asclepius the great physician | see my lord Menelaus some Trojan
or Lycian archer knows business well | shot him with arrow to his renown fell
our discomfiture" obediently | his squire set out made way through hastily
ranks of the bronze-clad Achaeans searching | for the lord Machaon found researching
plans with his men powerful shield-bearing | force that under his command there faring
from Tricce where the horses graze he went | up to him delivering message sent
"Quick my lord Machaon! Agamemnon | King sends for you see our great captain one
Menelaus some Trojan Lycian | archer who knows his business well stuck an
arrow into him to his own renown | our discomfiture" stirred by herald's frown
Machaon set off with him they threaded | their way through the army's great ranks serried
when reached spot where red-haired Menelaus | lay wounded all chieftains many layers
circled around him the admirable | Machaon passed through the rings was able
at once arrow from fastened belt extract | barbed points broke off as he with pull exact
undid glittering belt corslet under | -Neath apron coppersmiths made a wonder
when found place sharp point pierced flesh sucked out blood | soothing balm skill applied spot wounded good
from the supply with which Cheiron friendly | had equipped his father and then while he
attending Menelaus of the loud | war-cry Troy's battle-lines advanced aloud
to the assault the Achaeans once more | put on their armour turned their thoughts to war
King Agamemnon now showed his mettle | at once alert to battle fine fettle
no hesitation sign of fears nervous | for the fight and glory eagerness plus
decided not use horses chariot | inlaid pair led aside by squire with lariot
and as they went Agamemnon careful | instruct him Eurymedon son Ptol
-emy keep close at hand in case weary | at any point in long tour of army
then set off on foot go round of forces | and when he would come upon his horses
-loving Danaans who up and raging | he stopped and then was them encouraging
"Argives you have the right spirit do not | forget it now as perjurers will not
get any help from Father Zeus and men | who went back on their word and have broken

the truce going to have their own smooth flesh | devoured by vultures while we fully fresh
carry off Troy's little children and wives | they love on board our ships when we Argives
have sacked their stronghold" on the other hand | any found shrink from ugly boy band brand
of war got sharp rebuke and angry words | "Contemptible creatures you Total nerds
brave only with the bow! is there no shame | in you? why just stand there in a dazed frame
of mind like fawns that dash across the plain | and stop when they're tired as they have no brain
spirit? that's what you look like requiting | selves with a blank trance instead of fighting
do you wait for the Trojans to threaten | our good ships on the beach grey sea beaten
in the hope that Zeus will put out a hand | and protect you then?" this way played the hand
impressed his will on the men on his tour | of the serried ranks came too to the fore
the Cretans paraded there their soldiers | under the able Idomeneus
in forefront indeed Idomeneus | brave as boar his squire Meriones plus
commanded the company in the rear | the King quickly compliments leader dear
delighted see them "Idomeneos | now of all my horse-loving Danaos
there is not one I count on more than you | not just on the battlefield off it too
I'll show you this when we sit down to dine | and when of the elders the sparkling wine
mixed in the bowl for the very best men | when his portion each long-haired Achaean
has drunk your cup stands full like mine to drink | from as you wish off with you now to drink
in the battle be the man you've always | claimed!" "My lord Atreides on such days
you can rely on my loyal support | and solemn assurance gave you in port
when this business began now rouse the rest | of long-haired Achaeans so we may test
ourselves in battle right away now that | the Trojans have broken their oath for that
they have naught to expect except disaster | and death since oath keep loath will come faster
as broke the truce" well pleased with this reply | Atreides passed on and made way nigh
the crowd up to the two lords called Aias | the pair were arming themselves and the mass
of infantry behind loomed like a cloud | that sees from a lookout point goatherd proud
across the sea that down upon him bore | with at its back great West Wind's mighty roar
oncomes over sea whirlwind in wake which | darkening in distance 'til black as pitch
goatherd shudders at sight drives flock in cave | thus behind the two Aiantes the brave
youths moved out to battle their closed crowd shroud | set-ups bristle shields spears dark as a cloud
King Agamemnon rejoiced when saw them | paid a signal tribute saluting them
as leaders of his now bronze-clad Argives | "As for you two one order not applies
exhortation would be out of place your | very leadership inspires men in core
corps fight their best by Father Zeus Athene | Apollo the mettle I wish be seen
in all King Priam's city captured sacked | by Argive hands crack troops would soon have cracked"
leaving them with these words Agamemnon | King of Men passed on came to Nestor then
clear-voiced orator from Pylos sandy | whom he found preparing his men handy
for the fight and marshalling them under | their officers Pelagon Alastor
Chromius Prince Haemon Bias the great | captain charioteers he did locate
with their horses and cars up at the front | at back mass top-class infantry effront
-ery serve as rearguard in between he | placed inferiors even laggardly
shirkers would be forced to fight and he told | charioteers instructed first to hold

in horses not get entangled barbed wire | melee "Don't think that charioteer's fire
bravery skill entitles him break ranks | and on his John Stones fight the Trojan tanks
don't let one drop back and weaken whole force | when a man in own chariot perforce
comes within reach of an enemy car | it's time to try a spear-thrust as those are
the best tactics this is the discipline | spirit enabled forefathers break in
to walled towns by storm" so used that acquired | experience battles long past inspired
his troops it warmed King Agamemnon's heart | to watch him said what he felt for his part
"Venerable lord how happy I would be | if your admirable spirit could be
matched by the vigour of your limbs your strength | unimpaired but age which no-one has strength
to halt lies heavy on you if only | could pass on to someone else join friendly
ranks of youth!" "Ah my lord Atreides" | said the Gerenian Knight "I wish these
things most heartily too to be the man | I was when killed great Ereuthalion
but the gods don't grant us all their favours | at one time was a young man lord save us
for now age oppresses me yet for all | I'll be with my men chariot withal
and in command their plans and orders come | from me privileges one ageing some
even if now the handling of the spears | is left to younger men of lesser years
than myself with the vigour for the work" | content with what he had seen of the work
Agamemnon resumed his tour the next | visited Peteos' son Menest
-heus tamer of horses he and his | Athenian troops standing idle his
neighbour Odysseus of the nimble wits | his large Cephallenian force with its
leader also standing easy the call | not yet reached their ears go to battle all
for Trojan and Achaean regiments | only just begun take up their segments
so they stood and waited for some other | Achaean battalion take over
the advance against the Trojans begin | fight when noticed this the King did admin
-ister a severe rebuke "You sir Men | -estheus son of royal father then
and you Odysseus arch-intriguer you | always seek own advantage why are you
hanging back like this leaving others to | advance? because it is up to you to
take your stand in the front line welcome shock | of battle are you not the first shock jock
get my invitation when a banquet | all leading captains afoot etiquette?
on such occasions you are quite content | take fill mellow wine roasted pig me(a)(n)(t)
enjoy yet seem quite content to watch while | ten battalions in Achaean style
fall on oppos before you make a move" | this the resourceful Odysseus did move
gave a black look "My lord Atreides | accusations Total absurdities
can you now maintain that in pitched battle | we ever loiter in the rear? you will
have your wish if that is what's troubling you | see father Telemachus getting to
grips with front rank of these horse-(s)talking | Trojans meanwhile it's nonsense you're talking"
when Agamemnon saw that Odysseus | had got the hump smiles at him issues thus
apology "Royal son Laertes | Odysseus of ever nimble wits ease
I do not blame over-much and do not dwell | on spurring you on for I know you're well
disposed towards me in your heart in fact | we see eye to eye but enough post fact
-um I will make amends for anything | uncivil I may have been gainsaying
let the gods wipe it out" with this did text | them then went in search of others the next

came on was Tydeus' son the great | -heart Diomedes chariot of state
well-made standing horses yoked Sthenelus | stood close at hand son of Capaneus
Agamennon viewed Diomedes' | stance took him sharply to task "What does this
mean? the son of Tydeus that dauntless | charioteer shirking fight more or less
just watching? not Tydeus' habit | ever shrink back sally out just a bit
in front of all his friends and come to grips | this is what folk say who saw him when chips
down say he was superb but I never | knew him and set eyes on him not ever
although he did come once to Mycenae | but as a friend not as an enemy
with Prince Polyneices reinforcements | seeking avoid any impediments
time of their expedition against Thebes | Sacred Walls busy as Madchester bees
begged very hard for adequate support | we promised bee in any storm La-porte
but Zeus made us change our minds by showing | inauspicious omens so their going
from Mycenae but when had gone some way | reached the deep meadows banks and reedy sway
of Asopus Achaean commanders | put up Tydeus lord key-words banders
for a parley he went to Thebes and found | large group Cadmeians dinner around
in the palace of Prince Eteocles | as visitor may be wobbly knees
alone there among a crowd of strangers | even for gallant Tydeus dangers
but not at all challenged them to friendly | matches in every case won easily
with Athene's generous help that riled horse | -racing Cadmeians sent ahead horse
-racers to lay an ambush in his path | with forty two officers psychopath
Polyphontes hardened bully killer | as had also been before his father
and Maeon son of Haemon man of rank | however Tydeus dealt with them rank
brought them to an end indeed most ugly | but for one sent home killed the whole party
had warning from the gods let off Maeon | that sir Tydeus Aetolian
you are his son but don't fight like he did | though may be better when come to talk bid"
the staunch Diomedes made no reply | to this harangue accepted rebuke high
from the sovereign he revered but the son | illustrious Capaneus lid on
tongue could not keep "My lord you know the facts | don't distort them for I claim that the fact's
one's a far better man than one's father | DID take Seven-gated Thebes with weaker
force we stormed a more powerful defence | than they ever faced signs the gods sent hence
in Zeus we then put our faith whereas they | came to grief through their own presumptive way
never talk to me about our fathers | art in heaven in the same breath as us"
"Be quiet man and take your cue from me" | Diomedes interposed with angry
glance at Sthenelus "I am not erring | with quarrel with Agamemnon spurring
us on to fight our Commander-in-Chief | because it is he who will get the chief
credit if Achaeans beat the Trojans | take holy Ilium but Achaeans
defeated at same time he suffers most | come it is time for you and me to host
thoughts of war" and jumped down from chariot | in all his armour and as leapt riot
into action the bronze rang full G(r)imli | on the prince's breast stoutest heart might be
dismayed now battalion on battalion | into battle swept relentlessly on
like great waves of waves come onslaught hurtling | one top one on echo beach chortling
under a westerly gale and far out | at sea man their crests begin to rise out

of the waters and then in they come crash | down on the shingle with a mighty brash
roar or arch themselves to break on a cliff | and there send the sea foam flying skewiff
each of the captains shouted his orders | to his own command but men on borders
of silence moved quietly they obeyed | their officers and no sound there betrayed
came behind like army of the Somme dumb | the metalled armour they marched in rent numb
their eyes as it glittered on every man | but it was otherwise with host Trojan
they were like the sheep that stand in a rich | farmer's yard and their white milk then up pitch
go bleating incessantly on as hear | their lambs such a tower babel here
from the great Trojan army which hailed from | many parts being separated from
each other by lack of common language | thus used many different cries calls war wage
Ares War god spurred on forces Trojan | Athene of Flashing Eyes force Achaean
Terror and Panic were also at hand | Strife War-god's Sister gives him a big hand
in his bloody work once begun can't stop | at first seems little thing ere long moptop
hits high heaven with her head though feet still | on the ground swept in among all troops fill
-ing them full of hatred for each other | dying men's groans wished hear brother-brother
at the last armies met with clash bucklers | and of bronze-clad fighting men with their spears
then the bosses of their shields collided | great roar went up screams dying elided
with the vaunts their destroyers earth ran rain | of blood so winter then when two mountain
rivers flowing spate from the great springs culls | higher up tumbling as torrent mingles
at a watersmeet in some deep ravine | far off in hills herder some swine scene keen
hears their thunder thus tumult let loose slips | turmoil as the two armies come to grips
Antilochus the first to kill his man | Echepolus of Thalysius son
fighting in full armour in Trojan front | with first cast he struck him on the ridge front
of his crested helmet spear-point landing | forehead bone pierced darkness came crash-land -ing
down on his eyes collapsed in the melee | like a falling tower he was barely
down when Prince Elephenor Chalcodon's | son leader of fiery Abantes ones
seized him by the feet and tried to drag him | quickly out of range of armour spoil him
an enterprise he did not carry far | valiant Agenor from not afar
had seen him dragging the body away | with his bronze-headed shaft then fired away
caught him on left flank which was left exposed | by the shield as Elphenor in stoop posed
he collapsed and over lifeless body | grim struggle ensued between each army
Trojans Achaeans at each other leapt | like ravenous wolves men tossed men adept
now then Telemonian Aias downed | Anthemion's son Simoisius drowned
sturdy youngster took his name from River | Simois beside which born when mother
returning from Mount Ida where father | mother had taken see their sheep rather
too short was his life for he not repays | parents for their most loving caring ways
for ended when met great Aias' spear | for he had scarcely sallied out to here
when Aias struck him in the breast by right | nipple bronze spear went through shoulder quite right
down came in the dust like slender poplar | with a bushy top has shot up popped far
in the big meadows by a stream cut down | wainwright's gleaming axe later man line down
will make some felloes from it for the wheel | of a beautiful chariot but he' ll
leave it now to lie on bank and season | so Aias fell felled Anthemion's son

and now Priam's son Antiphus in his | shimmering cuirass javelin of his
sharp aimed across crowd at Aias himself | although Antiphus missed his man himself
he did make a hit for he caught Leucus | one of the comrades of Odysseus
in the groin as he dragged Simoisius | away body fell from hands of Leucus
and he himself came crashing down on it | Odysseus infuriated at it
seeing Leucus killed in his glittering | bronze equipment through front ranks skittering
his way right up to the enemy line | where he took his stand looked around one fine
cast of his shining lance he then did try | the Trojans leapt back as saw it come fly
but Odysseus had not thrown in vain | struck bastard son Democoon Priam's strain
who'd joined up from his stud-farm Abydus | only to fall then to spear Odysseus
chucked looked back in anger at comrade's death | the bronze point had struck on one temple death
came out at the other night descended | on his eyes fell thud armour clang out did
illustrious Hector whole Trojan front | fell back while Argives shouted triumphant
dragged the corpses in advanced still farther | Apollo from Pergamus filled rather
with indignation called to host Trojan | "On with you you charioteers Trojan!
never give the Argive best in battle | they're not made of stone iron or metal
their flesh can't keep out penetrating bronze | when they're hit and what's more Thetis' son's
not fighting he born she of Lovely Locks | but is sulking by the ships in dry docks"
thus redoubtable god them encouraged | from citadel while Argives more enraged
by Athene Daughter of Zeus the august | Lady of Triton went through the ranks just
by herself spurred on any laggards seen | now for Diores toils of Fateful scene
son Amarinceus by stone jagged | hit near ankle on right leg then ragged
he who threw it was the Thracian captain | Peiros son Imbrasus who came fron Aen
-us brutal rock shattered the two sinews | and bones and for Diores the sin news
fell backwards in the dust his hands stretching | out to his friends for lack of breath (w)retching
but Peiros ran up and struck his navel | with spear poured out on ground entrails Total
night descended on his eyes as Peiros | sprang away Aetolian Thoas
hit him in the chest with a spear below | the nipple and the bronze point sank full low
into the lung Thoas came up to him | pulled the heavy weapon out of him grim
drew sharp sword struck him full in the belly | killed him not get armour booty welly
as Peiros' men Thracians with topknots | on their heads surrounded him in top lots
they held their long spears steady in their hands | and then fended Thoas off though he stands
big strong formidable Thoas shaken | and stirred to withdraw so these two taken
Peiros and Diores stretched in the dust | at each other's side chieftains left to rust
one Thracian other bronze-clad Epean | but not only ones killed without paean
indeed this was not an idle skirmish | newcomer yet unhit hit and mash-mish
would soon have found had Athene not shielded | from the hail of missiles and then him led
by hand to the very thick of the fray | many Trojans and Achaeans that day
bit the dust and were stretched out side by side ...

πέντε

*Book 5*

# DIOMEDES FIGHTS THE GODS

*how Diomedes by his great valour*
*made havoc of Trojan host warrior*
*and Aphrodite wounded even seen*
*Ares hit as well with aid of Athene*

... Pallas Athene Diomedes inspired
son of Tydeus with audacity | resolution and in extremity
eclipse all his comrades-in-arms cover | self glory steady as Star of Summer
was the glow with which she then set blazing | shield and helm when rises from his bathing
in Ocean all other stars to outshine | such fire caused stream from head and shoulder shine
as thrust him in very heart of battle | a Trojan called Dares citizen weal
-thy of good repute priest of Hephaestus | had two sons Phegeus and Idaeus
and both in every kind of fighting trained | these two from the rest themselves entrained
advanced against him in their chariot | while Diomedes off meet them foot-hot
when in range Phegeus began the fight | hurled his long-shadowed spear with all his might
but point passed over Diomedes' | left shoulder now was Diomedes'
turn to cast weapon did not leave his hand | for nothing it struck Phegeus full hand
-some in the middle of the breast and out | tumbled from well-made chariot in rout
Idaeus also deserted leaping | to rear his brother's corpse over keeping
not daring Black Fate would have got him too | if Hephaestus had not come to rescue
wrapping him in night saving him so priest | aged of his might not then on grief feast
be utterly broken magnificent | Diomedes drove off the horses sent
them with his followers to hollow ships | and when the Trojans saw how bad the trips
Dares' sons had been on how one killed | beside his chariot the other stilled
put to flight they for all their bravery | were dismayed at this point Athene clearly
Bright-Eyed interposed laid restraining hand | on ferocious War-god's killing arm brand
"Ares" cried "murderous Ares Butcher | of Men and of Cities and Towns Sacker
is it not time for us let the Trojans | fight to the finish with the Achaeans
and see who Father Zeus intends to win? | let's leave the field before inspiring in
him anger" and led the impetuous | War-god from the fight made sit on famous

Scamander's grassy bank as a result | Argives Trojan line thrust back in tumult
with each of their leaders killing his man | begun by Agamemnon King of Man
in hurling the great Odius chieftain | of the Alizones from his car then
as Odius had been the first to fly | and as he turned Agamemnon let fly
and caught him right in the back with his spear | in the mid-point between each shoulder clear
drove it through his breast fell with a thud dull | and his armour did ring about him full
next up Idomeneus killed Phaestus | the son of the Maeonian Borus
who'd come from the fertile lands of Tarne | as Phaestus getting into his car nay
for the great spearman pierced his right shoulder | with long javelin crashed down from car cur
-sed and hateful night did then engulf him | retainers Idomeneus stripped him
then Menelaus son of Atreus | killed Scamandrius son of Strophius
with sharp-pointed spear great man for the chase | who'd been taught to hunt by Artemis ace
herself to bring down any kind of wild | game the mountain forest might yield wild child
Artemis the Mistress of the Bow though | not of any help to him now and no
either the long shots that had won him such fame | as Scamandrius fled before fame game
glorious spearman of Many Layers | struck with lance mid-back between the shoulders
drove it through his chest he fell face downward | and his armour upon him did clang hard
next Meriones killed Phereclus son | of Tecton himself the son of Harmon
carpenter could turn hand such curious | kind work so no greater favourite thus
Athene had 'twas he who'd built for Paris | those trim ships driven everything a-miss
proved a curse to the whole Trojan peoples | and self since knew nowt of the oracles
Meriones ran after him caught up | through right buttock stitched him quite rite right up
spear-head passed clean through right to the bladder | under bone dropped to knees he be lad a
scream gave and Death enveloped him then Meges | killed Pedaeus bastard Antenor he's
please her husband the gracious Theano | had brought up like a child of her own so
Meges mighty spearman caught up with this | man struck on the nape of the neck with his
sharp lance point came between the jaws severed | tongue at root fell in dust with severe-d
-eath bit the cold bronze with his teeth meanwhile | Eurypylus Euaemon's son mean style
Hypsenor killed son Dolopion proud | served priest Scamander River-god flood loud
and was worshipped by the people of Troy | as fled before Euaemon's high-born boy
Eruypylus gave chase slashed at shoulder | with sword the great man's arm shorn as-under
fell bleeding to ground Fate set her seal on | him and the shadow of death eyes fell on
and such was the execution then done | in the assault by front line Danaan
indeed as for Diomedes himself | you could not have told on which army shelf
the Trojan or Achaean he belonged | across plain winter storm torrent he longed
comes tearing down and flattens out the dykes | and against its sudden onslaught no Tykes
can stand backed too by heavy rains no dykes | meant hem it in sCalderdale nor the likes
Severn stone walls round vineyards their sturdy | trees it has its way and far and widely
the farmers see the wreckage work splendid | and so the Trojans in their ranks serried
collapsed before the son of Tydeus | unable withstand though so numerous
when noble Pandarus Lycaon's son | saw Diomedes storm the plain for fun
driving Trojan companies before him | lost no time bent crooked bow aimed at him

struck him as forged ahead in right shoulder | on a plate of his cuirass plate-piercer
the sharp arrow pressed straight on and blood spread | over the cuirass Pandarus rais-ed
great shout triumph over Diomedes | "Forward charioteers now so much ease!
forward and at them! the best man they've got | is badly wounded won't last a jot lot
longer if Apollo in earnest when | he sent ME to here from Lycia then"
Pandarus could boast yet Diomedes | was not beaten by the dart's bitter ease
fell back came to halt by his horses thus | chariot too and called to Sthenelus
son Capaneus "Quick dear Sthenelus | get down from the chariot and draw thus
this wretched arrow out from my shoulder" | Sthenelus leapt to the ground came over
to him and pulled out the arrow clean through | his shoulder and the blood came gushing through
his knitted tunic and Diomedes | of the loud war-cry offered in prayer these
words "Mark me unsleeping Child of Zeus who | wears the aegis if ever in past you
wished us well and then stood by my father | or indeed myself in heat of farther
action be kind to me again Athene | let me kill Pandarus bring me within mean
spear-cast of the man who shot me never | had a chance and now folk telling ever
that I'm as good as dead" Diomedes | prayer rose up air Pallas Athene's ears seize
and there and then made a new man of him | and so also came up to stand by him
spoke momentous words "Now Diomedes | no fear you can fight the Trojans at ease
for I have filled your heart with the boldness | illustrious father Tydeus yes
the great shield-bearing charioteer I | have also swept the deep mist from your eye
made you able distinguish gods from men | and so now I will tell you if and when
a god comes here to put you to the test | against the immortals you must give rest
just one exception if Aphrodite | Daughter of Zeus comes into fight flighty
use your sharp bronze and wound her" with that bright | -eyed Athene disappeared and back to fight
son of Tydeus went in front line mean | took place once more even without Athene
determined fall on enemy again | and now he was three times as bold again
as before like a lion a shepherd | charged with the woolly sheep on a farmstead
outlying wounded as leapt into yard | but failed to kill has only roused him hard
-er to greater fury and now he can | not keep him off but does them abandon
the sheep in their panic hide in stables | there to be mown down in heaps enables
and the still furious lion jumps hard | over the high wall thus gets out of yard
it was with such fury Diomedes | the mighty charged the Trojan line disease
began by slaying Astynous and a | chieftain Hypeiron struck one above a
nipple with his bronze-pointed spear other | with great sword on collar bone by shoulder
so shoulder severed from the neck and back | left them lying there to the chase cut back
after Abas and Polyeidus the sons | old Eurydamas who believed in tons
dream-power but no dreams to recount | these when set out for the front of blood fount
and so then the mighty Diomedes | killed both after that Xanthus and Thoon these
pursues sons of Phaenops a pair stripling | whose father now old man ailment crippling
had no other son to whom bequeath wealth | they next fell Diomedes took wealth health
clean away left father broken-hearted | flesh again never saw sons departed
home from the war was their cousins who stepped | into estate Diomedes' next

victims two sons Dardanian Priam | Chromius Echemmon both say I am
ride same chariot but like a lion | pounces on cattle in a glade backs on
opening in the forest breaks an ox's | or heifer's neck son Tydeus ax(l)es
them rudely from their chariot without | so much as a "by your leave" came the clout
Aeneas seeing how Diomedes | creating havoc in Trojans with ease
set out through melee and rain of missiles | seeks Prince Pandarus when number mobile's
noble found stalwart son of Lycaon | he went up ally to lay a one on
"Pandarus what are you doing now man | with bow winged arrows? aren't you the bowman
supposedly the best that Lycia | can boast better in Troy than any a
one? for Heaven's sake man raise a prayer to | Zeus and let fly at that fellow there to
the fore I don't know who it is but he's | having it all his own way and thus he's
done us too much harm already brought down | many of our best men from around town
yet be careful may be one of holy | immortals annoyed with us for faulty
performance of our rights we are being | punished perhap by god angry being"
Lycaon's noble son saluted man | Aeneas with the respect due Trojan
Councillor "If you ask me the man is | Diomedes himself recognise his
shield and crested visor of his helmet | know his horses too when I see them yet
I cannot swear that he is not a god | if who take him for of courage the mod
-el great Diomedes I see the hand | Heaven in this mad attacking band brand
some god surely must have been standing by | him enveloped in haze to have made my
arrow swerve as it hit him for I HAVE | shot at him and in the right shoulder have
hit him clean through the plate of his cuirass | certainly thought I'd seen off his queer ass
bad to Hades yet I did not kill him | so perhaps some angry god DOES shade him
and here am I without a chariot | and pair to carry me now hereabout
while all the time have eleven home some | splendid chariots wainwright's hands fresh come
cloths spread over them couple of horses | standing by munching rye and white barley fizz
in the palace before I left for front | Lycaon dad old spearman said upfront
time and again I ought from chariot | lead my men when seek to cause a riot
amongst the enemy but I would not | listen better if had listened to what
said thought of my horses who'd had always | enough to eat afraid the fodder trays
might run short in the congested city | Ilium on foot rely archery
not that archery was going to do | me any good already shot at two
of their best men Menelaus the lord | Diomedes and in each case I scored
a hit and drew blood no doubt about it | but that just roused them to raise their rate hit
yes did unlucky thing when took crooked | bow from its peg that day I first hook-ed
up with my company for your lovely | town so as Prince Hector to please solely
but if I ever get home again set | eyes on my own country and my wife set
foot in high-roofed house I'll be ready let | anyone there then cut off my head-set
if I don't smash this bow with my own hands | throw into blazing fire well off my hands"
"Don't talk like that" said commander Trojan | "and yet it's true enough that nothing can
be done to stop the man 'til you and I | in a chariot raise the hue and cry
and then attack him with other weapons | come mount my car and you'll see what happens

what the horses of the Tros breed are like | and how quickly can cover ground alike
makes no odds at all which way you drive them | in flight or pursuit can rely on them
to get us both safely back into Troy | if Zeus should give Diomedes the boy
of Tydeus another victory | yet come now take whip and reins and when timely
moment comes I'll dismount do the fighting | or let me care for the horses plighting
you to stand up to the man" "Aeneas | you must take rein your own horses alas
as they will better pull the chariot | if behind normal driver runs riot
if presently we have to run away | from Tydeus' son might fly away
when missed your voice and take us refused these | off the field and see then Diomedes
indomitable close in finish us | off drive off our horses so handle thus
your own chariot and pair when the man | comes up I will greet him as a spear-man"
this point decided they mounted the car | so resolutely drove their fast pair far
out of front line towards Diomedes | Sthenelus son Capaneus saw these
approaching promptly warned Tydeides | "My lord my most dear lord Diomedes
here come now two stalwarts bent on fighting | you most formidable pair us blighting
one is the bowman Pandarus who calls | himself Lycaon's son the other calls
self Aeneas who names lord Anchises | as his father and fair Aphrodite's
his Mother so quick now let us fall back | in chariot not be taken aback
storming about the front line any more | I beg or may die Troy's far foreign shore"
mighty Diomedes gave angry look | "Do not talk to me now of flight you schmuck
you won't persuade me not in my nature | flee fight run away strong as ever sure
refuse use chariot will go meet them | as I am as Athene lets me show them
no cowardice as for those two there their | horses may be fast but they won't save their
riders both from us get them home-some | even if one escapes now listen come!
and don't forget what I say if Athene | fullness her wisdom gives me win obscene
and kill them both leave our own horses here | we can tie the reins to the rail here near
concentrate on Aeneas' horses | seize THEM and drive them out of the courses
Trojan and into ours for I tell you | that they are bred from the same stock look you
as those that all-seeing Zeus gave to Tros | in return boy Ganymede to win toss
THEY were the best horses in the world whole | but later Prince Anchises the breed stole
by putting mares to them without consent | Laomedon the mares later on went
and foaled in his stables and of the six | horses he got out of them he then picks
four for himself reared them at the manger | but gave these two to minimise danger
in battle to Aeneas if we could | capture them in glory selves cover would"
in the meantime as they were so talking | other two the pair thoroughbreds stalking
came up at a gallop and Pandarus | noble son Lycaon called across thus
"So the stubborn Diomedes naughty | shot mine survived braves it out son haughty
Tydeus not to be felled by arrow! | well then I will try him with a spear now
see what that will do" poised and hurled the long | -shadowed javelin struck the shield be-long
Tydeides the bronze head pierced the shield | reached the cuirass shout of triumph did wield
over him noble son of Lycaon | "A hit" he cried "clean through the shield and on
through the flank you won't stand up to that long | what a triumph I'll thank you for ere long!"

"A miss! you never touched me" powerful | Diomedes said not perturbed awfull
-y "and what's more fancy before you two | have done that one or the other of you
will be proper done in and god glut good | of battle stubborn with his precious blood"
then Diomedes cast his spear guided | by Athene on head Pandarus struck did
by eye right on nose through his white teeth passed | and his tongue by the relentless bronze slashed
off at the root and the point then came out | at base of chin of chariot crashed out
his burnished armour scintillating rang | out upon him the horses shied up sprang
thoroughbreds though they were this was the end | Pandarus Aeneas to meet his end
perhap leapt down from the chariot shield | and long spear fearing that now in the field
Achaeans might try rob him of the corpse | bestrode like lion at bay in a copse
with pride in his power with spear covers | round shield determined to kill all comers
and uttering his terrible war-cry | Diomedes picked up a rock to try
to lift it feat beyond even the strength | any two men today though bred at length
but Diomedes handled it alone | without effort so struck home in the zone
hitting Aeneas on the hip where the thigh | turns in hip-joint 'cup-bone' name some apply
he crushed that and he broke both sinews too | skin jagged boulder lacerated through
the noble Aeneas sank to his knees | supported self one great hand like a tree's
but world went black as night before his eyes | indeed prince right up to it in his eyes
and would have perished there and then but for | quickness of his Mother Zeus' Daughter
Aphrodite who had conceived him for | Anchises when his cattle caring for
seeing what happened she threw her arms white | round her beloved son drew a fold white
then of her shimmering robe across him | so from flying weapons to protect him
and a fatal spear-cast one of the best | from Danaan charioteer in breast
and while Ahprodite was rescuing | son from field Sthenelus not eschewing
instructions he'd had from Diomedes | of the loud war-cry his horses' reins he's
tied to the chariot rail and left them | kicking their heels at some fair distance from
the scene of the turmoil mad dash seeing | for Aeneas' long-maned pair seizing
and drove them out of course Trojan into | Achaean course handed them over to
Deipylus friend felt well-adjusted | more than any man his own age trusted
and who had often proved his loyalty | saying drive pair back to ships black comely
beaked hollow gallant Sthenelus mounted | chariot grasped shining reins decanted
own powerful horses at a gallop | in quest of Diomedes would not stop
'til had rejoined him and Diomedes | gone in pursuit of her relentless he's
Cyprian Aphrodite realised | that was just some timid lass deified
and not one of those goddesses who play | dominating part mankind's battles say
like Athene or Enyo Sacker of Towns | post long time through the crowd chasing her down's
result then the son of the great-hearted | Tydeus caught up with quarry darted
to the assault and made a lunge at her | cut gentle hand with sharp-pointed spear cur
-sed at base of the palm his point tearing | the imperishable robe the caring
Graces had made for her in flesh sinking | where the palm joins the wrist and out pinking
then came the goddess's immortal blood | ichor runs in veins of happy godhood
not eating bread drinking our sparkling wine | and so bloodless of the immortal line

Aphrodite gave piercing primal scream | dropped son Phoebus Apollo took upstream
wrapped him in a dark blue cloud to save him | from a fatal spear-cast in the breast grim
Danaan chariots Diomedes | the loud war-cry over Aphrodite's
fall raised a great shout of triumph "Daughter | Zeus quit this battle leave alone slaughter
is it not enough for you to set your | traps for feeble womenfolk? for if you're
persisting in joining the fight you will | at very name war be taught tremble"
cowed then by his threatening attitude | distraught with pain the Aphrodite dude
hey Jude! withdrew her lovely skin was stained | with blood and the wound her grievously pained
but Iris of the Whirlwind Feet took her | in tow and out of the turmoil led her
left field Aphrodite found turbulent | War-god sat ground with spear fast horses lent
on a cloud sinking to her knees implored | her Brother a roan loan should be ensured
of his horses with the golden harness | on their heads "Save me please do your darnedest
dearest Brother let your horses get me | to Olympus where the immortals be
I am in great pain from a wound given | by mortal man son Tydeus even
who's in mood now fight Father Zeus himself" | lent horses golden harness Ares self
Aphrodite to car in great distress | Iris in beside as chariotress
took the reins in hand and flicked the horses | with the whip to make them start their courses
willing pair flew right off soon reached steep heights | Olympus where gods live in day-night flights
once there fleet Iris of the Whirlwind Feet | brought the gilded horses to halt meet neat
unyoked them then from the air-racing car | beside threw ambrosial fodder far
lovely Aphrodite went to Mother | sank down at knees Dione took Daughter
in her arms spoke to her in way most fond | at same time stroking her with her hand frond
"Dear Child! which of the Heavenly Ones has | hurt you now like this out of mere spite as
if you were only a branded felon?" | laughter-loving Aphrodite told on
"'Twas that bully the son of Tydeus | Diomedes who wounded me as thus
was rescuing my own son beloved | my favourite from the field ill-favoured
Aeneas this war has now ceased to be | a struggle the Trojans Achaeans v
Argives now fight against the gods themselves" | "Endure my Child face now your troubled selves
gallantly" replied the goddess gracious | "Many of us who live on Olympus
have long suffered here at the hands of men | in our try injure each other as when
Otus and the mighty Ephialtes | into chains threw the suffering Ares
spent thirteen months trussed up in a bronze jar | would have been the end of him and for war
great appetite if Eriboea | beautiful young giants' step-mother a
confession told Hermes what they had done | the strength of Ares very nearly done
at his last when Hermes spirited him | away the fetters near too much for him
Here suffered too powerful Heracles | Amphitriton's son struck with tentaCleese
three of a barbed arrow in the right breast | she in agony and the monstrous beast
Hades himself wounded with an arrow | and like the rest had to bear the sorrow
when that same man son of aegis-bearing | Zeus shot him at Gate of Hell ill-faring
among the dead left him to his anguish | sick at heart suffering a pain excruc
-iating Hades found way Olympus | of the heights and the Palace of Zeus thus
arrow had driven into his shoulder | muscles draining his strength soon keel over

however Paeeon the healer spread | soothing ointments on the wound soon cur-ed
for after all not made of mortal stuff | think of the audacity sure enough
and savagery of the man who cared so | little what wickedness set hand to so
he plagued the very gods of Olympus | with his bow! as for your trouble was thus
Athene of the Flashing Eyes who him told | chas(t)e you but the wool over eyes did fold
fooled again not know how short life for one | who battles against an immortal one
he no homecoming from terrible war | horrors little kids all call dad no more
prattle around him gathered at his knees | so strong as he is let Tydeides
take care none more formidable than you | come out to fight with him or one day too
Aegialea wise daughter trusty | of Adrestus and gallant wife mighty
horse-taming Diomedes will hear lost | her husband of Argives the best who bossed
and wake her household from their sleep with her | lamentations" all the while the ichor
as was speaking wiped from her daughter's hand | with both of her own healed wound of wrist brand
and the sting taken out of the pain keen | Here Athene had missed nothing of this scene
seized the chance for his former sarcasm | Zeus to repay so fathom this chasm
bright-eyed goddess Athene first stepped forward | "Father Zeus I hope that going forward
you won't take it amiss when I suggest | your Cyprian Daughter has done her best
again in luring women Achaean | into embrace of soldiery Trojan
she loves so dearly one of these ladies | wears a golden brooch evidently she's
Aphrodite the dainty hand scratching | when busy her stroking on it catching"
this only drew a smile from the Father | of men and gods he did call however
Golden Aphrodite to side "Fighting | my child's not for you YOU run side plighting
wedlock the tender passions that's your scene | the enterprising War-god and Athene
military affairs general take seize" | during heavenly talk Diomedes
of the loud war-cry flung self once more though | at Aeneas he knew that Apollo
had taken him under his protection | cared naught even over all direction
of that great god in effort persisting | killing Aeneas him suit de-listing
armour splendid three times he leapt at him | murderous fury thrice the god thrust him
back by his bright shield but when he charged fourth | Archer-god checked terrible shout held forth
"Think Tydeides and give way! do not | aspire equal gods immortals are not
made same stuff as men who walk on the ground" | when heard this fell back a bit to confound
the wrath of the Archer-god Apollo | removed Aeneas from battle to ho
-ly citadel Pergamus in place plus | where his temple stood there in the spacious
sanctuary Leto and Artemis | Archeress not only healed him team is
skilled made even more splendid than ever | meanwhile Apollo of the Bow Silver
created a phantom looked exactly | like Aeneas and was armed same as he
round this phantom the Trojans and the brave | Achaeans hacked each other's non-conc(l)ave
leather shields the great round bucklers or light | targets that they across their breasts held tight
but now intervened Apollo Phoebus | with appeal to War god tempestuous
"Ares murderous Ares you Butcher | of Men great and of Towns the Great Sacker
I call on you to take a hand and drive | this Tydeides from the battle-hive
in a mood to fight Father Zeus himself | he began with Aphrodite herself

wounding her wrist then at me flung himself | like a demon" and Apollo himself
withdrew sat on the heights of Pergamus | Ares the Destroyer as Acamas
disguised self the fiery Thracian captain | and then slipped in among the ranks Trojan
to put new heart in them he began by | exhorting royal sons Priam with cry
"Princes of royal blood how much longer | are you to let your men fall to slaughter
at hands of Argives? 'til their battle vies | at the town gates? see where Aeneas lies
son proud Anchises one we looked up to | as we so do to my lord Hector too
come on now rescue our gallant comrade | from this seething mass" with these words he made
fighting spirit soar one and all able | Sarpedon too joined in admirable
Hector rebuked roundly "Hector fiery | spirit of old where gone? of hold city
talked without troops allies single-handed | save for brothers sisters husband-branded
what's become of THEM? can't see single one | cowering like hounds before a lion
while we do the fighting though we came in | as allies only long long journey in
reinforcing you I made a far cry | from Lycia Xanthus of eddy high
where left my dear wife and my baby son | a shed-load too of goods land possession
many a poor neighbour itching get hold | and yet I make my Lycians hold bold
not slow myself meet my man in battle | though own nothing here goods cattle chattel
that the Achaeans could carry away | in the mean time you yourself just there stay
don't even tell your men to take a stand | womenfolk families defend lend hand
take care you and they don't get caught like fish | in dragnet would you all enmesh fin-ish
fall an easy prey to the enemy | who may be soon sacking your fine city
any time now you should be pondering | all these things day and night corresponding
with leaders of your glorious allies | plead make determined stand how one replies
to the hard things said about you the duke" | Hector was stung by Sarpedon's rebuke
jumped down from his car at once in all his | armour went round through the host brandishes
a pair of sharp spears in hand everywhere | driving his men on to stand and fight there
and their martial spirit then a-rousing | result as Trojans turned from carousing
faced the Argives but these too held their ground | closed ranks were by no means on the rebound
but as infantry again got to grips | wheeled round not withdraw the chariot ships
the dust horses' hooves kicked up among them | filled copper-bronze sky settled down on them
whitening the Achaeans like chaff-heaps | whitened then by the falling dust when heaps
of men winnowing and chaff blown across | the space sacred place by wind (w)hol(l)y cross
threshing floor dust-gust sent by auburn-haired | Demeter so from chaff wheat her repaired
so steadily then did troops Achaean | meet this shock but now the fierce Arean
ranging everywhere threw veil of darkness | over battle help Trojans out of mess
on the orders of Phoebus Apollo | of Golden Sword as P H Apollo
had told him put fresh heart into Trojans | when saw Pallas Athene on Danaans'
side withdraw moreover Phoebus himself | urged Aeneas to leave the rich shrine shelf
where self taken sanctuary filled the great | captain with fresh valour so although late
better than never took place with comrades | happy find him still alive not in shade's
form see him come back sound of limb good heart | not that they questioned at all or in part
for kept far too busy by Apollo | of the Silver Bow Ares Killer o'

Men Strife in her unquenchable fury | on their side Argives did spur stir furi
-ous on to battle two great Aiantes | indeed Odysseus Diomedes
but they needed little encouragement | no onslaught Trojan made them once relent
however hard was pressed home stood their ground | like the motionless clouds stationed around
with which Son of Cronos in calm weather | caps mounts angry airs Boreas boister
-ous friends all are sleeping no blustering | winds send dark clouds away de-clustering
so Danaans held firm against Trojans | did not flinch Agamemnon to each man's
giving straight way every exhortation | "My friends be of stout heart true men get on
in the field fear nothing but dishonour | in each other's eyes for when a soldier
fears disgrace then more are saved than are killed | neither honour nor salvation fulfilled
by flight" as he finished made a swift cast | with a trusty javelin struck stuck fast
Trojan officer Prince Aeneas' | company Deicoon Pergasus'
son and whose habitual gallantry | in the front line had earned honour mighty
from Trojans like unto one Priam's sons | was hit on the shield by Agamemnon's
spear and it failed to keep off the weapon | the bronze point pierced it and then it pressed on
through the belt and into his abdomen | fell with thud armour rang upon him then
yet Aeneas responded by killing | two champions the Danaans so stilling
the sons of Diocles Orsilochus | Crethon father's living locus focus
had been the fine town of Phere Diocles | man full substance then descent could trace he's
from line of god of River Alpheus | which as broad-flowing stream meanders thus
through Pylian territory the first | Orsilochus powerful chieftain thirst
-y son of this River had Diocles | great-hearted now Orsilochus had he's
and Crethon twins he trained them in all arms | and when of age embarked into the charms
of the hollow ships Achaean for Troy | the land of horses and so redeploy
satisfy calls of the Atreidae | Menelaus and Agamemnon high
but their adventure ended with them dead | as a pair of lions who have been bred
by their mother in the mountain jungle | plunder farmers' yards prey cattle bundle
sturdy sheep 'til they themselves fall victim | to bronze of man met fell fell victor him
and were felled like tall pine trees Aeneas | being the hand gallant Menelaus
with great pity filled at their fate abashed | straight away right of way through front rank dashed
in his bronze equipment all a-glitter | brandished his fine bronze-tipped spear big-hitter
Ares-emboldened who wished naught better | than of him see Aeneas get better
but great king Nestor's son Antilochus | observed then Menelaus' onrush
and thus followed him into the front line | fearing some calamity was in line
to overtake their leader and the whole | venture down into dark black soul sole hole
Menelaus Aeneas offering | fight already sharp spears at each proffering
as Antilochus neared his commander | took his place beside him as top-brander
when Aeneas saw this united band | he felt unable to against them stand
for all the daring he had shown before | as duo victorious you dragged your
two dead back into the lines Argive then | and after handing over to their men
the well-starred couple back to front once more | next killed Pylaemenes commander sure
redoubtable brave Paphlagonian | infantry standing still when great spearman

Menelaus son Atreus struck him | with a javelin collar bone bit him
meanwhile Antilochus dealing with squire | charioteer Mydon the brave whose sire
Atymnius and who was wheeling his | powerful horses round hit full on his
elbow with a lump of rock and the reins | white withal their ivory trapping veins
dropped from his hands he fell down as he must | thus Antilochus made him bite the dust
dashed in thrust sword into man's temple | with a gasp fell fell headlong from his full
well-wrought chariot buried head shoulders | in the dust for a little while moulders
stuck there as the sand happened to be deep | then his horses kicked him down to deep sleep
him laid flat on the ground Antilochus | gave them a touch of the whip sent them thus
into the Achaean lines but Hector | had observed these two and now he made for
them with a great cry and supported by | powerful following of Trojans nigh
who were being led by Ares himself | goddess Enyo shameless Panic herself
in her train Ares brandished in his hand | spear monstrous size strode behind boy-band brand
Hector now in front when Diomedes | of the loud war-cry then saw there Ares
filled with dismay like the improvident | traveller who after long journey spent
over plain finds way barred by estuary | fast-flowing river takes one look mighty
seething foam and then turns back in his tracks | thus Tydeides fell back on his tracks
but not without warning his men "My friends | no wonder we've been impressed by the fiend's
spearmanship daring always has a god | with him to save his skin the sneaky sod
see there's Ares too disguised as a man | keep face enemy retreat as one man
we must not offer battle to the gods" | and no sooner had he given these odds
than the Trojans were on them Hector killed | then Menesthes and Anchialus skilled
veterans both in the one chariot | Telamon(-)Aias a one-man riot
(-)Ian filled with pity when saw them fall | taking his stand close by them launched withal
force a glittering javelin struck son | Selagus one Amphius one rich man
who lived in Paesus owned many cornfields | but Destiny took off the battlefield's
far away to serve as ally Priam | sons Telamonian Aias struck prime
on the belt long spear stuck in abdomen | he fell down with a mighty crash but when
illustrious Aias ran up to strip | him of his arms the Trojans then let slip
a volley of glittering javelins | many of which he took on the shield's chins
and yet he planted on the corpse a foot | freeing body bloody bronze spear afoot
but could not get all armour off his back | javelins too much for him held him back
and was afraid of being surrounded | and by the eager Trojans confounded
overpowered as faced formidable | numbers with their spears ready and able
and thus they managed to drive him away | though big redoubtable in sturdy way
Aias shaken retreated such struggle | there where fight of hottest muddle muggle
meanwhile Tlepolemus tall handsome son | Heracles faced the god-like Sarpedon
brought together by the stern hand of Fate | these two a son and a grandson the great
Zeus Cloud-compeller made at each other | when in range of banter-bother brother
Tlepolemus gave challenge "Sarpedon | Lycian Counsellor what makes you then
come here just to hide yourself? you don't know | what a battle is and they ought to know
better than call you son aegis-bearing | Zeus the sons he used to have not nearing

like how different by all accounts from great | Heracles my dare-all lion-heart fate
-ed father who once came here for the mares | of Laomedon with just six ships' wares
and a smaller force than ours and yet sacked | Ilium the streets of the town well wracked
now YOU are a coward and your army | wasting away strong man that you may be
yourself and you have come all the way from | Lycia bolster Trojan storm form from
us but much good you'll do them! I'm tracking | you to fall to me so be sent packing
through the Gates of Hades" "Tlepolemus" | the Lycian leader responded thus
"You know so very well that Heracles | wouldn't have sacked Ilium of holies
the holy but for the stupidity | of one man Laomedon the haughty
who with insults repaid his services | refused let him have the mares' services
he'd come so far to get but as for you | I say here and now to meet your doom you
are due and to die at my hands unsteeled | by my spear your life you will soon now yield
to Hades of Fabled Horse the glory | to me" but by way of reply story
the other raised his ashen shaft and long | javelins leapt from both men's hands so long
for one and the same time Sarpedon struck | Tlepolemus middle of neck the shmuck
deadly spear-point passed right through and nether | darkness down on eyes came to end tether
same moment Tlepolemus' spear hit | Sarpedon in the left thigh the point bit
pressed furiously on and grazed the bone | but for a while Father destruction zone
saved him from the heroic Sarpedon | carried from fight by loyal hangers-on
the great spear weighed him down as dragged along | as in haste more than speed were not on song
had not noticed or thought of pull use | free ashen shaft from thigh and so leg use
they had their work cut out to see him safe | on side Tlepolemus re-laid ex-waif
from the field by the Achaeans bronze-clad | meanwhile the excellent Odysseus had
observed his fall but not to be dismayed | as the sight him into a fury flayed
though he was uncertain what to do for | a moment then debated fatal flaw
if should set off in pursuit of the son | Zeus Thunderer or do execution
further among the Lycians but Fate | not intend Zeus' son stalwart that date
to fall to sharp bronze of brave Odysseus | Athene on Lycians turned furious
he then and there and first killed Coeranus | and then next Alastor and Chromius
followed by Alcander and Halius | and next Noemon and Prytanis thus
indeed the noble Odysseus would | have gone on to shed more Lycian blood
but for quick eye Hector helm glittering | who when saw what game a-litter-rating
strai(gh)t way hot-footed it to the forefront | in his armour of bronze full resplendent
striking terror into host Danaan | arrival most welcome to Sarpedon
son of Zeus who appealed in his distress | "Prince Hector rescue me from this shit mess
don't leave me lying here at the mercy | of the Danaans then in your city
I shall be content to die if I must | as it is very clear that I am just
not meant to see my country home again | wife little son bring happiness a-gain"
Hector of the bright helm made no reply | but by way of answer though darted by
thrust Argives back kill as many as could | but removed Sarpedon the like god-hood
by his trusty followers and then laid | under a fine oak tree splayed sacred prayed
to aegis-bearing Zeus where the stalwart | Pelagon own squire withdrew shaft a-thwart

ashen from his thigh a mist descended | on his eyes fainted mind away wended
but presently came to as North Wind played | about him from swooning to self replayed
meanwhile the Argives faced by both Hector | in his arms of bronze and by Ares nor
fled back to ships neither counter-attacked | but instead they then steadily back-tracked
as became aware Ares' presence | on-side Trojan and who then in essence
first and last to fall to Hector great son | of Priam warring Ares the Brazen?
first was Prince Teuthras and then Orestes | the second tamer of horses with ease
a spearman from Aetolia Trechus | Oenomaus Oenops' son Helenus
he of the flashing belt Oresbius | who lived in Hyle shores lake Cephisis thus
where looked after his rich estate beside | his Boeotians in fertile countryside
when white-armed goddess Here saw slaughtering | Argives left right could not hide torturing
soul from Athene "Unsleeping Child of Zeus | aegis-bearing just disastrous us use
if let maniac Ares run amok | of the promise we made will make a mock
-ery when we told Menelaus he | would bring down the walls of Troy before he
left come it is high time we threw ourselves | into battle" she of the Flashing Elves'
Eyes nothing loth so Here Queen of Heaven | Daughter of Cronos then went to golden
harness her horses while Hebe deftly | quickly worked get her chariot ready
by fixing the two bronze wheels each spokes eight | on ends of the iron axle-tree plate
felloes of wheels imperishable gold | and with bronze tyres fitted on the rims bold
a wonderful piece of work while the naves | rotate on axles of fine silver staves
the car itself has a platform of gold | and silver straps there tightly interfold
with a double railing running round it | silver shaft running out from front of it
to the end of this pole Hebe tied gold | -en yoke beautiful and attached fine gold
breast-straps and Here there was all agog for | dread joy of the hurly-burly of war
meanwhile on her Father's threshold Athene | Daughter of aegis-bearing Zeus shed sheen
soft embroidered robe made with her own hands | donned a tunic in place and turned her hands
to equip self for the lamentable | work of war arms of Zeus of Cloud-compel
-'er threw round 'er shoulders formidable | tasselled aegis each point remarkable
with Fear beset and carries Strife and Force | and the cold nightmare of Pursuit perforce
therein and bears also the ghastly grin | in image of a Gorgon's head the grim
redoubtable emblem aegis-bear Zeus | on her head put her golden helm good use
with its four plates and double crest adorned | with fighting men from cities hundred-horned
then stepped into the chariot flaming | gripping the huge long spear with which aiming
break ranks many a noble warrior | almighty Father's Child roused to anger
Here lost no time flicked the horses with whip | the Gates of Heaven of own accord whip
asunder in thunder kept by the Hours | Wardens of broad sky Olympus towers
whose task to close entrance or roll away | the heavy cloud normal Olympic day
through gates goddesses drove their patient steeds | found the Son of Cronos tell their need deeds
he sitting aloof from the other gods | on Olympus' top peak in the gods
and the white-armed goddess Here brought her pair | to a halt and had a word with Zeus there
the Lord Supreme and the Son of Cronos | "Father Zeus aren't you moved by Ares toss
violence to indignation at sight | too of all these Achaeans brave in fight

whom he's slaughtered without rhyme or reason? | I can't bear to watch but your Cyprian
Daughter and Apollo of Silver Bow | seem to like it in fact it suits them so
to have let loose this savage who pays heed | to no law Father Zeus will you be peed
off with me if give him a sound thrashing | and him from the field be now soon trashing?"
"No get to work!" replied the Gatherer | of the Clouds "let Athene our warrior
deal with him no-one is a better hand | at twisting Ares' tail" this in hand
and no fault to find white-armed goddess's | used the whip Here now flicked on the horses
and the willing pair flew off on a course | midway between earth and sky's starry bourse
and since these horses of gods with their high | -thundering hooves cover at one bound nigh
the distance one can see into the haze | as look-out from the watchtower in a-maze
over the wine-dark sea they soon reached Troy | its pair of noble rivers selves deploy
at watersmeet Simois Scamander | the white-armed goddess Here took a gander
stopped her horses released them from the yoke | and she then hid them in a mist a toke
-n of her powers and Simois freed | ambrosia sprang up for them to feed
then the two goddesses set out on foot | strutting like pigeons eagerness afoot
to bring assistance to the Argive arms | made for that part of the field in whose arms
the pick of the Achaeans had rallied | round great Diomedes had not dallied
standing while new alliances forging | at bay like lions fresh from flesh gorging
or wild boars can be too formidable | there Here stopped and gave voice formidable
mimicking noble Stentor's voice brazen | who could raise a shout like to fifty men
together "For shame Argives! you creatures | contemptaile! yet so splendid features!
the days when great Achilles came out fought | the Trojans then never adventured aught
in issue from the Dardanian Gates | too fearful terrible spear's mighty fates
but fight far from town now by your black ships" | and thus she emboldened them amid-ships
put fresh heart into everyman meantime | Athene Flashing Eyes made a mean bee-line
for Diomedes son of Tydeus | found the prince airing the wound Pandarus
had given him with his arrow under | the broad shoulder-strap of his round buckler
the sweat was irking him troubled by this | and weakened in arm had lifted up this
strap and the dark blood was away wiping | goddess hand on his horses' yoke gri(p)peing
"Tydeus had a son but how unlike | himself! Tydeus small man but how like
unto a fighter! he even fought when | I had such like expressly forbidden
and did not want him make display even | when sent alone with a crowd Cadmeian
to parley Thebes and I told him to sit | eat dinner in palace quiet a bit
yet what must he do but challenge the young | Cadmeians like old lion-heart of young
self as was and beat them all easily | with the help that he also had from me"
how different from you! I stand beside you | and from all sorts of harm I do shield you
and then I tell you to fight the Trojans | with all of my blessing from the heavens
but you're exhausted can't lift a finger | after all you've done! paralysed with fear
perhaps are you? if that is the trouble | I no longer take you for a double
son descended from the line Tydeus | a grandson of the doughty Oeneus"
"I recognise you goddess" said stalwart | "of the great aegis-bearing Zeus the Daught
-er you are and thus I can speak to you | without reserve I am not unmanned you

ought to know by fear or by exhaustion | all I do is keep in mind your caution
the limits you yourself imposed on me | for you told me not fight against any
blessed gods except for Aphrodite | the Daughter of Zeus you said that if SHE
came into the fight then I could wound her | with spear but it's Ares the carrier
all before him when I saw that I fell | back the rest to rally round me did tell"
"My dearest Diomedes a true son | of Tydeus!" cried Flashing Eyes Athen
-'e "I understand with me at your back | though you need not fear Ares and so lack
fear of any other god so quick now | and at him! drive up don't stop anyhow
to think "This is the redoubtable War | -god" but then let him have it at close quar
-ters look at the maniac over there! | do you know just the other day that there
pestilential double-dealing villain | gave Here and me his word oath sworn even
to fight against Troy and help the Argives? | and now he's fully neglecting their lives
forgotten all he said strength now playing | on the Trojan side" and as so saying
she reached out dragged Sthenelus back hustled | him out of the chariot as bustled
about he only too glad to leap down | the eager goddess took his place at crown
of car beside noble Diomedes | the beech-wood axle at the weight of these
two groaned aloud goddess formidable | and a mighty man of arms well able
Pallas Athene seized reins whip drove Ares | direction and at that moment Ares
despoiling the gigantic Periphas | the noble son Ochesius alas
the best man in Aetolian force | spattered with blood busy stripping perforce
the armour from his victim and she hid | her approach from god fearsome hot-headed
by invisibility cap on head | but when the Butcher Ares saw ahead
the gallant son of Tydeus he left | Periphas to lie where met his life theft
bereft headed straight for Diomedes | the tamer of horses and then when these
two had right quickly come to close quarter | Ares starts fight blow mortal meant slaughter
with bronze spear he thrust at Diomedes | over the yoke and the horses' reins with ease
but Athene of the Flashing Eyes catching | the shaft with her mighty hand dispatching
up above the chariot where it spent | its force in the air made in him no dent
Diomedes of loud war-cry now when | brought his spear into play so Athene then
drove home against lower part Ares' | belly where he wore an apron round his
middle and there the blow landed wounding | War-god fair flesh not abjuring
Diomedes drew out his spear Brazen | Ares let forth a yell loud as even
nine or perhap ten thousand battling men | every Achaean and every Trojan
quaked with terror at that cry appalling | god of war never for his fill calling
then like the column of black air issues | from the clouds when a tornado fissures
up after heat Diomedes Brazen | War-god saw whirl up off into heaven
in a welter of misty haze Ares | travelled rapidly soon as reached gods' ease
the home high Olympus sat down by Zeus | son of Cronos in sorry state showed Zeus
immortal blood pouring from his injury | and recounted his story dolefully
"Father Zeus does not the sight of all this | violence cause indignation crisis?
see what we gods have to suffer at each | other's hands whenever occurs one reach
out do mankind favour fault lies in you | as we are all at loggerheads with you

for having cursed the world with that crazy | Daughter of yours who to some devilry
or other always up to rest of us | including every god on Olympus
bow to your will and stand in awe of you | but whenever a question of her you
neither say nor do anything to check | the creature who thus does just what the heck
she wishes to you let her have her head | because she's a Child of your own godhead
and was born for mischief see how she's thus | encouraged the cursed son Tydeus
insolent Diomedes run amok | among the immortals of godhead stock
he began by charging Aphrodite | on her wrist inflicting a cut mighty
then flung himself like a demon at ME | I'm quick enough on my feet happily
to have escaped otherwise should have had | long painful time among the grisly dead
or come off crippled for life by his blows" | Zeus Cloud-gatherer gave him bloody nose
with black look "You turncoat don't come to me | whine naught you enjoy as much as bloody
fighting quarrelling also that is why | more than any god on Olympus high
I hate you Your Mother Here too has a | headstrong and ungovernable temper
I've always found it hard to control her | by word of mouth alone I suspect her
of starting this business and getting you | into trouble but don't intend let you
suffer any longer since you are my | own flesh and blood as your Mother is my
Wife yet if any other god fathered | such a pernicious prat brat god-w(a/i)(y)(s)e erred
long since would have found self in deeper hole | than the Sons of Uranus" make him whole
thereupon Zeus told Paeeon who spread | soothing ointment on the wound it heal-ed
for Ares was not made of mortal stuff | made the fierce War-god well quickly enough
in the time that the busy fig-juice takes | to thicken milk and curdle as one shakes
and stirs the white liquid Hebe bathed him | then lovely clothing to put on gave him
and sat down by Zeus the Son of Cronos | all his former self-esteem back bonus
then the two goddesses Here of Argos | Alalcomenean Pallas palace
of almighty Zeus meanwhile had returned | Butcher's murderous career scene interned

ἕξ

*Book 6*

# HECTOR AND ANDROMACHE

*how Diomedes and Glaucus making*
*ready to fight then acquaintance making*
*parted friends and Hector in the city*
*bade farewell to his wife Andromache*

so the soldiers Trojan and Achaean | grim struggle left alone to carry on
battle sways to and fro across the plain | bronze-tipped spears many a-rraign counter-rain
mid-point Simois and streams of Xanthus | bulwark Telamonian Aias plus
of Achaeans first to break a Trojan | company and his friends new hope open
when struck fighter who best of Thracians did | Acadamas the son tall and splendid
of Eussorus Aias let fly with spear | hit man on the ridge above visor clear
of his plumed serpent helm bronze point landed | in forehead pierced bone and night descended
on his eyes next Diomedes of loud | war-cry Axylus son Teuthranus ploughed
under from the pleasant town Arisbe | wealthy man lived well in house builded he
by the roadside had made self popular | as of all comers an entertainer
but no teammate now make forward tackle | on oppo save him from a spear-tackle
dreadful Diomedes killed him and squire | Calesius charioteer to wire
it went right down both to the world below | Euryalus killed Opheltius blow
Dresus and chased Aesepus Pedasus | Water-nymph Abarbarea borne thus
peerless Bucolion Bucolion | of the haughty Laomedon a son
he the first offspring of a secret love | shepherding when met and lay in her love
-ing arms she conceived bore twin boys as well | 'twas these now who to Euryalus fell
son of Mecisteus who cut them off | in their gallantry and strength and stripped off
the armour from shoulders Astyalus | to the last steadfast did not outlast thus
Polypoetes Pidytes Percote | of with bronze spear Odysseus fell him smote
noble Aretaon fell to Teucer | and Antilochus the son of Nestor
with a glittering lance killed Ablerus | Agamemnon Men's King slew Elatus
lived by lovely waters Satniois | hill-town Pedasus the noble Leitus
killed Phylacus who'd taken to his heels | Eurypylus Melanthus' life steals
meanwhile Menelaus of loud war-cry | managed take Adrestus alive full-cry

the man's horses bolting across the plain | met tamarisk branch that did them detain
snapped the shaft where fixed to the curved body | of the chariot and galloped off free
towards the city joining the others | in a wild stampede but on his uppers
master been tumbled out of chariot | beside wheel flat on face in dust laid out
soon Menelaus son of Atreus | standing over him long-shadowed spear plus
in hand Adrestus threw his arms around | Menelaus' knees prayed to him sound
"My lord Atreides take me alive | and then an ample ransom you'll derive
for my father is rich and has plenty | of treasure in his house bronze and gold he
wrought irony he'd pay princely ransom | if he heard about my treatment handsome
taken alive to the ships Achaean" | so endeavoured his captor's heart soften
and indeed Menelaus just about | then to tell his squire to now take him out
to ships Achaean when Agamemnon | came running up his brother to remon
-strate with "My dear Menelaus why so | chary of taking men's lives now slow so?
did the Trojans treat you as handsomely | when they came and stayed in your house? no we
aren't going to leave single one alive | down to the babies in mother's womb hive
not even they must live and the whole folk | must be wiped off the face of the world's yoke
none be left to think of them shed a tear" | the justice of this remark made tear tier
in mind Menelaus thrust Adrestus | from him with his hand at that moment just
as Agamemnon struck him in the flank | man collapsed Agamemnon as swank prank
put his foot on his chest and withdrew his | ashen spear from wound then Nestor made his
call to the Achaeans in a loud voice | "Friends Danaans countrymen no invoice
now for looting! lingering behind to | get back with the largest share of kind to
the ships! let us kill men and afterward | at ease you can strip corpses from field hard"
put new heart daring into everyman | and it looked as though the army Trojan
defeated disheartened would be thrust back | into Ilium by the winners Ach
-ean but at this juncture Priam's son | Helenus the best augur in Troyton
sought out Aeneas Hector and appealed | "You're both in supreme command in the field
we put you there because you've never failed | us in the council-chamber or the field
now prove us right make a stand here don't yield | yourselves visit every part of the field
and check the troops before they reach the gates | in fell panic fall into the arm-gates
of their women and make the enemy | happy men and when you've rallied every
one of our companies we'll stand our ground | fight the Danaans here although down ground
as we are we've no choice in the matter | meanwhile go into the city Hector
and speak to our mother tell her collect | the older women at temple elect
Bright-eyed Athene on the Acropolis | unlock the doors of the shrine her polis
-y should be choose a robe from her palace | the greatest and of the loveliest lace
and the one of the most value to her | lay it on Lady Athene's knees let her
promise to sacrifice in her temple | dozen yearling heifers of whom temple
untouched by the goad if only she will | have pity on town and Trojans' little
children wives and keep the savage spearman | Diomedes great panic-making man
clear of holy Ilium seems as though | he's become our most redoubtable foe
we were never so terrified even | of Achilles called a goddess' son

and prince of fighters that he was fact is | Diomedes has run amok there is
no man who can hold him" promptly Hector | acted on the advice of his brother
leapt down in all his armour from his car's | frame brandishing a couple of sharp spears
went everywhere among men urging stand | rousing fighting spirit brothers' band brand
result Trojans turned round faced Achaeans | who now gave ground and killed no more Trojans
indeed Trojans rallied to such effect | Argives thought from starry heaven effect
rescue some god must have come down in swoops | there Hector crying aloud to his troops
"Gallant Trojans wond'rous allies be men | my friends fight with the resolution then
you've always shown while I to Ilium | tell our Elders and wives they must make some
propitiation of the gods promise | them they will make a sacrifice" with this
Hector of the flashing helmet went off | toward the town the dark leather rim of
his bossed shield tapping above and below | on the back of the neck and ankles low
and now Glaucus son of Hippolochus | and Diomedes son of Tydeus
approached each other in the space between | the two armies and offered battle scene
when they'd come within range Diomedes | of loud war-cry other challenger's he's
"Who comes here? give me your name horse-master | if you are a man for I have never
seen you 'til now in the field of honour | and yet in facing long-shadowed spear dour
in my hand you've shown far greater daring | than any of your friends fathers faring
badly of men meet me in my fury | liable to weep but if one of ye
immortals come down from the sky I'm not | one fight against the gods-in-heaven lot
not even Lycurgus the powerful | son of Dryas survived his own quarrel
with the gods of Heaven for very long | as he had chased the nursing-mothers long
of frenzied Dionysus through holy | Nysa hills and their holy of wholly
magic wands cast to the ground from their hands | all as the murderous Lycurgus lands
ox-goad blows upon them and strikes them down | Dionysus fled found sanctuary down
below salt-sea waves where Thetis took him | trembling completely cowed to her bosom
such the effects of the man's chastisement | immortals though easy livers resent
what he'd done Son of Cronos struck him blind | and after that did not long a life find
what with all the deathless gods against him | so must not count on me should it come grim
to that to fight with any Blessed One | but if you are like us a mortal one
who ploughs the earth for food come on and you | will meet your doom the sooner than think you
"My gallant Tydeides" then chipped in | son of Hippolochus "What does my lin
-eage matter to you? for men in their | generations are like to the trees bare
When The Wind Blows one year leaves scattered good | on the ground but the trees burst into bud
and put on fresh ones when the spring comes round | and so does one generation abound
and another nears its end yet if you | wish to hear about my family you
shall hear the tale most know it already | in deep Argos there's a place Ephyre
called where the horses graze lived a villein | named Sisyphus as cunning a villain
as ever was father's name Aeolus | and Sisyphus had a son called Glaucus
in his turn father of Bellerophon | incomparable save misfortune one
to be a subject of King Proteus | far more powerful noble than he plus
fell foul of him expelled from Argive state | Queen Anteia wife of potentate

had fallen in love with the youth handsome | endowed with every manly grace and some
begged satisfy in secret her passion | but of sound principles Bellerophon
refused she went to King with lying tale | "Bellerophon has tried to me assail
kill him or die yourself" the King enraged | when heard this infamous tale but he gauged
not to kill him a thing he dared not do | but he decided to pack him off to
Lycia with sinister credentials | gave him folded tablet whose essentials
a number of devices traced by him | bearing a deadly meaning and told him
he must hand this to his father-in-law | the Lycian king thus own death ensure
Bellerophon's journey was forwarded | by the gods in perfect way as they did
when he reached Lycia and the Xanthus | river as an honoured guest welcomed thus
by the king of those broad dominions host | entertained him for nine days was the most
slaughtered nine oxen for him but when tenth | day came in the first rosy zenith strength
of Dawn examined him and asked to see | exactly what kind of credentials he
-(he!) had brought from son-in-law Proteus | and when fatal message deciphers thus
King's first move order kill the Chimaera | gods had foisted on man monstrous creature
she had a lion's head a serpent's tail | body of a goat breath came out in hail
flail of terrible blasts of burning flame | but let self be guided by the gods' game
caught her by tail gave good hiding killing | second test famous Solymi stilling
he said was the most terrific battle | he had ever fought then third task to kill
Amazons fight as man keep a-breast man | but the King had now thought of a new plan
set cunning trap to catch him on way back | from this adventure stationed at his back
in ambush best men in all Lycia | not a one came home the income-para
-ble Bellerophon killed them all in end | King now knew was true son of a godsend
pressed him to stay in Lycia offered | his daughter's hand half his kingdom proffered
while the Lycians also him granted | for his personal use estate splendid
comprising vineyards cornfields aplenty | princess bore three children to the doughty
hero Isander and Hippolochus | Laodameia slept with Zeus thus
by the Counsellor mother Sarpedon's | become the mighty Prince of the mail bronze
but the time then came when Bellerophon | incurred enmity of all the gods on
high wandered off in solitude across | Aleian Plain eats heart out so cross
and so avoiding all contact with men | insatiable Ares killed his son then
Isander in battle with the famous | Solymi Golden-Reins Artemis thus
slew Laodameia in anger | Hippolochus was the last remainer
and I am his son he sent me to Troy | he used often to say to me "My boy
let your motto be 'I lead' strive to be | the best because your forefathers proved be
best men in Lycia and Ephyre | never disgrace them such my pedigree
that is the blood-line that I claim as mine" | and Glaucus' tale now went down just fine
with Diomedes of the loud war-cry | stuck spear into the earth with delight high
in cordial terms to Lycian prince | spoke "Surely by ties established long since
your family and mine are linked for Oenus | my noble grandfather once peerless plus
Bellerophon entertained in palace | and for twenty days kept him there in place
post which gave each other the splendid gifts | that host and guest exchange thus Oenus gifts

his friend a belt stained with bright purple dye | his friend gives gold two-handled cup which I
left in my house when I set out as for | father Tydeus have no recall for
I was just a baby at time when he | joined an expedition Achaean the
one that came to grief at Thebes but I've said | enough show in me you'll have a good head
start friend in heart of Argos and there'll be | you in Lycia if to that country
ever go so let's avoid spear sallies | each even in melee Trojans allies
famous their a-plenty for me to kill | if I have the luck speed my boots to fill
and plenty of Achaeans to slaughter | if you can and let's exchange our armour
so all may know our grandfather's friendship | made friends of us" each leapt from his car-ship
clasped hands pledged each other but with dry wit | Zeus turned Glaucus into a Total twit
because he exchanged with Diomedes | gold armour for bronze hundred oxen's fees
for the value of nine meanwhile Hector | the oak tree at Scaean Gate now set for
at once besieged by Trojan wives daughters | ask if war sons husbands brothers slaughters
and friends all to pray recommending them | to the gods and one by one dismissed them
but not before many heard news grievous | made way Priam's palace luxurious
magnificent house fronted with marble | colonnades in main building a marvel
were fifty apartments of stone polished | grade 1 listed and 2 not demolished
where Priam's sons slept with their wives daughters | of his had their own separate quarters
on the opposite side of the courtyard | where twelve adjoining bedrooms built of hard
polished stone and well roofed in Priam's sons | -in-law slept here with wives who loved those sons
Hector met at palace gracious mother | coming in with Laodice daughter
of hers by far most beautiful "Hector!" | cried put hand in his "what have you come for
my child in the middle of pitched battle? | it is true then those abominable
Achaeans wearing us down walls storming | and the spirit was in you performing
moved come in lift hands in prayer to Zeus on | Acropolis but wait a moment on
while I fetch you some mellow wine so you | may be the first to make libation to
Father Zeus and the other immortals | and then if you like enjoy a mortal's
cup wine a great comfort to weary man | and after fighting hard for everyman
dear you must be exhausted" "My lady | mother" said Glittering Helmet bring me
no wine or you will rob me of the use | of my legs leave me feeble unmanned use
-less nor offer organic sane sparkling | wine without viral hands sanetising
a man cannot pray to Son of Cronos | Lord of Black Cloud when clean on him onus
but bespattered blood and filth it is you | who must pray find the older women too
to go with offerings to the temple | Athene the Warrior take an ample
robe loveliest greatest you can find in | house and one you put the most value in
yourself lay it on Lady Athene's knees | promise sacrifice her shrine heifer sees
yearling dozen untouched by goad if she | only on the city will have pity
and on the Trojans' wives little children | and that she will keep that savage spearman
son Tydeus mighty panic-maker | clear of sacred Troy offerings taker
Athene Warrior go then to her shrine | while I go to try to make Paris shine
in battle though doubt he'll listen to me | I wish that the earth would open he be
swallowed up the gods brought him to manhood | to be a thorn in the flesh of the good

Trojans my royal father and his sons | if I could see him bound for the dungeons
of Hades I should then say good riddance | bad rubbish" Hector's mother palace stance
gave instructions to her maids while these were | going round town to gather the older
women went down to the scented storeroom | where she kept her embroidered robes the loom
-work Sidonian women Prince Paris | himself ships over from Sidon when is
on cruise brought him home with high-born Helen | from wardrobe Hecabe chose for Athen
-e as gift most richly decorated | and longest dress under all the rest laid
and now this jewel-like a star glittered | set out several other women skittered
along at her side Athene's temple reached | Acropolis the doors Theano breached
of lovely cheeks of Cisseus daughter | wife Antenor charioteer slaughter
and who'd been made priestess of Athene by | the Trojan people and with a loud cry
which all joined the women lifted their hands | to Athene Theano takes in her hands
the robe lays it on knees Lady goddess | to Daughter almighty Zeus prayer address
"Lady Athene mighty goddess Cities | Protectress break spear of Diomedes
bring him crashing down before Scaean Gate | and we will sacrifice to you by fate
here now in your shrine twelve heifers yearling | the touch of the goad never unfurling
if you take compassion on the city | Trojans' wives and little children pity"
thus Theano prayed but Pallas Athene | in answer made a shaking of head scene
while the women praying to the Daughter | of almighty Zeus made his way Hector
unto splendid house where Paris live did | Paris had himself this house constructed
with the best workmen to be found fertile | land of Troy for him they built with fur(red) tile
complete with hall courtyard sleeping-quarters | Priam's Hector's Acropolis nears
the royal Prince Hector stepped indoors he | carried spear eleven cubits long be
bronze point glittered before him there a gold | ring round was set the top of the shaft bold
found Paris in bedroom exam mining | brill armour shield cuirass examining
his curved bow while Argive Helen beside | him sat with her ladies-of-the-bedside
and superintended their fancy-work | when Hector saw Paris sharp made short work
"Sir you do disgrace yourself by skulking | like this when our men round town fall skull king
and at the very walls it is your fault | city's invaded battle sound default
you'd be the first to quarrel with any | -body who you found shirking his duty
in the field off with you now before town | goes up in flames!" "Hector to do me down
you've every right I deem but listen I | must explain that I am not s(k)ulking I
bear no grudge against the people Trojan | I came here to indulge my own chagrin
however has just been urging wife my | not without eloquence be making my
return to the front I think she is right | the same man does not always win the fight
give me a moment while I arm now so | for battle or go on and I'll follow
can soon catch you up" this drew no reply | from Hector flashing helm plume nodding high
Helen to placate made effort gracious | "Brother know I am indeed a shameless
evil-minded despicable creature | how I wish the very day birth feature
my mother the Storm-fiend had swept me off | to mountains or roaring sea into coff
-in and waves had overwhelmed me before | all this could happen and then what is more
since the gods have ordained this evil end | wish I'd found better husband in the end

one with some feeling for the reproaches | contempt from his fellow men approaches
but as it is this husband a creature | inconstant will never change that feature
though one day will suffer for it if I | am not mistaken but come in now my
brother sit on this chair no-one in Troy | greater burden to bear than you Oh Boy
all through my own shame and the wickedness | of Paris star-crossed C(a/o/ou)pul(a/e)t(e) no less
tormented by Heaven to feature in | the songs and the stories not yet written
by people and poets as yet unborn" | "You're kind Helen" Flashing Helm of time shorn
"but do not ask me to sit down I can | but refuse already late return an
-xious to help out the Trojans who miss me | whenever I am away terribly
what you can do is speed this fellow up | and he had now himself better buck up
then could catch me up before I leave town | since I intend to look in at house own
to see my servants and wife and little | boy for I cannot tell whether I will
ever come back to see them again or | fall to Argives very day doomed for"
with this Hector of the glittering helm | took leave soon reached his own glittering realm
not find white-armed wife Andromache home | up onto the city wall in did home
with her child and a maid her attending | there standing in tears misery pending
and so failing to find his good wife there | he went to the threshold to inquire where
of the maidservants "Maids tell me what has | happened lady Andromache where has
she disappeared to from house? visitor | one of my sisters alone again or
wife of one of my noble brothers? or | has she gone to shrine of Athene wherefore
rest of the Trojan ladies intercede | with the august goddess "Because you need
the truth" one of his busy maids avers | "she's not visiting one of your sisters
or noble brothers' wives and not gone then | to Athene's shrine with rest of the women
to pray to august goddess ascended | great Tower of Ilium as heard did
that our men being worn down and army | Achaean had won a great victory
she rushed off to the walls like one distraught | and the nurse followed with baby and caught
her up" and when Hector heard this he raced | from the house down the well-built streets retraced
his steps he'd crossed the great city had reached | the Scaean Gate by which then would have reached
the plain when Andromache his richly | -dowered wife came running to meet him she
daughter Eetion Cilician King | great-hearted Under-hill Milk Wood living
of Placus in Thebe-under-Placus she | came to meet her bronze-clad husband nurse she
carrying a little boy in her arms | their baby son and Hector's darling charms
as lovely as a star Hector calling | Scamandrius rest Astyanax "King
City" as dad the defence Ilium | Hector looked at his son and smiled but glum
his wife bursting into tears went to him | and put her hand in his then addressed him
"Hector you're possessed this bravery of | yours will be your end you do not think of
your little boy or your unhappy wife | who you will soon make a widow for life
someday Achaeans are bound to kill you | in a massed attack and when I lose you
I might as well be dead be no comfort | when you have met your doom but grief left naught
for I have no father and no mother | now that the great Achilles felled father
when sacked our lovely town Cilician | Thebe of the High Gates though killed Eetion
he was too chivalrous to despoil him | in his decorated arms he burnt him

built a mound above him and the mountain | Nymphs Daughters of Zeus of aegis refrain
planted elms around it I had seven | brothers too at home in one day even
they went down shades to Hades' House all | great Achilles swift-footed killed them all
among their shambling cattle and white sheep | as for mother who was Queen in Thebe's keep
Underhill-woods of Placus Achilles | brought her here with rest of his duty-frees
but from spoil toil frees for princely ransom | she smitten in father's house by Artem
-is the Archeress and so you Hector | to me father and mother and brother
as well as my beloved husband so | have pity now stay here and do not go
from this tower make your boy an orphan | your wife a widow call rally Trojan
by the fig-tree there where wall's easiest | to scale and the town to assault of rest
most open thrice already their best men | under the two Aiantes Idomen
-eus the famous the Atreidae | formidable Diomedes war-cry
loud have attacked that point tried to break in | one who knows the oracles and steeped in
its history must have told them or there | were reasons of their own to attack there"
"All that my dear" said great Glittering Helm | "my sure concern but if I hid from realm
battle like a coward refusing fight | and so leaving the Trojans to their plight
I could never ever face them again | nor women in their trailing gowns the grain
against would be besides I've always trained | myself like a good soldier not refrained
from place in the front line to win glory | for my illustrious father and me
deep in my heart I know the day's coming | when holiest Ilium is going
to be razed with Priam and the people | of Priam of the good ashen spear cull
yet I'm not so much distressed by the thought | of the suffering on the Trojans wrought
Hecabe herself King Priam or all | my gallant brothers to enemy fall
flung down in the dust as by thought of you | dragged off in tears by some Achaean who
will turn you into a slave I see you | in Argos some other woman has you
toiling at the loom water-carrying | from alien well hapless harrying
helpless drudge no will of your own 'There goes | the wife of Hector' will say when one knows
just who you are "he was the champion | first of the horse-taming Trojans when yon
-der Ilium was besieged' and each time | they say it you will feel another chime
of pain at the loss of the one man who | might have kept you free may the earth lie too
deep on my dead body to hear the screams | as you're carried off!" held out arms live-streams
as finished did glorious he to take | his boy who with a cry shrank aback-take
to bosom of the girdled nurse alarmed | by father's appearance he was disarmed
by the bronze of the helm and the horsehair | plume saw nodding down at him so to scare
his father lady mother had to laugh | noble Hector fast took helm off fixed gaffe
by putting the dazzling thing on the ground | kissed son then in his arms dandled around
and then prayed to Zeus and the other gods | "Grant that this boy Zeus and the other gods
may be like me pre-eminent in Troy | as strong and brave as I a mighty boy
City King of Troy may people say when | he comes back from battle 'Well so here then
is a far better man than his father' | and let him bring home the bloodstained armour
of the enemy he's killed make mother | happy" Hector handed boy to mother
took him to her fragrant breast and she was | smiling through her tears and when saw this was

much moved stroked her then with his hand "My dear | I beg you not to be too much in fear
no-one's going send me down to Hades | before my time but Fate even shades these
can't escape let alone man of woman | born as hero or a coward craven
go home now and attend to your own work | the loom and spindle and see that the work
of the maidservants is carried out war | is men's business this particular war
the business of each man in Ilium | myself above all" helm of horsehair plum
-'e as spoke took helm she set out for home | great tears many backward looks soon got home
and then there in the palace of Hector | killer of men she soon found a number
of her women-servants and stirred them all | to lamentation and so they mourned all
for Hector in his own house though was still | alive thinking not survive the viol
-ence and fury that the Achaeans wield | and come back to home from the battlefield
Paris had been quick too and not lingered | in his tall house directly he'd fingered
his splendid armour with trappings of bronze | and off he then hurried through the town one's
folk and at full speed like a stallion | who breaks halter at his manger where one
keeps fattening him gallops off across | the fields in triumph head giving a toss
to his bathing-place in the delightful | river and he knows just how beautiful
he is mane back along shoulders flying | away he goes feet the ground bare plying
to the haunts and pastures of the mares' rut | so Paris Priam's son came down hotfoot
from the high citadel of Pergamus | resplendent in his armour amorous
like the dazzling sun laughing as he came | soon caught up with brother of great fame name
just as leaving the spot where he had talked | with his wife before Hector could speak balked
by Prince Paris then starting to excuse | himself "My dear brother such a recuse
-ant I have been too leisurely kept you | waiting when you wanted to be off too
I have not been as punctual as you | wished" "Sir" said the Glittering Helmet "you
have lots of courage no reasonable | man could make light of your great in-battle
achievements but too ready to give up | when suits you refuse be up for the cup
of glory and find it mortifying | hear the Trojans your name vilifying
those that you yourself have brought to this pass | but let us be off let no more time pass
later I'll make up for any dire thing | I may have said if Zeus OKs driving
the Achaeans from our soil celebrate | our deliverance with drink-offerings spate
in our own palace then a safe haven | to the everlasting gods of Heaven"

ἑπτά

*Book 7*

# AIAS FIGHTS HECTOR

*of single combat Hector and Aias*
*the burying of their dead there alas*
*and of the construction of a great wall*
*about the hollow Achaean ships all*

Prince Hector said no more but quick passes | out of the gate with his brother Paris
both eager for fight to the expectant | Trojans their reappearance jubilant
just as welcome as a breeze from heaven | to sailors numbed leg arm from strain leaven
from smiting the sea-water with their blades | of polished pine victims fell to their blades
at once when Paris killed Menesthius | who lived at Arne son King Areithous
the Maceman and the ox-eyed lady Phyl | -omedusa Hector a sharp spear-kill
when Eioneus got it in the neck | under the bronze rim of his helm a wreck
heck-y-thump brought him down while son Glaucus | Hippolochus captain Lycian thus
casting spear across crush struck Iphinous | on the shoulder he son of Dexius
just as was mounting behind his mares fast | fell from car to ground crumpled at the last
when the bright-eyed goddess Athene saw them | slaughtering Argives in fierce assault then
she sped down from the peaks of Olympus | to sacred Ilium Apollo thus
as he desired a Trojan victory | who'd seen her from Pergamus starts banshee
pursue intercepted by the oak-tree | Apollo Son Zeus immediately
accosted her "Daughter of almighty | Zeus why have you come down in so spritely
a way from Olympus? what high purpose | in mind? since the suffering and pure loss
of the Trojans moves you not the slightest | I take it you've come throw your weightiest
into the scales make the Danaans win | but listen to me put better plan in
let us stop the fighting for a moment | another day they can regain moment
-um until they reach their goal Ilium | since you won't be happy 'til Ilium
razed to the ground" "So be it Archer-King" | said Athene goddess of the Eyes Flashing
"that's what I too had in mind when I came | from Olympus watch the battlefield game
but how do you propose stop the fighting?" | "Could rouse of horse-taming spirit fighting
Hector make him challenge one of mighty | Danaans to mortal combat so see
Achaeans be put on their mettle punt | on a champion who would take a punt

at Prince Hector" this was his idea | Flashing Eyes Athene made no demur here
and Priam's son Helenus was able | devine what these divines would enable
and he went straight to his brother Hector | "Now will you in your wisdom Prince Hector
let yourself be guided by your brother? | I suggest you make take sitting cover
Trojans Achaeans challenge champion | Danaan then to meet you man to man
you need have no fears for your life your time | has not yet come because I have this time
-line straight from deathless gods themselves" Hector | was delighted and stepped out into war
no-man's-land grasping his spear by middle | cleared line huddle muddle fiddle diddle
did they all sat down and Agamemnon | did the same with the soldiers Achaean
Athene and Apollo of Silver Bow | sat down in form vultures ready to crow
in tall oak sacred aegis-bearing Zeus | enjoyed sight all warriors out of use
sitting there on the plain ranks upon ranks | bristling with shields helmets spears and their tanks
like darkened surface sea when West Wind main | starts to blow ripples spread across the main
and Hector stood between the two hosts' arms | "Trojans you Achaean men-at-arms
hear a proposal that I wish to make | from on high for Heaven's and Zeus' sake
our truce has not been permitted to last | clear he means us to suffer to the last
day when you bring down the towers of Troy | or succumb by your much-travelled ships' b(u)oy
you have in your army the finest men | now of all Achaea is there one then
prepared to fight me? if so let him step | forward from among his friends now next step
your own champion against Prince Hector | here are my conditions holding Zeus for
witness if your man kills me with his long | -pointed spear he can strip off my belong
-ings and take them to your hollow ships but | he must allow them to bring home my butt
so the Trojans and their wives may burn it | in rite way but should Apollo let it
be me win and I kill your man I'll strip | his armour off bring into sacred ship
of Ilium where I shall hang it on | the wall of the Archer-King's shrine then on
to your well-found ships I'll send his body | so the long-haired Achaeans may bury
him to rites make a mound above him by | the broad Hellespont so when passes by
one day some future traveller sailing | good ship across line fine wine availing
sea will say 'This of an earlier day | the monument to some warrior say
been killed in single combat by Hector | famous' thus name kept alive forever"
speech received in silence by enemy | ashamed refuse challenge but mind did flee
from accepting at last Menelaus | many inward-struggles many layers
rose to his feet reproached them bitterly | "What does this mean Achaea flowery
women I can't call you men who used be | bitter threats battery ever-ready
so not one Danaan who'll meet Hector? | infamy degradation infector!
very well then sit and rot you whole crowd | inglorious to a man each coward
so I will arm myself fight him then | the issue lies with the gods in Heaven"
began to put on his splendid armour | that O Menelaus would have been your
end at the hands of Hector because he | far better man if not leapt up you free
Achaean kings from falling off cliff shelf | imperial Agamemnon himself
Atreides had not just then seized you | by the right hand and there restrained you "You
are mad lord Menelaus no call wish | for you to attempt such a thing foolish

withdraw now however mortifying | do not let ambition get you trying
a better man you'd not be the only | one who's quailed before Prince Hector son he
chief of Priam even Achilles filled | with fear make that encounter honour's field
and he a better man than you by far | so you go back now and sit down afar
among your men and the Achaeans will | find another swallow this bitter pill
he may be fearless eager for his fill | of trouble but think even Hector will
be glad to take it easy if away | alive from stern ordeal asked for come may"
in face of his brother's wise remonstrance | Menelaus gave way to acceptance
much relieved were his attendants who took | the armour from his shoulders Nestor took
then to his feet addressed limp Argive leaves | "This is too much and so Achaea grieves
how too Peleus old charioteer | would grieve great orator commander dear
of the Myrmidons who took such delight | when I stayed with him once have shone the light
parentage pedigree every Argive | if came to ears those same men were downjive
-ed before Hector he would lift up his | hands to the gods and beg them to let his
spirit leave his flesh down to House Hades | Father Zeus Athene Apollo days these
such like make me wish could as young being | as when Pylian levies trial seeing
with spears men Achaean at swift River | Celadon below walls of Pheia
by the streams of Iardanus! were challenged | by Ereuthalion had it then legend
their best man like a god and on shoulders | bore armour King Areithous the bolder's
greatly named Maceman by compatriots | girdled wives alike as never fought lots
with bow or long spear but would break the ranks | oppo iron mace Lycurgus with thanks
killed him not by superior strength but | by stratagem narrow pass caught his butt
spot where his iron mace could not save him | before mace in play Lycurgus on him
he pierced him through the middle with his spear | brought crashing to ground on his back-end clear
stripped him of the armour Brazen Ares | had given to him then wore it when he's
ever going into battle later | when Lycurgus by then grown much older
he then let his squire Ereuthalion | wear it and so challenged our champion
in Areithous' armour and no-one | then and there dared to take the challenge on
were all thoroughly scared but the spirit | of adventure worked within me and it
gave me the ballsyness to take him on | though I the youngest of all and so on
we fought and Athene gave me victory | and yet the tallest and strongest man he
I've killed he looked like a giant sprawling | there in all his height and breadth galling
if only I were still as young with all | my powers intact! Hector of the All
Flashing Helm would soon have his fight as is | see before me best men host Argive is
set to offer and not one has the will | to stand up to Hector!" the old man's shrill
reproaches brought nine men to their feet then | first to spring Agamemnon King of Men
and he was followed by Diomedes | mighty son of the great Tydeus he's
and then these two by the two Aiantes | and so full of martial valour were these
and these again by Idomeneus | Meriones squire Idomeneus
a peer of the man-killing War-god thus | Euaemon's highborn son Eurypylus
Thoas son of Andraemon got up too | and the good Odysseus when all these to
fight Prince Hector had volunteered horseman | rose again Nestor the Gerenian

"You must decide by lot who have honour | for the one chosen will not just render
a service to Achaean arms but reap | rich reward in his own heart to heap keep
if he escapes alive from the ordeal | stern that awaits him" each one made the deal
marked his own lot cast into the helmet | of King Agamemnon the son well met
Atreus while troops to the gods raised hands | and prayed looking up into the broad bands
in and of the sky "Father Zeus Aias | let it be or Diomedes alas
Mycenae's King of the great halls Golden" | as they prayed Nestor the Gerenian
charioteer shook the helm and the lot | of Aias jumped out very one the lot
of them had hoped for a lot a herald | bearing it from left to right round circled
showing it to each Achaean chieftain | and each in his turn denied it then when
he failed to recognise his mark at last | in course his tour the herald with the last
lot came to the man who'd marked it and cast | into helm illustrious Aias fast
himself so then reached out and the herald | came up to him and put the lot fabled
in his hand Aias recognised his mark | and threw the lot at his feet in a mark
of rejoicing "Friends the lot has fallen | on me I'm delighted to be chosen
for I think I shall defeat Prince Hector | I only ask of you while I arm for
the fight to pray to Zeus the Royal Son | of Cronos but let your praying be done
in silence so Trojans not overhear | or pray aloud! for no-one do we fear
whoever as no-one is going to | have his way with me and make me run too
either by brute force or skill after all | hope I too can fight as fool not at all
in Salamis born and bred" so they prayed | to King Zeus Son of Cronos and displayed
up into the broad sky said "Father Zeus | rule from Ida of most glorious use
and so grant Aias a great victory | but if you love Hector too let none be
beaten and the fight drawn and while they prayed | Aias his flashing bronze armour displayed
and when it all was slung on he sallied | like monstrous Ares in fury rallied
armies hurled at each other by mighty Son | Cronos in soul-destroying hate for one
another thus the gigantic Aias | a bulwark most mighty of Achaea's
risen went into battle with a smile | on his grim face and brandishing the while
his long-shadowed spear as he forward strode | the Argives when saw him overjoyed mode
not a Trojan whose knees did not tremble | even Hector's heart flutters dissemble
but it was too late for him to turn tail | slink back among ranks he'd made call avail
as challenger and now Aias drew near | carrying a shield like of a tower sheer
made of bronze and seven layers leather | for Tychius the master-currier
from Hyle made this glittering shield for him | with the hides of seven big bulls for trim
an eighth layer of bronze holding this shield | Telamonian Aias bold revealed
went right up Hector before on going | to defy him "Hector you're now going
to discover in single combat what | sort of champions Danaans have at
their disposal even when they can't count | on Achilles the lion-hearted fount
of man-breaking at the moment lying | idle by seagoing ships still plying
a quarrel with Agamemnon and yet | we have men who can stand up to you yet
yes plenty of them so take the first cast | start the fight" in response to this first cast
Hector of the flash helm said "Prince Aias | royal son Telamon you can try as

you may to scare me like a feeble child | or a woman who knows naught of field wild
of battle to me battle and slaughter | things of very familiar quarter
I know well enough how to swing my shield | of toughened oxhide to right or left field
the mark to my mind seasoned warrior | know how dive in when charioteer for
be on the move in close fighting I know | all the dance steps the War-god has to show
but enough for seeing the man you are | I don't want play part sniper from afar
and nick a shot at you so watch me cast | and may my cast go home!" he poised and cast
his long-shadowed javelin struck the shield | seven-fold formidable that did wield
Aias on its metal sheath outermost | eighth layer the untiring bronze that host
tore through six of its layers but held up | by the seventh hide then Aias held up
and hurled his long-shadowed spear the weapon | heavy struck the round shield of Priam's son
pierced the gleaming shield forced way through ornate | cuirass and then in onward pressing straight
tore the tunic on Hector's flank but swerved | had he in that sway fate date death deferred
now pair when each had pulled out his long spear | assaulted like flesh-eating lions rear
or wild boars strength not to be derided | Hector struck Aias spear-missile guided
in the middle of the shield but bronze | did not break through the stout shield turned point bronze
then Aias leaping in caught Hector on | shield brought him up short and the spear passed on
clean through the shield with force enough left reach | his neck and make the dark blood from the breach
gush out yet even so Hector flashing | helm did not give spirit not dashing
drew back a little and with his great hand | picked large jagged piece black rock from the land
hurled it at Aias' formidable | seven-fold shield struck it in the middle
on the boss making the bronze ring out but | Aias picked even bigger rock shot-put
he swung and hurled at Hector with such a | tremendous force that the giant boulder
crumpled his shield and swept him off his feet | Hector jammed in shield on back lay flat neat
but Apollo soon had him up again | and so now they would have closed in again
and hacked at one another with their swords | but for ambassadors of Zeus' words
two heralds Talthybius Achaean | side and Idaeus on the side Trojan
had the wisdom come up and intervene | to-ward the combatants raised staves between
latter herald of ripe experience | acting as spokesman "Dear sons at once hence
give up and break off the fight Zeus the Cloud | -gatherer loves you both this not allowed
both fine spearmen we all of us know that | another good reason to stop is that
it's near dark" Telamonion Aias | "It was" making answer said "Idaeus
Hector who asked for this duel tell HIM to | call it off if he makes the first move to
do so I'll take my cue from him" Aias" | said the great Hector of helm flash alas
"you are big strong and able and the best | spearman on your side that said I suggest
we cease fighting for the day for we can | always meet again on the field go on
'til the powers above decide between | us both also the light losing its sheen
we'd do well take the hint let an end be | Achaeans would be glad at your ships see
you back and your own friends and followers | above all while I should Troy's Two Towers
get very warm welcome from folk Trojan | and in their trailing gowns ladies Trojan
assembled for thanksgiving to the gods | on my behalf but first let's even odds
by exchanging gifts of honour so that | may be said by our two sides alike that

we fought tooth and nail but were reconciled | presently at last as friends domiciled"
he gave Aias his silver-studded sword | which he handed over with scabbard broad
well-cut baldric and Aias gave Hector | his brilliant purple belt this vector
saw them part Aias back to Achaean | lines while Hector rejoined forces Trojan
his men delighted when saw him return | alive and whole safe from a fury turn
and unconquerable hands of Aias | escorted him back to the city as
one they'd given up for dead meanwhile on | other side Aias to Agamemnon
King soldiers led buoyed by victory when | they reached royal huts Agamemnon then
King of Men offered a five-year-old bull | on their behalf to Son of Cronos full
mighty they flayed prepared it by chopping | carcass to small pieces deftly lopping
these they pierced with spits carefully roasted | then withdrew from fire with their work hosted
meal prepared fell to with a good will on | the food shared alike although noble son
Atreus Agamemnon paid him | the honour to the long chine helping him
when their thirst and hunger were satisfied | discussion by old man Nestor incised
with a proposal to lay before them | often proved itself in past his wisdom
was their loyal counsellor and was then | in this spirit he rose and addressed them
"My lord Atreides and you other | chieftains long-haired peoples of Achaea
we've had heavy losses the cruel War-god | darkened with our dead combatants' blood-shod
the banks of the Scamander and their souls | have gone down the House of Hades halls' holes
I suggest therefore that at dawn you should | announce a truce and then all of us could
work together cart the bodies in here | with oxen and mules burn them fairly near
to the ships arranging in each case for | friends of the dead to bring the bones home for
their children when return to our country | over pyre let's make one barrow only
with such material as plain provides | with mound as base let's quick-build high wall hides
the ships and ourselves strong gates let into | leaving carriage-way chariots into
little way outside let's dig a trench deep | parallel with walls to serve as a keep
obstruction stop chariots infantry | if Trojans get out of hand way any
press us hard" such was Nestor's scheme each king | indicated it was to his liking
meanwhile at the door of Priam's palace | mighty Ilium's Acropolis space
the Trojans also holding a meeting | but one marred by an outburst not fleeting
of bitterness 'twas Antenor able | who set off stir up troubling fable
"Trojans Dardanians allies hear me | now proposal make the Fates compel me
let's cut the crap give Argive Helen back | to the Atreidae with baggage-pack
of all her property by fighting on | as we are doing the guise taking on
of oath-breaking fools and there's no good that | I can see will ever now come of that
we have no choice but to do as I say" | Prince Paris Husband of Helen straight 'way
leapt up dealt with man bluntly of rote quote | "That speech of yours has really got my goat
you might have thought of something much better | but if really mean this utter fetter
and propose this move then the very gods | have addled your brainbox with odds and sods
and it's time for me to let the gallant | Trojans know what I feel and thus I plant
my feet firmly against surrendering | my wife but I'm willing be sundering
self from all the goods I brought home with me | from Argos and more from my treasury"

he sat followed Priam Dardanian | wise as the gods counsel's The Guardian
stepped in "Trojans Dardanians allies | and listen how now to me advice lies
for the moment take your supper in town | as usual not letting your guard down
so needing every man to stay alert | and at dawn down to the hollow ships pert
let Idaeus go convey to my lords | Agamemnon Menelaus the words
heard from Paris starter of the quarrel | and he can do another thing useful
ask Atreidae whether have yearning | refrain from fight 'til after the burning
of our dead later we will fight again | 'til the powers above let one side gain
the winning hand" the King's advice was well | received and they acted on it as well
the troops took their supper in their several | messes dawn the herald went to the hull
-ow beaked ships where found war-chiefs Danaans | in conference by stern Agamemnon's
ship joined the circle delivered message | clear enunciation of herald sage
"My lord Atreides other feted | fated princes Achaeans united
Priam and all the other lords Trojan | told submit for your consideration
Paris-made offer starter of our feud | all the property he brought back purlieued
to Troy in his hollow ships – and would to god | that he had been the first to bite the sod -
willing to return additions of own | so though do so at urging Trojans own
won't give up lord Menelaus' wife | and furthermore on a matter of life
death whether you have yearning will burning | to refrain from the fight while we're burning
our dead and afterwards we can fight on | 'til the powers above decide who's won"
received complete silence Achaean chiefs | loud war-cry Diomedes the relief's
"At this stage let none think of partaking | anything from Paris or of taking
Helen either any fool can see that | the doom of the Trojans is sealed" at that
Achaean chieftains applaud to man one | the tamer of horses Agamemnon
– Achaeans not only nifty Paddlers | but of horses too the mighty Saddlers –
King of Men himself the herald addressed | "What Argives think have heard for yourself stressed
you have your answer with it I concur | burning of corpses another matter
to that I raise no objection when men | dead and gone one can't grudge them the boon then
of a quick cremation and so a truce | then and let the Thunderer mighty Zeus
and Lord of Here witness it" and as spoke | for all the gods to see lifted bespoke
sceptre up Idaeus left went back to | sacred Ilium where the Trojans too
had mustered with the Dardanians all | seated in the splendid conference hall
awaiting the herald's return and when | he reached them he went to the centre then
of the gathering and there he declared | the result of his mission they prepared
themselves at once double task to come some | to scour the field and bring in the dead some
to fetch wood while on other side parties | Argives despatched same duties the hearties
from well-found ships now Sun again alighting | from deeps on quiet Stream Ocean lighting
the fields with his first beams when the Trojan | parties met their counterparts Achaean
even so found hard recognise dead good | before had washed away the clotted blood
with water then as lifted them onto | the waggons the hot tears flowed out there too
King Priam had forbidden his men to | cry out loud so heaped the corpses onto
the pyre in silent grief after they did | consume them in the flames they then headed

back to holy Ilium so too on | their side the Argives piled their dead on
a pyre with heavy hearts when they had burned | them in the flames remains-ers had returned
to black bleak ships before dawn following | when night day struggling to be swallowing
detachment of Achaean troops gathered | by pyre set to work over it fathered
single barrow such material all | as plain provided first off built a wall
with high ramparts protect good wooden ships | fitting strong gates so the twin-wheeled land-ships
could pass in and out outside parallel | with wall dug deep trench along broad ample
ditch the Argives planted a row of stakes | the long-haired ones toiled at task high stakes takes
were observed by the gods who'd sat down with | Zeus the Lord of the Lightning Flash and with
amazement watching work of the bronze-clad | soldiers Poseidon Earthshaker voiced had
first his feelings "Father Zeus is there none | left now in the whole wide world with just one
jot of decency tell us of his plans? | have you seen that the long-haired Achaeans
have thrown a wall round their ships and dug a | trench along without offering proper
sacrifices to the gods? people will | talk in the future about this wall still
of theirs as far as light Dawn's spread afield | the wall Archer and I built in the field
with such labour for King Laomedon | will be in that future time forgotten"
Zeus Cloud-compeller indignant being | "Imperial Earthshaker misgiving
absurd leave it to other gods who are | less powerful resolute than you are
to be alarmed at this new contraption | rest assured wherever Dawn light traction
yours the name that will be held in honour | what's to stop you once long-haired a goner
Argives sail home? why not break down the wall | and then scatter the bits and pieces all
in the sea cover the long beach once more | with sand? and after that you could be sure
the great Achaean works would be no more" | and while the gods were talking on some more
sun set and Achaeans finished their task | and in their huts took some oxen to task
took their supper now a number of ships | had just put in from Lemnos cargo ships
for bearing certain volumes at this time | a mighty weighty heavy fine line wine
they had been sent by Euneus the son | whom Hypsipyle had borne to Jason
the great captain and he had included | amphorae thousand gallons protruded
as special gift for the Atreidae | Menelaus Agamemnon the high
from these the long-haired Achaeans sup-plied | themselves now with wine with bronze they replied
for some some with gleaming iron others | with hides or live cattle again others
for slaves was very a sumptuous meal | they sat down to and it was the real deal
whole night long-haired Argives feasted themselves | while Trojans and allies feasted themselves
but all night long Zeus Thinker chundering | ill heart for them Greta Thun(berg)dering
there then kept maintaining ominously | and their cheeks turned pale with fear creepily
and they poured wine on the ground from their cups | no man dared sup even when in his cups
before he had first made a libation | to Lord Zeus the almighty Son of Cron
-os but at last the clan able lie doon | and of restful sleep enjoy the great boon

ὀκτώ

*Book 8*

# THE TROJANS REACH THE WALL

*how Zeus bethought self of his promises*
*to avenge arite wrongs Achilles'*
*on Agamemnon bade war abandon*
*the gods facilitate a win Trojan*

as Dawn over world saffron mantle spread | Zeus who delights in the thunder of dread
called the gods to conference on highest | of Olympus' many peaks choicest
he opened it himself all attended | carefully "Listen you god-desses" said
"while I tell you now what I have resolved | to bring this business that I think I've solved
to a speedy close with that end in view | I give you my ruling not one of you
must defy must accept it all of you | and if I should find any one of you
taking independent course of your own | helping your Trojan or Danaan own
you will be thrashed ignominiously | and packed off to Olympus speedily
or I will seize him/her and hurl into | the gloom of Tartarus far far into
the ground where the deepest of all chasms | yawns below the world and where the spasms
of the Iron Gates lie in wait Brazen | Threshold distant Hades as earth heaven
far will teach you by how much I'm the most | powerful of all the immortals(') host
but perhaps you gods would like to put me | to the test and yourselves satisfied be?
suspend a golden rope from heaven lay | hold of it together try as you may
you will never drag Zeus High Counsellor | from heaven to Earth for if I therefore
take a hand pull in earnest from my end | haul you up all together in the end
thereupon I should make the rope fast to | pinnacle of Olympus leave all to
dangle in mid-air by so much my strength | does exceed of both gods and men the strength"
Zeus finished and they all then held their tongues | because he had spoken as if in tongues
with tremendous force left them dumbfounded | at last Athene Flashing Eyes rebounded
"Father of ours Cronos Son Lord Supreme | we all know well your invincible seam
but we are sorry for the Danaan | spearmen left as will be to destruction
and a miserable fate but we'll refrain | from fighting and shall retain selves restrain
to giving helpful advice to Argives | so through your anger not all grieve lost lives"
Zeus the Cloud-gatherer then smiled at her | "Have no fear Lady of Trito and dear

Child of mine as I was not in earnest | don't mean to be unkind to you dearest"
harnessed to his chariot his two swift | horses with their brazen hooves they could really shift
gift golden flowing manes clothed self in gold | and then he picked up his splendid whip gold
-en mounted chariot started horses | with a flick willing pair at their courses
flew midway between earth and starry sky | to Gargarus peak he eyed eyrie high
Ida many springs mother of wild beasts | where has a precinct fragrant altar feasts
there the Father of men and gods pulled up | his horses freed from yoke and wrapped them up
in a dense mist then sat down on the height | exulting in his glory and his might
looking out over the Trojan city | and Argive ships in mean time hastily
long-haired Achaeans prepared ate breakfast | in their huts armed selves after fast axe fast
while on their side in the city Trojans | prepared too to fight were fewer Trojans
yet for all that were eager to grapple | driven by need to fight for wives and chil
-dren gates were all thrown open with great din | whole army infantry and horse poured in
to the plain thus the converging forces | met again with crash spears bucklers' forces
bronze-clad fighting men bosses of their shields | collided and that a great roar then yields
and the screams of the dying were mingled | with the vaunts of the victors out singled
and the earth ran with blood right through the morn | while the blessed light of the day from dawn
grew stronger volley and counter-volley | found their mark men kept falling in folly
field but at high noon the Father held out | his golden scales either pan put rout clout
as sentence of death one side for Trojans | horse-tamers other bronze-clad Achaeans
raised the balance by middle of the beam | down on Achaeans' side came the beam scream
spelling a day of doom for them sentence | set on bountiful earth while Trojans whence
went soaring their side up to the broad sky | and thus Zeus then thundered out from Mount I
-da sent a flash of lightning down among | the Achaean troops who confounded stung
by it and terror drained cheeks every man | Idomeneus nor Agamemnon
neither had the heart then to hold his ground | and neither two Aiantes courage found
even though henchmen of Ares they were | only Nestor Warden of Achaea
lingered but that not of his own free will | but because his third horse in trouble ill
Prince Paris the Lady Helen's husband | hit him with an arrow on the headband
where mane starts to grow on a horse's head | very deadly spot agony rear-ed
for the point sank into his brain writhing | round the dart the other horses driving
into confusion Nestor was slashing | at the reins with his sword when up dashing
through turmoil came the horses of Hector | redoubtable charioteer Hector
himself behind the old man there and then | would have lost his life but for veteran
Diomedes' quick eye Odysseus | called in a resounding voice "Odysseus"
shouted "my noble and resourceful lord | with your shield behind you like a coward
in the crowd where are you off to? take care | or as you run away a ploughed spear share
will catch you in the midriff for heaven's | sake stop and help me keep off the old man's
back that savage" but the much-enduring | Odysseus then out of hearing during
speeding on his way back to Achaean own | hollow ships left thus to resources own
Diomedes drove to point of attack | posted self Nestor's chariot at back
and brought reassurance to the old king | "These young warriors" he said "are proving

too much for an old man like you my lord | with all those years bear you're put to the sword
dead-beat squire of yours is hopeless and your | horses too slow get in my car and you're
going to see what horses of the breed | of Tros are like and how fast such a steed
can cover the ground in flight or pursuit | it makes no odds and I took them as loot
from Aeneas only the other day | these fighting thoroughbreds let our squires pray
take charge of your horses while you and I | drive this fabled pair tight into the eye
-teeth of those there Trojan charioteers | and teach Hector a lesson that my spear's
also active in my hand a-tingling" | Nestor Gerenian Knight back mingling
not loth so two gallant squires Sthenelus | gentle Eurymedon of horses thus
took charge while Nestor and Diomedes | mounted chariot of Diomedes
Nestor took up the polished reins started | the horses with the whip and soon darted
within range Hector Tydeus' son | let fly as the other came charging on
missed him but instead got Hector's squire dear | who was acting as his charioteer
Eniopeus a son Thebaeus | the proud hit him by the nipple his breast plus
also had the horses' reins in his hands | the man fell headlong went down with all hands
from the car making his horses shy died | where fell that his charioteer had died
wrung Hector's heart but sorry as he was | for his former comrade-in-arms he was
left lying there as Hector went off in | search of a charioteer dashing in
-to host fast horses not long no driver | as he soon found Archeptolemus he
son of Iphitus and made him get in | behind the pair got him hands take reins in
irreparable disaster threatened | now Trojans and they might have been battened
back into Ilium as lambs to pen | had not the Father of gods and men then
been alert and acted quickly with a | terrific thunderclap he then launched a
dazzling bolt guided it to earth yearning | front of Diomedes' car burning
sulphur's dreadful reek filled air horses shy | and backed themselves under they did go shy
the chariot the polished reins dropped from | Nestor's hands in terror turned to Diom
-edes "My lord Tydeides wheel your | horses round and fly don't you see that you're
not going to get any help from Zeus? | at the moment Son of Chronos makes use
of Hector lets before him carry all | but just for the day our turn will call fall
another day if he's kind however | bold a man may be he cannot counter
will of Zeus who is far more powerful | than us" Diomedes loud war-cry "Full
true is that good sir and yet it cuts me | to the quick to think that Hector will be
holding forth and saying to host Trojan | 'Listen how Tydeides from me ran
he didn't stop until he'd reached the ships' | he's sure to brag like that I've had my chips
when he does may the earth swallow me up!" | "What nonsense dear sir" Nestor followed up
"from the son of the doughty Tydeus | he can dub you a milksop coward thus
to heart's content but won't convince Trojans | and Dardanians nor each proud spearman's
wife whose loving husbands you have flung down | in the dust" wheeled horses roundly backed down
and drove them back in flight across the rout | from what had been a fighting retreat bout
Hector and the Trojans followed them up | and an almighty uproar then went up
with a hail of deadly missiles the great | Hector glittering helmet raised a great
shout of triumph over Diomedes | "The Danaan horsemen Tydeides

honoured you with the best seat at table | the first cut off the joint and a stable
never-empty cup they will not think so | well of you today after all you're no
better than a woman so off with you | big girl's blouse no-coward me won't let you
climb our walls or carry off our women | in your ships I'll see you off to heaven
-'s dungeon first" when Tydeides heard this | he then had half a mind to turn round his
horses and meet Hector face to face thrice | he was on the point of doing so thrice
Counsellor Zeus thundered from Mount Ida | that the victory to the Trojans a
sign with help from him and there was Hector | calling out aloud to every vector
"Trojans Lycians and Dardanians | your hand-to-hand-loving fighting legions!
be men friends do justice to your valour | I'm convinced that Zeus is on my and our
side he has assured me a victory | triumphant and disaster to crazy
Danaans fools that they are to have gone | and made those flimsy futile walls not one
moment delay us as for trench they've dug | our horses will jump over with a shrug
and once I get among the hollow ships | let the watchword 'Fire!' be upon your lips
I want to see those ships go up in flames | Argives lurching round in fume-filled bare frames
falling dead beside the hulls" he turned to | his horses called each by name them talked to
"Xanthus Podargus Aethon and Lampus | noble repay me now for lavish plus(h)
attention paid you by Andromache | great king's daughter always had your back she
hastened to put honeyed wheat before you | and to drink at your pleasure wine mix you
before she thought of serving me who claim | to be her loving husband now chase fame
at the gallop let's take Nestor's famed shield's | talk of Heaven itself solid gold wields
they say shield bars and all armrods inlaid | breastplate Hephaestus himself for him made
from shoulders horse-taming Diomedes | and if we could capture these two pieces
I should hope to make the Achaeans flight | take in fast now-full ships this very night"
his vainglorious tone met resentment | from the Lady Here with an impatient
movement on throne made high Olympus quake | turned to great god Poseidon Lord of Quake
"Imperial Earthshaker I'm distressed | to see that you not greatly impressed
by piteous plight of the Danaans | even though they make at altar stations
pleasing offerings Helice Aegae | can't bring self to wish them victory? why
if we who're on their side minds so making | keep all-seeing Zeus from mischief-making
thrust Trojans back what a sorry god cowed | he'd be sitting there lonely as a cloud
on Ida!" "Here" said Lord of the Earthquake | "these were wild words indeed that you spake
even from your unruly tongue far be | it from me join others' conspiracy
against Zeus the Son of mighty Cronus | so much stronger than all the lot of us!"
while these two talking to one another | between the ships and trench whole enclosure
by the great wall was filled with a medley | of chariots armed men penned in as be
sheep by that peer of the impetuous | War-god Hector son Priam Zeus pious
with the upper hand had him ignited | he would have on the trim ships alighted
now going up in flames if Lady Here | had not made Agamemnon's head go clear
rally the Argives before was too late | went along past the huts and ships of fate
a large purple cloak clutched in his great hand | climbed up the bulging black hull on the strand
of Odysseus' ship in the centre | so a man's voice entire length line enter

would carry to the end huts of Aias | Telamonian Achilles' ass
who'd had confidence enough in their own | bravery and strength to draw up their own
trim ships on the extreme flanks from this point | Agamemnon forcefully made his point
voice rang out to whole Danaan army | "Shame on you Argives" he cried out loudly
"contemptible creatures splendid only | on parade! where's the assurance that we
the finest force on earth? what of idle | boasts you made in Lemnos while did idle
the time you spent gorging yourselves on the beef | of straight-horned cattle and with such belief
drank from bowls brimful of wine? then you said | each of you could stand up to a hundred
nay two hundred Trojans whereas today | the whole crowd of you have nothing to say
against Hector alone he before long | will have the ships going up in flames' tongue
Father Zeus was ever a great king fooled | like this and of all his glory de-tooled?
yet I can claim that on my unhappy | journey a-ship not one of the mighty
fine altars of yours did I overlook | and on every one did I (e/o)vercook
the fat and thighs of bullocks so eager | was I to bring down the not so meagre
walls of Troy ah Zeus this prayer grant at least | let us escape with our lives if deceased
the rest don't let Trojans overwhelm us | like this" Agamemnon made his prayer thus
the Father moved by his tears with a nod | head salvation army vouchsafed by god
and at the same time sent out an eagle | best of prophetic birds of a nimble
doe an offspring a fawn in its talons | and it dropped the fawn where the Achaeans
sacrificed to Father of Oracles | by splendid altar Zeus when oracle's
become clear that the eagle was Zeus' | fell on the Trojans with better uses
of their zest recalled the joy of battle | and then not one of the many battle
-hard Danaan charioteers could boast | he'd raced Diomedes to the trench coast
driven out first engage the enemy | Diomedes was the first certainly
to kill a Trojan man-at-arms victim | was Agelaus the son of Phradmon him
who had swung his horses around for flight | no sooner had wheeled than caught by spear flight
in the back midway between the shoulders | and driven through his breast boulders
bold as brass crashed from chariot his armour rang | about him after Diomedes sprang
Agamemnon lion Menelaus | the Aiantes resolute and dauntless
Idomeneus squire Meriones | peer the man-killing War-god peerless he's
Eurypylus Euaemon's noble son | then ninth to sally forth with a bend on
his incurved bow Teucer took usual | place behind the shield of Aias son Tel
-amon Aias would move shield aside slow | Teucer would peer out for target to show
in the crowd and shoot then as the man hit | dropped down dead like a child running for bit
'er shelter to mum's skirts Teucer cover | took once again with Aias hid under
his glittering shield and who was first host | of the Trojans to fall to the foremost
Teucer? Orsilochus then Ormenus | Ophelestes Daitor and Chromius
god-like Lycophontes Amopaon | Polyaemon's son Melanippus on
each other hard fell and swift brought down on | the bountiful earth King Agamemnon
delighted when saw what a shock | strong long bow runs amok wreaking havoc
in the Trojan ranks went up to him said | "Teucer son Telamon my belov-ed
prince shoot on as now and you may well bring | salvation to the Danaans lending

fame to your father Telamon who took | you under his roof though bastard did look
after you repay him now with glory | though he long way away this scene gory
I'll tell you what I undertake to do | if aegis-bearing Zeus and Athene do
ever let me sack lovely town of Troy | I'll first prize of honour to you deploy
after my own say a tripod at head | or horses with car or woman share bed"
"My noble lord Atreides why flog | a willing horse? as I've been on job blog
without rest from the moment when we thrust | them back towards the town to chance I trust
watching with my bow and picking men off | and eight long-barbed arrows I have shot off
each found its mark in the flesh of some fighting | youth yonder but here now us benighting
a mad dog I can't hit" aimed at Hector | who he yearned to bring down sent new vector
arrow flying from string missed but pierces | breast one of Priam's noble sons peerless
Gorgythion whose mother the lovely | Castianeira with figure comely
as a goddess had come up from Aesyme | wed the King but weighed down by helm did seem
Gorgythion's head then dropped to one side | like the lolling head tired of Somme-tied tide
poppies weighed down by war seed and showers | of spring and his eagerness empowers
him get him Teucer aimed at Hector sent | an arrow flying from his string but went
astray this time too for Apollo turned | his dart aside Archeptolemus burned
Hector's daring charioteer beside | the nipple on his breast as he did ride
into the fight crashed from his chariot | made his horses shy and died on the spot
the death of his charioteer did wring | Hector's heart but sorry as was being
left him there and called upon his brother | Cebriones happened be near other
to take the horses' reins Cebriones | heard him then and obeys with no delays
Hector from his resplendent chariot | leapt to the ground with a terrible shout
picked up a lump of rock and made straight for | Teucer who he'd determined to do for
Teucer had just taken a sharp arrow | from his quiver and put it to the bow
as he drew back the string and aimed at him | struck by Hector flashing helm shoulder him
with the jagged stone on the spot weakest | where clavicle leads over to neck breast
the bowstring snapped his fingers and wrist numbed | he sank down to his knees and the bow thrummed
dropped from hand Aias did not disregard | his brother's fall came running up to guard
over bestrode covered him with his shield | and two of their trusty men from the field
Alastor and Echius' son own | Mecisteus lifted him from ground groan
-ing heavily bore to hospital ships | for Olympian Zeus with that the chips
were down put fresh heart into the Trojans | who now from this start drove the Achaeans
right back to their own deep trench and Hector | irresistible now mad war vector
full of the joy of battle led the van | a hound in full cry after a lion
or a wild boar snapping at buttock flank | following each twist and turn of prey rank
hung on heels of long-haired host Achaean | killing the hind-most all the time as ran
before him fled across trench palisade | suffering heavy losses as they made
to escape didn't stop 'til reached the ships | calling each other for aid amid ships
everyman lifted up his hands poured out | prayers to the gods but Hector was about
them wheeling long-maned horses to and fro | glaring at them with the eyes of Gorgo
-'n's gaze or murderous War-god white-armed | goddess Here was with great sorrow disarmed

when she saw their plight and did not hide her | distress from the goddess Athene "Daughter
of aegis-bearing Zeus can you and I | look on without making a final try
while the Danaans perish? for they will | and miserably too culled by a single
man see what he's done to them already! | there's no stopping him in his mad eddy"
"Nothing could please me more" said the bright-eyed | Athene "than see mad bad stampede be-tied
stamped out have him killed on his native soil | by Argives but Father's in evil toil
mode obstinate old sinner that he is | and always my plans is ready to diss
never thinks of the many times I went | to his son Heracles' rescue sent
by him when was defeated by the tasks | Eurystheus set Heracles just asks
whimpering to Heaven Zeus would send me | speeding down to free of difficulty
if my prophetic heart given warning | all this when Eurystheus suborning
him down to the House of Hades Warden | Gates bring from Erebus The Guardian
Hound of Hell would never again re-cross | the cataracts of Styx but now Zeus cross
with me is letting Thetis have her way | because she kissed his knees with hand in play
on his chin when she begged him to support | Achilles sacker of towns sport disport
merily verily day will come he'll | once again call me his Flashing-Eyed heal
-ing darling meanwhile please get our horses | ready while I to palace of aegis
-bearing Zeus and arm for war want to see | how pleased this son of Priam of flashy
helmet will be when the two of us show | ourselves athwart the ranks for it's now so
the Trojans' turn to fall dead by the ships | Achaean glut dogs birds of prey with strips
of fat and flesh" the white-armed goddess made | no demur here Here Queen of Heaven maid
so with the Daughter of mighty Cronos | went away to put the golden harness
on her horses while on Father's threshold | Daughter aegis-bearing Zeus shed soft-fold
embroidered robe had made with her own hands | put on tunic equipped herself so hands
down then the lamentable work of war | with the arms of Zeus the Cloud-compeller
stepping into the flaming chariot | gripping the huge long spear that runs riot
among the ranks of noble warriors | when she her Father's Child to war angers
no sooner in Here starts horses with whip | Gates of Heaven thundered open that trip
of own accord kept by the Hours Wardens | of the broad sky and the Olympic dens
task close entrance roll away heavy cloud | through Gates drove their patient double-steed shroud
but when Father Zeus saw them from Ida | he was enraged and at once gave order
Iris Golden Wings convey a message | "Off with you Iris and speed your passage!
make them turn back do not let them meet me | face to face terrible thing it would be
for them to fight with Zeus tell them from me | who make no idle threats and so it be
I will hamstring the horses they're driving | them both from their chariot be driving
break the chariot up ten rolling years | would pass they not be healed of wound tear tears
my thunderbolt would deal them would teach | the Lady of the Flashing Eyes to breach
her Father's writ as for Here not so much | hurt angry HER instinct's defy me much"
Iris of the Whirlwind Feet sped off thus | from peaks of Ida to great Olympus
on the rugged heights met them at the gates | themselves stopped them and Zeus' message states
"Whither away? and what is the object | of this mad foolish and reckless project?
the Son of Cronos forbids aid Argives | hear what he threatens to do to your lives

and you know that Zeus keeps his word he will | hamstring the horses you're driving and hurl
you from the chariot and break it up | and ten rolling years you would then pass up
and be left still suffering from the wounds | his thunderbolt would deal terrible wounds!
and that Lady Flashing Eyes would teach you | what it means to fight your Father it's you
not Here who habitually defies | his orders who makes his hurt anger rise
so much due to your brazen and graceless | impudence if you really dare brandish
that giant spear of yours at him" Iris | Fleet-Footed took her leave then Here marks this
to Athene alarmed "Daughter of aegis | -bearing Zeus I've changed my mind won't do this
not go to war with Zeus on man's behalf | let chance say who's to live be cut in half
Zeus must decide in his own mind between | the Trojan and the Danaan last scene
as is only right" as spoke she turned their | chariot back and the Hours unyoked their
long-maned horses and tethered them at their | ambrosial mangers awaiting there
tilted chariot against wall burnished | by the gateway while the two refurnished
the immortal gods in great chagrin sat | on golden chairs Zeus from Ida out flat
to Olympus fast chariot horses | he also would receive such services
when he arrived at the home of the gods | from illustrious Earthshaker the god's
unyoked horses put chariot on stand | cloth covered all-seeing Zeus all in hand
sat on his golden throne great Olympus | quaked beneath his feet thus away from Zeus
Athene and Here sitting by selves saying | no word to him asking not essaying
but he knew what was passing through their minds | "Athene and Here why so down in your minds?
not worn out surely by the glorious | battle in which you killed notorious
Trojans so many of those you loathe? I | now could never be forced aside from my
path by all the gods in Olympus such | the strength of my unconquerable clutch
but you two were trembling in every limb | before even saw field out on a limb
of horrors let me tell you what would've | happened to both of you if you'd not've
changed your minds my thunderbolt then would've | wrecked you and if you HAD got back would've
been then in somebody else's chariot" | this drew mutterings from them where sat plot
together still for Trojans trouble all | however Athene held her tongue for all
her annoyance with Zeus her Father none | the rejoinder though seethed indignation
but Here could not contain her rage burst out | "O Dread Son Cronos now here Here hear out
this is intolerable! we know as well | as all the rest you're all-powerful fell
and not to be challenged as such but we're | feeling so sorry for Danaan spear
-men left as they will be to destruction | and miserable fate on your instruction
if it's your wish we'll refrain from fighting | content ourselves sound advice imparting
to Argives so may not all come to grief | through your anger" Zeus referred to his brief
"Here Here my ox-eyed queen you'll have at sun | -rise opportunity to see the Son
almighty of Cronos do yet greater | execution even among the spear
-men of the Argive force for I tell you | the mighty Hector is then going to
give his enemies no rest 'til the swift | Achilles returns again to his shift
by the ships where very stern(')s the fighting's | in dire straits most desperate alighting's
fell over the body of Patroclus | that's decreed by Heaven and as for fuss
anger of yours leaves me at my calm most | for all I care you to the nethermost

pit can go join Iapetus and Cronos | who don't enjoy Hyperion Sun's toss
of beams nor any breezes sunk as are | in the depths of Tartarus you as far
down as you can go and your angry will | leaves me manifestly unconcerned still
there are no limits to your impudence" | this time the White-armed goddess no response
made and now the bright lamp of the sun dropped | and so then into Ocean gently plopped
and so then drawing black night in its train | across the fruitful earth giver of grain
against the Trojans' will who'd not wanted | day to end but to Achaeans who did
yearn for this dark relief much thanks came like | a tardy answer to their prayers a-like
illustrious Hector pulled host Trojan | from the ships summoned meeting in open
arena beside the swirling river | where the terrain there was of corpses clear
they got down from their chariots to hear | Hector hectoring them he held a spear
full eleven cubits long the bronze point | before him glittered gold ring around point
at the top of the shaft as he addressed | his troops his weight on the spear he did rest
"Friends Trojan Dardanian allies please | listen to me had hoped trash enemy's
ships the whole host with them before going | home to windy Ilium light going
too soon though and that more than anything | Argive fleet sea-shore delays everything
end now can only do as night suggests | prepare for supper while day one digests
unyoke your long-maned horses put fodder | by them then quickly go bring some udder
cattle and fat sheep from town supply your | -selves with a mellow wine and bread from your
houses and collect a good quantity | of wood so we're able to have plenty
of fires burning all night 'til dawn lights up | whole sky in case long-haired Argives try up
sticks make a dash for home despite the dark | sail away in their hallowed hollow (b)ar(k)que
we must certainly not leave them embark | at their ease let's give them something stark dark
to digest at home arrow or sharp spear | in the back as they jump aboard teach fear
and other people too think twice about | the miseries of war before raise shout
of assault against horse-taming Trojans | in Troy itself let our heralds' summons
call out the young lads and grey-headed old | men on walls built for us by the gods bold
all around the town to bivouac while our | womenfolk each home keep fire full power
burning and regular guards be mounted | to see enemy has not dismounted
in town from horse Trojan troops when away | those brave Trojans my orders for today
may hold sway anyway for the moment | I think that we can say that 'It all went
well' in the morning then I will enhance | the soldiers further disposition stance
hope pray to Zeus and all the other gods | I'll be able drive off these hellhound sods
that the Fates have brought here in their black ships | night now must guard against any own slips
when sun peeps piper at the gates of dawn | we'll arm selves attack them with Total brawn
by the hollow ships then I'll see whether | the mighty Diomedes can weather
my onset or drive me back from the ships | to the wall or whether cash in his chips
with my sharp bronze bear off his bloodstained arms | he'll learn dawn if has in him Fate's charm balms
to stand up against my spear more likely | as tomorrow's sun ascends he will be
bleeding lying in battle-front half-ish | company dead round their leader I wish
I were as sure of immortality | and ageless youth with a lasting glory
like Athene's or Apollo's as I am | that this day will be a disastrous sham

-bles for the Argives" the Trojans greeted | this harangue from Hector applause tweeted
they freed their sweating horses from the yokes | tethered thongs and with all the jo(c)key blokes
by their own chariots then quickly hie | to town bring oxen fat sheep and sup-ply
selves with mellow wine and at same time bread | from their homes and they also collected
large quantities of wood and presently | smell of roast meat was rising languidly
to high heaven on the breeze all night long | they sat across the corridors elong
-ated of battle great thoughts there thinking | poems their many fires b(r)ight kept (tw)inkling
there are nights when the upper air's windless | and the stars in heaven stand out peerless
in their full splendour round the bright moon's sheen | when every mountain-top headland ravine
starts into sight as deeps sky infinite | torn open in mighty rents so finite
to the very firmament when each star | is seen the shepherd rejoices afar
such and so many were the Trojans' fires | twinkling in front of Ilium's great spires
midway between the ships streams of Xanthus | and there were burning fires a thousand plus
on the plain round each one sat fifty men | in the light of its blaze the horses then
stood beside their chariots munching rye | and white barley waiting there on stand-by
for Dawn to then ascend her golden throne | rosy-fingered coming into her own

## ἐννέα

*Book 9*

# OVERTURES TO ACHILLES

*how Agamemnon beseeched Achilles*
*be appeased denied hid did Achilles*

while the Trojans were there their watch keeping | Achaeans Panic-gripped shudder shrieking
deadly she who treads on the heels of Rout | all their best captains the tortures of doubt
dark despair their hearts storm-tossed like fish-bass | -delighting sea when Zephyr Boreas
the winds that blow from Thrace do pounce on it | alternate squalls and the black rollers hit
their crests pile seaweed all along the beach | Agamemnon wandering on the reach
distraught in grief told clear-voiced team herald | to summon every man by name herald
-ic to meeting but not to shout aloud | a leading part in work himself endowed
sat down to Assembly in sorry mood | Agamemnon rose address them sore moved
mighty tears ran down his face like water | trickling from a spring in streaks black torture
down a precipice "My friends and Captains | hard at hand Counsellors of Acheans
Zeus the great Son of Cronos has dealt me | a crushing blow cruel god who assured me
solemnly that I should bring down the walls | of Ilium before I left but all's
changed in his mind to my disappointment | bitter now bids me Argos retrenchment
in disgrace half my army lost it's clear | that unconquerable Zeus who did clear
out high towers many a great city | and who will destroy others yet clearly
has decided in his omnipotence | so now let every man of you commence
follow my lead aboard the ships I say | and let's go home to our own country yea!
broad-streeted Troy will never fall to us" | outburst received complete silence soldiers
Achaean long time sat speechless unease | dejection but at last Diomedes
of the loud war-cry clambered to his feet | "My lord Atreides it is most meet
first and foremost this imbecility | yours contended where it just so to be
even now in the assembly (wherefore | your lordship knows privileges we draw)
and you must not be offended as you | took it on yourself the other day to
reprimand me in front of the whole troupe | said I was a coward and nincompoop
as every Achaean heard young and old | but does not Zeus in his wisdom withhold
gifts from YOU? imperial sceptre gave | and that which it brings with it the homage
yet did not give you courage and courage | is the secret of power in this age

sir do you really believe the Argives | to be the cowards even the low-lives
that your words imply? for if by your leave | have set your heart now on taking your leave
why not be off? the road is clear your ships | standing by the sea whole great fleet that ships
from Mycenae followed but rest of long | -haired Achaeans 'til we sack Troy will long
to stay nay they too can take to the ship | like you scuttle home but in comradeship
we two I and Sthenelus will fight on | until we reach our goal city Trojan
as it's by Heaven's will that we are here" | then the Achaeans were all of good cheer
with Diomedes shouted approval | Charioteer Nestor sought approval
"Tydeides a great man in a fight | no rival of your age in debate might
be sure not one of us here will cavil | at your speech nor gainsay a word as ill
but your words stopped too soon the fact is though | you talk sense to the Argive kings and though
you were right saying what you did at need | you are still rather young you might indeed
have been my youngest son and I who am | so much older than you yourself are am
left explain the speech's implications | work out in detail the complications
when I come to do so I shall count on | everyone's support King Agamemnon
even for that man is an enemy | of his clan and hearth and indeed country
who enjoys bitter taste of civil war | but enough for the moment let's take for
our cue the dark night prepare for dinner | so sentries must be posted at inter
-vals close along the trench outside the wall | duty I leave to younger then withal
sorted Atreides as overlord | you must give a lead ask each senior lord
to a banquet a proper thing for you | to do and one too that cannot hurt you
day by day ships bring wine to you and yours | over the seas from Thrace those huts of yours
full of it as King of this great people | it is for you to offer hospital
-ity and when you have gathered us all | as one must listen to the man whose call
is most apposite God knows we Argives | need best and cleverest words of our lives
given all these enemy fires so near | to the ships to no-one do they appear
as a pleasant sight and this very night | will make or break the expedition's might"
Nestor's advice well received and promptly | followed at the double team armed sentry
went out under chief Prince Thrasymedes | Nestor's son with noble Lycomedes
Creon's son Ascalapus Ialmenus | children of the War-god Deipyrus
Aphareus Meriones seven | captains of the guard a hundred young men
marched behind each with long spears in their hands | midway between trench and wall took their stands
each party lit a fire and everyone | prepared their dinner as Agamemnon
led whole party senior commanders | to his hut savoury meal commandeers
to be served up they helped selves to good things | spread before them when all satisfyings
of hunger and thirst done old man Nestor | took the floor as at heart had more care for
their interests this not the time only | his wisdom won the day "Your majesty
Agamemnon son of Atreus King | of Men with you my speech is beginning
and it will end with you for you are King | of a great people for whose governing
wise Zeus has put the sceptre in your hands | entrusted you with the laws of the lands
so it behoves you above all both to | give and listen to advice also to
carry out the suggestions others may | feel bound to put forward in such a way

that to your own interest then deploys | you'll get the credit for whatever ploys
originate with THEM and now I will | tell you what I think best sure no-one will
hit on a better remedy than mine | it was long ago I made up mind mine
and I have not altered it since in fact | your majesty not since that lack of tact
when you infuriated Achilles | by seizing lady Briseis' knees
we were all against it and I for one | did my utmost to try to dissuade one
but your arrogant temper bettered you | a man of the highest distinction you
degraded who the gods themselves esteem | by confiscating his prize lovely dream
-boat to your own profit which brings me to | my point even now let's take bold steps to
approach and placate him with a humble | apology and peace offerings full"
"My venerable lord" said Agamemnon | "of blind folly the account you've given
is wholly true blinded I was I do | not deny it myself for the man who
Zeus has taken to his heart and honours | as he does Achilles and dishonours
to that point the Achaeans for his sake | is worth an army as I did forsake
the true path and gave into an impulse | lamentable committed this repuls
-i've acted ill will now go back on it | and make particular amends for it
with a handsome indemnity before | you all I will enumerate the score
of all the splendid gifts that I offer | seven tripods untarnished fire-power
ten talents of gold with twenty cauldrons | of gleaming copper and twelve stallions
powerful prize-winners with nothing more | then than the prizes they've won fighting for
me so a man would not be badly off | nor the precious gold any shortage of
also I will give him seven women | skilled in the fine crafts they are Lesbian
I chose for their exceptional beauty | these he shall have from me and with them she
who I took away from him the daughter | of Briseus and I'll give moreover
my solemn oath never been in her bed | and slept with her as a man when does bed
a woman these shall be put in his hands | at once then if the gods let us lay hands
on the great city of Priam let him | come in with us when we share out the trim
spoils load his ship with gold and bronze to his | heart's content and at a choosing of his
for himself own twenty Trojan women | loveliest found save Achaean Helen
and if in due course we do get back to | Achaean Argos richest of lands too
he can become my son-in-law and I | will treat him in just the same way as I
do Orestes my own beloved son | who is now being brought up there full on
in lap of luxury number three is | daughters in my palace Chrysothemis
Laodice and Iphianassa | of these he shall choose whichever lass a
-takes his fancy take to Peleus' | house without making usual gifts his
indeed I will pay HIM a dowry a | generous one bigger than ever a
-warded with a daughter not only that | I will give him seven fine towns the flat
Cardamyle (in the far far distant future to be | home museum Ire/Eng/Greek god Pat Leigh
-Fermor) grassy Hire also Enope | Pedasus rich in vines holy Pherae
lovely Aepeia Antheia | with its deep meadows and they are all near
the sea in farthest part Pylos sandy | rich in flocks cattle their citizens he
they'd do homage to pay tribute to him | and indeed they would make a god of him

acknowledging his sceptre prospering | under his paternal sway proffering
all this promise will do if he relents | let him surrender and why one resents
Hades more than any god I don't know | but it may be perhaps that he is so
adamantine and unyielding? so let | him submit himself to me who am yet
his senior by so much both as king | man" "Your majesty Agamemnon King
of Men son of Atreus " replied ye | great charioteer Nestor "nobody
can say your offer to Prince Achilles | is not generous well then let us seize
the time with all speed send deputation | to the hut complex Peleus' son
I am ready to nominate the men | myself they must not refuse duty then
first of all Phoenix the venerable | he can go in advance then the able
Aias and the noble Odysseus | heralds Eurybates and Odius
are the men to go with them but first let | someone fetch water for our hands and let
call for silence so we may pray to Zeus | Son of Cronos implore trace grace face truce"
each one satisfied Nestor's arrangements | and heralds hastened to pour unguents
over their hands while their squires filled the mix | -ing bowls to the brim with drink after fix
-ing a little first in everyman's cup | served them all with wine when they had raised up
in libation drunk as much as they wished | the envoys from Agamemnon's hut dished
up their errand post the Gerenian | charioteer Nestor had once given
them full instructions glancing from man one | to another as he exhorted one
and all to do their utmost to placate | the peerless Achilles but with eye-state
mostly on Odysseus was firmly found | he and Aias walked down shore of the sound
-ing sea together with many a prayer | to great Sea-god who girdles the layer
of the world that the task of so moving | the proud heart of Achilles not proving
too hard when they came to the Myrmidons' | huts ships found prince with songs were lutey ones
the time beguiling about famous men | and was accompanying himself then
on a tuneful lyre a beautifully | ornamented instrument silvery
crossbar he'd chosen from the spoils when he'd | to Eetion's city gone destroy he'd
he now alone except for Patroclus | sat opposite eyes on Achilles thus
quietly awaiting him stop singing | envoys neared Odysseus message bringing
halted before prince surprised Achilles | sprang to his feet lyre in hand and chilled he's
for now forward from chair where been sitting | and Patroclus too got up so hitting
on men with fist-bump gesture of greeting | Achilles the great runner word greeting
"Welcome – to two dear friends! time someone came | and as angry as I am all the same
no two Achaeans I love more than you" | the noble Achilles led them into
his hut seated them on chairs with purple | coverings turned quickly to Purtrucle
standing by "Bring out a bigger bowl pray | my lord P less water in the wine say
a cup all for here are my dearest friends | under my own roof" P carried out friend's
orders set fleshing-block in the firelight | laid on it backs of sheep fat goat not light
and the chine of a great hog rich in lard | Automedon held these for him well hard
Achilles jointed them and then carved them up | the joints and the slices then spitted up
in the meantime Patroclus royal son | of Menoetius sent the fire full on
when it had burnt down again the embers | scattered made space for animals' members

laid the spits above them on dogs resting | after meat un-holy salt attesting
when he'd roasted it and heaped it up on | platters fetched some bread and set it out on
the table in handsome baskets and then | Achilles divided the meat portion
-style took a chair by the wall opposite | King Odysseus told friend P-erform rite
of sacrifice to the gods Patroclus | threw on the fire ritual pieces plus
they all then helped themselves to the good things | spread before them when the food and drink things
were sorted Aias nodded to Phoenix | Odysseus saw the signal in the mix
having filled his cup with wine drank "Your health | Achilles! and now with all this great wealth
of appetising dishes to dispose | of can't complain of our rations' repose
either in my lord Agamemnon's hut | or here in yours this very moment but
pleasures of table are far from our thoughts | confronted virual disaster of sorts
of magnitude appals us so unless | you now rouse yourself to fight we have less
than an even chance to save our brave ships | or see them sacked by those insolent slips
of Trojans and their allies infamous | bivouacking close to wall and ships famous
their camp is bright with fires and they're convinced | nothing left to stop a win be evinced
swooping down on our black ships Zeus the Son | of Cronos indeed encouraged them on
with lightning flashes on the right Hector | has run amok triumphant all-power
-ful he trusts in Zeus fears not man nor god | in the frenzy in which he is now shod
his one prayer's for the early approaching | gracious Dawn for he itching encroaching
on us hack ensigns' tops from our good ships | and send up in flames those very same ships
to smoke us out slaughter us by the hulls | and I'm terribly afraid as one mulls
this over that the gods may well let him | carry out his threats that may be our grim
fate to perish here so far from Argos | where the horses graze then cast off the dross
if even at this late hour you want to | rescue the exhausted troops from the too
great Trojan fury and if you refuse | you yourself will regret you did not choose
that course for when the damage has been done | there will be no chance of mending it son
bestir yourself before that stage we reach | save the Argives from catastrophic breach
on the beach my good friend when your father | Peleus sent you off from Phthia
to join Agamemnon did he not e'en | these words admonish you 'My son Athene
and Here if they wish you well are going | to make you strong what YOU must be doing
is to keep a check on that proud spirit | a better thing than pride a kind heart fit
of quarrels deadly be reconciled now | all the Argives young and old will and how
look up to you the more?' those were the old | man's precepts which you've allowed to grow cold
yet even so it's not too late to yield | give up this bitter hatred that you wield
Agamemnon is ready to make you | ample compensation the moment you
relent if you will listen I'll spell out | the gifts that he's destined to you dish out
seven tripods untarnished by the flames | ten talents gold twenty cauldrons in frames
of copper twelve powerful prize-winning | race-horses and he said that with nothing
more than a man won for him as prizes | not bad off under him no surprise is
or short of precious gold in addition | he said he will give you seven women
skilled in the fine crafts Lesbians who he | had picked for their exceptional beauty
as his part of the spoils when you yourself | took the city of Lesbos lacked life-shelf

you shall have these from him with them woman | who'd commandeered from you King of Man
daughter of Briseus moreover he | will give you his solemn oath he's never
been in her bed and slept with her as he's | wont to as a man your majesty these
gifts shall all be put at once in your hands | later if the gods let us get our hands
on Ilium Priam's great city you're | to come in with us when we start up shore
and share the spoils load your ship with gold bronze | to heart's content and select twenty bronzed
and brazen for yourself Trojan women | loveliest around save Argive Helen
and if in due course we manage get back | to Achaean Argos the richest track
of all those fair lands you can be his son | -in-law treat you as he does his own son
his beloved Orestes who's being | brought up there lap of luxury being
and he has three daughters in palace his | Iphianassa then Chrysothemis
and Laodice of these you shall pick | the one you like the best and take the chick
house Peleus not give usual gifts | in fact he will give YOU generous gifts
bigger than anyone's ever given | with his daughter you'll also get seven
lovely towns Cardamyle Enope | and grassy Hire Pherae the holy
and Antheia of deep mead meadows | the beautiful Aepeia and those
rich vines of Pedasus all near the sea | in the richest furthest reaches sandy
Pylos people rich in flocks and cattle | and they will do homage to you and'll
pay you tribute as though you were a god | acknowledge sceptre figurehead of god
prospering under your paternal sway | and all this he will do for you to sway
you relent yet if your hatred displayed | for Atreides has all else outweighed
pity some the rest of the united | Achaeans lying in their camp now dead
-beat and they will honour you like a god | you could then find yourself indeed well shod
in glory in their eyes for now's the time | when you could get Hector for at this time
he fancies he has no match among all | the Danaans the ships brought here may call
you venture near in his senseless fury" | "Royal son Laertes nimble wits he"
replied Achilles the great runner" to | save you sitting there in turns trying to
coax me I had better tell you point-blank | how I feel and what I have in the tank
I loathe like Hell's Gates he who thinks one thing | and says another so now I'm giving
my decision and you can take it that | neither my lord Agamemnon for that
nor the rest of the Argives are going | to win me over time seeming showing
man gets no thanks struggling with enemy | and yet the share of the spoils ends up be
same whether sits at home or fights his best | it seems that cowards and brave men the best
are equally respected and death comes | alike to one whose life nothing up sums
and one who has toiled hard in the risk ring | all I have suffered constantly risking
my life in battle's left me no better | off than the rest I've been like an otter
bringing every fish she gets to her kitts | no matter how hard with HER it then sits
I have spent many a sleepless night fraught | many a bloody day against men fought
like us for their womenfolk I've taken | twelve towns from the sea also eleven
I took by land deep-soiled realm Ilium | I'll have you know from each got tidy sum
of loot all of which I brought back each time | gave my lord Agamemnon (the swine!)
son of Atreus who had stayed behind | by the black ships and who in tiny mind

parcelled a few little bits of it out | kept the lion's share and what did give out
a portion to the princes and kings in | recognition of their rank is safe in
their possession and I'm the only one | he's robbed not as though no wife he HAS one
of his own choice so let him sleep with her | and be content and now for that matter
what drove the Argives to make war on Troy? | Atreides raised a force for what ploy
if not for Helen of the lovely hair? | and can it be Atreidae fare fair
as only men on earth who love their wives? | and do not all men who conduct their lives
in a right-minded way love and cherish | each own woman as I loved Brieseis
with all my heart though captive of my spear? | but now out of my arms he's snatched her dear
and swindled me don't let him try his tricks | on me again I know too well his kicks
and pricks won't succeed no Odysseus he | must look to you and other kings if he
wants to stop the ships going up in flames | he's already done marvels when my name's
not in the lists he's built a wall with trench | dug all along it indeed fine broad trench
complete with palisade but even he | can still not keep out the murderous He
-ctor! why in the days when I took the field | with the Argives it would not have appealed
to him to throw his men into battle | at any distance from the wall civil
he came no farther than the Scaean Gate | and the oak tree where one day had a date
alone and he was lucky to get home | alive but things have changed now not to home
in on my lord Hector *t*hat is my choice | tomorrow to Zeus I make sacrifice choice
and all the other gods then lade and launch | my ships the very first thing in the staunch
morn's light if you're curious enough see | you'll watch them breasting the Hellespont sea
where the fishes play and my men inside | straining at the oar in three days betide
given good crossing by the great Sea-god | I should on Phthia of the deep sod
set foot I left a rich home there when I'd | the misfortune to come here and now I'd
enrich it further with what I bring back | the gold the red copper from the towns' sack
the girdled women and the grey iron | that fell to me by lot thus every one
of the prizes save the one of honour | given me thus for me does diss-honour
in insult withdrawn by one and same man | the lord Agamemnon the king of Man
son Atreus tell him all I've set down | tell him in public so the rest may frown
on any further efforts he may try | overreach Danaan royalty high
unconscionable schemer he always is | and yet he would never dare for all his
impudence to look me straight in the eyes | no I will help him not by advice wise
nor in the field he's broken faith with me | played me false never again shall I be
deceived by what he says so much for him | to perdition go quietly let him
Zeus in his wisdom has addled his brain | already as for his gifts I disdain
them just as I disdain the man himself | not if he were to offer me himself
ten times or twenty times as much as he's | got or could raise elsewhere thus with all these
revenues Orchomenus Thebes Thebes | Egyptian its houses stuffed to the eves
with treasure and through every one of a | hundred gates two hundred warriors sa
-lly out with their chariots and horses | and not too even if his gift-horses
were as many as the grains of sand or | dust particles would win me over for
first he must pay me in kind for bitter | humiliation endured big hitter

like me will not have a daughter of his | for my wife could be as lovely as is
golden Aphrodite and skilful as | Pallas Athene of Flashing Eyes art has
and yet I would not marry her he can | to some other of brothers Achaean
more royal than me and on a level | with himself and then if the gods level
with me allow me to get home safely | Peleus won't need help in finding me
a wife throughout Hellas and Phthia's | a bounty of Achaean girls daughters
of the noblemen in charge of the forts | I've only to choose one for home comforts
make her my own for there were times often | at home when had no higher ambition
than to wed some suitable girl of my | own station and enjoy the fortune my
old father Peleus had made for life | as I see it's more important than strife
-gathered hoard of fabled wealth either Troy | the most splendid in peace before the boy
Argive came or counting all the treasure | that is piled up in rocky Pytho sure
behind the stone threshold of Archery | -King Apollo for cattle and sturdy
sheep can be had for the taking tripods | and chestnut horses you can get with wads
but you can't steal or buy back a man's life | when once the breath has left his lips in strife
my divine Mother Thetis of the Feet | Silver tells me that Destiny does meet
out to me on my journey two courses | but to the grave if stay in the courses
play my part in siege of Troy there's no home | -coming though shall win undying fame home
and away but if home to own country | my good name will be lost from history
though I'll have long life spared an early death | one more point for the sake of your life-breath
I recommend that all the rest of you | embark forthwith and set sail for home too
because you will never reach your goal in | the steep streets of Ilium as all see-in'
Zeus up above his loving hand did weave | town and its folk have taken heart so leave
me now and report to the Argive lords | in open council because you my lords
as seniors have the right to do they must | think of some better way to save the trust
-y ships now and all the troops beside them | now that these overtures to me find them
-selves blank refusal but Phoenix can stay | and spend the night with us then sail away
for home with me in the morn if he's on | for that as there will be no compulsion"
Achilles had finished and they were stunned | by his bleak no a long silence no fun-d
had the old charioteer Phoenix was | first to break silence in such terror was
for the Argive ships he burst into tears | "If so think lord Achilles idea's
sailing home as so obsessed by anger | that you will not any more consider
saving the gallant ships from going up | in flames what for the book is a turn up
for me without you my dear child? how could | I possibly stay here alone? and would
not the old charioteer Peleus | make me your guardian when he sent us
from Phthia to join Agamemnon? | you were a mere lad had no handle on
the hazards of war or even debate | where people make their mark to make you great
in these things to make a speaker of you | and man of action he sent me with you
I could not bring myself to let you go | and stay here not if God himself were so
to strip me of my years turn me into | the sturdy youngster I was when first to
the outside world went thus leaving Hellas | the land of lovely women O a-lass!
I ran away as a quarrel went on | with father Amyntor Ormenus son

the reason why we were at daggers drawn | he was making love to a courtesan Dawn
beautiful neglecting wife my mother | who kept begging me to turn my father
against courtesan by foreskinning him | spend night in her arms before inning-him
I consented and did so my father | knew at once and as a solemn curser
called on the avenging Furies to see | to it a son of mine never should he
have to take on his lap and as time showed | his curses the gods allowed to corrode
by Zeus of the Underworld and august | Persephone so angry my first t(h)rust
instinct then was to put him to the sword | but one of the immortals gave me word
made me think of public opinion | of the obloquy that I would summon
on myself and the horror appalling | compatriots me parricide calling
yet I could not bear prospect of hanger | -about angry dad's house any longer
of course friends and kinsmen who'd out sallied | in their efforts allied round me rallied
to importune me then to stay at home | fat sheep shambling kine crooked horn genome
were slaughtered without end many a fine | fat hog extended over fire the swine
to have his bristles singed many a jar | the old man's mellow wine did not go far
for nine nights they camped beside me taking | it in turn to go on guard and making
two fires burn one under the colonnade | walled yard other in forecourt outside played
the door of the sleeping-quarters but on | tenth night which was pitch dark I burst open
the stout doors of my bedroom and escaped | found it easy climb wall of courtyard scaped
none of the maidservants or men on guard | spotted me so in earnest fled yards hard
right across Hellas and its spreading lawns | to deep-soiled Phthia mother of dawns
and sheep where I then presented myself | to Peleus the King and he himself
took me to heart loved me as a father | loves only son who's cherished heir father
to a great estate made me man rich one | by giving me a populous region
to rule I settled down on the borders | of Phthia King of Dolopesers
and since then most worshipful Achilles | all my loving devotion gone to these
goals fighter-speaker and do you recall | how you'd not go out to dinner at all
or touch your food at home with anyone | but me how I would always take you on
my knees pamper you by cutting titbits | for you from my meat and up to your lips
holding my cup? you often soaked the front | of my tunic with wine that from that font
then from clumsy little mouth did dribble | for you struggled in truth no mere dribble
worked so hard and I felt that since Heaven | not going to send me a boy Evan
better make YOU my son most worshipful | Achilles so from an end miserable
you could some day save me conquer your pride | Achilles you've no right to play the wide
-boy in stubbornness the very gods for | all their greater excellence power
and majesty are able to be swayed | even they from their course have often strayed
waylaid by sacrifice and prayers humble | libations burnt-offerings when stumble
sinners and miscreants bend knee to them | in supplication and don't you know them
those Prayers as Daughters of almighty Zeus? | with halting gait downcast eyes creatures use
wrinkled make it their business to follow | Sin about but Sin is hard to follow
strong and quick enough to leave them behind | stealing a march on them and all mankind
brings to grief as roams around world routing | PRAYERS come when trouble-shooting out shouting

the man who receives these Daughters of Zeus | with humility when come up their use
he's greatly blessed by them his petitions | granted but when man hard repositions
his heart and rebuffs them they go and pray | to Zeus the Son of Cronos that he may
himself be visited by Sin and punished | through his fall and this rule undiminished
applies to you Achilles you must give | their due to the Daughters of Zeus and give
in to them and so being placated | happens withal men noble-heart fated
if lord Agamemnon had not made you | generous offer with promise to you
of more to come but had then persisted | in his rancour I'd be the last one bid
you cast your anger to the winds and aid | Argives however great need as they fade
but as is he's not only admitting | a great deal now but also committing
himself to future liberality | besides choosing plead his cause key aides be
the most distinguished men in the whole army | who're your best friends in Argive family-tree
their pleas and pilgrimage here are the things | you must not dismiss as mere sweet nothings
though no-one can blame you for resentment | you've felt 'til now heard of noblemen spent
in comparable tales in times olden | who'd worked themselves up into a passion
yet proved amenable to gifts yielded | to persuasion my looking back yielded
over time a case I recall myself | we're all friends here and I'll tell you the self
-same story the Curetes were fighting | the warlike Aetolians siting
the city of Calydon losses were | heavy for both Aetolians were
defending their lovely town Curetes | were doing all they could to crater these
town walls and the trouble had started when | the goddess Artemis of Throne Golden
took offence and thus let a monster loose | on Calydon because King Oeneus use
-less had failed to make her any harvest | -offering on sacred hill estate crest
all other gods enjoyed sacrifices | rich of almighty Zeus was only this
Daughter to whom he had offered nothing | perhaps forgot her perhaps his noting
wrong but in either case fatal mistake | for the Lady of the Bow did this take
personal sent a creature of the gods | ravenous wild boar whose tusks bore poor odds
settled down to ravage the royal pounds | and with the tall fruit trees he strewed the grounds
he brought them tumbling down rooting them up | with their blossom on the twigs still stuck up
at last Oeneus' son Meleager | killed him but he was forced to beleaguer
a posse of huntsmen hounds from cities | all around because the vile creature is
too powerful for a handful and brought | a number of them to an end distraught
even then Artemis started the lass | real battle-royal over the beast's carcass
set Curetes Aetolians proud | each other's throats for shaggy hide head shroud
in the war that ensued so long as ye | redoubtable Meleager took part he
war went against Curetes unable | sit in siege town for all available
numbers but many a sensible one | is at times overmastered by passion
and that's what happened now to Meleager | enraged by Althaea his mother
at home with wife lay in idle quarter | very lovely Cleopatra daughter
of Marpessa of the slim ankles her | -self daughter of Euenus the father
of Cleopatra Idas in times past | had been upon the earth the man strongest
had faced Lord Phoebus Apollo with bow | for sake Marpessa lovely ankles show

Cleopatra's parents in their home say | her given nickname was Alcyone
memory mum's life as queen-kingfisher | and plaintive calls uttered when the Archer
-god Phoebus Apollo carried her off | Meleager took her to his bed shake off
with her his nursed soul-destroying anger | mother's curses made him bitter banger
he had killed her brother she in her grief | had begged of the gods in search of relief
kill her son falling on her knees failing | deluging her lap with tears and flailing
the ground with her fists as called on Hades | august Persephone of the shades she's
and Fury who walks in the darkness thoughts | unbending from Erebus heard retorts
before long the Curetes were storming | at the gates one could hear them de-forming
walls Aetolian Elders induce | tried him now to come out and break his truce
to save the town sent a deputation | the leading priests liberal donation
promised could choose estate acres fifty | for his own use one half a vinery
other open ploughland to be carv-ed | out of the richest part of the Calyd
-onian plain the old charioteer | Oeneus to theirs added own prayer here
he stood on Meleager's bedroom's threshold | lofty shook the wooden doors solid gold
begging and beseeching his son and his | sisters and mother earnestly urged his
return though just made him more obstinate | thus comrades-in-arms and many a mate
the dearest and most loyal friends he had | resisted their efforts with all he had
'til the very last moment Curetes | had scaled walls firing the quarters with ease
of the great city missiles hailing down | on his very room in that part of town
and at that point his lovely wife approached | in tears all the miseries reproached
pictured people suffer when town captured | the slaughter of men the city immured
in dust and ashes by flames alien | the enemy bearing off the children
and the womenfolk in their gilded gowns | and thus her sad recital of the downs
-(l)ide to come touched his heart and he came out | and donned his gleaming armour all about
saved Aetolians from disaster | own conscience being dictator master
and that being so they gave him none of | the many splendid gifts they had made of
-fer of he saved them but got naught by it | my friend do not think as he did of it
feel inspired to follow his example | for because when the ships for example
are already on fire will be harder | then to save them no come while gifts offer
still to be had and the Achaeans will | treat you like a god if you risk battle
with no such inducement they will not view | you anywhere near so well although you
turn defeat into victory" Phoenix | had done Achilles great runner nix fix
"My lord Phoenix my dear old friend I've no | use for the Argives good opinio
-'n I'm content with the approbation | of Zeus which will retain me on station
by my beaked ships as long as breath remains | in my body and limb function maintains
what's more I wish you to know I object | to your new currying favour abject
with lord Agamemnon by this attempt | to upset me with a displayed contempt
of maudlin emotion be careful how | you give that man your heart or you may now
change my love for you to hate the right thing | for you to do then would be the crossing
of the man who crosses me for I have | now decided and these men shall then have
to tell him so I'd rather give you half | my kingdom than relent you have not half

comfortable bed to sleep on so stay | here yourself and we will decide at day
-break whether to go home or not" so stalled | Achilles surreptitiously signalled
Patroclus with a movement of eyebrows | make the bed for Phoenix so others' brows(e)
might think of getting on their way as soon | as possible Aias the royal son
of Telamon who first made to move on | and thus turning to Laertes' son
"My lord Odysseus of the nimble wits | let's go then for it now to me seems it's
doomed to failure at this time | anyway bad as the news is quick time
we must report it to the Danaans | who're no doubt sitting up thinking what plans
they need make but I can't help thinking on | the rancour arrogance combination
Achilles has displayed ruthlessness too | no thought for the affection of friends who
made him the idol of our camp! the sheer | inhumanity of it! common here
quite even in some cases of murder | for someone for a son or a brother
accept blood-money no need killer flee | indeed does not have to leave the country
even if he pays up to next of kin | whose pride and injured feelings are akin
to being appeased by indemnity | but you Achilles god only knows see
does the why of it worked self up into | this fiery fury implacable too
over a girl a single girl and here | we are offering you seven of sheer
best and a great deal more too be a bit | more forbearing and think to do your bit
as our host we are under your roof we | were picked from the whole Danaan army
we wish nothing better than to remain | your closest and dearest friends Achaean
out of all of them " "Your highness Aias | the royal son of Telamon alas
there's much in what you say but my blood boils | when I think of what happened all my toils
through the vile way in which Atreides | treated me in public like some Hades
reject go now report my decision | no thought of war until Prince Hector son
of wise Priam reaches the huts and ships | Myrmidon on one of his killing trips
of Argives and destroys the fleet by fire | I have a notion however dire ire
of his furious onslaught may be Hector | brought up short by own hut vector therefore
stopped by own black ship" then each visitor | after taking up two-handled goblets for
making libation made way back along | line ships of line Odysseus as the prong
Patroclus told his men and maidservants | quickly make a bed of comfy implants
for Phoenix when the women had carried | out his orders and on the bedstead spread
fleeces a rug and sheet of fine linen | old man lay down on it waited come in
the blessed light of dawn then Achilles | himself slept in a corner with his squeeze
a woman he'd brought from Lesbos beside | daughter of Phorbas Diomede on(e)side
of the lovely cheeks and Patroclus slept | in the corner opposite and he kept
a companion too Iphis of the robe | girdled who Achilles had made disrobe
to him when he captured the high fortress | Scyros city Enyeus of the press
the envoys reached the hut Agamemnon | no sooner inside than lords Achaean
leapt to their feet on every side pledging | with golden cups and with questions sledging
Agamemnon the most urgent of all | "Illustrious Odysseus of cheval
-ry Achaean the flower tell me now | from being burnt will he save the ships' prow
or is that proud spirit implacable | still?" steadfast excellent well-capable

Odysseus made report "Your majesty | Agamemnon son of Atreus ye
King of Men the man has no intention | of relenting he's even more intent on
rejecting you and your gifts than ever | says that for yourself you can discover
with the assistance of your friends how to | save the ships and men and he threatens to
drag own curved ships into the sea at dawn | and advised the rest of us to be gone
as well said 'You will never reach you goal | in the steep streets of Ilium as all
-seeing Zeus has stretched out a hand over | that city and its people moreover
have taken heart' those were his words of my | fellow envoys heralds you can rely
on both and Aias here to bear me out | but the old man Phoenix is sleeping out
there Achilles pressed him to stay so he | could embark for home in the morn if he
wished although he would not force him he said" | when Odysseus done not a word was said
his message and its blunt delivery | left the Argive lords aghast a gloomy
long silence followed not broken until | at last Diomedes of war-cry shrill
ventured "Your majesty Agamemnon | the King of Men and of Atreus Son
it's a thousand pities that you brought your | -self to plead with Achilles and made your
so princely offer he is a proud man | at best of times and now you've allowed an
even more grandiose conceit of self | let him be whether he stays on the shelf
or sails he will fight again when his own | conscience speaks and the spirit moves to own
and now I hope you'll all follow my lead | for now go to bed you've enjoyed the feed
and the wine that a man needs to keep up | his strength and courage but then when comes up
the first fair light of Dawn you sir must take | action let your infantry and horse take
position before the ships and inspire | them with your word of command and higher
by fighting in front line yourself each king | expressed approval for this good thinking
he of the loud war-cry Diomedes | made their libations and did retire these
to their several huts where they lay down deep | and enjoyed the generous boon of sleep

δέκα

*Book 10*

# NIGHT INTERLUDE

*Diomedes Odysseus slew Dolon*
*spy Trojan themselves spied on camp Trojan*
*and in faraway part of it stealing*
*horses Rhesus negative Thracian king*

the chiefs of the Achaeans united | the rest of the night in the unblighted
soft arms of sleep but Agamemnon son | of Atreus c-in-c too much on
his mind for restful sleep groan after groan | from depths being heart so soon s(o/e)wn moan mown
through with fear as the sky's pierced by lightning | when the Lord of the Lady Here's inciting
a hailstorm torrential rain or blizzard | to mantle fields with snow or play hazard
by unleashing the dogs of war on some | unhappy land and when he glanced out from
his hut across Trojan plain he was thus | confounded then by the fires numberless
burning before Ilium by music voices | of the troops when looked back over choices
at the ships and his own army he plucked | hair from his head by the roots to Zeus looked
up to heaven so Zeus could see and his | proud heart came close to breaking and in his
panic could think of nothing better than | to go to Nestor Neleus' son
in the hope together they might hit on | some way of saving the expedition
from disaster then sat up on his bed | and with his tunic he himself garb-ed
he bound a stout pair of sandals on his | comely feet at the last cast over his
shoulders glossy pelt great lion tawny | fell right down to his ankles not scrawny
spear then picked up meanwhile Menelaus | was also finding it as onerous
as his brother snatch a moment of sleep | too obsessed by an anxiety deep
for the Achaeans who for his sake bold | had unsheathed sword to Troy across the old
wilderness of water cast a spotted | leopard's skin round his broad shoulders potted
his bronze helmet on his head picked a spear | in great hand set out rouse brother dear near
the overlord of every Achaean | who the folk worshipped found him by the stern
of ship slinging armour on his shoulders | glad to see him though Manos the bolder's
-of the loud war-cry – the first to speak though | "My dear brother why are you arming so?
had you now thought of sending a man out | to spy on the Trojans? I greatly doubt
you'll find anyone willing to accept | the duty would indeed take the precept

of a stout heart to venture out alone | through the mysterious night as spy own
enemy camp" "Menelaus what | you and I must do is to rack somewhat
our brains to find some way of relieving | the Achaeans and ships save from grieving
now that Zeus has turned against us it's clear | the offerings of Hector more dear
to him than ours and that a single man | and he is not a son of the gods can
do such damage just one day en-during | as Hector's done to us such a flooring
quite outside my experience the fact | remains that he has performed such an act
as we shall feel to our cost for many | a long day to come quickly and manly
I wish you now to run by the ships call | Aias and Idomeneus withal
I'll go to the excellent Nestor tell | him to get up and he might very well
pay a visit to the outposts which are | so important ensure the sentries are
up to the mark as they will pay greater | attention to him than any other
for own son and Idomeneus' | squire Meriones the squads' onus's
on as leaders "Ok but what of my | -self? what do you wish of ME just and why?
shall I keep with them wait your us joining? | or simply straight away to come running
back to you when they have got their orders?" | "Keep with them or we may spark disorders
by missing each other on the way there | are many paths to follow everywhere
in the camp and give your man a shout each | and as you call him up when within reach
mention his lineage and father's name | let them have their dignities all same fame
and do not be proud as we too must work | Zeus seems to have picked us out not to shirk
trouble from the moment we were born" he | dismissed his brother after carefully
instructing him went in search of Nestor | the shepherd of the people without door
on a soft bed beside his hut prost(r)ate | and own black ship by side lay his ornate
arms a shield two spears and shining helmet | besides these too the glittering belt yet
the old man would put on when he prepared | to lead his men into battle he dared
whatever the danger took no account | of his age and here he made an account
himself raising on his elbow lifts his | head up on high he called out challenges
Atreides "Who goes there wandering | round camp alone at ships' borne one daring
at dead of night when everyone's asleep? | are you looking for a stray mule or sheep
or one of your friends? speak up and do not | advance on me before give answer what
do you here?" "Nestor son of Neleus | of Argive chivalry locus focus
surely you recognise Agamemnon | Zeus has singled out for persecution
long as breath in this body there remains | and still now a stealthy health there pertains
in his limbs I'm on the move as you see | as too much troubled by anxiety
of war and Achaeans' plight to enjoy | moment's sleep and the concern I deploy
for my people is so acute I am | no longer master of myself I am
in torture and my heart hard thrusting | as though from my breast would soon be bu(r)sting
knee-trembler underneath undermines me | I see you can sleep no better than me
if you want something to do come with me | and pay a visit to see no sentry
has been overcome by fatigue fallen | asleep with all their duties forgotten
the enemy are sitting very near | and of their plans we've no clear idea
and they might even launch a night terror" | "Your majesty Atreides" Nestor

Gerenian horseman said "I'm quite sure | Zeus the Counsellor will not let Hector
realise all the high hopes he may be | entertaining now on the contrary
I fancy he'll have more to worry him | than ever if Achilles chooses trim
his anger of course I'll then go with you | but let us wake some of the others too
Odysseus the gallant Diomedes | Aias the Runner the stalwart Meges
and it would also be good if someone | could go along and call up Telamon
-ian Aias King Idomeneus | whose ships are at the end of the ithsmus
some way off but what of Menelaus? | I like respect but does men 'e lay us
open to danger and I must say so | even if it makes you mad for being so
heedless as to be sleeping at such | a moment leaving all the work so much
needed to you at time when he withal | should now be completely engaged with all
senior officers imploring them to | do their best as situation is too
desperate for us not to" "Sir there are | times when I'd indeed be glad see you are
taking him to task as he is often | inclined to do nothing and that is when
things slide but it is not through laziness | or because he is any way brainless
but because he looks to me and relies | on my initiative but did arise
tonight before me and then self attached | to my quarters I've already despatched
him to call up the two men you mentioned | so let's be off with the pickets stationed
outside the gates I told them to fall in" | "If he is going to do that well in
this hour" said Nestor "none will have a word | to say against him and thus not reward
his leadership" speaking he got into | his tunic bound well-made sandals onto
his comely feet next donned a purple cloak | fastened with a broach 'twas a double cloak
a thick nap on the wool did spread it out | picked strong spear with sharp bronze point and set out
on his way along the ships of the bronze | -clad Achaeans first man of the key ones
Nestor wakened was Odysseus whose thoughts | were like unto of mighty Zeus the thoughts
shouts woke him instantly came out of hut | questioned his visitors so this he put
"Why do you wander round like this at dead | of night by huts and ships unattended?
what brings you here? it must be serious" | "Royal son of Laertes Odysseus
of the nimble wits" then Nestor answered | Gerenian charioteer "annoyed
be not with us Argives are indeed in | serious doodoo but come now join in
with us and let's wake some of the others | consult whether to be fighter brothers
or fleers" when he heard this Odysseus | cunning of the nimble wits went back thus
into hut slung on his back ornate shield | followed them next found lying in the field
with his armour Diomedes the son | Tydeus sleeping round him his men on
their shields for pillows their spears stuck on end | so had in the ground the sharpened butts' end
bronze points flashed in the distance like lightning | from Father Zeus now prince benighting
enlightening beneath him hide farmyard ox | glossy rug drawn under hard yard head box
Nestor woke him with a touch of his foot | to rouse him further flung a taunt afoot
"Wake up Tydeides why should you sleep | in comfort all night long? is sleep so deep
it's escaped your notice the Trojans are | sitting on the plain above us thus are
barely a stone's throw from the ships?" answered | then with some feeling Diomedes who'd
awoken and leapt up in a trice "You're | a hard old man sir also you never

take a moment's rest are there not younger | men in the army to do a rounder
and summon all the kings? there is no hold | -ing you down my venerable lord old"
"My friend I admit that you are right I | have my most excellent sons also I
have troops in plenty to go the rounds call | people up but we're in a criti-call
position our fate is balanced on a | razor's edge an appalling end for a
generation Argive or salvation | but if you're sorry for me younger one
as you ARE go yourself and wake Meges | and Aias the Runner" Diomedes
cast round his shoulder the skin not scrawny | glossy feet reached of great lion tawny
picked up his spear and went on his errand | and when in their huts had the task in hand
brought the two along with him party then | visited outposts failed catch any men
officers of the watch on watch asleep | they were sitting there in their weapons' keep
on alert like dogs that uneasy keep | watch in a farmyard over flock of sheep
thought of sleep no more as they have heard some | savage animal that down now doth come
through the wooded hills with the hue and cry | of men and hounds behind him sentry nigh
duty went keeping watch through that evil | night banishing sleep from their eyes all ill
turning constantly toward plain to catch | first sign of movement on the Trojans' patch
the old warrior with his inspection | of the outposts was pleased his confection
a word of encouragement "That's the style | my lads keep up or enemy's bile vile
will swallow us up if one takes a nap" | he then passed quickly out across the sap
followed by Argive kings summoned council | and Meriones and Nestor's noble
son they'd asked to aid at their conference | and leaving the trench behind them thence
sat down in an open place where the ground | was not littered with bodies of earth-bound
dead very spot where Hector had there paused | his slaughter of Argives when night had caused
battlefield blackout and he had turned back | after sat awhile tossed forward and back
ideas Nestor then called for silence | "I wonder if enough self-reliance
and pluck any man here has to pay these | arrogant Trojans a visit and seize
perchance a straggler from the enemy? | might even talk overhear oversee
plans they may have whether they mean to stay | in their advanced stance or to go away
back into town after their victory | if he could learn that and return wholly
intact there's not a man in the world who | would not hear of your achievements and who
will be well-rewarded too the leaders | of the expedition signal honours
indeed will each give to you a black ewe | with its suckling lamb and moreover you
will be invited to all their banquets | ceremonial and feasts" the quiet's
for all save Diomedes of the loud | war-cry who ventured speak aloud allowed
"Nestor this adventure appeals to me | the Trojan camp is very near so be
it I will visit it and yet I wish | another man could go with me I wish
to be more comfortable and would be | more inclined take a risk together we
two men seize advantages one would miss | out on whereas a man on his own is
liable to hesitate if and when | sees a chance and makes stupid mistakes then
several wished to go with Diomedes | both the Aiantes henchmen of Ares
Meriones and Nestor's son eager | Menelaus too of the famous spear
also Odysseus the much-enduring | Odysseus said would like to be boring

deep into the Trojan camp adventure | always dear to him King played part venture
"Diomedes great son great Tydeus | my heart's delight thus you shall have from us
whichever companion you may prefer | best of the volunteers who on offer
are plenty and you must not let respect | for persons leave the better not expect
to take the lesser don't be influenced | by a man's lineage though more nuanced
in royalty than the one of your choice" | he said this in his terror for the choice
of his red-haired brother Menelaus | Diomedes lay of many layers
decision soon before them "If right on | that your wish is I choose my companion
myself how could I overlook god-like | Odysseus Athene's favourite alike
that gallant soul that no adventure finds | unready? and together with our minds
could go through blazing fire and yet come home | he has the quickest brain so in the zone
of any man I know" the all-daring | Odysseus "There's no need for you fair sing
my praises or criticise me either | you're talking to men who know me rather
well let's be off my lord Diomedes | night's already well advanced and dawn's ease
near the stars past their zenith a good third | double of night gone leaving us the third
watch only" said no more but slung on their | formidable arms and then the veter
-an Thrasymedes gave Tydeides | double-edged sword because his own blade he's
left behind beside his ship along with | a shield on head put an oxhide casque with
-out peak or plume of the kind called "skull-cap" | that young gallants wear their heads fully cap
and then Meriones a fine gift made | Odysseus a bow quiver and sword laid
a leather helmet on his head inside | a strong lining of interwoven hide
straps under which a felt cap was sewn in | and then the outer rim was adorned in
cunning style on either side with a row | of white flashing boars' tusks this helmet so
originally came from Eleon | where Autolycus had at first stolen
it from Amyntor son of Ormenus | by breaking then into well-built house plus
Autolycus gave to Amphidamas | of Cythera take to land Scandea's
and Amphidamas gave it to Molus | for his hospitality and Molus
in his turn gave it to Meriones | now it was the head of Odysseus he's
protected and so armed in this manner | formidable pair then left their manor
to chieftains Pallas Athene now witch sent | a lucky omen a heron which went
to their right the night was too dark to see | the bird but heard it squawk Odysseus he
well pleased by the omen offered then | a prayer "Hear me Daughter of Zeus Athen
-'e who stand by my side during all my | adventures indeed can't get nigh sky-high
venture without your seeing me tonight | show me your special favour make it right
we come back some signal deed to our score | one which will make the Trojans very sore"
Diomedes of the loud war-cry made | a prayer of his own "Daughter of Zeus Maid
of Trito hear me also be with me | as were with my noble father when he
Tydeus once went into Thebes as an | ambassador for army Achaean
while leaving their soldiers on the bank | of the Asopus went there with a frank
and friendly offer to the Cadmeians | a great terrible thing on his return's
to do in which you helped him out Lady | goddess support ever ready steady
go so stand by me now watch over me | with the same devotion you'll have from me

a yearling heifer that's broad in the brow | no-one's broken in nor yet set 'til now
beneath yoke to you shall be sacrificed | gold foil on horns" so orificed sufficed
as Pallas Athene heard them and when their | petitions to the Daughter of Zeus there
finished they set out a pair of lions | black night battlefield remaindered irons
picking their way among corpses blood-stained | arms and the lordly Trojans also gained
scant time for sleep Hector would not let them | he called together all the leading men
the Captains and Counsellors Trojan when | he had gathered them all around him then
he told them of an idea he had had | "There's work to be done rich reward be had
this is the offer I guarantee to | the man who does the job who would like to
volunteer? quite apart from the kudos | he'll gain for himself if he wins this toss
I'll give him the best chariot and pair | of thoroughbreds in the Achaean lair
to the man who dares to reconnoitre | around the ships and try to exploit a
weakness see if fleet guarded as normal | or whether as a result of their fall
at our hands they're already discussing | departing or so worn out not fussing
to keep watch at night" Hector's challenge thence | was at first received in complete silence
but among the Trojans present a man | called Dolon the son of Eumedes one
of the sacred heralds a rich man with | plenty of gold and bronze unattractive
his appearance to be sure but he was | fast on his feet in family of six was
the only son this man came forward now | took the floor "Hector this adventure how
it appeals to me I volunteer to | reconnoitre around the ships for you
but first will you hold up this staff and swear | to give me the inlaid chariot pair
of horses peerless Achilles drives too? | I shall not be useless I promise you
as a spy or fail your expectations | I'll go right through camp to Agamemnon's
ship where I guess the senior officers | will be for fight or to be off from us"
Hector's answer taking the staff in hand | to Dolon letting his solemn oath stand
"Let Zeus himself Consort of Here and Lord | of the Thundercloud hear me swear aloud
that no other Trojan shall ride behind | those horses and delight in them you'll find
for the rest of your days" later events | gave a twist that he in no way invents
to this promise but it sent off Dolon | who straight away slung his curved bow upon
his shoulders threw the pelt of a wolf grey | over it ferret-skin cap on loaf grey
put picked up a sharp javelin left the camp | towards the ships though not destined re-vamp
back from them with news for Hector however | the crowded camp once behind sped eager
on his way Odysseus saw him coming | to his companion remark "In-coming
here I see a man from the enemy | Diomedes spy on our ships maybe
or else to strip some of the corpses one | can't say shall we let him pass and go on
a little way? then we could make a dash | pounce on him but if he's a too fast flash
for us you must threaten him with your spear | and head him off all the time so to near
the ships and away from the encampment | not slip through hut-town by some enchantment"
agreed they turned off among the dead by | the path Dolon innocently passed by
at a run and when he'd left them behind | as far as the width of fallow mules find
they can plough in a day (and are better | than oxen at the jointed plough ever
could be at dragging through deep fallow ground) | two gave chase Dolon stopped when heard on ground

footsteps behind him supposing these were | friends coming from the Trojans and who were
intent on turning him back as Hector | had taken further thought and had counter
-manded his mission but when were a spear | -cast off or even less he knew then fear
they were enemies so took to his heels | peeing with panic both straight on his heels
Tydeides and Odysseus sacker | of cities chased as any top tracker
relentless as two sharp-toothed sporting dogs | of a roe or hare will hang on heel-togs
as flies before them through country wooded | screaming as goes the whole time they fended
him off from his own folk in fact fleeing | as he was towards the ships soon seeing
a run into the outposts when Athen | -'e gave Tydeides extra strength then
to make a spurt so none of the bronze-clad | Argives should be able to claim he had
hit Dolon before Diomedes could | reach him dashed up Diomedes who would
cry out "Stop! or I will now soon get you | with my spear and I think I will lay you
dead soon enough" as spoke let fly but missed | him on purpose head of polished spear hissed
over his right shoulder stuck in the ground | he stopped terrified by the hunting hound
white with panic stuttered his teeth chattered | the pursuers came up panting shattered
arms his clattered gripped he burst into tears "Take me | alive and I'll ransom myself plenty
of bronze and gold wrought irony at home | from which father would pay a goodly tome
if he heard that I'd been taken alive | to the hollow beaked good black ships Argive"
"Pull yourself together man" said crafty | Odysseus "don't be troubled by any
thought of death answer my questions see here | tell the truth just what was your idea
in leaving camp and coming to the ships | at dead of night when each man dream-sleep ships?
strip out some of the dead while by night hid? | or on reconnaissance by the ships did
Hector send you? or did you come on your | own initiative?" knees quaking "Hector
dazzled me against my better judgement | by promising the horses resplendent
and inlaid chariot of Achilles | the glorious he wished me a-fill these
eyes with whether the ships were guarded as | is normally the case or whether as
a result of their defeat at our hands they're | already discussing that maybe they're
going to fly and are so exhausted | to keep watch at night they can't be arse-ed"
then Odysseus of the nimble wits smiled | at the man "So you were the most beguiled
by the idea of laying your hands | on that doughty prince's horses many hands
high? a fine prize to be sure! but they're hard | to master and drive at any rate hard
for a mere man or anyone except | Achilles whose mother has the precept
of a goddess now answer my questions | and tell me the truth in full not sections
where did you leave Hector your C-in-C | when you came here just now? and in what see
is his equipment lying? where are his | horses? and how are the Trojans' sentries
disposed? where are the rest of them sleeping? | and just what is the next step they're steeping?
are they to hold their advanced positions | or retire into the strong bastions
of the city after this victory | over the Achaeans?" "Now truthfully
I'll answer your questions firstly Hector's | in conference with all his advisers
by the barrow of King Ilus away | from all noise you asked of the sentries' way
my lord no special guard was mounted watch | the camp or indeed lookouts to keep watch
each family has its fire the men detailed | for duty stay awake exchange re-ta(i)led

halloes keep each other alert in heart | as for the allies from many a part
come leave it to us while they're asleep | keep watch because at hand don't close keep
THEIR women children" but cunning deeping | Odysseus not happy "Are they sleeping
in the same parts of camp as the Trojan | charioteers or somewhere else? be on
the mark I want to know" "Once more I can | tell you everything the host Carian
and Paeonians of the crooked bows | lying by the sea with Leleges those
the Caucones and the most excellent | Pelasgi whereas the Lycian bent
the lordly Mysians the horse-taming | Phrygians and the chariot-aiming
Maeonians were allotted ground in | Thymbra region but why would you go in
-to all these details? if your idea's | raid our positions what of newcomers
the Thracians who're on their own over there | right at the end of the line? Rhesus their
king the son of Eioneus is there | loveliest biggest horses anywhere
whiter than snow and they run like the wind | his chariot is beautifully lim(b)ned
with gold and silver and he brought too some | gigantic parts golden armour handsome
a fantastic sight men shouldn't really | wear such things they are only fit for ye
immortal gods well now will you take me | to the ships or tie me tight and leave me
here while you go and satisfy yourselves | about me? you'll soon find that which resolves
the truth about what I've told you" now | the mighty Diomedes a grim brow
"Dolon you've given us news excellent | but don't imagine you'll be freedom sent
now that you have fallen into our hands | if we did set you free tonight no hands
barred to prevent you coming down once more | to the Achaean ships on the sea shore
either to play the spy or to meet us | in battle but if I kill you to us
you will never be a nuisance again" | Dolon was raising his great hand in vain
for as just about to touch captor's chin | plead for mercy was there and then done in
Diomedes fell on him with his sword | struck him full on the neck without a word
cut through both sinews his head met the dust | before he ceased speaking they took the (t)rust
-y ferret-skin cap from his head and stripped | him too of wolf's pelt his bow incurved gripped
and his long spear then noble Odysseus | held up in hand taken trophies a plus
Pallas Athene see as she the goddess | of Spoil "Let these gladden your heart goddess
you were the first of all the immortals | in Olympus to whom for help made calls
now help us again raid in sleep laying | Thracians with their horses" finished praying
he raised up the bundle clear of his head | dumped it in a tamarisk bush gather-ed
a handful of reeds fresh tamarisk twigs | put on top to mark the spot so he twigs
where they are as they come back through the dead | dark of night and now the two went ahead
thread their way there among the arms blood-stained | soon reached place where the troops of Thrace slept drained
so were they tired out by their exertions | their fine gear neatly piled in three portions
on the deck beside them pair of horses | stood by each man centre slept Rhesus his
fast horses by him were tied by the reins | to end of chariot-rail trail trains veins
Odysseus saw him first pointed him out | "There's our man Diomedes and flat out
and the horses Dolon told us about | before we killed him and so now put out
all your strength no need to stand there fumbling | with your arms quick now! the horses tumbling
or kill the men yourself and I'll take care | of the horses" Diomedes there stare

with fury filled by Athene Flashing Eyes | laid about him 'til he was up to his eyes
in gore hideous groans from dying men | came up and the earth ran red with blood then
the son of Tydeus dealt with those men | from Thracian country like a lion when
he's found some sheep and goats un-shepherded | pounces with murder in heart slaughter did
twelve of them and as he came to each and put | to sword Odysseus of nimble wit foot
of every body seized then from behind | dragged it out so the spot not be man-mined
way left clear for each pair long-maned horses | who unaccustomed to new master is
might be frightened if treading on a corpse | thirteenth man that Tydeides did corpse
was King Rhesus who's breathing heavily | when he robbed him of his sweet life for he
enduring an evil dream that had come | to him that night and had taken form loathsome
of Diomedes son of Tydeus | through Athene's machinations Odysseus
all-daring meanwhile released the stamping | horses from chariot at bit champing
tying together with thongs drove them out | of the crowded space with a little clout
from his bow for he had not thought of late | take shining whip that lay in the ornate
chariot directly he was clear he's | given a whistle let Diomedes
know but Diomedes in no hurry | he was wondering how he could worry
in the most outrageous way so whether | to take hold on the chariot ever
lay the ornamented armour drag out | by the shaft or hoist it up carry out
or do further murder of the Thracians | wise Diomedes still weighing options
when Athene beside with word came down did | of warning "The son of the great-hearted
Tydeus would be well advised to think | of getting home to the ships in the blink
of an eye or may reach them in full flight | there are other gods you know and they might
wake the Trojans up" when heard this address | recognising the voice of the goddess
he mounted at once Odysseus with bow | struck the horses to the ships off flew so
Apollo now he of the Silver Bow | had been keeping his eyes open also
and not for naught when he saw how Athene | on Tydeides a dancing queen keen
he was enraged with her and descended | on the great Trojan army attended
one of the Thracian leaders Hippocoon | who of Rhesus a noble kinsman soon
waking suddenly he leapt up and when | he saw the empty places before them
where the horses had stood and men gasping | out their lives in hideous last-grasping
killing-zone gave groan called his friend by name | this brought the Trojans running to the game
with a fearful hue and cry and there looked | with amazement at the horrors been cooked
up by the two men before escaping | to the hollow ships the two when scaping
the spot where they had killed Hector's spy King | Odysseus pulled up their cantering
horses Tydeides jumped down handed | up the blood-stained arms and then he mounted
again and flicked the horses they flew on | with a will towards the hollow ships on
the beach eager to reach their journey's end | Nestor first catch what distant wind did send
to them "My friends Captains and Counsellors | of the Argives could it be the error's
mine or am I right? for I could swear e'en | can hear now the sound of the full-on scene
galloping horses think what it would be | to see Odysseus and the mighty
Diomedes come dashing right in here | with some fine horses from the far too near
Trojan camp! but I'm horribly afraid | the Trojans are on the warpath have made

trouble for our two best men" the last words | were not out of his mouth when the two lords
then arrived and they jumped down to the ground | welcomed by friends much shaking hands around
and many exclamations of delight | no-one more keen to learn of their fight flight
than Nestor "Tell me O illustrious | Odysseus flower of resourcefulness
Achaean how did you get hold of those | horses? you went in from under the nose
Trojan and took them or did some god meet | you on the way and deem that it was meet
to make you a present? and they shimmer | like sunshine I meet the Trojans ever
in fact I can claim that I never stay | behind at the ships old as I now may
be for a fighting man but I've never | witnessed or imagined horses ever
like these come now you met a god and he | gave them to you? Zeus Cloud-gatherer he
is very fond of you both and so his | Daughter Athene of the Flashing Eyes is"
"Nestor son Neleus who the Argives | love to honour" Odysseus replies
the gods now have greater powers than men | and if one wished make us a present then
he could easily produce an even | finer pair but to answer your question
my lord these horses have only just now | arrived and they are Thracian and just how
excellent is Diomedes? he killed | their master beside him the twelve most skilled
men in his company we killed fourteen | men in all for we caught a spy sent e'en
to reconnoitre our camp by Hector | and the other insolent Trojans there"
then he drove the thoroughbreds through the trench | laughing the other Argives followed hence
in gay mood when they'd reached the comfy hut | of Tydeides tied up with well-cut
thongs at the mangers where Diomedes | had his own fast horses standing and these
were munching their honey-sweet barley then | Odysseus put the blood-stained equipmen
-tof(f) Dolon in the aft part of his ship | 'til such time as could make sacrifice hip
to Athene then they went into the sea | from shins necks and thighs all the sweat wash free
when the waves had removed the sweat from their | bodies felt ever so much fresher there
and went and soaked themselves in polished laths | from washing rubbing with olive-oil baths
sat down to eat and from a full mixing | -bowl wine libations Athene affixing

ἕνδεκα

Book 11

# ACHILLES TAKES NOTICE

*despite glorious deeds Agamemnon*
*Trojans press hard on army Achaean*
*and the far long-fated starting (b)locus*
*of evil begins come on Patroclus*

when Dawn arose from the bed where she sleeps | with the Lord Tithonus there then seeps creeps
light for the immortals also for men | Zeus sent down to Argive ships demon then
Strife the banner of battle in her hands | on bulging black hull of ship on strand stands
Odysseus' which lay in the centre | of line so shout carries entire venture
-length huts of Telamonian Aias | and those of Achilles as each one has
confidence enough in own bravery | and strength draw up their trim ships extremely
at the flanks stood there the goddess uttered | great and terrible war-cry so guttered
thereby inspiring every Argive heart | with a firm resolve then not to depart
from the war carry on relentlessly | soon enough more in love became to be
with thought fighting than of sailing away | in black ships own country style file away
Atreides in a loud voice gave troops | order prepare go through fight hoop loop gloops
and then himself put on his bronze gleaming | he began by around his legs teaming
pair splendid greaves fit silver clips kick-ass | for the ankles next put on the cuirass
Cinyras had once presented to him | as a friendly gift for news had reached him
distant Cyprus of the great Achaean | expedition with Troy destination
and so Cinyras had sent to the King | this cuirass as a gracious offering
it was made of parallel strips dark blue | enamel ten gold twelve tin twenty too
on either side three snakes rose up in coils | toward the gap for neck enamel's foils
iridescence gave them a rainbow look | like the one the Son of Cronos oft took
out and hangs as a portent on a cloud | to mankind below Agamemnon bowed
his sword from his shoulders and studs golden | glittered on the hilt but silver token
was the sheath attached with golden baldric | manly man-covering shield did up pick
'twas a nobly decorated item | having concentric rings bronze ten of them
and twenty knobs of tin made a circle | white rite right around dark boss enamel
central figure on it grim Gorgon's head | such compelling eyes only to awe led

on either side of her Rout and Panic | depicted fitted with silver baldric
round which writhing snake of blue enamel | twisted the three heads grew from its reptil
-ion single neck head Agamemnon | put on this helmet having its four plates set on
its double crest sporting its plume horsehair | nodding fair defiantly in air fare
finally picked up the pair strong sharp bronze | -headed spears and beams from this ported bronze
into the distant sky brightly flashing | in answer Here Athene mighty crashing
by way of salutation to the King | Golden Hall Lion Gate Myscene's setting
charioteers all left cars drivers' charge | with instructions in proper order charge
'em up trench-foot-points they themselves with din | bustle smote without warnin' new mo(u)rnin'
sky fell in on foot at double full kit | formed line here as a result chic lit
longing trench feat some time before drivers | lagging lot arrears reverse gears diverse
dread Son of Cronos the war-fever fanned | in their hearts then a bloody dew out-spanned
over them from high Heaven the fall-out | sent so many radiated out rout
a soul to Hades on their side in fell | Trojans too on high ground plain's well fell swell
around the great Hector and Aeneas | to whom the Trojan folk gave honour as
a god peerless Polydamas along | with Antenor's three sons Acamas young
godlike Polybus noble Agenor | but 'twas Hector with his shield circular
conspicuous among their champions | like a baleful star one moment glistens
in all its splendour from behind a cloud | the next is hidden by a misty shroud
Hector to be seen up with the foremost | company now again with the hindmost
spurring them on and in his panoply | of bronze like lightning flashing dazzlingly
from the hand of aegis-bearing Father Zeus | starting on opposing sides the reaper's use
grim of a rich man's field who bring barley | or wheat tumbling down in armfuls barely
bearable 'til their swathes unite Trojans | fell on enemy so too Achaeans
to destroy their numbers there 'bout equal | panic on either side unthinkable
rushed in like wolves and Strife the heart-breaker | rejoiced when saw them for only to her
fate of the gods this action to witness | on the field being no other god-dess
take homely leave ease each in house lovely | constructed on folds Olympus (w)hol(l)y
all at loggerheads with Zeus of Cronos | the Son and Lord of the Black Cloud because
he wished to give the Trojans a fair win | but the Father cared nothing for their din
he had long slipped away alone sat down | exulting in his power looking down
on the town of Troy and the ships Argive | on the flashing bronze killers who there thrive
and on the killed rite on through the morning | blessed light of day grew stronger mourning
volley-after volley counter-volley | found their mark men fell still willy-nilly
but round the time when a woodman who fells | the tall trees high up in a mountain dell's
growing weary in arm and so feeling | he's done enough yields to appealing
thought of food and prepares himself a meal | the Danaans across the ranks appeal
to their friends put forth all their strength and broke | back oppo's battalions going for broke
Agamemnon dashed in first of them all | Trojan captain Badgerr ex cull fate fall
after him comrade driver Oileus | had leapt from his chariot Oileus
to oppose him as moved go head-to-head | Agamemnon struck him on the forehead
with his sharp spear for all its weight of bronze | the helmet unable to stop the bronze

-tipped spear pierced both the metal and the bone | spattered inside helmet with brain nose cone
of Oileus and his attack la fin | then Agamemnon alors Roi Humains
after stripping off both of their tunics | just left them lying there with their pubics
gleaming in the sun and went on to kill | Isus Antiphus sons Priam fell ill
one a bastard other legitimate | sharing the one chariot inti-mate
and driving it was the bastard Isus | fighting-man beside noble Antiphus
couple once Achilles apprehended | as their flocks on hills of Ida tended
tied them up with pliant twigs of willow | but later accepted ransom let go
and now they met the son of Atreus | imperial Agamemnon Isus
he with his spear above breast nipple hit | Antiphus beside ear with his sword bit
and then hurled him out of the chariot | with all speed the splendid armour stripped out
from the pair recognised them as so did | as by his own fast ships before he did
see them when Achilles the great runner | had conveyed them there from mighty Ida
all this as easy for Agamemnon | as break into lair doe nimble lion
crush her unweaned fawns seize them in his jaws | powerful rob them of tender life joys
as even if the doe is close at hand | she can't help in their terrible last stand
she is terrified herself off dashing | straight through the forest undergrowth crashing
in her haste to save herself fear sweating | from claws of beast formidable getting
near so with these two there not a Trojan | anywhere then could save from destruction
Trojans in rout before host Achaean | attacked Peisander next Agamemnon
stalwart Hippolochus who were the sons | of Antimachus astute nobleman's
had beady eye then on Paris' gold | in the hope of lavish bribes getting hold
had been more eloquent any than then | defeating proposals give back Helen
to red-haired Menelaus now each son | had been captured by King Agamemnon
in one chariot both had been trying | control their spirited horses shying
in confusion as polished reins had slipped | from the driver's hands and so Atreid
-'es lion sprang from the car it legging | not even for mercy him were begging
"Take us alive Lord Agamemnon you'll | have a ransom that you'll find substantial
father Antimachus rich has plenty | treasure in-house gold bronze wrought irony
he'd pay princely sum from hoard if he'd heard | taken alive horde Argive seaboard word"
such was their tearful appeal to the King | in-tone totally ingratiating
answer not "If you two Antimachus | sons really man once had the brass neck us
argue Troy assembly Menelaus | come on embassy with King Odysseus
should be killed on the spot not let return | to Argos you will now pay in your turn
for your father's infamy" no sooner | had he said this than he struck Peisander
on breast with spear flung out of chariot | and brought him to earth on his back flat out
Hippolochus leapt down him killed on ground | slashed off arms and head with a two-sword bound
sent body rolling like rounded boulder | through the crowd Agamemnon cold shoulder
gave them dashed in where the hottest fightin' | rest of bronze-clad Argives behind right in
infantry fell on infantry cut them | to pieces species all fled before them
charioteers with their bronze made havoc | of other charioteers them did crock
from ground below them rose a cloud of dust | kicked up by thundering hooves of death lust

of their horses themselves and all the while | Agamemnon to Argives shouting style
followed up killed like a forest virgin | fire ragin' hither thither vergin'
conflagration wind swiftly assaults the trees | and thickets topple headlong to their knees
before the onslaught of the flames routed | Trojans mown down totally flank-outed
onslaught Agamemnon son Atreus | and so many a pair lost horses thus
tossed their heads rattled empty chariots | down the channels of battle lariots
missing master hand their charioteers | lay sprawling on the ground well in arrears
more enticing spectacle to vultures | than to their wives in-different cultures
but from the flying missiles and the dust | from the slaughter turmoil and the blood-lust
Hector was withdrawn by the hand of Zeus | and thus Atreides left to cut loose
to sweep on to such effect did inspire | his men by noon fleeting Trojans aspire
via their eager speed to get to town | past barrow made golden olden past town
days for Ilus of Dardanus the son | and past the wild fig-tree and half-way on
over plain still chased by Atreides | with his terrible war-cry and still he's
bespattering each invincible hand | with gore but when the Scaean Gate at hand
beside old oak tree they came to a stop | gave their slower friends a chance catch-up op
for many in panic were still flying | over the open plain with high-flying
Atreides these cattle on sweeping | as a lion does on hindmost leaping
when stampedes herd at dusk and sudden death | comes to a solitary heifer breath
last post its neck pounced on broken with jaws | stonky before settles down paw-pause paws
devours her blood entrails Agamemnon | thus dealt with them from car by him down done
on back/face many a charioteer | so all-devouring vehemence spear
and they had almost got to the shelter | of town of walls that frown when the Father
of men and gods down from Heaven with a | thunderbolt in his hands sat on Ida
the Mount of the heights of the many springs | and sent out Iris of the Golden Wings
as his ambassador "Off with you now | Iris as fast as you can be sure how
you give to Hector this message from me | as long as Agamemnon he does see
storming in the front line mowing down so | the Trojan ranks then let him give ground though
telling his men to keep the enemy | closely engaged the while but directly
the King is hit by a spear or arrow | and takes to his car I'll give Hector now
strength to kill 'til reaches the well-found ships | the sun there sets and the blessed fillips
of darkness intervene" so fleet Iris | made no ado sped down from peak Isis
Iraki Ida to sacred Troy where | found Hector wise Priam's son standing there
among the horses and the wooden cars | she went up saluted him by the bars
of his princely titles after his name | "Father Zeus has sent me down to give name
to his will as long as you see the King | Agamemnon storming in front mowing
down the Trojan ranks refrain from fighting | but at the very same time inciting
your men keep enemy engaged closely | when King hit and takes to car directly
Zeus will give you strength to kill 'til you reach | well-found wooden ships on the beach's reach
sun sets blessed dark intervenes anew" | job done Iris the Nimble-Foot withdrew
and Hector at once jumped down from his car | in all his armour swinging pair at par
of sharp spears in his hand went everywhere | among his men urging them then and there

make a stand rousing their spirit martial | Trojans no more turned away green turtle
but confronted the Achaeans but they | on their side had reinforced their ranks play
battle set the armies faced each other | Agamemnon to be foremost eager
led them all off by charging at the foe | say Young Cowgirl Muses In The Sand snow
of your home on Olympus the first man | just who was he to face Agamemnon?
Trojan or an ally great renown id? | why he was the tall and handsome Iphid
-amas a son of Antenor was he | had been reared in rich-soiled Thrace mother she
of sheep where Cisses his mother's father | and also of Theano the father
she of the lovely cheeks had brought him up | from infancy in his palace grown up
to the heyday of his youth done his best | to keep him at home would even invest
his daughter's hand but Iphidamas had | no sooner wed her than enticement had
whisked from her arms by news expedition | Achaean and he sailed with a squadron
of twelve beaked ships and left the trim vessels | in harbour Percote and he himself fell's
reached Ilium on foot this was the man | who now confronted Agamemnon son
of Atreus when come to quarters close | King starts fight but with miss spear's not close
gone astray Iphidamas in his turn | belt under cuirass Agamemnon earn
a stab did but though followed up full pelt | kept grip on spear failed pierce glittering belt
utterly spent when spear-point met silver | it was bent like a bit of lead Imper
-ial Agamemnon grabbed hold of shaft | pulled it towards him with fury fast haft
of a lion dragged it from the man's grasp | and then with his sword gave him his last gasp
hit him on the neck and brought him to earth | thus Iphidamas fell for all his worth
sank into the sleep that is not broken | unlucky man! was not just a token
but fighting for his country far from wife | just wed but had no joy of her in life
though he had given so much to win her | paid hundred head cattle venture merger
promise of a thousand beasts to follow | mixed goats and sheep from his flocks not hollow
now Agamemnon son of Atreus | stripped his corpse off with armour fabulous
into the ranks and the admirable | Coon Antenor's eldest son able
in the melee to see what had happened | his eyes were dimmed as anguish did append
for his fallen brother and he came in | on the off side and holding his spear in
his hand caught the noble Agamemnon | unawares struck below the elbow on
the middle of the forearm the gleaming | spear-point passed right through Agamemnon King
of Men shuddered but far from giving up | withdrawing charged at Coon holding up
his wind-devouring spear Coon had hold | of Iphidamas' foot making bold
dragging sibling into crowd calling on | all his best men be helping one on
with his father's son and as he did so | Agamemnon King of Men struck him so
hard with a bronze-headed spear under his | bossed shield and brought him to earth after this
ran up cut head off over the body | Iphidamas at the hands of the we
royal Atreides Antenor's sons | fulfilled their destinies there fated ones
and went down into the House of Hades | as long as blood was still running with ease
from his wound Agamemnon carried on | harrying with spear sword and bo(u)lder on
all fronts the enemy ranks but when blood stanched | and the wound began to dry then he blanched
at a stabbing pain as sharp as the pangs | which seize a woman in childbirth the pangs

bitter sent then by the Eileithyiae | the travail-makers Here's Daughters sent by
to dispense labour pains Atreides | overcome by the agony of these
pains leapt into his car told his driver | to make for the black ships in his bitter
distress sore called aloud to Danaans | "Friends Captains and Counsellors now the van's
up to you to save our sea-going ships | from the fury of war Zeus in the grips
of his wisdom will not now let me fight | the Trojans from dawn right through to the night"
Agamemnon said no more driver whipped | his pair of long-maned horses and shipped
them towards the thousand-face fleet flew off | with a will and their great breasts bore flecks of
foam their bellies grey with dust as carried | from the field Agamemnon wound-harried
when Hector saw Agamemnon withdraw | called to Trojans Lycians from great jaw
in a loud voice "Trojans and Lycians | revellers-in-a-fight Dardanians
be men my friends and recall your valour | martial the best man they've got's lost power
Zeus the Son of Cronos has given me | a great victory so now drive for me
your good horses straight at host Danaan | mighty win greater victory even"
thus he roused them put fresh heart into each | and as a hunter now releases each
of his snarling hounds against a savage | wild boar or lion Hector son of sage
Priam forceful as the furious War | -god proud Trojans onward did spur therefore
against the Achaeans took his own place | in the forefront and high thoughts then did race
though his heart flung himself into battle | as swoops down from the high mountains a squall
and lashes the blue waters of the sea | and who were the first and last then to see
their end at Hector's son of Priam's hand | now that Zeus had given him the command
of victory? the first was Asaeus | followed by Opites and Autonus
Dollops son Cliteris Opheltius | and Agelaus Aesymnus and Orus
and staunch Hipponous these the Danaan | leaders Hector killed fell like possessed man
on the rabble like a full gale when hits | from the West scatters into little bits
the white clouds that the South Wind has marshalled | when the great billows their march not forestalled
the foam flies high on the wings of the wind | so and in such a number did unwind
enemy as fall before the onslaught | Hector Argives threatened with the unthought
irreparable disaster as in flight | would soon have reached the ships and met their night
had not Odysseus to Diomedes | son of Tydeus called "Tydeides
what's the matter with us? how one forsakes | the former resolution? for Gods' sakes
my good friend come make a stand beside me | think of Hector inflicting infamy
on us if the Flashing Helm takes the ships" | "Indeed I" great Diomedes re-ships
reply "will stand take what comes but our poor | friends will not benefit by that for sure
for long for sorted Cloud-gatherer Zeus | would rather see Trojans cut us loose use"
with this he flung his spear at Thymbraeus | hit him on the left breast brought him down thus
from his car while Odysseus for his part | dealt with Molion the prince's great-heart
squire leaving these where they fell and for them | there was no more fighting the pair of them
dashed into the crowd ran riot couple | of wild boars turn in high fury double
back to attack the hounds that have chased them | thus rounded on the Trojans pair of them
trashed their attackers giving the Argives | welcome pause for breath in flight for their lives
from illustrious Hector chariot | two chieftains fell to them straight on the spot

and they were sons of Merops of Percote | of the day the ablest prophet won vote
had forbid his sons go off to the war | throw their lives away but these from afar
beckoned by the black hand of Death demurred | however the famous spearman not erred
Diomedes took life arms despoiled | glorious Odysseus was not foiled
killed stripped Hippodamus Hypeirochus | looking down from Ida Son of Cronos
stabilised the battle now for a bit | slaughter mutual Tydeides hit
Agastrophus noble son of Paeon | hip joint hip javelin nigh right full on
this man had been unable to escape | left his chariot in bit of a scrape
made fatal mistake leaving it behind | in charge of his squire charging up behind
to the front line on foot cost was his life | Hector with a glance assessing the strife
now seeing where lay the glaring weakness | made for Diomedes and Odysseus
with a great shout that brought the companies | Trojan after him grim Diomedes
of the loud war-cry was shaken even | when he saw him turned to Odysseus then
close at hand "We too in double trouble | for here comes Hector the formidable
don't let's move we'll stand drive him off" swung up | his long-shadowed javelin and hurled it up
at Hector's head and did not miss struck on | the crest of the flash helmet but his bron
-ze spear turned by Hector's never touched flesh | it was prevented by helm flash's mesh
its triple plates and visor that Phoebus | Apollo had given him Hector thus
promptly ran a long way back took cover | with his men sinking to his knees over
-come supporting himself with one great hand | on the ground just a moment beforehand
the world went black as night before his eyes | now follow-up spear Tydeides eyes
went right across the front lines to the spot | where he had seen the weapon lose the plot
so Hector had time to come to when had | leapt into car drove off into crowd had
thus escaped destruction then but the great | Diomedes rushing up with spear late
had something yet to say to him akin | to "You cur once more you have saved your skin
but only just for Phoebus Apollo | takes care of you still you say prayers no
doubt to him before you venture again | earshot of the spears but we'll meet again
and then I'll finish you if I also | can find a god to help me for now though
I shall try my luck against the rest" thus | resumed the stripping of Agastrophus
spearman he'd killed but now Paris husband | of Helen of the lovely hair whose hand
had drawn her from Argos and now drew so | on great captain Tydeides a bow
leaning for cover against the column | on the mound which those mighty men of some
bygone age had made then for their chieftain | Ilus son of Dardanus and so when
Diomedes was engaged in pulling | the burnished cuirass from the full-lulling
Agastrophus' breast shield from shoulder | the heavy helmet from his head bo(u)lder
now Paris drew the centre of his bow | and shot not for nothing did the arrow
leave his hand but hitting Tydeides | on the flat of his right foot and with ease
went right through and stuck in the earth Paris | with a happy laugh then leapt out from his
ambush gloated over Diomedes | "Youre hit so I did not shoot" cries words these
"in vain I only wish I had shot you | in the belly and indeed had shot you
dead Trojans who quake before you like some | bleating goats before a lion get some
respite from blight" unperturbed with great art | Diomedes replied "Bowman braggart

with your pretty lovelocks and your glad eye | for the girls if you were to face me nigh
man to man with real weapons you would find | bow and quiverful would not be a kind
defence as it is you flatter yourself | all that you've done is to scratch my good self
on the sole of the foot I care no more | than if a woman or naughty boy sore
slightly had made me shot from a coward | milksop does no harm going forward hard
still but MY weapons a much better edge | one touch from them a man is off the ledge
his wife has lacerated cheeks and his | children have no father earth red with his
blood and there he rots with fewer girls than | vultures at his side" the renowned spearman
Odysseus had come up and covered him | Diomedes sat down behind him grim
-ly withdrew the sharp arrow from his foot | pain stabbed his flesh in great distress set foot
into his car told his charioteer | to drive back to the ships no Argive here
to support him now all panic-stricken | Odysseus of great renown even
was perturbed and took counsel with his soul | indomitable "What" he asked self whole
with a groan "is coming to me next? would | be infamy take to my heels scared good
by the odds against me but even more | unpleasant to be caught alone for sure
now that Zeus has set on the run the rest | of Argives but why discuss it? let rest
do I not know that cowards leave their post | whereas the man who claims to lead the host
is in duty bound to stand unflinching | kill or die?" while impingeing self pinching
in this infernal internal debate | shield-bearing Trojan companies great rate
bore down upon him and surrounded him | caught tartar in their net on a whim grim
like the moment when the strong young huntsmen | with their hounds bait a wild boar in its den
whetting his white tusks and his crooked jaws | comes out from the depths of his lair paws pause
jaws yawning they rush him from every side | there is a noise of snapping jaws beside
but formidable as is hold their ground | so when the Trojans had circled him round
began harry him but he started well | leaping at Deiopites noble fell
with his sharp spear wounded him in shoulder | from above and next killed Thoon bolder
and Ennomus and then Cherisdamas | who had jumped down from his chariot and has
struck him hard with his spear in the navel | was all at sea an engagement naval
beneath his bossed shield and Cherisdamas | fell in the dust clutched at the earth's last gas
-p leaving them where they fell Odysseus | with spear stabbed Charops son of Hippasus
he was a brother of wealthy Socus | a gallant nobleman who hastened thus
to help confronted Odysseus arch-speaker | "Illustrious Odysseus arch-schemer
arch-adventurer today you'll either | two sons of Hippasus triumph over
and boast about the splendid pair you've killed | stripped or by my very spear heart be filled
and die yourself" he cast struck the round shield | glittering to the bronze the shield did yield
weighty spear passed pressed through cuirass ornate | and into his flank then did penetrate
ripped the flesh clean off but Pallas Athene | did not allow a bowel movement scene
Odysseus knowing that it had not touched | key spot drew back to Socus on sore point touched
"Now my unhappy friend your doom is sealed | my fight against Trojans you might have s(t)e(e/a)led
but I tell you that here and now you are | going to meet your fate and die you are
to be conquered by my spear and shall yield | your life to Hades of the Fabled Field
Horse and the glory to me" Socus reeled | started to run but had no sooner wheeled

round than Odysseus caught him with his spear | in the back midway between shoulder ear
blades and drove it through his chest he came down | with a thud and great Odysseus was down
on him in triumph "Ah Socus son dear | Hippasus doughty driver now so clear
after all Death was too quick for you you | did not escape YOUR eyes poor wretch that you
are won't be closed by your father mother | because the carrion birds will gather
round you with their flapping wings tear your corpse | to pieces but "I" if I die a corpse
that shall have the full funeral honours | from my noble countrymen" spear's onus
on him pull from own wound and bossed shield blood | gushed up as the point came out and he stood
in great distress when the companies Trojan | saw his blood across melee run called on
each other attacked him in a body | he gave ground shouting to friends for help he
called out at very top of his voice thrice | and Menelaus hearing those calls thrice
turned quickly to Aias who by fate near | "My royal son of Telamon I hear
the dauntless Odysseus now crying out | it sounds as though Trojans have cut him out
of his company in heat of the fight | and are overpowering him we might
do well to dash to the rescue I fear | he will come to grief if we don't get near
and what a loss to the Danaans if | so fine a trooper fell!" he set off swif
-tly god-like Aias went after him | they soon found the King Odysseus at him
on either side the Trojan host | and there followed on there such a scene most
as enacted in the hills when at dawn | an antlered stag is surrounded by tawn
-y jackals the stag who has been wounded | by a huntsman's arrow so confounded
but he ran fast enough for as long as | the warm blood flows also for as long as
his legs will carry him but when arrow wound | has sapped his strength mountain jackals have found
him in the twilight of the woods tearing him | to pieces with their carrion jaws grim
when of a sudden a hungry lion | enters stage left scene jackals flee lion
now takes his turn to use his jaws and thus | while Trojans storming round wise Odysseus
of the many wiles and that gallant man | by lunging with his spear kept host Trojan
death at bay Aias with towerlike shield | came up and covered him the Trojans yield
scatter all directions Menelaus | favourite of Ares took Odysseus
through the crowd by the arm supported him | until they reached his own chariot trim
which his squire drove up then Aias flinging | himself on the Trojan jackals killing
Doryclus a bastard son Priam he's | then wounded Pandoclus and Pylartes
Pyrasus Lysander as a river | swollen to the full by heavy winter
rains rushing down in spate from mountain zines | to the plain sweeps up the dead oaks and pines
and carries tons of silt into the sea | lustrous Aias stormed the plain site to see
fell on enemy trashing man and horse | Hector knew naught of this did not endorse
as on far left by banks of Scamander | engaged where heaviest slaughter slander
and a desperate fight had flared up there | round fierce Idomeneus great Nestor
Hector was busy here doing marvels | with javelin and car on his travels
and so mowing down the young Achaeans | yet even so those brave Argive-Ians
not have retired had not forsaken lout | Paris Lady Helen's spouse taken out
Machaon great captain there bearing grim | the brunt of the onslaught by striking him
with a three-barbed arrow in right shoulder | the Argives who'd been fighting the bolder

for their chief now filled with anxiety | as they thought he might soon a captive be
as fight swayed Idomeneus at once | called out to the noble Nestor "At once
my lord Nestor flower of Achaean | chivalry! to your car fetch Machaon
drive with all speed to the ships a surgeon | worth whole regiment Nicola Sturgeon
if can cut out arrow heal whole wounded | with his ointments Nestor promptly mountedd
his car and Machaon son of peerless | and famous physician Asclepius
got in beside Nestor touched the horses | with his whip and the willing pair races
off towards the black ships nothing better | had they wished for Cebriones driver
for Hector at present saw the Trojans | on the other wing were now also-rans
and drew Hector's attention to the fact | "Here we are engaged in a remote tact
-ical battle while our other-wing troops | are being routed pell-mell in great groups
Telamonian Aias up sweeping | easy recognise it's him grief heaping
by the broad shield on his shoulders let's drive | over there and where the stiffest fight dive
in with infantry and charioteers | where men killing men and battle's roar rears
unceasing" he touched long-maned horses' fears | with whistling lash the pair no sooner hears
the stroke than they sweep the fast chariot | off at a gallop towards the combat
trampling on corpses and shields so causing | the axle-tree below and rails coursing
round it to be sprayed with the blood thrown up | by their hooves and the tyres Hector well up
for it and get among throng of fighting | men to leap in and breakthrough inciting
but though his coming did bring confusion | to the Argives spared javelin use on
not at all but he avoided battle | then with the mighty Aias son of Tel
-amon attacked elsewhere spear sword boulder | but in the last knockings it was Father
Zeus himself on his high throne caused Aias | to turn tail lost his nerve halted alas
then with an anxious glance at the numbers | around swung seven-fold shield round shoulders
turned in retreat and step by step ground gave | as wild beasts oft look behind to selves save
he was like a tawny lion driven | from cattle-yard by farming men riven
with fear and dogs who've stayed awake all night | save from his maw the fattest heifer might
so hungry for meat the lion charges | showers darts blazing faggots discharges
at him the group's strong hands scare him for all | his eagerness and at dawn slinks off all
down-jived and so in such discontent | withdrew from the Trojans towards his tent
much against his will and acutely aware | of the danger to the Argive ships there
even so was stubborn as a donkey | who so gets the better of the monkey
boys in charge of him turns into a field | they're passing and helps himself to the yield
there and so many sticks have been broken | on his back that their cudgelling token
leaves him unconcerned 'til they drive him out | at last with much ado but not without
having eaten all that he wants and so | proud Trojans and their far-famed allies so
hung on the heels of Telamonian | Aias pricking the centre of his iron
-like shield with their arrows at times in fit | of renewed fury he'd wheel hold unit
whole of the horse-taming Trojans at bay | turn once more resume retreat from affray
thus he managed to fend off the whole force | that was then threatening the ships perforce
standing and laying about him single | -handed as was midway between shingle
Achaean shore plain Trojan and launched by | brawny arms many spears held on high by

his ample shield though they hankering go | further still and many another so
short fell without a taste of his white flesh | stuck in the earth deprived of the feast fresh
that it craved when Euaemon's highborn son | Euryplyus saw Aias labour on
under this hail of missiles he ran up | to support his glittering spear sent up
struck the chieftain Apisaon the son | of Phausius under midriff in on
to liver bringing him forthwith to ground | dashing up began take armour trove found
but as he stripped the man he was spotted | by Prince Paris quickly bent bow potted
him then with an arrow in the right thigh | but Eurypylus though leg hampered by
the broken shaft saved self from death certain | taking cover with his company's men
but gave a great shout to the Danaans | "My friends all you Counsellors and Captains
you Argives turn in your tracks make a stand | to save Aias from a disaster strand
-ed shot at as he is can't see how he | can disengage himself so now then rally
round the great Aias son of Telamon!" | thus the wounded Euryplyus had done
his bit they closed in and rallied round him | each crouching behind his sloping shield rim
spears at ready Aias made his approach | towards them and once he'd managed to broach
their friendly line he faced about once more | and stood so the fighting went on once more
just like a fire inextinguishable | while the mares of Neleus breed able
were sweating as they ran bearing Nestor | from field Machaon folk's shepherd in car
also it was that the great Achilles | of nimble feet been watching the crises
of the battle and lamentable rout | from stern ship saw him took note he's put out
called at once bosom-buddy Patroclus | shouting for him from the ship Patroclus
hearing him in the hut came out swinging | look like the god of war this beginning
of the end for him before Achilles | could explain himself he said "Achilles
why did you call? what do you want me for?" | and Achilles the great runner therefore
"My dear prince heart's delight at last I see | the Achaeans gathering at my knee
to abase themselves as in doodoo high | however what I wish you to do my
lord Patroclus is go and ask Nestor | who is the wounded man he's taking for
treatment from the field for seen from behind | he looks exactly like Machaon kind
son of Asclepius but the horse-pair | passed by me in such a great flurry-fare
that I did not see his face" Patroclus | obeyed his friend at once and set off plus
at a run along huts ships Achaean | in a while Nestor and Machaon
reached Nestor's hut where stepped down from the car | onto the fruitful earth the horses are
unyoked by Eurymedon old king's squire | then stood in the breeze the sea shore dryer
to blow the sweat from their tunics and there | -after into hut each sat easy chair
pottage prepared for them by Hecamede | Nestor had had from a Tenedos deed
when Achilles sacked the place the daughter | great-hearted Arsinous from the slaughter
been chosen by the Argives as tribute | to their counsellor the one most astute
she starts by moving up to them handsome | a polished table with its legs some-what come
-ly well-enamelled put a dish bronze on | with as flavour for the drink an onion
yellow honey and sacred barley-meal | beside wonderful beaker the real deal
adorned with golden studs which the old man | had brought from his sandy home had four han
-dles each supported by two legs on top | of each facing one another a top

class pair golden doves feeding there meeker | kind of person would've found the beaker
very hard to shift from table when full | but old as he was he without trouble
could lift it comely attendant in cup | mixed pottage and Pramnian wine served up
after making it ready by grating | with bronze grater goat's milk cheese and sating
with white barley on top invited drink | had quenched their parching thirst having a think
when Patroclus then suddenly appeared | in the doorway looking like a god reared
up the old man then rose from polished chair | drew him forward by the hand and begged there
him be seated but Patroclus he is | not keen come more in made his excuses
"I've no time to sit down my venerable | lord and you also will not be able
to persuade me I've too much reverence | respect for master who now sends me hence
on my errand which was to ask of you | who the man who was wounded was who you
brought in but I see it's lord Machaon | I will go back at once and report on
this to Achilles you know well enough | my venerable lord what a hard and tough
man he is quite capable of finding | fault without reason ""I'm not clear-minding"
said Nestor "why Achilles is so much | concerned about one casualty as such
while ignoring the disaster total | army has suffered our very best all
lying shipside struck by spear's bitter ease | arrows breeze the mighty Diomedes
has been hit Odysseus the great spearman | has been wounded so has Agamemnon
Euryplyus an arrow in his thigh | and now here is another victim nigh
I've just brought in hit by arrow a-new | yet Achilles though he's a fighter too
for the Achaeans pity not a mite | or concern is he waiting 'til in spite
of all we can do our brave ships go up | in flames by the sea our army cut up
peacemeal? I cannot take his place my limbs | aren't so supple now my old strengths just whims
-y ah me if only were still as young | and vigorous as was when when far out strung
with the Eleans as we came to blows | for the lifting of some cattle my blows
killed Itymoneus the gallant son | of Hypeirochus then a denizen
of Elis by way of reprisal I | was raiding his herds he resisted I
brought him down with a javelin rustic | levies straight away scattered in panic
what a haul of booty we rounded up | from the field fifty herds of cattle up
to as many flocks of sheep droves of pigs | and scattered herds of goats also the gig's
yielded a hundred and fifty chestnut | horses all mares with foals lots from the rut
in the night we drove them to the city | Neleus Pylos sandy salt-gritty
and Neleus was delighted that an | unfledged warrior as I was back then
should have had such luck at dawn town-criers | summoned all the folk who had debt-flyers
in Elis to attend the leading men | in Pylos held a great meeting and then
divided the spoils which came in handy | as the Epeans in debt to many
of us indeed we in Pylos in a bad way | and so the few who were left anyway
after the mighty Heracles had come | and done his very worst to us and some
in previous years and all our best men | killed Neleus most excellent of men
had had twelve sons but I alone survived | all the rest of life long since been deprived
as a result the Epean soldiers | had become unbearable treated us
with contempt and oppressed us shamefully | but old king Neleus got a goodly

flock of sheep also a herd of cattle | from our spoils picked three hundred as chattel
for self along with their shepherds by way | of recouping heavy loss come his way
in the good land of Elis when he'd sent | four race-horses with a chariot meant
to run in the games there and compete for | the tripod King Augeas kept them for
self sent back driver sorry man horseless | with an insulting message Neleus
resented the wording of this as much | as the King's high-handed action as such
so now he helped himself liberally | to the booty left the community
divide rest in such a way that no sort | of person of proper share should go short
we had just accomplished the last details | of this business which entails the entrails
sacrifice to the gods at various | points in town third day whole strength Elis thus
horse and foot bore down on us in haste hot | with the two Moliones who were not
men and had no experience of war | an outlying stronghold Thryoessa
is perched on a steep hill overlooking | the Alpheus and Pylos nigh brooking
aimed to destroy this place did it surround | and overran also the plain around
however in the night Athene speeding | down from Olympus on high need heeding
us to get under arms not unwilling | us whole force she raised in Pylos willing
for the fight but Neleus did not wish | me go as knew naught of serious-ish
fighting and he hid my horses from me | though went on foot Athene arranged did she
the affair so that managed to outshine | our own greatest charioteers that time
even there's a river Minyeius | that into the sea near Arene falls thus
horse Pylian stopped here 'til dawn when foot | battalions came rolling up from that foot
-hold a rapid march in battle order | brought us by noon to the sacred River
Alpheus and we sacrificed there to | almighty Zeus offered too a bull to
the River-god a bull to Poseidon | and then a heifer to Pallas Athen
-'e ate supper in our several messes | and then after we had done the dishes
we settled down for the night on the banks | of the stream on each man his armour clanks
the Epeans meanwhile beleaguering | fortress confidence over-eagering
and determined on its downfall had no | idea of trouncing were going so
to get instead no sooner had Sun shown | his face above distant horizon zone
than we gave battle with prayer to Zeus's | name and to Athene and when the armies
came to grips the first man there fell to me | and then I the new owner came to be
of his excellent horses spearman one | called Mulius of Augeas a son
-in-law married to his eldest daughter | Agamede of the auburn-haired laughter
knew each magic herb grows in whole wide world | and as he came at me I at once hurled
my bronze-headed spear and he fell headlong | to ground I took his car and went along
to take my place in the front line the proud | Epeans frightened scattered in a crowd
in all directions when saw the captain | of horse and best fighter meet fate certain
but I was after them like a black squall | I took fifty cars by each one did fall
couple men by my spear there bit the dust | and if left to me would have killed not just
those men but the twin Moliones too | of House of Actor if Poseidon who
their Father Imperial Earthshaker | had not hid them in a thick mist cover
rescued them from the field yes Zeus gave us | a great victory chased them we ravers

across open land killing men gathering | their splendid arms 'til our cars lathering
through the cornlands of Bupraison and we | got to the Olenian Rock eyrie
place called Alision Hill at that point | Athene saw fit to halt us and then point
us back there I killed and left my last man | our chariots withdrew from Bupraison
and drove back to Pylos we all giving | glory Zeus among gods among living
men to Nestor thus did I acquit me | among the men of my day so surely
now look at Achilles he's a brave man | yet who will profit from that other than
he? and mark my words he too will shed tears | when the army is destroyed they'll be tears
of remorse my friend and do you recall | clearly Menoetius your father what call
made that day he sent you from Phthia | to join King Agamemnon's adventure?
I and King Odysseus were in the house | and heard it all on a recruitment joust
across the fertile land of Achaea | when we arrived at the splendid manor
of Peleus where we then found the lord | Menoetius and yourself and my lord
Achilles with you Peleus the old | charioteer burning fat from bold rolled
ox's thigh in honour of mighty Zeus | the Thunderer in his stable-yard use
had in his hand of chalice golden | the burnt offering by a libation
accompanied of the bright sparkling wine | while you two were preparing the meat line
at that moment Odysseus and I | appeared at the gate Achilles did cry
in astonishment took us by the hand | and brought us inside and gave us chairs grand
withal usual hospitality | offered us refreshment and thus when we
had so satisfied our hunger and thirst | I disclosed point of our visit first
urged you Achilles then and there enlist | more than willing even only half pissed
and your fathers both gave you their blessing | while the old man Peleus was spelling
out to boy Achilles always strive for | the first place outdo any peer in war
Menoetius son of Actor was giving | you his own advice I now reliving
his words 'My son Achilles is of birth | nobler than you and is in fighting worth
by far the stronger but you are older | for you to better advise him bolder
set him an example and take the lead | he follows to his advantage will lead'
those were your old father's precepts which you | have forgotten but not too late for you
to talk to Achilles in this fashion | he might well have sense enough to listen
who knows? the advice of a friend's often | the most effective you may coax action
from him with a little luck yet if he | secretly deterred by some prophecy
perhap some word from Zeus that his lady | Mother has told him of let him maybe
at the very least let YOU take the field | with the Myrmidon force and so be healed
the Danaans perhaps to salvation | and indeed let him give you to fight on
own glorious armour so the Trojans | may take you for him break off their actions
and so then give our weary forces time | to recuperate even a short time
-break makes all the difference in war think | Trojans themselves have fought too to the brink
of exhaustion and you being so fresh | might well drive them back to the town afresh
from the ships and huts" Patroclus's pent | emotions profoundly stirred by words went
off at the double along the ship-line | to rejoin his royal master by time
he'd reached ships of Odysseus feet fleeting | still place where held the Assembly meeting

legal sessions and had put up altars | to the gods Eurypylus avatar's
high-born son of Eumaeon met limping back | from the fight with an arrow-wound in back
of thigh sweat pouring from head and shoulders | the blood ran dark from the wound that smoulders
with pain but his mind was not affected | gallant Patroclus was much affected
by compassion for him in his distress | pictured Argive Counsellors Captains' stress
-ed all far from their dear ones and the land | of their fathers filling all the Troyland
nimble dogs with their white flesh he appealed | to Eurypylus "Can our wound be healed
my noble lord and the monstrous Hector | be checked or all fall to his spear vector
be desTroyed today?" "My lord Patroclus" | responded the wounded Eurypylus
"there's no salvation for an Achaean | now they will fall by their own black wooden
ships with all our former champions flung | there already by slings arrows stung
outrageous fortune Trojans grow stronger | but at least you can preserve ME longer
see me safe to black wooden ship I wish | you to cut this arrow from my thigh swish
off the blood with warm water spread soothing | ointment on wound some sooth(-ing)-saying
that you have some excellent prescriptions | you learnt from Achilles whose descriptions
instructions Cheiron civilised centaur | I cannot appeal to our surgeons for
I hear that Machaon's lying wounded | in the camp in need of a well-r(ou/u)n(e)d(ed)
physician himself Podaleirius | the other is still hotly engaged thus
in the field" "This is intolerable" | Menoetius's gallant son just able
to exclaim "what are we to do my lord | Eurypylus? I'm en route to my lord
Achilles my wise master messenger | for Nestor the Warden of Achaea
all the same I'm not going to leave you | in the lurch exhausted as I see you
indeed are" as he spoke he put his arm | round great captain's waist to his hut with charm
supported and Eurypylus' squire | when saw him spread hides on the floor entire
and there Patroclus laid him down and cut | the sharp point of the bronze-tipped arrow butt
out of thigh with a knife and the dark blood | from the wound with warm water then did flood
away teased out root of a bitter herb | in his hands and applied it was the verb
-al hit spot for it was a sedative | wight white witch banished pain way creative
and so with this wound then began to dry | and the blood ceased to flow so stopped the cry

δώδεκα

*Book 12*

# HECTOR STORMS THE WALL

*how the allies and main body Trojans*
*broke within the wall of the Achaeans*

while the gallant Patroclus attending | to Eurypylus's wound unbending
fight went on Achaeans Trojans throwing | in all their men and there was no showing
that the trench of the Argives and thick wall | behind would hold out much longer at all
because when they built this wall for the ships | with the trench alongside made fatal slip's
failure to make ritual offering | to the gods so safe haven proffering
fleet sheltering and vast spoils they'd taken | the wall built without goodwill of Heaven
not last long but while Hector was alive | and Achilles s(k)ulked and while host Argive
couldn't sack Priam's city Achaean | great wall held but later when all Trojan
best were dead many of the Argives too | though some were left when Priam's city too
had been sacked in the tenth year of the siege | had sailed home expedition Argive liege
Poseidon and Apollo selves plighted | destroy wall turn against it united
waters of all the rivers that run down | Ida range sea lovely Scamander's down
and Simois's on whose banks many | shields and helmets lay and also many
a warrior of that most heroic | generation had met his end tragic
Rhesus Heptaporus Caresus grand | Rhodius along with Granicus s(tr)and
Aesepus then all these rivers Phoebus | Apollo brought together one isthmus
for nine days flung their waters at the wall | while Zeus without ceasing made the rain fall
submerge it quicker with nuke sub Trident | in hand the Earthshaker himself torrent
directed washed out to sea all wooden | and stone foundations army Achaean
had laid down with such labour and levelled | shore of Hellespont that fast flowed bevelled
all when the wall had disappeared he turned | on green magic wide beach to sand and returned
the rivers to the channels down which their | limpid streams had been running before there
all this still to be done by Poseidon | Apollo but for now wall carried on
unimpaired scene tumultuous battle | wordsworth's wood-smith's-work two towers rattle
resounding to the enemy's missiles | for the Argives who were cowed in the aisles
by the lash of Zeus penned in held beside | the ships in fear of Hector for their hide
mighty panic-maker raging prowling | as ever with fury of a howling

gale he like a wild boar or a lion | when he turns this way and then that amon
-g hounds and huntsmen to defy them grim | in his strength they close their ranks confront him
like a wall pelt him with showers of darts | but no fear or thoughts flight any parts
of his dauntless heart his very courage | kills him time and again he turns in rage
and tries some new point in the ring of men | wherever charges the ring gives way then
Hector darts to and fro among the toss | -ing wave of men goading car drivers cross
-ing the trench but when it came to the point | own fast horses did jib at this fell joint
frightened by its width halted on the brink | neighing shrilly horse lead to water think
indeed the dyke was by no means easy | take at bound cross anyway so queasy
squeezy overhang both banks all along | watchtower top row of pointed stakes strong
and close-set the Argives had planted their | enemies to keep well off over there
and thus this was not a place where horses | could break in towing behind their boxes
but the troops were keen to try the passage | and thus Polydamas with this message
to lion-hearted Hector suggested | Troy's chiefs allies ingested digested
"It would be folly now to cross trench hence | in our chariots for the strong defence
of the palisade on top makes it well | nigh impossible by wall hard nigh well
thus leaving the charioteers no room | whatever to dismount and around zoom
to fight in fact so narrow a strip I | am certain they would come to grief nearby
if Zeus the Thunderer is really on | our side and wishes the host Danaan
to be utterly destroyed well and good | there's nothing I want more than that they should
perish far from Argos right here and now | and be forgot but what if they do now
round on us? if we're driven from the ships | get selves entangled in hip trip-wire lips
of the trench I do not think a single | man would escape news to Troy to bring ill
I've a better plan that hope you'll adopt | let our squires take charge of our horses opt
stay by trench while we on foot in full gear | follow Hector and there create such fear
that the Achaeans then will not stand up | to us if their number is really up"
this advice seemed excellent to Hector | he jumped down straight away in full armour
from his car and all the other Trojans | abandoned their chariot formations
when they saw Prince Hector dismount leaping | out they told their drivers to be keeping
their horses drawn up in order proper | by side of trench then stood clear and proper
sorted themselves out and fell in behind | their own captains in five companies lined
the best and biggest was that of Hector | peerless Polydamas none was more for
throw themselves in-to breach the wall and fight | by the ships and Cebriones whose might
needed Hector left less valuable man | with his chariot as he third chief man
the second company led by Paris | Alcathous and Agenor the third is
led by two of Priam's sons Helenus | godlike Deiphobus with Asius
the noble son of Hyrtacus third did | hold command and whose big glossy rapid
horses brought from Arisbe and River | Selleis and of the fourth the leader
Aeneas handsome son of Anchises | backed by Archelocus Acamas these
two sons descended from Antenor's line | in all kinds fighting experience fine
Sarpedon last led allies glorious | and had appointed Asteropaeus
warlike and Glaucus under his command | because he considered them the outstand

-ing men among the allies after him | he the finest soldier of the whole gym
-nasium come into formation shield | touching each oxhide each making a shield
-wall and then advanced on the Danaans | resolutely sure no enemy plans
actions could stop them now from swooping down | on the black ships as to their own took down
the tactics deemed by the ab(d)ominable | Polydamas the Trojans and noble
allies all save Asius Hyrtacus | son as a ruling prince objected thus
not wanting to leave chariot behind | with his squire in charge decides to go blind
drive right up to the hollow ships full tool | equipage however he was a fool
not destined to evade his evil fate | and drive back his chariot and pair late
in triumph from the sad ships to windy | Ilium in the spear of the weighty
Idomeneus Deucalion's son | abominable doom was waiting on
to engulf him for his drive was teeing | up the left flank of the ships there being
a causeway Argives used when returning | from the plain and here Asius turning
drove horses and car over and coming | to the gateway found the doors welcoming
no long bar in place defenders holding | open to give the stragglers not holding
the field last gasp chance to reach the ships so | Asius in his car made straight to go
through the gate followed by his company | they of utterly-piercing-war-cry be
these foolish folk thought that host Achaean | could no way stop them now from swooping on
the black ships but at the gate they met | two champions scions both an outlet
of warlike Lapith race stalwart poet | son of Peirithous one Polypoet
-'es and Leonteus a peer of Ares | murd'rous War-god pair firmly sturdy knees
had planted there in front of the high gate | lofty mountain oaks that resist the fate
of wind and rain Forever Changes Love | anchored by long sturdy roots and above
mighty branches thus the two relying | brawny arms beserkers set defying
the onslaught of the doughty Asius | stood firm the Trojans round King Asius
massing and Adamas son Asius | Thoon Orestes Oenomaus Iamenus
held up their leather shields with a mighty | shout made straight for the wall and but briefly
the two Lapithae encouraged the men | -at-arms Danaan inside to fight then
and there for the ships however when saw | Trojans storm wall heard fateful fatal flaw
of disorder indeed panic among | the Danaans behind them quit the throng
came right out and fought in front of the gate | pair of wild boars in a dire mountain strait
facing a noisy mob of dogs and men | charging away to either flank and then
crushing and rooting up the undergrowth | round them sound clattering tusks fight not loth
'til at last hit by javelin and killed | so shining bronze on the breasts of the skilled
Lapithae rang out as it met each blow | Trojan for they put up a superb show
trusting in their own strength and in their friends | on the wall above to not meet their ends
battling for camp and the gallant ships' hearts | flinging stones down from the well-built ramparts
the Trojans too hurled stones showers rock frack | -ing both sides now from battle back pack track
came pelting to ground much like the flakes | in a blizzard when the dark cloud-host snakes
before the wind and the bountiful earth | blanketed in snow bossed shields helms unearth
-ly loud rang out as the great boulders hit them | Asius son of Hyrcatus was then
in despair groaned slapped his thighs cried out hot | "Ah Almighty Father Zeus I knew not

you too were such a lover of the lie | these two withstand our fury high nigh I
never thought felt us irresistible | but look at them now ready both to kill
or be killed ere they give way from the gate | supple-waisted wasps or bees that with mate
built in a hollow by a rocky path | won't be driven out of their own homes' path
but stay and fight it out with the huntsmen | bold for the sake of all of their children!"
Asius' outburst had no effect | on Zeus who had decided to let Hect
-or have the gory glory and meanwhile | other companies Trojan rank and file
had carried the fighting to other gates | but how can I picture these many states?
would take a tell-tale god to tell the tale | all along the watchtower the stone wall wail
fierce fires had broken out hard-pressed Argives | were compelled to fight for their very lives
and ships all the gods who had taken sides | with them were broken-hearted that besides
'twas the two Lapithae who now attacked | Polypoetes cast his spear and smacked
Damasus on his bronze-sided helmet | metal spear not checked when metal helm met
point went right through pierced bone spattered inside | the hel-met with his brains did thus betide
the end of Damasus in the onslaught | next Polypoetes killed Pylon caught
Ormenus with a fatal strike meanwhile | Leonteus an offshoot Ares-style
had flung his javelin at Hippomachus | hit on the belt son of Antimachus
then he drew his sharp sword from its sheath dashed | into the throng the first man with whom clashed
Antiphates closing he struck with sword | and brought him crashing down on the greensward
flat on his back and in swift succession | brought Iamenus Orestes and Menon
nearer than they'd been to the kindly soil | while the Lapithae were stripping the spoil
from these men all their resplendent armour | under chiefs Polydamas and Hector
the young warriors who formed best biggest | of the companies had shown the greatest
eagerness breach wall and set ships on fire | standing at the trench not enough on fire
to advance just as were going to cross | a portent appeared to them on the cross
an eagle flying high along their front | from the left clutching a blood-red serpent
in his talons the monster was alive | still gasping showing signs wished live did writhe
back then and bit his captor on the breast | beside the neck then the eagle distressed
in pain released his hold let snake drop droop | among whole troop with a loud cry did swoop
away down the wind Trojans did appall | when saw snake lie shimmering amid all
indicating will aegis-bearing Zeus | Polydamas straight to he dauntless use
Hector(ed) "Hector as a rule you object | when I offer good advice in effect
at our Assemblies and you consider | impertinent that a mere commoner
should disagree with you in the council | chamber or in the field indeed counsel
your authority always be upheld | but once more I'm going to say what's held
by me be best advice we ought not to | advance and dispute the ships as I DO
know in truth what will happen exactly | if portent does not lie just as ready
to cross the eagle then appeared to us | clutching a monstrous blood-red serpent thus
in talons flew on left along our front | the snake alive to eagle took affront
bit it so dropped before he reached his nest | failed to get it home give it to the rest
of his family and in the same way | even if by great strife we find a way
of breaking down the Argive gate and wall | and the enemy then does give way all

our flight from the ships over same ground | will prove disastrous Argives on home ground
fighting for their ships will kill number | of our men they will be in dead lumber
we'll have to leave behind for that is how | a prophet who really understood now
such omens and had army's confidence | would interpret this portent's importance"
Hector flashy helm gave him a black look | and replied "Polydamas I do look
on this interference with resentment | surely you've somewhat better to invent
as if you really do mean what you say | the gods themselves with your brains have made hay
Zeus the Thunderer in his own person | in all solemnity made me certain
promises and these you bid me forget | instead you would have me use as target
for my acts a flight of birds winged creatures | for me have no interesting features
in fact I do not care whether they fly | to the right towards the morning sun sky
or to the left into the western gloom | let's weave our future fate on Zeus' loom
he who rules all mankind and the gods too | fight for your country the best in my view
and only omen and yet why should you | of all men hold back from fighting anew?
even if rest of us slaughtered wholesale | by the Achaean ships you need avail
not of fear for your own safety you're not | the man to stand up firm fight it out hot
nonetheless if you do shirk or dissuade | any of the rest from the escapade
I'll not hesitate strike you with this spear | and take your life" thereupon Hector here
signalled the advance with a mighty roar | his men after him from Mount Ida soar
-ing Zeus who delights thunder unleashing | a gusty wind the dust there releasing
blew it straight at the ships bewildering | the Achaeans wide eyes be wild erring
advantage Hector Trojans serve trusting | in this token of god's good-will thrusting
on in their strength made determined efforts | breach wall tearing at the parapet forts
and trying to pull down the battlements | lever up projecting buttresses e-vents
these the Argives had let into the ground | outside to support the towers make sound
in the hope that by these undermining | the wall itself might be dissed-inclining
yet for all that the Danaans would not | yield them entrance closed up each broken spot
with oxhide screens and from the battlements | pelted the enemy with the remnants
as they came up under the wall the two | Aiantes everywhere round on top to
and fro directing defence on urging | Achaeans some were mildly scourging
but to those others who had abandoned | all resistance harsher terms were sanctioned
knowing also that to make an army | it takes all kinds they appealed not only
to their picked men but those of average | ability and below average
"Friends Achaeans and fellow countrymen | know today that there is work for all men
as you know this well enough yourselves | none listen to those rebel evil elves
the Trojans and their threats and turn his face | to the ships instead forward in a face
-to-face with two-faced enemy cheering | each other on as in trust adhering
to Olympian Zeus Lord of Lightning | will let us counter-attack chastening
them back to their town" thus the Aiantes | held together strength of Achaeans' knees
with their exhortations by now the stones | were falling down fast as thick as hailstones
on a stormy day when Zeus the Thinker | has begun to snow let see him tinker
with the javelins of his armament | when he has laid all the wild winds dormant

and snows without ceasing 'til he's coated | the high hilltops of the coast the bold head
-lands the clover meadows the farmers' fields | 'til even shores inlets of grey sea-fields
filled with snow only the breakers fend off | as they come rolling in remorseless off
the mighty deep all else blanketed | by the overwhelming fall banqueted
from Zeus' hand such the showers of stones | were being hurled in both direction zones
as the Achaeans pelted the Trojans | and the Trojans likewise the Achaeans
'til the whole length of the wall was thundering | to volleys there their life-lines sundering
but even now illustrious Hector | and his Trojan troops would not ever
have broken down the stout gate in the wall | long bar had not Zeus Counsellor of all
inspired his son Sarpedon to fall on | the Achaeans as a lion falls on
cattle Sarpedon thus swung his round shield | around to the front his splendid great shield
of beaten bronze hammered out by the smith | and backed with hide after hide and forthwith
stitched together with gold wire that ran right | around the circle and with the shield right
in front of him and brandishing two spears | he set out like a mountain lion who nears
starvation long lacks meat hardihood-led | prompts assault very walls of a homestead
explore the pens even if finds herdsmen | on the spot guarding the sheep with dogs then
and spears has no mind to be chased away | without having a tumble in the hay
either leaps in and pounces on a sheep | or himself indeed struck down in a heap
on meeting the defence by a javelin | from quick hand so godlike Sarpedon in
to assault felt impelled the wall break through | the battlements he turned to Glaucus though
Hippolochus' son "Glaucus why do | the Lycians at home distinguish you
and me with marks of honour the best seats | at the banquet the first cut at the (m)eats
of the joint and the cups never empty? | they all look up to us as gods but why?
and why were we made the lords of that great | estate of ours on the banks incarnate
of Xanthus with all its lovely orchards | splendid wheat fields indeed not meagre shards?
are we not obliged to take our places | now in the vanguard and turn our faces
to the flames of battle? only so can | we hope to make our soldiers Lycian
say this of us when they discuss each King | 'Living on fat of land ruling drinking
the mellow vintage wine they do but they | pay for it in their gory glory they
are mighty men of war and wherever | Lycians fight you will see them ever
in the van' ah my friend if after having | survived this war could be sure of having
ageless immortality I'd neither | take my place very front line nor either
send you out to win honour in the field | but things are not like that for death doth yield
a thousand pitfalls for our feet and no | -one can save himself and cheat him and so
in we go whether we yield the glory | to some other or win for us only"
Glaucus indeed did heed Sarpedon's call | the two went forward with at their heel all
the great Lycian force when he saw them | Menestheus son Peteos ahem
in shock shuddered as against his sector | of Argive ramparts that viral vector
was directed looking along the wall | for some commander who could save them all
from disaster saw the two Aiantes | legends who were for battle gluttons these
standing quite near with Teucer who'd just come | from his hut but shouting then would not come
across noise so great could not make them hear | and the very sky was assaulted here

by din smitten shields and helmets crested | let alone pounding of the gates tested
as these were all closed now and the Trojans | had come up to them and knocked out their pans
to break them down and force their way inside | Menestheus had to quickly decide
what to do so sent herald Thootes | message Telamonian of the Aiantes
"An errand for you my good Thootes | run and call Aias or the Aiantes
preferably as we'll soon be wiped out here | the Lycian captains head right for here
and we know what savages Lycians | can be when come with a strength like lion's
but if the two of them over there are | as hard put to it as we ourselves are
let us have the brave Telamonian | Aias at least and bring the great bowman
Teucer with him" the herald on errand | set out promptly length of wall quickly spanned
and when reached the Aiantes accosted | them at once "My lords commanders" started
"Menestheus my noble master begs | you to come over if only for dregs
of time lend him a hand in his dire straits | preferably both of you really states
that's what he'd like best of all for we will | soon be wiped out yonder one and all ill
captains Lycian now heading straight | for our sector we all know what a state
these savage Lycians can get into | when they come to grips but if you are too
hard-pressed he hoped you my lord son | of Telamon would come the great bowman
Teucer too" mighty Telamonian | Aias did not refuse assist this plan
turning to Oileus' son did spell | it out carefully "Aias you as well
as our stalwart Lycomedes I want | to stay here and see that our people want
for nothing to keep enemy engaged | while I go and aid those being upstaged
over there I will be back directly | I've saved our friends" and with that he quickly
set off and his brother Teucer the son | own father went with him and Pandion
attended carrying his crooked bow | since they were making for a spot of so
intense pressure they went along inside | the wall and so reached the sector beside
led by Menestheus the great-hearted | found redoubtable vanguard stout-hearted
captains of the Lycians now storming | the battlements like a tempest de-forming
the darkness and thus they then hurled themselves | at the enemy tumult further swells
Telamonian Aias first to kill | Sarpedon's mate generous Epicl
-'es hit him with a jagged lump of rock | he'd picked up inside battlements' block stock
from top of the heap by an embrasure | this great chunk sturdiest youngster for sure
of our generation would have found hard | to lift with both hands Aias heaved well hard
above his head hurled crushing the helmet | with its quadruple ridge smashing well-met
skull to bits he dropped from the high tower | spirit leaving his bones like a diver
meanwhile Glaucus of Hippolochus son | stalwart by Teucer fight termination
as he charged Teucer saw his arm exposed | and struck it with an arrow from his bow's
twang spoiled fight for Glaucus who drew back that | hastily unobtrusively so that
Argives might not see that he was wounded | and thus gloat over him and so Sarped
-on suffered keenly when he realised | Glaucus gone yet dematerialised
not was his ardour thus thrust up with a spear | at Alcmaon mighty son Thestor clear
struck him and tried to drag the weapon out | the man came with it falling headlong out
of the wall his ornate bronze equipment | rang upon him Sarpedon battlement

got his giant hands on and gave a pull | and so then a length of battlement full
of breastwork fell exposing top of wall | made breach big enough for company all
but still had to reckon one and same time | with Aias and Teucer's arrow did chime
with the bright baldric run across his breast | supporting his man-covering shield vest
and although Zeus saved him from destruction | not wishing then that the doom of his son
should be met there by the sterns of the ships | Aias charging down struck him amidships
shield again weapon failed to penetrate | but staggered him then in his onset great
and was forced to withdraw a little bit | from the battlements though taken a hit
Sarpedon not go right back still filled field | with hopes of glory he was so he wheeled
round shouted to his godlike Lycians | "Why have you let your resolve Lycians
seep away like this? strong as I am I | can hardly breach the wall make a path by
myself to the black ships after me then! | the more the merrier" Lycian men
took the King's rebuke to heart on either | side arraigned about their royal leader
they attacked with a greater vehemence | than ever for their part the Achaeans
did then the companies behind the wall | reinforce ensuing battle for all
desperate as neither could the stalwart | Lycians break Achaean wall a vile wart
at all establish a rout(e) to the ships | nor Argives thrust Lycians back from ships
once they had gained a footing on the wall | divided by the battlements withal
and they were like two men quarrelling poor | over fence in the common field next door
in hands yardsticks each fighting for fair share | in a narrow strip no duty of care
across the breastwork hacked at each other's | leather shields and the enormous bucklers
or the light targets held across their chest | cruel bronze bit into many a man's breast
flesh not only when a man swung round bared | his back often through shields selves straight home fared
and therefore shields themselves all along the watchtower | battlement were drenched in a great shower
of mingled blood Trojans and Achaeans | and yet still unable were the Trojans
to set their great enemies on the run | for the Achaeans managed to hold on
the battle nicely balanced as the scales | in which an honest working woman bales
out the wool against the weights to make sure | of the meagre pittance she's to procure
for her children as the struggle was as | equal as that 'til moment when Zeus has
given mastery to Hector Priam's | son he who was easily the primus
inter Par(i/e)s the first to leap inside | the Argive wall he used his voice beside
and sent it ringing through the Trojan ranks | cried "On with you you Trojan mark 4 tanks!
down with Argive wall and let's see the ships | go up in flames" no Trojan ear that ships
not his stirring call massing together | now then charging the rampart endeavour
scale the parapet with sharp spears in hand | but Hector seized and brought along in hand
a rock that was lying before the gate | broad at the base though running to a fate
-al point it would have taxed the strength of two | best men in any city these days to
lever it up from the ground and onto | a cart but Hector without much ado
handled it alone Zeus in his wisdom | made it light for him within his fiefdom
as easily as a shepherd taking | up a ram's fleece in one hand and making
away with it scarcely feeling the weight | lifted up the great rock brought it by fate
to bear on the panels that did there fill | the morticed framework doors high double-ill

held on the inner side by two sliding | bars locked by single bolt right up sidling
taking a firm stance with legs well apart | make sure a powerful throw filled the part
hit the doors full in the middle and broke | the hinges off on either side did choke
its own momentum carried the rock in | -side from gate there's a great rock 'n roll-din
as panels smashed to splinters by impact | of the stone and the bars gave way in fact
glorious Hector leapt inside a look | like sudden nightfall on face stricken stuck
two spears in hand the bronze on his body | shone with a baleful light and then as he
sprang in through the gate none save for a god | could have met and held this all-killing bod
and now with the fire flashing from his eyes | turned to the crowd behind called on the guys
Trojan to surmount the wall and his men | responded promptly with some of them then
swarming over the wall others pouring | in through the gate in panic outpouring
Danaans fled among the hollow ships | all hell let loose all too soon came to grips

δεκατρία

*Book 13*

# THE BATTLE AT THE SHIPS

*Poseidon stirred Argives defend ships plus*
*subsequent valour Idomeneus*

when Zeus had brought Hector and host Trojan | up to the ships he left them thereupon
with their enemies to the agony | and toil of the unending struggle he
turned his shining eyes into the distance | where surveyed lands horse-breeding Thracian stance
the Mysians who prefer hand-to-hand | fight lordly Hippemolgi in the land
where they drink mares' milk and the Abii | who on earth the most law-Abiidi
and not another glance of his bright eyes | did he give to Troy nor even surmise
that any of the immortals would now | come down to help either side anyhow
but the Lord Poseidon at his own post | kept far sharper look-out than most each host
he too had sat down on the highest peak | of Samothrace and was watching the peak
of the battle spellbound he had risen | from the sea and sought out this spot given
from here whole of Ida as well as town | of Priam ships of the Argive sea-town
could be seen pitied host Achaean then | in their hour of defeat and was most en
-raged with Zeus now he got up came swinging | down the rocky slope and all a-ringing
trembling at deathless feet of descending | god the high hills and forest lands ending
in three strides only fourth reaching Aegae | his destination where stands deep nearby
in the lagoon his famous palace built | of gleaming gold will stand there in the silt
forever harnessed to his chariot | brazen-hooved golden flowing-maned and hot
swift horses two clothed himself now in gold | and then he picked up his well-made whip gold
-en mounted chariot drove across waves | each monster of the sea comes out and waves
not failing to recognise their ur-king | on all sides from caves lurking issuing
and were gambolling there at his coming | the sea itself in its delight coming
on to him makes way so much that bounding | horses flew along bronze axle sounding
dry below as they carried him to-ward | Argive fleet midway between rugged hard
Imbros and Tenedos an almighty | cavern down in a deep sea-pool mighty
Poseidon the Earthshaker here unyoked | and left his horses beside them invoked
some ambrosial fodder and tying | legs with golden hobbles no untying
nor shaking off to ensure their staying | 'til their master's return he awaying

then to the great Achaean camp here like | high wind or conflagration in wake-strike
of Hector son of Priam host Trojan | indomitable fury sweeping on
wasting no breath on their normal war-cry | hopeful of capturing the ships so nigh
killing all the best Argives beside them | but at this moment Poseidon did then
emerge from depths of sea put a fresh dash | of heart into the Argives of Calchas
borrowing the form and tireless voice key | Worker-shaker and Girdler of the World he
first accosted the two Aiantes who | he found in little need be pushed anew
"My lords U 2 too can save host Argive | if keep your courage high no craven d(r)ive"
thought of panic entertain host Trojan | has in large numbers the great wall climbed on
but irresistible as they seem now | I'm not concerned about rest front row row
where the bronze-clad Achaeans will hold them | in check it is here I dread the end then
where that madman Hector who now pretends | father's mighty Zeus for own fake news ends
storming in the van like a raging fire | if some god could just make you see higher
this the place for you two to stand fast | rally the rest you might yet at the last
fend him off from the gallant ships for all | his fury and from Great Zeus himself all
the encouragement he gets" thereupon | Earthshaker World-Girdler lighting upon
them with staff with dauntless resolution | filled them made new men of them solution
with speed of striking peregrine who leaves | his post high on a precipice's eaves
rocky poises swoops to chase some other | bird across the plain did the Earthshaker
then disappear from their ken Poseidon | of the two it was Oileus' son
the Runner who first knew him for a god | turned at once to Telamon's son a prod
"Aias 'twas one of the gods who live on | Olympus who urged us just now fight on
by the ships he did take the seer's form yet | was not Calchas our diviner prophet
his heels and the backs of his knees were proof | enough for me he was indeed a spoof
it is not hard to recognise a god | and not only that for I feel an odd
change in my heart I am twice as eager | as I was for fight then somewhat meagre
my feet and hands itching to be at them" | first Aias agreed "I feel the same tem
-plate my mighty hands itching on my spear | my spirit is aroused and my feet here
dancing to be off and single-handed | I should now be happy to be landed
with Hector Priam's son in his fury" | while the Aiantes were getting furry
savouring the joy of battle the god gird | -ing their loins giving heart anew the Gird
-ler of the World stirred up host Achaean | in the rear who were then seeming keen on
recovering their spirits by the ships | gallant not only unmanned in full grips
of exhaustion also demoralised | by sight of enemy who'd realised
crossing of the great wall in such numbers | looked at them eyes filled with tears dead lumbers
for they saw then no hope now of salvation | but with the ease of a god Poseidon
went among the ranks and hounded them on | Teucer the first visited rounded on
roused with lord Peneleos and Leitus | then the turmoil-makers Antilochus
Meriones Thoas Deipyrus | and with his stinging words he now put thus
fresh heart into them "Argives shame on you! | are you raw recruits? the very men you
are on whose gallantry I had relied | to save our ships if YOU have not now tried
because the fight is so severe the day | for our loss to the Trojans underway

ah what a portent for my eyes fearful | thing I never dreamt of seeing tearful
the Trojans at our ships! in old days those | behaved exactly like cowardly does
that trot through the woods in their weak aimless | ways just cannon-fodder for pantheress
jackals and wolves no fight in them at all | that's how used to behave the Trojans all
taking care never for a moment to | stand up to us and to meet us hand-to
-hand now they've left their city far behind | indeed come fighting all around behind
the fast ships all through the incompetence | of our Commander-in-Chief slackness hence
of the troops who're so sick of their leader | that than fight to save the ships they would rather
die by them yet even if the whole blame | does lie with our overlord to his shame
Agamemnon son of Atreus who | insulted Achilles we have no new
excuse whatsoever for giving up | the struggle but brave men can always up
their game let's be quick to repair our faults | it is not pretty to see your default's
cowardice sirs deemed some of best soldiers | whole force be slacking selves so sold err thus
could forgive some feeble wretch throwing up | the game but you're not such a way made up
and so with you I quarrel heartily | my friends such a lack of activity
in you is half-way to a far worse thing | does it not occur to each man thinking
the shame and obloquy that his conduct | may bring him in a crisis he has ducked
when great Hector has broken down the gate | and the long bar and his war-cry of late
is sounding by the very ships?" with these | stirring words rallied the Argives with ease
so effectively that they lined up on | sides two Aiantes such strong formation
as would have given pause to very War | -god himself or Athene the Marshaller
of the Host and there stood the very pick | of their best men awaiting the oil slick
Hector the Trojans impenetrable | huge hedge of spears and sloping shields buckle
-r to buckler helm to helm man to man | so close the ranks then that when as a man
they moved their heads the bright glittering peaks | of their plumed helmets met their cheeks to cheeks
overlapping as they swung them forward | in their sturdy hands they maintained a hard
-y look to their front eager for the Clash | now the Trojans came on in a great mass
with Hector in the van sweeping forward | bolder boulder down rocky sloping sward
when a river swollen by winter rain | has washed away its supports once in train
and then the misbegotten thing sweeping | over brow of hill high in air leaping
and hurtles down through the echoing wood | and runs on unchecked until it is stood
on level ground having stopped its rolling | much against its will thus Hector trolling
threats makes for a while reach the sea with ease | through the Argive huts and ships as you please
killing as he went but when ran into | that solid block he stopped short hard put to
go on and the Achaeans facing him | swords double-pointed spears lunged at him grim
thrust him off he was shaken and fell back | but in a loud voice to his men called back
"Stand by me now Trojans and Lycians | and you hand-to-hand men Dardanians
the Achaeans won't hold me up for long | packed together though they are in a throng
like stones in a wall they will give before | my spear if true I was brought here for sure
by the best of all gods the Thunderer | and Lord of Here" his call the inspirer
rousing everyman in the company | and his brother Deiphobus manly
strode out among them with high heart swinging | his rounded shield to the front as winging

airily forward advancing under | its cover Meriones soft thunder
glittering lance let fly at him no miss | as struck rounded oxhide shield with hiss kiss
save that the long shaft far from passing through | broke off at the socket the shield held true
by Deiphobus at arm's length having | good reason fear piercing lancing having
from the doughty Meriones so that | nobleman took cover once more back sat
with the friends behind him he was angry | at missing a win and lance gone dangly
and so off he went at once to the camp | ships fetch long spear and so once more up ramp
from his hut but the rest fought on tumult | of battle filled the air Teucer of cult
Telamon was the first to kill his man | then who was Imbrius the great spearman
son of horse-fancier Mentor liv-ed | at Pedaeum before the venture livid
Achaean had arrived and he was wed | to Medisicaste out of wedlock si-red
by Priam but when did Danaans come | in their rolling ships went to Ilium
and won there a place of honour for him | -self among Trojans live with Priam trim
treated like one of his many children | Teucer below the ear hit this man then
with a long lance which he had just pulled out | Imbrius fell out with a mighty clout
like an ash that has stood as a landmark | on a high hilltop 'til axe makes its mark
and brings it down where it then sweeps the ground | with its delicate leaves that all around
abound thus Imbrius fell his ornate | bronze equipment rang upon him the late
Teucer ran up eager to strip armour | as he did so Hector with a glitter
of spear let fly but Teucer was looking | out and by just a hair's breath brooking
no contact and thereupon went on struck | Amphimacus son Cteatus Ac
-tor House in the breast as he rushed into | the fray and he fell with a thud onto
the earth and his armour rang about him | as Hector dashed in to tear tight helm trim
from his temples Aias then aimed at him | with shining spear but no part of him grim
was exposed he was completely hidden | by a gaunt daunting sheath of bronze brazen
all Aias hit was the boss of his shield | yet of such force the blow he had to yield
ground leave the two dead men to be relayed | by the Argives Antimachus arrayed
within their lines by Stichius and Prince | Menestheus captains Athenians
while the two Aiantes all the hazards | disdaining possessed themselves of the shards
of Imbrius's corpse like a couple | of lions who've snatched away a supple
goat from under the noses of goatherd's | snarling dogs and lift it clear of the herd's
ground as they carry it off in their jaws | through undergrowth helmed Aiantes' claws
held Imbrius aloft stripped him of arms | but death Antimachus alarms disarms
so son of Oileus in his fury | hacked Imbrius' head from neck furry
and with a swing hurling sent it whirling | through crowd in dust Hector's feet dropped twirling
but when Poseidon saw his grandson killed | in this encounter with bitter bile filled
went along by huts ships of Achaeans | stir 'em up brew trouble for the Trojans
he met Idomeneus the famous | spearman with member Idomeneus
of his own company had been who'd just | come out of the fight with a spear-wound thrust
in the ham man had been carried in then | by his brothers-in-arms and Idomen
-eus after instructing the surgeons | was off to his hut with all intentions
of returning to fight when the Royal | Earthshaker stopped him and taking the style

of voice of Thoas son of Andraemon | who was the great king of all of Pleuron
and mountainous Calydon and worshipped | all Aetolians rule well equipped
"Idomeneus Chief of the Cretans | what's become of the threats we Achaeans
were always making against the Trojans?" | "Thoas" answered the King of the Cretans
"from what I see no individual | to blame we are veterans all equal
no-one is unmanned by fear or has run | away from this terrifying action
in panic I can only think it must | be the will of Cronos' son that doest
damn the Argives to end inglorious | this remote spot far from the Argos truss
but you have always been a man steady | putting heart into folk good and ready
you see them breaking down don't slacken now | put the men on their mettle and how!"
"Idomeneus" replied Poseidon | the Earthshaker World Girdler "may the one
who does not fight his best today never | come home from Troy but stay here forever
to delight the dogs! come now take your arms | follow me we must put our backs no qualms
into this business together if we | are to be of any use even see
poorest fighters turn into brave men then | when they stand side by side and we've taken
our place in battle by the very best | always" the god returned to join the rest
in the tumult and Idomeneus | made way to well-built hut put on his plus
fours splendid armour seized a pair of spears | then came out looking like as when appears
the Son of Cronos with lightning in hand | when he has a message mankind to hand
discharges from the glittering summit | Olympus flash in distant sky plummet
so bronze flashed on his breast as he ran then | however he'd hardly left his hut when
met by Meriones his noble squire | come fetch himself member of bronze spear choir
"My dearest comrade-in-arms brother's son! | Idomeneus exclaimed "Meirion
-es of the nimble feet! why have you left | the battlefield? are you by wound bereft?
worn out by the pain from an arrow-head | perhap? or a message for me as head
of the company? I assure you *I* | have not the least desire to sit in my
hut but am very eager for the fight" | "My lord and commander" replied aright
Meriones who understood him well | "I've come for a spear hoping find one fell
in your hut as the one I had did yield | when hit that prat Deiphobus' shield"
"If it's a spear you want" said chief Cretan | you'll find twenty not only one meet an
example leaning against burnished wall | entrance to my hut Trojan spears from all
men I kill I don't believe in fighting | enemy any distant site sighting
hence my collection of spears and bossed shields | helms glittering cuirasses also fields"
"I too" Meriones quick to reply | "in hut Trojan weapons piled plenty high
and in my black ship also but not where | I can source them at once from over there
away yonder moreover I do not | consider myself to have failed to spot
and carry out my duty any more | than you and so in field of honour sure
I take my place in the front whenever | battle is joined and I would moreover
have expected any other soldiers | bronze-clad Argives to be blind to powers
prowess of my arms rather than you who | have seen it for yourself" "No need for you"
said Idomeneus "to dwell on that | I know well your mettle and just how that
would be proved true if any nobleman | were being detailed by the ships for an

ambuscade there's nothing like an ambush | for bringing one's worth from behind a bush
and picking out the brave from the coward | changes colour all the time does coward
cannot sit still for nervousness but squats | first on one heel then on the other twot's
heart's thumping in breast as he thinks of death | in all its forms teeth chattering last breath
one can hear but brave love never changes | colour at all and mood not far ranges
from the moment when he takes his seat in | ambush with the rest puts his prayer in
for to come to grips with the enemy | as quickly as may be and nobody
on such an occasion would think lightly | of your bold strength even if in any
event you were hit by arrow or spear | it would not be behind on back of ear
or neck that the weapon would fall would strike | in front as you rushed forward like the shrike
keep your tryst with the others in the van | but must not stay here natter like old man
or folk may be scandalised go into | my hut and get a heavy spear" now too
Meriones bold as god of battles | snatches up a bronze spear and off rattles
after Idomeneus with high heart | bent on war the two were like the Death Fart
Ares and his son indomitable | and fierce Panic-maker no man able
to withstand even staunchest warrior | turns tail when those two as hen harrier
march flying from Thrace join Ephyri | or the Phrygians to bring victory
to one side turn deaf ear prayers others thus | Meriones and Idomeneus
leaders of men set out for the battle | thus in their resplendent bronze "Just what'll
be the point" said Meriones " where you | enter the fray? in the centre or to
our right wing or on the left? it is there | I imagine the point of defence where
the Achaeans are most likely to break" | the chief replied "There are others to take
care of the ships in the centre the two | Aiantes are there so is Teucer too
the best bowman we have and a good man | in a scrimmage as well they'll give that man
Hector right bellyful fighting mindful | formidable though he s finding it full
hard for all his rage to break the spirit | of those men and wear down to the limit
their indomitable strength as he must | before he can turn the good ships to dust
unless the Son of Cronos helps and throws | a burning brand among them and he knows
Telamonian Aias will never | yield to one who eats the bread ever
Mother Earth can be cut by bronze brought down | by a rock and he'd not even stand down
to Achilles breaker of the battle | -line at least not in a standing struggle
though nobody can run like Achilles | let's see on the left wing what the will-i(e)s
we'll soon find out if we're going to win | glory from some other man or he win
it from us" eager as the War-god | Meriones led given the nod
by his chief and they reached the front and when | the Trojans saw Idomeneus then
fierce as a flame and his squire with him too | in their decorated arms they called to
each other across the ranks and attacked | in a body fight became general stacked
by the sterns of the ships their battalions | were rolled up together could see no joins
just as the dust when lies thick in roadways | on stormy day caught by blustery plays
of wind rolled into a great solid cloud | in that chaotic mass much like a shroud
the one main aim of each man was to stab | his neighbour the field bristled with long slab
-cutting spears and the eye was dazzled by | the glint of bronze from great assembly nigh

of so many shimmering helms burnished | cuirasses and resplendent shields furnished
spectacle enjoy not been so moved then | none but the most insensible of men
and thus the two mighty Sons of Cronos | taking different sides brought such chaos
and much tribulation to men-at-arms | Zeus had in mind a win for Trojan arms
and Hector with a view to exalting | Achilles nimble feet still defaulting
yet not for that the Argive army be destroyed | utterly before Ilium so buoyed
Thetis and her strong-willed son Poseidon | on the other hand had come stealthy on
up out of the grey surf join the Argives | inspire them distressed him to see their lives
lost to the Trojans furious with Zeus | yet descent parentage the same though Zeus
the older and wiser for which reason | Poseidon careful not to give open
help to the Argives took form of a man | in that disguise spurring on troops to a man
kept moving to and fro on the go thus | the gods saw to it rope did evil truss
for this desperate even tug-of-war | thus tautened either way in this jaw-jaw
the rope was unbreakable and no-one | could undo the knot but many a one
it undid but Idomeneus though | no longer a young man threw himself so
into the fight with a shout to his troops | and struck panic into the oppo groups
by killing Othryoneus ally | who'd joined Trojans from Cabesus drawn by
news of the war a newcomer to Troy | who had asked Priam the hand to deploy
Cassandra most beautiful of daughters | instead of paying for promised slaughters
marvellous drive the Argive from his shores | the old king welcoming these offered chores
pledged daughter's hand on this understanding | he be part of the fighting grand-standing
but Idomeneus glittering spear | cast caught him as along did swagger near
bronze cuirass he was wearing served him ill | as the spear-point landed in the middle
of his belly fell to earth with a crash | Cretan mocked him in a flash like a rash
"Othryoneus I congratulate | you on betrothal Priam's daughter('s) mate
subject of course to your part of the deal | being now duly fulfilled and made real
could WE do business some similar sum? | if you'll help sack citadel Ilium
we'll send over to Argos for daughter | loveliest of Atreides halter
and make her your bride step this way with me | to our ships that go off to sea where we
can now come to terms about your wedding | you'll find our bride price not too forb(i/e)dding"
taunting him so lord Idomeneus | seized him by foot began drag Asius
though through crowd to the rescue did rush | on foot in front of chariot did push
and the driver kept it so close to him | that his shoulders were all the time a-skim
with horses' breath Asius did utmost | to despatch Idomeneus but host
too quick for him he hit him with a spear | throat under chin near oh dear so clear shear
deep point went right in through Asius fell | like oak poplar or towering pine fell
woodmen in the mounts with whetted axes | to make timber for a ship task tax(i/e)s
lie stretched before chariot horses doest | groaning and clutching at the blood-stained dust
driver losing such wits as he possessed | with panic and chaos was so obsessed
did not even have the presence of mind | to turn the whole carboodle around find
way to slip out of the enemy's hands | but spear cool-headed Antilochus lands
in his middle bronze corslet no avail | belly up middle for diddle failed sail

with a gasp fell headlong from well-built car | Antilochus son noble Nestor far
then drove his horses out of the Trojan | line-up and into the one Achaean
Deiphobus distressed death Asius | then came up close to Idomeneus
launched a shining lance Idomeneus | though looking out avoided onrush fuss
by sheltering behind the shield rounded | always carried concentric rings bounded
of oxhide and also glittering bronze | fitted with a couple of crossbars fronds
as crouched under cover of this bronze spear | flew over him drew deep note as it sheer
grazed edge of the shield but it had not flown | for nothing from Deiphobus' own
sturdy arm because it struck a chieftain | Hypsenor of Hippasus was a son
in the liver just under the midriff | and this bitter blow brought him down forthwith
Deiphobus elated by triumph | cried "Asius without revenge triumph
does not lie! even on way to Hades | Warden of the Gate I feel his shade he's
to travel with a light heart now that I've | given him an escort" army Argive
heard the jubilation with disgust plus | none with such loathing as Antilochus
the doughty who did not forget his friend | in his sorrow but ran now to defend
his body bestride covered with his shield | then two of their trusty men in the field
Mecisteus the son of Echius | and the worthy Alastor the corpus
lifted from the ground groaning heavily | carried it off to the ships by the sea
but no pausing for Idomeneus | in the high fury that possessed him thus
his one desire was to bring down black night | on a Trojan's eyes or go down in fight
to save the Achaeans from destruction | next victim the noble Alcathous son
royal Aesyetes son-in-law a | Anchises whose Hippodameia
eldest daughter was his wife this lady | as a girl in his palace had been she
darling of father and gentle mother | moreover there was indeed no other
woman of her age with such beauty skill | brains small wonder best man in broad realm still
of Troy had married her man who now fell | to Idomeneus albeit well
helped by Poseidon for the god cast spell | on Alcathous' bright eyes so befell
on his legs a slumber so could neither | leap aside or escape to rear either
he was standing still as a monument | or a tall tree with leaves as ornament
crowned when Idomeneus' great spear | hit him struck full in the chest pierced through clear
coat of bronze he was wearing hitherto | had saved his flesh from harm but sharp anew
now rang out as the spear rent it he fell | with a crash and the spear was fixed fell well
into his heart which had not stopped beating | yet to the very butt still tweeting
'til the god of battle stilled it with his | heavy hand Idomeneus in his
triumph called aloud "Deiphobus three | killed for the one you so bragged of so we
may call quits but why don't you tackle me | yourself my friend and learn the quality
one of Zeus' stock who's ravishing | your land as it was Zeus establishing
our line made his son Minos the Cretan | King his son the peerless Deucalion
and I Deucalion's succeeded him | King of a great people in our trim prim
spacious isle now my ships have brought me here | be a curse to you your father sow fear
in everyone in Troy" this challenge left | Deiphobus in two minds hope bereft
fall back and call on one of his gallant | compatriots support so important

or see what could do alone deciding | better get help as onto a hiding
sought Aeneas found him standing idle | back of crowd always bore vital viral
ill will against Priam as he made so | little of him as good as any though
Deiphobus went up to him appealed | as one of leading men in Trojan field
"Aeneas you are badly needed for | the rescue now of your brother-in-law
Alcathous if you care at all about | your family come and help me bring out
your sister's husband who lived in your house | cared for you as a child in his own house
has just fallen to the spear of the great | Idomeneus" his heart stirred with hate
made straight for Idomeneus in mood | ugly but Idomeneus not shooed
off like a little boy waited for him | with self-reliance was full to the brim
like a mountain boar when caught by a crowd | of huntsmen in some lonely spot not cowed
as he faces the hue and cry's gristling | with eyes all aflame and his back bristling
his tusks whetting in eagerness take on | all comers hound man renowned spearman one
Idomeneus thus waited earth-bound | Aeneas' onslaught and gave no ground
at all but did call for support looking | first Ascalaphus but sought booking
Aphareus also Deipyrus | with Meriones and Antilochus
to these tried men he made urgent appeal | "My friends" he cried "come to my help I feel
very alone and am dreading attack | by the swift Aeneas now on my track
as I know him for a killer mighty | in a fight and has advantage flighty
youth and if our ages were matched now as | our mood soon be a win for Aeneas
or myself" with one accord they all closed | in and around Idomeneus posed
crouching behind sloped shields but Aeneas | his side called too on friends and allies as
looking to Paris and Deiphobus | the excellent Agenor his pro-plus
fellow leaders in the Trojan army | who moreover backed him to hilt very
sheep follow keep close behind bellwether | go to drink at a stream from the pasture
and Aeneas was as happy o'ersee | main body behind as shepherd to see
his sheep volleys long javelins exchange | over the site of the corpse at close range
of Alcathous the bronze rang grimly on | their breasts as all across the throng cast on
but there were two warriors Aeneas | and Idomeneus of Ares peers
who surpassed all the rest in their keenness | tear their flesh with finesses of remorseless
bronze Aeneas at Idomeneus | cast but looking out Idomeneus
dodged his bronze spear which flew by and quivered | in the ground from his strong hand delivered
nothing then Idomeneus replied | full into belly Oenomaus spear plied
breaking the plate of his corslet through which | javelin-point let his bowels rich out-pitch ditch
Oenomaus fell down in the dust clutched | at the ground and Idomeneus crutched
his long-shadowed spear out of the body | but overwhelmed by missiles as was he
unable strip splendid arms and armour | from the man's shoulders he was no longer
nimble enough to put on a fast spurt | following up his own cast or to skirt
someone else's and being too slow to | save his life by running made practice to
fight where he stood and so keep death at bay | however now as moved slowly away
Deiphobus who was still nettled by | his taunts a shining spear at him let fly
for second time missed Idomeneus | hit a son of Ares Ascalaphus

the heavy weapon went right through shoulder | fell in dust another clutcher-boulder
on the ground and it was only later | Ares of the Brazen Voice great Father
heard that his son had fallen in action | at the moment was sitting high up on
Olympus under the golden clouds where | was held by writ of Zeus together there
with the rest of the immortal gods for | whom it was out of bounds the Trojan war
now over Ascalaphus fought forlorn | hand-to-hand Deiphobus had just torn
off the glittering helmet from dead head | when Meriones swift as War-godhead
leapt in and struck his arm near the shoulder | with a spear the helm with heavy visor
dropped from his hand and rang loud on the ground | Meriones swooped back in with a bound
like a vulture hopping up to its prey | withdrew spear and retreated from the fray
then taking cover with his friends again | Polites brother Deiphobus then
putting his arm round his waist supported | him out of the turmoil and transported
him to his fast horses who selves plighting | in a quiet spot behind the fighting
with their driver and his well-painted car | carried him off to the city afar
worn out with pain and heavily groaning | for blood from the fresh wound in arm foaming
the rest fought on tumult intensified | Aeneas now with spear incentifised
struck Aphareus son of Caletor | on the throat by fate just happened therefore
be turned towards him and the man's head lolled | one side under shield helm crumpled did fold
soul-devouring Death did him engulf then | meanwhile Antilochus seized time gulf when
Thoon's back turned his way leapt in not in vain | quickly and struck and cut clean through the vein
that runs right up through the back to the neck | Thoon dropped backwards in the dust a wreck
stretching his hands out to brothers-in-arms | Antilochus fell upon him strip arms
and armour but keeping a wary eye | Trojans coming up on all sides pricked high
and wide glittering shield but could not get | behind or even scratch smooth-skinned neck yet
of his with their cruel bronze for Nestor's son | protected by Earthshaker Poseidon
even in such hail of darts as this one | unable shake off foes faced them on one
side now another spear was never still | for a moment but followed his thoughts still
swinging round in his hand as he effaced | a distant enemy or then menaced
to lunge at a one near just preparing | cast into crowd where in hope wayfaring
for a chance Adamas son Asius | leapt in struck centre of his shield A-plus
with spear but Poseidon of Sable Locks | did grudge it then the life of Antilocks
caused it to miscarry result that half | stuck in shield like a charred stake other half
fell to ground Adamas to save self tried | back among his men tired he now retired
but Meriones followed as withdrew | caught him with a javelin that he threw
half-way between navel and private parts | for a wretched soldier receiving darts
the most painful spot to be hit weapon | went home there to have dire straits effect on
Adamas collapsing writhed around it | as a bull twists when herdsmen have caught it
roped up in hills bring in against its will | so stricken man writhed but not long just 'til
the lord Meriones came up pulled spear | out of his flesh and so night did appear
now to his eyes and then Helenus closed | with Deipyrus struck temple exposed
with big Thracian sword shearing off his helm | it fell to the ground and the dislodged helm
picked up by an Achaean as it rolled | among the fighters' feet then of Death scrolled

out the unlovely night on the eyes of | Deipyrus then Menelaus of
the loud war-cry son Atreus grieved when | he witnessed this and made for Prince Helen
-us with a menacing shout brandishing | a sharp spear Prince replied by furnishing
burnished bow so two ready to let fly | at the same moment one with sharp spear try
the other with an arrow from his string | Helenus son of Priam then did sting
Menelaus on the breast keen dart ping | -ing striking plate corslet rebounding
as the black beans or chickpeas on a broad | threshing-floor leap from the shovel's broad board
and with whistling wind and winnower's force | behind them the deadly arrow perforce
bounced sped off from corslet illustrious | Menelaus a son of Atreus
though Menelaus of loud war-cry st(r)and | did better struck Helenus on the hand
in which was holding his polished bow | bronze spear clean through hand into bow a blow
Helenus in fear for his life fell back | among friends with his hand hanging down back
by side dragging the ashen spear along | the spear withdrawn from the wound before long
by the noble Agenor who bound up | the hand with a bandage of fine spun-up
wool it was really a sling Agenor's | squire was able to lend him Peisander's
now made a bee-line for illustrious | Menelaus 'twas an evil Fate thus
led him down this plath with death at the end | death Menelaus to them you would send
the two men closed Atreides began | with a miss his spear errant but Peisan
-der better he struck shield illustrious | Manos yet without sufficient force thus
to drive the bronze point right through the broad shield | held it up spear at the socket did yield
snapped yet Peisander well pleased confident | of victory but Atreides went
on the charge with his sword silver-studded | then Peisander from under his shield did
bring out a fine bronze axe with long smooth haft | of olive wood at close quarters craft laughed
Peisander struck the cone of other's helm | on top just below the horsehair plume realm
yet Menelaus now caught Peisander | as he came on the forehead just under
the eye socket the bones cracked and his eyes | all bloody drop at his feet in the dust sighs
reels and falls fell Menelaus put boot | in on chest and as stripped him of his loot
triumphed over him "The nearest you'll come | to the black ships of the horse-and-homesome
-loving Danaans insolent Trojans | always spoiling for blood of Achaeans
and more again not that there aren't other | forms of infamy along with other
vices you dabble in witness the shame | you caused me you curs curse you when the name
and laws of hospitality you broke | wrath of Zeus the Thunderer did invoke
he who made them and before long going | to bring your mighty city bedoinging
you stole my wife when she was your hostess | gaily sailed away to my great distress
with her and half my wealth and now you will | not be satisfied 'til our well-travel
-ed ships go up in flames and have slaughtered us | and yet for all your fury unrighteous
you shall be stopped ah Father Zeus they say | you're wiser than any man or god nay!
all this is your work! why so indulgent | Troy bullies for destruction effulgent
such a passion and who enjoy the din | pitched battle so much continue their sin
forever? people tire of everything | sleep love sweet music dancing very thing
even perfect gig things take far longer | than battle to make one cry 'No longer!'
but these Trojans are not your normal son | each one of them is for war a glutton"

as he spoke the peerless Menelaus | stripped the blood-stained armour many layers
from the corpse and handed it to his men | he went off and took his place again then
in the front line no sooner was he there | than attacked by Harpalion the fair
son of King Pylaemenes who had come | with his father to fight for Ilium
not to return to own country this one | closing now with Manos Harpalion
struck the centre of his shield with a spear | not enough force drive through mask-shielding gear
he thought he'd save himself by slinking back | into his company minding his back
looking around for dart coming his way | Meriones while he was on his way
back shot at him a bronze-headed arrow | hit him in the right buttock the arrow
went clean through his bladder came out below | bone Harpalion collapsed forthwith so
gasped out his life in the arms of his friends | lay stretched out on the ground like a worm ends
the dark blood poured out of him soaked the earth | the Paphlagonians of gallant worth
gathered round lifted him into a car | and with heavy hearts then drove him afar
to holy Ilium weeping father | went with them leaving his son's death rather
unavenged but Harpalion's slaughter | roused Paris up all into a lather
this Paphlagonian had been his guest | shot an arrow avenge friend and late guest
there was an Achaean called Euchenor | son of Polyidus a soothsayer
man of substance and good birth inhabited | Corinth and when for Troy he departed
knew well enough the melancholy end | awaited father'd oft foretold that end
he die in bed of a painful illness | or killed Troy in Achaean distress mess
so went saving his wealth from fine heavy | that upon him they would have made levy
and himself from a loathsome malady | and the pain that he did not wish to see
or bear now Paris with an arrow struck | under the jaw and ear by luck not stuck
with a lingering death quickly engulfed | unlovely darkness both sides battle wolfed
down went fire-fight inextinguishable | but Prince Hector who had not been able
to be kept informed had no idea | on the left of the ships the enemy
wreaking such destruction among his men | indeed 'twas near upper hand Argive then
to such effect did Earthshaker Girdler | of World inspire them besides supporter
of them exerting his own strength Hector | thus that part of front still the attacker
he'd broken the shield-bearing Danaan | companies stormed gate and wall Achaean
where Aias and Protesilaus' ships | were drawn up on the sea shore there the chips
were down as the protecting wall had been | lower than any other place had seen
the Danaan infantry and their cars | putting up fiercest defence all wall bars
at this point Boeotians Ionians | with their long tunics splendid Epeans
Locrians Phthians had the utmost | difficulty in holding Hector's most
ardent assault on the ships unable | quite to thrust him back like immutable
fire he came at them from Athens picked men | holding the defence there then led by Men
-estheus son Peteos backed by three | Pheides with Stichius and the hardy
Bias the Epeans commanded by | Amphion Dracius Meges son Phy
-leus and the Phthians by Medon | and by the staunch Podarces now Medon
was a bastard son of King Oileus | a brother of Aias the Runner thus
but he had been exiled for homicide | having killed a kinsman step-mother's side

Eriopis the wife of Oileus | and Podarces a son of Iphiclus
the son of Phylacus these two in their | full armour fought to defend the ships there
in van of the great-hearted Phthians | and side-by-side with the brave Boeotians
Aias the Runner son of Oileus | was never separated from Aias
Telamon's son for a moment even | made one think of a pair of dun oxen
at the ploughshare in fallow ground straining | each still struggled as hard after training
at the base of their horns outpouring sweat | only the polished yoke kept separate
press on down the furrow 'til brought up by | the ridge at the end of the field stuck by
each other these two and cheek-by-jowl stood | but there was this difference understood
between them Telamon's son was backed by | retainers in strong well-trained body nigh
always ready relieve him of his shield | when done in by heat or fatigue in field
whereas of Oileus the gallant son | not accompanied by host Locrian
of his no stomach for hand-to-hand fight | as the usual arms they put to flight
plumed bronze helmet rounded shield ashen spears | put trust in bow so create archer fears
and of the sling fine-spun wool these weapons | followed their chief with to Troy's bastions
and there were indeed several occasions | a Trojan company cut to ribbons
by their volleys while heavy-armed Achaeans | in the front line then engaged the Trojans
and the bronze-clad Hector the Locrians | kept firing from safe rear 'til the Trojans
thrown into confusion by the arrows | began to find relish for fight narrows
in fact they might have had to leave the ships | and huts cash in their discomforted chips
retreat to windy Ilium save for | Polydamas formidable Hector
went to once more "Hector you're still one then | obstinate man on advice though Heaven
has made you a magnificent fighter | still like to think a know-better blighter
than anyone in how plan a fight too | however you cannot possibly do
everything by yourself people differ | in their gifts one man can fight another
dance or play the lute and sing another | yet is endowed by Zeus the all-seer
with a good brain oft to the advantage | of friends who betimes are saved from carnage
because HE knows far better than they do | however I will speak my mind to you
and say what I think best the fighting's spread | all round you in a ring our men instead
stormed wall gallantly but having done so | standing idle under arms or are so
scattered among the ships they risk being | overwhelmed as bad odds they now seeing
I suggest you break away and call on | all your best men and have a discussion
to settle the whole question whether to | fall on the well-found ships so hoping to
secure a decisive victory or | failing that fully intact to withdraw
I for one afraid that the Argives grave | aim to make us pay for what we them gave
yesterday they've a man lying idle | at the ships who's a glutton for battle
and I can not believe he will keep out | of the whole fighting" Hector had no doubt
about this advice and so answers as | sure without pause "Stay here Polydamas
and keep all the best men round you while I | go face the situation yonder I
will soon be back when I've set our folk there | to rights" with that he sped away from there
glittering like a snow-capped peak and as | passed swiftly through Trojan ranks as well as
those of their allies shouted to his men | and from their stations they all ran up when

heard his voice massed round Panthous' son | amiable Polydamas but on
went Hector a-questing down the front line | see if of Deiphobus could find sign
anywhere and stalwart Prince Helenus | Adamas son Asius Asius
himself the son of Hyrtacus he soon | to learn that not a one still shared the boon
of being now both alive and unhurt | two fallen lay dead by yurt ships' skirts curt
-ailed while others lay back within Troy's wall | at both long or short range were wounded all
but he did find one man quickly enough | on left bank flank where they had had it tough
the noble Paris husband of Helen | of the lovely hair urging on his men
driving them into battle when Hector | came up to him roundly gave him what for
"Paris you pretty boy you woman-struck | seducer I ask you now where you the fuck
are Deiphobus great Prince Helenus | Adamas son Asius Asius
son of Hyrtacus? and what have you done | with Othryoneus? Ilium's done
its topmost towers down so no gaming | for you now save death" "Hector you're blaming
an innocent man in your rage if I | have ever shrunk from the battle-call I
have not done so today for I too can claim | I was not born to see the utter shame
of the name of coward from the moment | when you decreed that our men should be sent
to attack by the ships we've held our ground | here engaged the Danaans in the round
the friends you ask about have died of late | save Deiphobus Prince Helenus great
who've withdrawn each wounded by a long spear | in the arm but had the luck to get clear
lead us now wherever you wish we shall | follow with a will and I say no shall
-ow courage either so far in us lies | yet man can't fight beyond his power size
however keen" thus Paris pacified | his brother and they went off side by side
into the very heart of the battle | raging there at full throttle death rattle
round Cebriones the admirable | Polydamas Phalces the most able
Polyphetes Orthaeus and Palmys | the sons of Hippotion Kelly Morris
and Ascanius who'd arrived from deep | -soiled Ascania role relief trench keep
the previous morning now felt impelled | to join in the Trojans as if propelled
like an angry squall that swoops down from a | thunder-laden sky strike salt-water bay
bringing an indescribable turmoil | to the moaning sea where great waves toil roil
and hiss and arch their foaming backs in a | never-ending procession of slaughter
came on behind Somme officers rank on | serried rank glittering with bronze the son
of Priam Hector as murderous War-god | in their van before held rounded shield-hod
with its close layers of hide and ample | sheath of beaten bronze and on each temple
his burnished helmet swayed time and again | dashed up probed enemy line for a gain
at various points in hope that before | him would break as charged under cover sure
shield but shook not Argive resolution | one Aias stepped out into the open
with great strides and challenged him "Hey you there | come closer now give up this futile fare
trying to make the Argives run away | for we do know something about the way
of war and if we did take a thrashing | it was Zeus in wicked scourge mode trashing
who gave it us I guess you imagine | going to destroy our shipping line in
a trice? but we too have deck hands ready | to fight for them and long before likely
you get the ships to capture your fine town | and sack it as for you this I lay down

the time is drawing nigh when in your haste | to save yourself yourself you will abase
before Father Zeus and the other gods | praying then that they will give you good odds
on making your long-maned horses faster | than falcons as they gallop with master
back home to Ilium in clouds of dust" | a lucky omen in eagle form just
then flying high on the right enlightened | these words and the troops Argive were heartened
by the sight shouted for joy but Hector | illustrious would not be silenced for
a moment "Arrant nonsense Aias what | one expects from a clodhopper and clot
but you surpass yourself of one thing I | am sure just as sure as I am that I
should love to spend my days as son aegis | -bearing Zeus the Lady Here and with this
the honours of Athene and Apollo | and THAT is that this day shall be no show
for the whole Argive force and you will die | with the rest if dare try deny reply
to my long spear which is going to tear | your lily-white skin yes you shall fall there
by your own ships your flesh and fat shall but | the Trojan dogs and the birds of prey glut"
with that Hector led a charge and his men | came after with roar fit deafen Heaven
while the whole force behind took up the cry | the Argives answered with their own war-cry
and summoning up their courage awaited | the onslaught of the Trojans' best fated
clamour from hosts upper air revolted | and the very lamp of day assaulted

■ δεκατέσσαρες ■

*Book 14*

# ZEUS OUTMANOEUVRED

*of how Zeus beguiled by Sleep and Hera*
*into slumber on the heights of Ida*
*Poseidon spurred Argives resist Hector*
*and then of how was wounded said Hector*

the din was so great it reached Nestor's ears | in his hut near drinking away his fears
turned in alarm to son Asclepius | "My lord Machaon now the two of us
must consider what to do battle sounds | are growing louder by the ships but zounds!
sit here for now and drink your sparkling wine | while the lady Hecamede takes some time
to heat water and wash the clotted blood | from your wound I'll go quickly to some good
place where I can get a view discover | how things now are" and as spoke did uncover
picked up a well-made shield of gleaming bronze | that was lying in the hut and belongs
to his son Thrasymedes horse-tamer | as he using the shield of his father
took a strong spear with a sharp point of bronze | and no sooner steps out of hut than one's
gaze falls on a lamentable sight | for his Argive comrades were in full flight
the insolent Trojans close on their heels | so Argive wall finally reels heels keels
there are times when the great sea is darkened | by soundless swell as to call it's hearkened
so felt the gale on the way but that's all | it knows and the waves can't begin to fall
this way or that until the wind sets in | steadily from one side or other in
such a way then the old man now faltered | between two courses his mind was altered
from whether he should join the horse-taming | Danaans in the fight or go aiming
Agamemnon son Atreus find his | Commander-in-Chief in end concludes his
best move to go to Agamemnon | meanwhile the fighting and slaughter went on
and the hard bronze rang out on men's bodies | as met thrust swords double-pointed spear-bodies
on way fell in with the royal lords these | who had been wounded there Diomedes
and son of Atreus Agamemnon | Odysseus too as they were coming on
up from their ships stationed on shore of grey | sea a long way from the great furore
being the first row that had been drawn up | on land whereas the wall had been built up
along those that were farthest from the sea | because the beach itself wide though it be
had been unable to hold all the ships | and the Argives had drawn them up in strips

layered along whole seaboard of long bay | from headland to headland so that they may
get a view of the fight kings making way | inland together use spears in stave way
and in a sorry frame of mind when there | encountered then the old man Nestor their
hearts sank King Agamemnon did question | him straight away "Flower of Achaean
chivalry son of Neleus Nestor | what have you abandoned the carnage for
and come down here? for I fear that Hector | the redoubtable's going to do for
us as he said he would one day when he | was speaking to his men and swore that he
would never fall back from the ships to Troy | before in flames for good could them desTroy
slaughter us as well that was the promise | he made them and all that he said now this
coming true I've the unhappy feeling | that the whole Argive army is reeling
to disloyalty me like Achilles | if they now refuse and disobey these
orders to make a stand at the outer | limits ships" Nestor "Some such disaster"
Gerenian Knight said "is upon us | for certain and not even Zeus for us
himself could avert such a great defeat | because we thought that the wall for the fleet
and us was an impregnable defence | however that has now fallen and hence
our men are bound to a desperate fight | beside the ships look as hard as you might
you can't tell whether the Achaeans are | being harried from front or rear afar
so confused the slaughter overwhelming | the din maybe by thought overwhelming
if can do some good put heads together | but the one bit of advice I offer
is not to throw ourselves into battle | no wounded man can bear such death rattle"
"Nestor" said Agamemnon King of Men | "since the fighting has now arrived even
at the outer line of ships and neither | what cost us such toil strong wall nor either
the trench has been of any use although | we looked upon them as a defence so
impregnable thus saving fleet and us | I must conclude almighty Zeus with us
displeased so Achaeans should perish here | far from Argos and simply disappear
I had this feeling when he was aiding | Argives with all his heart but degrading
us then I know now when he's exalting | the Trojans to level of the vaulting
gods and us to impotence reducing | you must all do as I say deducing
inducing us drag down ships that were drawn | up by the sea on good water forlorn
launch them moor them well out 'til friendly night | lets us drag down the rest unless the fight
carries on and even then there is naught | to be feeling any shame about aught
run from disaster even by night fraught | better run to save one's skin than be caught"
"My lord" said Odysseus of nimble wits | "you must have lost your wits to nit-wits twits
what fatal leadership! you should have had | command whole posse so cowardly bad
instead of leading people like ourselves | lot from youth to age see struggles us elves
through to their bitter end 'til one by one | we drop so this is how you propose one
bid farewell to broad-streeted Ilium | which we have found such a hard conundrum!
you had better hold your tongue or the men | may get wind this crazy opinion then
which no-one with any sense would have put | into words least of all a king been put
in command of a huge army like yours | you can have no brain in that head of yours
to make such a suggestion to expect | during a full-pitched battle to elect
to drag our ships into the sea and put | the Trojans who have already now put

us to arrow spear sword into even | more exploitative hotspot uneven
enable zap whole expedition then | and do you imagine that all our men
are going to maintain a steady front | while their ships in what looks like an affront
are being dragged down to the sea they'll choose | nothing but look behind them and so lose
all heart for the fight and so that will be | the fatal outcome of your strategy
my Commander-in-Chief" "A harsh rebuke | Odysseus! but deem has the look no fluke
of wisdom very well I won't order | them to drag their ships against their better
judgement into the sea but one of YOU | now must come forward with something brand new
sounder than mine and seniority | doesn't matter I'll be pleased hear any
idea" emboldened Diomedes | of the loud war-cry "The man that one needs
is close at hand we shan't have far to seek | if I convince you and no fit of peak
at my being the youngest among you | and yet I can boast of noble birth too
my father was Tydeus whose bones line | ground under mound in Thebes he of the line
Portheus who had three excellent sons | living in Pleuron and in Caldyon's
hard land Agrius Melas the high | Oeneus the car driver who was my
father's father and the bravest of all | he didn't move from his old home at all
but Zeus and the other gods must have planned | a different life for the way that it panned
out Tydeus migration Argos thus | where he wed a daughter of Adrestus
and settled down in luxury with a | house with some good corn land and many a
private orchard also plenty livestock | and no Achaean of spearman-ship stock
to compare with him but you must have heard | all this and know that I speak a true word
so you can't take exception to any | proposal I put forward but only
if it's a good one on the grounds that I | am a baseborn commoner so what I
now suggest is visit the battlefield | indeed we must even though wounds do field
when there let's not partake in the fighting | keep out of range or may be inviting
a second wound and yet what we CAN do | is press others to fight those I mean who
have had a grievance to nurse and kept out | of it the other chieftains had no shout
against his suggestion so did accept | Agamemnon led and they all forth stepped
none of this had escaped the vigilant | eye of the great Earthshaker vigilant
-'e disguised old man caught them and taking | hold of Agamemnon's right hand talking
to him as one who knew "My lord no doubt | Achilles rejoicing evil redoubt
of heart as sees the Argives put to flight | slaughtered the fool that he is no foresight
or grain of sense well let's hope his folly | will at the end of the day finally
destroy him and Heaven will cast him down | and you my lord don't let it bring you down
because the happy gods are not feeling | just ill will towards you day appealing
coming still on contrary when Trojan | captains chiefs fill whole wide plain with curtain
of dust and you with your own eyes will see | their flight from ships and huts to their city"
when Poseidon had spoken he sped off | across the plain and a great shout let off
as loud as the war-cry of 9,000 | troops joined in strife or even 10,000
and such was the cry that came from the throat | Royal Earthshaker each heart did emote
Argive in the field so greatly lifted | withstand oppos cite site fight sight gifted
now Here of the Golden Throne looking out | from where stood Olympus' top peak far out

quick to spot two things saw how Poseidon | Brother and Brother-in-Law busy on
the field of battle and she rejoiced but | saw also Zeus sitting on topmost butt
-end peak Mount Ida of the many springs | filled ox-eyed Lady with fear and loathings
began wonder how to bemuse the wits | of aegis-bearing Zeus so that the twit's
at her beck and call she would deck herself | out to full advantage visit himself
on the mountain if he succumbed to her | beauty as well might be wished to fold her
in his arms she would benumb his busy | brain close his eyes forgetful dream-easy
sleep accordingly made her way to her | bedroom that had been built for her by her
own Son Hephaestus who'd fitted the stout | doors hung on posts secret lock not without
which not any other of the gods could | open went in closed polished olive wood
doors behind her began by removing | all stains most comely being improving
even ambrosia anoints able | self with delicious imperishable
olive oil of hers perfumed had only | to be stirred within Palace of Bronzey
Floor for its scent to spread throughout heaven | and earth with this rubbed her lovely skin then
she combed her hair with her own hands plaited | her shining locks from her immortal head
let them free-fall in their divine beauty | donned a fragrant robe of delicacy
of material that Athene's skilful | hands had made for her and had lavished full
its embroidery fastened it over | Amazon breast golden-clasped drew over
her waist a girdle from which a hundred | tassles hung pierced lobes ears affix-ed
two earrings each a thing lambent beauty | with a come-hither cluster of drops three
she put on a beautiful new headdress | as bright as mighty sun's white gold red tress
and then last of all the Lady goddess | on her shimmering feet fine pair sandl-ess
bound her toilet perfected left the room | beckoned Aphrodite across room zoom
social distance other gods had a word | with in private "I wonder" double-word
"dear child if you will do me a favour | or refuse as you're annoyed with me for
helping the Danaans while you're on(e)side | Trojan" so Aphrodite did blindside
replied "Here Queen Heaven Daughter of yore | of mighty Cronos tell me what's on your
mind and I'll gladly do what you ask | if I can and not impossible task
the answer of Queen Here's calculated | deceive "Give me Love and Desire" stated
"the powers by which you yourself subdue | mankind and gods alike for I am due
to go to the ends of the fruitful earth | to visit Ocean the forbear by birth
of all the gods and Mother Tethys who | treated me kindly and brought me up too
in their home on taking me from Rhea | when great Zeus made Cronos a prisoner
under the earth and the barren sea I'm | going to visit them as my aim this time
to bring their interminable quarrels | to an end and they have been like devils
for a long time now in the bitterness | of their hearts have called time on the sweetness
sleeping together if by discussing | the matter I could maybe be cussing
them round and induce them once more to sleep | in each other's loving arms I should keep
their affection and esteem forever" | "To refuse a request from you ever
sleeper-Queen in the King of Heaven's | arms would be impossible for heaven's
sake and wrong" replied the laughter-loving | Aphrodite from bosom removing
the girdle curiously embroidered | where all her royal magic resided

Love and Desire the sweet words bewitching | turn wise man into bitching fool (t)witching
"There" handing it to Here "take this girdle | and keep it well stowed in your bosom full"
and as pointed out stitches curious | added "all my power resides here thus
I have no fear that you will then come back | from your mission unsuccessful" smiled back
the ox-eyed Lady Here and as she tucked | it in her bosom smiled again that's fucked
unsuspecting Aphrodite Daughter | of Zeus who went home whereupon Hera
sped down from the summit of Olympus | first she dropped down to the range mountainous
Pierian and Emathia lovely | passed fast over snowy mounts of the free
horse-breeding Thracians highest peaks sweeping | but a foot on the ground never steeping
from Athos travelled over the foaming | sea so came to Lemnos city loam-King
Thoas where she then found the god of Sleep | brother Death took by hand told her need deep
"Sleep Master of all the gods all mankind | if ever past to me listen had mind
do what I ask of you now and I'll feel | grateful to you forever pray so pray seal
the bright eyes Zeus for me in sleep just when | in his ever-loving arms I've lain then
in return I'll give a beautiful chair | imperishable gold will never wear
which the lame god Hephaestus my own son | will make for you as cunning craftsman one
with a footstool underneath on which you | can rest your comely feet when food served you"
sweet Sleep "Here Queen of Heaven and Daughter | of the mighty Cronos a small matter
I should think it to put any of gods | immortal to sleep and even the god's
forbear of them all Ocean Stream himself | but I dare not go near to Zeus himself
the Son of Cronos or send him to sleep | unless asks me himself to send him deep
under I've learnt my lesson from the task | you set me once before bit of an ask
when so arrogant Heracles his son's | sailed from Troy after sacking the Trojans'
town you decided to do some mischief | with my gentle ministrations the chief
aegis-bearing I lulled to sleep while you | raised a tempest on the sea with which you
carried Heracles off to the peopled | isle Cos away from every principled
friend Zeus enraged when he awoke he threw | the gods about in his palace anew
sought me everywhere as chief offender | should have been cast from heaven forever
into the sea never heard of again | if Night who dictates to both gods and men
had not rescued me I found sanctuary | with her and Zeus though for all his fury
had to stop and think twice before doing | something swift Night would be wrong way viewing
and now you come once more with another | impossible request!" "Sleep" said ( m)other
Here "Why do you harp on about this task | and its dangers so small a thing to ask?
can you suppose that all-seeing Zeus will | exert self as much re Trojans' ill
as he did when it was the abduction | that enraged him of his very own son?
come do as I wish and I'll give you one | of the young Graces in marriage that one
shall be called the wife of Sleep" "Very well" | said Sleep who by her offer very well
attracted "by the inviolable | waters of Styx grasping the bountiful
earth with one hand and shimmering sea's sheath | with the other so the gods underNeath
with Cronos may then be our witnesses | swear and promise one of the young Graces
you will give me Pasithee with whom I | have been so deeply in love for all my
life" the white-armed goddess agreed gave him | her oath in the way prescribed verbatim

named all the gods under Tartarus who | are called Titans when duly sworn the two
wrapped themselves in mist and set out leaving | Lemnos and Imbros far behind cleaving
fast they reached Ida of the many springs | mother wild beasts and many other things
by way of Lecton where they left the sea | passed over the dry land causing the tree
-tops to sway beneath their feet but now to | avoid the eye of Zeus Sleep then came to
a halt and climbed up into a tall pine | -tree tallest there pierced lower airs did pine
for upper air shot up into the sky | and there he perched the branches hidden by
in form of a songbird of the mountains | bronze-throat to the gods nightjar to humans
meanwhile Here fast drew near to Gargarus | loftiest crest Ida Zeus did her suss
the Cloud-compeller saw her but at first | look his heart was captured again by thirst
for her as in the days when they had first | enjoyed each other's love and fit to burst
gone to bed together without parents' | knowledge he rose to meet her in torrents
of desire "Here what business brings you here | from Olympus and why no horses here
and chariot to drive in? Lady Here | gave him a crooked answer "I from here
on my way to the ends of the fruitful | earth to visit Ocean the bountiful
forbear of the gods and Mother Tethys | who did me kind in the gentle tethers
of their home I am going to see them | from interminable quarrels free them
they have been estranged for a long time now | and their hearts with bitterness they did plough
and ceased to sleep with one another my | horses by Ida of the many high
springs wait to take me over the water | and the solid land but I have sought a
moment Oympian here to see YOU | fearing if I paid the visit and you
did not know you might be angry with me" | "Here" said Cloud-gatherer "that's a journey
you may well postpone today let's enjoy | the delights of love never such uncoy
desire for goddess or woman flooded | and overwhelmed my heart not when love did
Ixion's wife even bore Peirithous | whose wisdom to rival the gods forsooth
or Danae of fair ankles of slim girth | daughter of Acrisius who gave birth
to Perseus top hero of his time | or daughter of Phoenix of far famed line
who bore me Minos and so godlike he | Rhadamanthus or Semele or Alcy
-mene whose son lion-hearted Heracles | Semele bore Dionysus pleasure's ease
to give to mankind or Demeter Queen | of the Lovely Locks or of finest sheen
Leto or when I fell in love with you | never have I felt such love and so too
sweet desire as fills me now for you" "Dread | Son of Cronos you still amaze me" said
the Lady Here dissembling still "suppose | we do as you wish and take our repose
in each other's arms on the Ida heights | where no privacy whatever alights
what happens if one of the eternal | gods sees us asleep and runs off to tell
the rest? I certainly do not relish | idea rise from bed we so cherish
and then we going back to your palace | think of the scandal back at your place ace
no if it really is your pleasure to | do this thing you have your own bedroom to
use your own Son Hephaestus built for you | and the doors he made are solid let you
and I lie down there if that is the use | wish make out of it" Cloud-compeller Zeus
responded "Here you need not be afraid | any god man will see us in cloud laid
golden too thick for that I shall hide us | even the Sun through the mist won't see us

whose rays provide him with the keenest sight | in all the world" as he spoke with delight
Son of Cronos took his Wife in his arms | and the gracious earth then sent up its charms
fresh grass beneath them crocuses dewy | lotus a soft crowded bed of lovely
hyacinths lift them off the ground so laid | covered by beautiful golden cloud plaid
whence a rain of glittering dew-drops fell | and so while the Father full peaceful fell
peaked on Gargarus with his arms around | his Wife by love and then by sleep unbound
gentle god of Sleep flew off to Argive | ships to tell the Earthshaker the new live
titbits went up to Girdler of the World | and his great secret to him then unfurled
"Poseidon you may help the Danaans | now with all your heart have the upper hand's
for a short time only 'til Zeus awakes | caught did I in deep gentle sleep sweep-stakes
after Here had tricked him into her arms" | and Sleep then went off to deploy his charms
with all the famous nations of mankind | left Poseidon even more of a mind
to champion the Danaans he sprang | beyond the front rank and his orders rang
out "Argives are we going once more to | leave the victory to Hector and to
let him take the fleet and reap the glory? | he says so but only gory story
of such boastful talk is based on the fact | that Achilles still refuses to act
sits in deep dudgeon by his hollow ships | yet he won't be missed much if each one chips
in rouses self and helps one another | listen you all to my plan it further
we must now equip ourselves with the best | biggest shields in the camp and for the rest
put dazzling helms on our heads go into | battle longest spears can lay hands onto
I myself will take command and I do | not think Prince Hector will stand up to
us for long for all his fury thus let | each man who's proved his worth fighting and yet
carries a small buckler then hand it to | a weaker soldier equip himself too
with a larger shield" they took Poseidon | gladly at his word and the kings took on
though wounded preparation of their men | for the fight Odysseus and King of Men
son of Atreus and Tydeides | visiting the different ranks within these
interchanging arms so the best soldiers | now the best equipped to inferiors
giving then their inferior weapons | when all of them hand donned their gleaming bronze
they set out the Earthshaker Poseidon | long daunting sword in great hand led side on
this sword like a lightning flash sacrilege | to touch in battle men shrink from its edge
in terror on the other side Hector | illustrious formed battle line vector
now most appalling fight of all able | -y staged by Poseidon of Locks Sable
and glorious Hector one for Argives | other Trojans no-one quarter gives lives
as they met with a clamour deafening | sea up to Argive ships huts leavening
but neither the thunder of the breakers | on the beach blown in from deep sea acres
by a northerly gale nor roar of flames | when fire attacks forest in the domains
of a mountain's ravines nor the wind's moan | in high foliage of the oaks when groan
then rises to a scream in its anger | swells so loud as the terrible utter
-ance of the war-cry that the Achaeans | raised along with the opposing Trojans
as they fell upon each other Hector | illustrious began with spear-vector
cast at Aias as he faced him full on | he did not miss but hit Aias full on
where two baldrics for shield silver-studded | sword across breast fully outstretched thudded

saved his tender flesh but Hector angry | at having made a powerful mighty
spear-cast to no purpose then sought cover | again Kompany men in fear over
his own life and as he withdrew the great | Telamonian Aias up to plate
stepped picked up one of the many boulders | that had been used to prop up ships' shoulders
had rolled among the feet of the fighters | then on the chest under the neck Hector's
struck over rim of shield making him spin | and whirl round like a top thus Hector in
his gallantry brought down in dust profuse | by as sudden a stroke as that of Zeus
when he uproots an oak unnerving all | near by violence of bolt and the apall
-ing reek of sulphur it gives off Hector's | second spear falls from his hand the vector's
crumpled up under his shield and helmet | the bronze trappings of his armour then met
with a clang the Achaean men-at-arms | rushed at him triumphant cries in swarm's charms
hoping to drag him off and discharging | volley of javelins but there their charging
no chance of either spear or dart touching | the C-in-C as he was now clutching
support surrounded gallant lieutenants | Sarpedon King of Lycian remnants
the admirable Glaucus Aeneas | noble Agenor and Polydamas
and of the rest was not one neglected | their commander they all him protected
with their rounded shields held in front of him | and then putting their arms underneath him
his comrades lifted him up carried him | from fray to horses who'd waited for him
in a quiet spot behind the fighting | with driver and painted car now flighting
him off groaning heavily toward town | but when they had eventually come down
to the ford of the eddying Xanthus | the noble River whose Father's Zeus thus
the immortal Hector's men lifted him | from out of his chariot and laid him
on the ground and poured water over him | straight away consciousness came back to him
sat up on his heels vomited dark blood | then he sank back once more on the ground good
the world went black as night before his eyes | hadn't yet recovered from the surprise
when the Achaeans saw Hector withdraw | they fell on Trojans with a new will raw
better bitter and recaptured their zest | Aias son of Oileus first to test
famous spearman the runner to draw blood | charged forward with spear sharp-pointed aim good
struck Satnius a flawless Nymph had borne | to father Enops when was on the horn
with his herds on banks of Satniois | Aias Satnius of Satniois
hit flank collapsed fierce tussle round ensued | Polydamas son of Panthous rescued
the great spearman struck Prothoenor son | of Areilycus with a blow full on
the right shoulder the heavy spear pursued | its course through his shoulder and thus ensued
his fall in the dust and clawing of earth | then Polydamas for all he was worth
uttered great yell of triumph over him | "Another spear from the strong arm trim grim
of the proud son of Panthous that did not | go astray but found home target hot got
an Argive's flesh can use it as a staff | as makes his way down to Hades' Gaffe"
the Achaeans heard his jubilation | with disgust none resented more than son
doughty of Telamon other Aias | nearest place where Prothoenor alas
fallen made swift cast with glittering spear | at Polydamas as then sought get clear
of field the latter avoids certain death | by leaping to one side spear of last breath
hit son of Antenor Archelocus | because the gods meant him to die he thus

was struck where the head meets the neck the last | segment of the spine both sinews aghast
as fell forehead mouth and nose hit the ground | before shins knees unbound down the ground found
turned to utter a shout then fell Aias | called across to peerless Polydamas
"Think it over Polydamas tell me | now if this death does not make up frankly
for death Prothoenor to judge by his looks | was certainly no craven and he brooks
no base birth maybe more like a brother | or of great lord Antenor son other
for the family likeness is striking" | Aias knew well enough when this liking
who he'd killed the hearts of the Trojans sank | but Acamas stepped up out of his rank
then bestrode Archelocus his brother | when a Boeotian tried drag his brother
out of legs brought that one Promachus down | with spear insolent triumph formed a crown
over his victim he shouted aloud | "You Achaeans who are so brave and proud
with your bows and free with your threats don't think | that troubles and disasters just us sink
we have had our losses yours are coming | your man Promachus sleep overcoming
via my spear in prompt repayment for | my brother's death what a wise man prays for
a kinsman survive and avenge his fall" | Argives revolted by boastful talk all
the doughty Peneleos specially | prompted by it into a reply he
made straight for Acamas but Acamas | did not place himself against his attack mass
and thus it was Ilioneus who fell | to King Peneleos worked on the fell
was a son of Phorbas a sheep-owner | in Troy of the god Hermes found favour
latter'd made him a rich man but mother | of Ilioneus gave no child other
to Phorbas and so now this only son | of hers was struck by Peneleos un
-der the eyebrow in socket of the eye | and the javelin has dislodged the eye
-ball pierced the socket came out nape of neck | he sank down stretched out both hands on the deck
but Peneleos drawing his sharp sword | hit him full on neck brought forward foreword
head and helm tumbling to ground heavy spear | still stuck in eye as he lifted it clear
like a poppy-head for Trojans to see | and exulted over his enemy
cried "Trojans be so good as to instruct | father and mother of this de-construct
and to start lamenting him at home prom | that's only fair because the wife of Prom
-achus son Alegenor will never | in any future have the great pleasure
of seeing HIM again when Argive greaves | sail from Troy" this made Trojans' knees quake grieves
everyman peers round to find some bolthole | hide-away from the sudden death of soul
pray tell me now you muses who live on | Olympus who was first Achaean son
to take a full set of blood-stained armour | from the foe now that mighty Earthshaker
had swayed the battle then in their favour? | Telamonian Aias the flavour
striking Hyrtius son of Gyrtias | leader of lion-hearts of Mysias
next Antilochus killed Phalces then on | to Mermerus and Morys Hippotion
slain by Meriones Teucer sent on | Prothoon and Periphetes and so on
Atreides hit on Hyperenor | the great captain in the flank the bronze tore
its way in and thus let out his entrails | and his soul then incontinently sails
through the gaping wound darkness came down on | his eyes but was to Aias the fleet son
of Oileus the greatest number fell | for when a panic had set in pell-mell
there was no-one like Aias for chasing | the routed enemy by foot-racing

πεντεκαίδεκα

*Book 15*

# THE ACHAEANS AT BAY

*Zeus wakes bids Phoebus Apollo for sure*
*fortunes of Hector and Trojans restore*
*and in the Trojan onslaught with great loss*
*fire thrown on the ship Protesilaos*

the fleeing Trojans cross the palisade | once more and trench and suffer a severe degrade
at the hands of the Argives didn't stop | 'til reached their cars as paused there on the hop
shattered and pale with terror Zeus lying | still on heights Ida lying still dreaming
beside Here of the Golden Throne awoke | of a sudden leapt to feet at a stroke
took good Wood-stock of battle this what saw | the Trojans thrown back in full mode withdraw
the Danaans in hot pursuit the Lord | Poseidon helping in the chase the lord
Hector lying on the ground his comrades | sat round he barely breathing in spades' shades
with great difficulty spitting blood mess | he had not yet regained full consciousness
for the man who'd hit him was by no means | the feeblest of all the Achaeans
the Father of men and gods was filled then | at sight of him with great compassion yen
turning on Here with a black look and voice | terrible as he gave her the invoice
"Here you are incorrigible I'm sure | that this is your doing and it's through your
wicked wiles Prince Hector has been (f)l/outed | in way fighting his folk have been routed
I've half a mind to strike you with my bolt | let you be first reap ripening fruit volt
of your unconscionable tricks have you then | forgotten altogether the time when
I strung you aloft with anvils hanging | from your feet and with your hands there dangling
tied with a golden chain you could not break? | new-fangled entangled up in air shake
in anger among clouds and gods on high | Olympus although they rallied round nigh
in indignation found impossible | set you free any individual
I caught in the attempt I seized and hurled | far away from the threshold of my world
when reached the ground to respond s/he too weak | even that did not relieve heartache bleak
I still felt for the godlike Herakles | who you to aid you in evil schemes these
by suborning the Winds had sent scudding | over barren seas before your blooding
northern gale to sweep him off in the end | to the peopled Isle of Cos a godsend
I rescued him from Kos and brought him back | to Argos where horses graze the outback

safe after all he'd been through I am now | reminding you of this so as somehow
to put a stop to your intrigues and teach | you how little you can rely on each
loving embrace you enjoyed when you came | here from Olympus and cajoled me tame
into your arms" the ox-eyed Lady Here | as she listened to this shuddered with fear
and hastened to reassure him "Let my | witnesses be Earth wide Heavens on high
and the falling waters of Styx (greatest | oath the blessed gods can take and the test
most solemn) both your sacred head our own | bridal couch by which never on my own
would dare forswear myself that it's not on | any prompting of mine that Poseidon
Earthshaker harms Hector and the Trojans | at the same time helping the Achaeans
I can only suppose he felt sorry | for them when he saw them pressed so hardly
by the ships acted of his own free will | I'm quite ready to remonstrate and will
pack him off if you just say where he shall | go Lord of Black Cloud" this drew smile not shall
-ow from Father of men and gods replied | to her much more mildly "Here my ox-eyed
Queen if from now on I could count on you | to support me in the god Council too
Poseidon would soon come round and see eyes | to eyes however much might otherwise
be inclined however if you have been | honest and told the truth about the scene
go back now to the gods order Iris | Apollo Archer here I wish Iris
to visit the bronze-clad Achaeans tell | Poseidon cease fight go to own home well
-watered Phoebus Apollo bring Hector | back into the battle only after
putting fresh heart in him making forget | the suffering that was making him fret
and Phoebus must then introduce panic | to the Achaeans and make them manic
-ally take to their heels they will fall back on | the well-found black ships of Achilles son
of Peleus who'll send friend Patroclus | out into the battlefield Patroclus
after killing a number of stalwart | enemies including my own stalwart
son Sarpedon will then fall to the spear | illustrious Hector before Troy clear
-ly infuriated Prince Achilles | by Pat's death sees Hector despatched with ease
from that moment on I shall cause the tide | of battle ebb from ships recede betide
steadily 'til the day the Achaeans | take the high fortress though machinations
of Athene and yet in the meantime I | remain hostile to the Argives and I
will not let any other immortal | come down to aid them in their struggle 'til
the wishes of Achilles are fulfilled | in accordance with the promise I willed
him and confirmed with a nod of my head | that day when divine Thetis turned my head
putting her arms round my knees imploring | me take the lead in honour restoring
her son" city-sacker Zeus had spoken | white-armed goddess Here took up the token
set out from Ida for high Olympus | flying in her haste a magnum opus
with the speed of thought like one who's travelled | widely and with fond memories (f/l)abled
of many places has but to retire | within himself and say "I wish I're
in that spot or in that' and he is there | reaching peak Olympus Lady Here there
presented self to the gods immortal | who in Zeus' palace did assemble
when they saw her they all leapt to their feet | pledged her with their cups ignoring this feat
Here now accepted a cup from The(m)is(s) | of the Lovely Cheeks who then the first (m)is(s)
to come running up to her with questions | pouring from her lips "Here! for what reasons

are you here looking like someone distraught? | the Son of Cronos has left you quite fraught
though he IS your Husband" "Lady The/m(is)s | no questions on that I pray" goddess m(is)s
of the white arms replied "you know yourself | just how harsh and unbending he himself
is liable to be but if you will | give the other gods a lead to table
in the hall you and the rest shall hear all | about the mischief he plans for us all
and in case there are any who still think | all's well in the world as they on the brink
of their dinner I can assure you | that the news will not suit everyone's view
on Olympus or on earth" with this Queen | of Heaven took her seat up and down scene
in hall Zeus gods filled with consternation | for although a simile smile formation
on Here's lips belied by dark brows forehead | it was a very angry goddesshead
addressed the company "What fools we were | what lunatics launch quarrel with Zeus near
yet here we are itching to get at him | still to stop him if not by a talk whim
then by force and all the while he sits there | by himself quite unperturbed but aware
snapping his fingers at us well he may | since he knows that for brute strength he is way
beyond the rest of us an excellent | excuse for you all to take troubles sent
lying down! and that reminds me Ares | if I'm not mistaken already he's
been punished as a son favourite bright | Ascalaphus has fallen in the fight
my lord the god of war does claim to be | his Father does he not?" Ares then he
flew into a passion when heard this news | with the flat of his hands slapped sturdy thews
"Gods of Olympus you can't blame me now | if I drop to the Argive ships and how
to avenge there the slaughter of my son | even though be my fate to be undone
by Zeus's bolt lie among the corpses | in the blood and dust" to harness horses
he called to Terror and Panic while he | put on his glittering arms now we see
another quarrel bitterer and more | disastrous than last would have come to fore
between almighty Zeus and the immortals | if Athene in her terror for the hall's
community had not leapt from her chair | and dashed after Ares harsh words to share
she snatched the helmet from his head the shield | from his shoulder and the bronze spear did yield
from his sturdy hand as put spear away | showed the impetuous War-god the way
her mind was working "Maniac! Blockhead!" | she cried "you will only be rendered dead
have you no ears to hear with? have you no | sense and no restraint? and do you not know
what we were told by the white-armed goddess | Here straight from Olympian Zeus no less?
or is it your wish to get a flailing | be chased back to Olympus tail trailing
between your legs while the rest of us reap | the whirlwind you've sown? for Zeus will not keep
away he will leave the Trojan gallants | and Achaeans then without a moment's
pause overwhelm us here in Olympus | innocent guilty alike seizing us
each in turn take my advice set aside | all thoughts of avenging your son beside
many a finer stronger man than he | has been killed long before now and will be
killed hereafter as we can hardly be | expected to check on the pedigree
of every man on earth" so Athene led | back to chair impetuous War-godhead
Here then asked Apollo and Iris who | in role of go-between gave service to
the immortal gods to accompany | her out of doors and there she faithfully
delivered message "Zeus commands you to | go now with all speed the pair of you to

Mount Ida and when you have reached the place | and encountered him in a face-to-face
you will carry out whatever command | he gives you" Lady Here regains command
of hall sat down on her throne while the pair | flew off through the air on their errand there
when they reached Ida of the many springs | mother of sheep great Zeus the all-seeing's
sitting on Gargarus' high summit | full enveloped mist perfumed did emit
they presented selves to Zeus compeller | -Cloud waited to see what may be his pleasure
Zeus noted their arrival and discerning | no issue with their despatch intern thing
re his Consort's commands starts by applying | to Iris her orders "Off with you flying
as fast as you can Iris convey my | words in full now no mistakes mind to my
Lord Poseidon tell stop fighting retire | from the field then he either I require
to other gods withdraw or into his | own sacred sea but if he then chooses
to ignore my explicit instructions | let he himself consider his actions
and decide powerful as he is whether | dare stand up any way whatsoever
to an attack by me who claim to be | by far the stronger god and also be
his senior by birth on that account | not that hesitates self equal to count
in his behaviour to me of whom all | the other gods in dread enthral in thrall"
wind-swift Iris of the Fleet Foot obeyed | promptly set out for sacred city glade
Ilium in her eager haste dropping | like snow or chilling hail harsh axe chopping
from clouds when squall comes down from North bitter | she then went straight up to the big-hitter
great Earthshaker said "Girdler of the World | god of the Sable Locks into your world
I have come with a message from aegis | -bearing Zeus and he commands you in this
to stop fighting to retire from the field | join the other gods or to own field yield
to the sacred sea withdraw and if you | disregard his orders he will face you
in this field warns you not to come to grips | with him maintain that when all the chips
are down he is by far the stronger god | he says not that you seem to give a sod
as equal with him you've oft claim-ed | of whom the other gods all stand in dread"
the great Earthshaker's infuriated | "It's outrageous!" he enunciated
"Zeus may be powerful but it's sheer bluster | to talk of forcing me the Earthshaker
who enjoy the same prestige as he does | to bend my will to his there's three of us
Brothers all Sons of Cronos and Rhea | Zeus me and Hades King of the Not Here
each of us was given his own domain | when the world was divided once again
we cast lots and I received the grey seas | as my inalienable realm Hades
drew the nether dark while Zeus allotted | the broad sky home plotted that was slotted
into the clouds in the upper air realm | but the earth was left as a common realm
for all of us and high Olympus too | and because of this I'm not going to
let Zeus have his way with me powerful | as he his let him stay in his lawful
third of the world quietly and don't let | him try to terrify me with the threat
violence as though I were an arrant | coward he would do better I warrant
to give his Sons and Daughters some advice | he is their Father they'll have to be nice
listen hard when he orders them about" | "Girdler of the World" she of Fleet Foot shout
"do you really wish me to convey so testy | even indeed reply peremptory
to Zeus? won't you change your mind? a true track | of excellence to be able change tack

and you know how the Avenging Furies | always have back of elder brothers' knees"
"Lady Iris you're right in what you say | and how excellent it is may I say
an ambassador showing discretion! | but galls me cuts me to bone dissection
to be bullied and scolded by a god | with whom Fate has decreed that such a sod
and I should share the world on equal terms | however I will for now take these terms
though not without resentment let me add | a word of warning about my own bad
feelings for if Zeus against my wishes | those Warrior Athene Hermes dishes
Here Lord Hephaestus citadel should spare | Ilium whose sacking would then there
have given Achaeans resounding | victory let him know will be sounding
irreparable breach between us two" | the Earthshaker left the army much to
the regret of those gallant men withdrew | to the sea Zeus of Cloud-compeller crew
instructed Apollo "I now wish you | dear Phoebus to seek out Hector anew
of the bronze arms Earthshaker and Girdler | of the World is by now a retirer
into the sacred sea so to avoid | the severity of my wrath covoid
indeed if we had come to blows whole world | would have heard even the gods in the world
below with Cronos but was far better | for both of us despite his great anger
that he yielded to me without feeling | my strength would surely been much ill-feeling
and sweat before we reached a settlement | take my tasselled aegis in your hands it's meant
to strike panic into the Achaean | chieftains by having it fiercely shaken
make illustrious Hector chief concern | my Archer lord and fill him with a stern
and desperate courage until such time | as Argives get to end of the ships' line
and Hellespont in rout and at that point | I myself will decide and make appoint
of what must be said and done to give them | respite from their punishment only then"
thus had spoken Zeus and Apollo turned | no deaf ear but like a peregrine burned
swooped down from mounts of Ida with the speed | of a dove-destroying hawk which indeed
is the fastest thing on wings Prince Hector | son wise Priam no more victim vector
prostrate when he found him but sitting up | his consciousness had now at last turned up
he could recognise the friends about him | having ceased pant and sweat no sweat for him
the moment aegis-bearing Zeus had willed | recovery Apollo him full filled
"Prince Hector just why are you sitting here | in such a sorry state and nowhere near
your troops? have you been hurt?""What god are you | my lord?" said Prince Hector "and why do you
come to me for news?" in a feeble voice | don't you know Aias of the death in-voice
and the loud war-cry as I was killing | his men by line of the ships outspilling
struck me on the breast with a rock? there was | no fight left in me indeed I thought was
very day I was set to breathe my last | go down to the dead in Hades' fast"
"Courage!" said the Archer-King Apollo | trust the confidant the Son Of Crono
-oso sends from Mount Ida take his place | beside you and protect you Phoebus ace
Apollo of the Golden Sword and who | in days gone by have saved not only you
but your citadel high as well up now! | tell your many charioteers just how
you want them to drive at the gallop right | up to the hollow ships and I'll go right
away ahead of them making the whole | way smooth for their horses' feet putting whole
company of Achaean lords to flight" | and Apollo as he spoke breathed power right

into the Trojan chief who now ran off | nimble feet limbs weight taken shaken off
like a stallion leaves halter in tatter | -'s where keep at manger make him fatter
gallops off across the fields in triumph | to bathing-place normal in the triumph
-al river and he tosses up his head | his mane back along the shoulders is spread
he knows how beautiful he is away | he goes skimming the ground along the way
with his hooves to the mares' haunts and pastures | thus Hector sped new pleasures well past yours
when heard the god speak lead charioteers | into battle until now oppo tiers
Danaan had been advancing in mass | formation using their fencing-sword pass
and double-pointed spears to good effect | but now they behaved as a rustic sect
with a pack of hounds who have been hunting | an antlered stag or wild goat but brunting
no success have lost him in a dark wood | or some rocky fastness when bearded hood
-ed lion sudden aroused by their cries | makes his appearance in their path and shies
whole party scuttling back no more stomach | for the chase and were so taken aback
the Danaans when saw Hector once more | marshalling his men and were filled full sore
consternation hearts sank Achilles heels | now it's Andraemon's son Thoas who feels
need to give a lead to the Danaans | by far finest of Aetolians
skilled with the javelin good hand-to-hand | also few of Achaean boy band brand
could beat him when the younger orators | with each other vying as debaters
now came forward did his best for each friend | "A miracle!" cried "and a most unfriend
-ly one for us! Hector back from the dead | and just when we all had it in our head
Telamonian Aias had disposed | of him some god who to him not opposed
has taken him in hand brought back to life | as if he'd not already taken life
enough of us and more of that to come | Hector would not have managed such a come
-back to the front line threatening us like this | if Zeus the Thunderer had not let this
happen well now so this is what I think | we should do let's let the main body shrink
back to the ships while we who claim to be | the best make a stand spears at the ready
in hope of holding Hector's first attack | he will certainly do his best to sack
our shield-wall citadel but I have an | idea he'll think twice before make an
attack main body" tactics adopted | at once and their best men then co-opted
to face Hector and his Trojans massing | them all around the main men Aias King
Idomeneus Meriones lad | Teucer Meges compeer of War-god mad
behind the main force retired on the ships | the Trojan host came on had got to grips
with a tight formation Hector striding | in van before even him presiding
with a mist round his shoulders Phoebus is | Apollo with the all-winning aegis
grimly resplendent with its tasselled fringe | the very aegis on all did impinge
that Master-smith Hephaestus had given | to Zeus then to strike panic into men
this in hand Apollo led the Trojans | but had kept selves together Achaeans
awaited them a deafening roar from both | went up now the arrows leapt out from bowth
-strings and then launched by brawny arms | many a spear now displayed its full charms
in a young warrior's body many | another white flesh not tasting any
fell short stuck in the earth balked of the feast | it craved as long as kept aegis beast yeast
steady in his hands volley and counter | -volley found their mark and men fell under

but the moment came when looking the horse | -loving Danaans full in the face hoarse
went with a great shout shaking it at them | their hearts turned to water courage from them
ebbed away like a herd of cows or some | great flock of sheep suddenly face awesome
attack at dusk when the herdsman's not there | and stampeded by mighty black brown bear
the Argives quailed and fled 'twas god-Archer | who turned them into cowards gave Hector
and his Trojans victory ranks having | been broken the Trojans began shaving
off the Achaeans singly Hector killed | Arcesilaus and Stichius the skilled
one leader of the Boeotians bronze these | clad the other of great-hearted Menes
-theus a loyal follower meanwhile | Aeneas slew Iasus Medon not vile
illegitimate son King Oileus | and he was a brother of Aias thus
but he had been exiled for homicide | for killing kinsman on step-mother's side
Eiriopis the wife of Oileus | an Athenian officer Iasus
his father Sphelus son of Bucolus | then Polydamas killed Mecisteus
their first clash Polites felled Echius | and noble Agenor killed Clonius
and Deiochus as joined other leaders | in their flight struck from behind at shoulder's
base by Paris whose bronze passed clean through him | while victors stripping the dead of each limb
the Achaeans flung back onto the trench | and the palisade and had been thrown thence
into total disorder had perforce | behind wall become a take-refuge force
seeing this Hector called to Trojan thains | in loud voice to leave the blood-stained remains
press on to the ships "Any straggler I see | or anyone does not now follow me
forthwith there I will there then put to death | on the spot and what is more such a death
shall get no funeral from his kinsmen | womenfolk dogs outside Troy shall rend open"
swinging his arm right back whipped his horses | sent a great cry down the Trojan courses
charioteers gave an answering shout | and they all drove off to a mighty rout
horses and chariots in line with his | and in their van Phoebus Apollo whiz
with the ease of a god kicked down the banks | of the deep trench and then piled them in ranks
in the middle made broad ample causeway | wide as the space that a warrior may
cover with a spear-cast when he's testing | his strength then they began breasting cresting
across squadron by squadron all led by | Apollo with aegis of glory high
and then with equal ease the god knocked down | the wall like a boy at a seaside town
playing childish games with the sand building | a castle just for fun then sand building
whole destroying with hands and feet that's how | you Lord Apollo spoilt Argive works now
started panic in the men who had toiled | at it so painfully thus they recoiled
once more to the ships halted beside them | and there they called to each other and then
every man lifted his hands up poured out | prayers to all the gods none keener shout-out
than Gerenian Nestor the Warden | of the race who stretched out his arms far then
to the sky that holds the stars cried "Father | Zeus if ever any of us farther
over in wheatlands Argos did burn you | the fat thigh of ox or sheep as prayed you
for a safe return and you promised it | with a nod of your head remember it
now Olympian save us from this day | fatal don't let the Trojans have their say
so completely and thus overwhelm us" | and in this way then did Nestor pray thus
Zeus the Thinker thundered loudly when heard | prayer aged son Neleus wise old bird

but when the Trojans hear the thunderclap | from aegis-bearing Zeus in wonder clap
their zest renewed fell on the Achaeans | more fiercely than ever and they gave ans
-wer with a roar sweeping across the wall | like billows on the high seas that roll call
before the wind great wave-maker tumbling | over the bulwarks of a ship rumbling
drove their horses in too in a moment | hand-to-hand at the ships fighting foment
Trojans from their chariots with double | -pointed spears the Achaeans in trouble
from high on the black sterns where they'd up-shipped | with great poles built up of many lengths tipped
with bronze they kept on board for fights at sea | but Patroclus for as long as did see
Trojans Argives disputing wall able | some way from ships sat with amiable
Eurypylus and while then entreating | him with his talk was with ointment treating
his severe wound the sharpness to deaden | of the pain but when he saw Trojans then
swarming across the wall heard Argives yelling | as fleeing gave a groan thighs wellying
with the flat of his hands "Eurypylus" | cried aloud deep distress "Your 'ip ply peel plus
I can't stay here with you any longer | however much you need me great danger
is upon us your squire must give comfort | while I haste back to Achilles' fort
do my best to get him to fight who knows? | the opinion of a friend can do those
sorts of things with a little luck no hoax | I may yet into action just him coax"
before he'd finished speaking his feet shoot | off on the move meanwhile the resolute
Argives blocked way for all-encumbering | Trojans but although them outnumbering
they had not the strength to prise them apart | from the ships however nor for their part
were the Trojans ever able to break | the Argive lines penetrate havoc make
among the ships and huts and so it played | to a nicety so that the front swayed
no more than the line that is stretched along | a ship's timber to prove that it is strong
and true by a most skilful carpenter | mastered his trade in school of Athena
while parties of men attacked other ships | Hector straight away went to get to grips
with illustrious Aias there ensued | between them for a single ship a feud
Hector strove vainly to drive Aias off | the ship set it on fire to get him off
his back Aias equally unable | once brought to the spot by god Locks Sable
however Aias did kill Caletor | son Clytius struck breast spear metaphor
as he was carrying fire to the ship | fell with a thud the brand slipped from his grip
Hector upon seeing his cousin fall | in the dust by the ship issued a call
loudly to the Trojans and Lycians | "Trojans Lycians and Dardanians
who love close fighting don't yield an inch in | this tight corner we now find ourselves in
rescue Caletor or the Argives will | have his armour off him as he lies still
among the ships" at Aias flung a bright lance | but missing him with a blow that did glance
struck Lycophron son of Mastor a squire | Cytherian of Aias came to hire
himself out after he'd killed a man then | in sacred Cythera standing near when
Hector's sharp bronze hit him above the ear | and he tumbled backwards from the ship's rear
to the ground gave up his life in the dust | Aias shook at the outcome of the thrust
called out to his brother "My dear Teucer | we have lost Lycrophon son of Mastor
a faithful friend who came from Cythera | to live with us who we thought as much a
one of us as own parents great Hector | has just killed him so where now your vector

-deadly arrows and the bow you had from | Phoebus Apollo?" Teucer emerged from
pack hastened to his side with incurved bow | and a full quiver at the troops below
began at once to fire arrows first struck | Cleitus the noble son of out-of-luck
Peisenor and squire to Polydamas | the proud Teucer managed to catch him as
he had the reins in his hands in trouble | with his horses came into the huddle
of troops who themselves in some disorder | with the idea of doing Hector
and the Trojans a good turn punishment | was swift and one from which no friend ardent
could save him as the arrow with its load | of grief struck him in back of the head mode
brought him crashing down from his chariot | horses shied ran away the empty-lot
-car rattling behind them 'til their master | Polydamas first clocked the disaster
made a move planted himself in their way | so that they could no longer have their sway
handed them over to Astynous son | of Protiaon careful stress this "Son
you must watch my movements and keep them | close at hand" he went back to his place then
in the front line he aimed his next arrow | at Hector in his arms of bronze and so
would have put an end then to the battle | by the ships had he struck managed to kill
Hector in the hour of his great glory | but Zeus who of being caught too wary
was looking after Hector had kept eye | on Telamonian Teucer his shy
he robbed him of breaking the cord twisted | of his strong long bow as try persisted
in plan fire at his man and thus arrow | with its load of bronze went wandering so
and the bow fell then from his hand to the ground | he shook with oath to brother did expound
"Some evil Power's everything blocking" | he exclaimed "we try today! now knocking
the bow from my hand breaking a fresh string | that I had only bound on this mo(u)rning
to carry the many arrows I meant | to shoot" "Well my friend" said Aias "you're meant
to lay down your bow and all those arrows | now that some god some one of us harrows
has made them useless take up a long spear | instead sling a shield on your shoulder here
and so meet the enemy give a lead | to our men the Trojans now have the lead
but we can at least show them once more how | we can fight and make them pay dearly now
for the well-found ships" he laid down his bow | in hut slung four-fold leather shield just so
on his shoulder put stout helmet on co(a)rs(e) | -air sturdy head and had a crest of horse
-hair whose plume from the top nodded grimly | took strong spear sharp bronze axe-pointy Gimli
ran out in a moment Aias' side | however Hector now when he espied
something amiss with Teucer's archery | to Trojans Lycians cried in joy "Ye
Trojans Lycians host Dardan-Ian | hand-to-handers now be men and Ian
my friend show your prowess here by the ships | I saw how one of their best men then slips
stopped there from shooting any more by Zeus | for there is no mistaking help from Zeus
makes it plain both to the side for which he's | planning victory and to those who he's
leaving in the lurch see how he's breaking | Argive resistance our cause up taking
stick together then and attack the ships | if any of you meets his fate and ships
an arrow or a spear well let him die | he will have fallen for his country high
and that is no death dishonourable | leave wife children good health safe enable
and his house and a bit of land secure | forever once these Argives leave our shore"
thus did Hector encourage his men then | with that he put fresh heart in each of them

Aias Hamlet Horatio calling | to the fleet flagging Nelson out calling
"ArgEngland expects do duty this day! | we've no choice but to try to save the day
and the ships and live or here now perish | or do you believe you will all relish
returning back home on foot if Hector | of the shining helmet takes the ships? for
he is itching them to set his fire on | can you not hear him driving whole host on?
and believe me he is not inviting | them to join in a dance he is plighting
them into battle and therefore we must | make up our minds and thus now put our trust
in meeting them man-to-man hand-to-hand | whether we live or die matter in hand
it's better to settle once and for all | than a weaker foe in this feeble call
let squeeze us to death in a struggle long | by the ships" Aias' urgent call strong
put new life into all his men but now | the Prince Hector killed Schedius by prow
son Perimedes Phocian chieftain | Aias killed Laodamas noble thain
of Antenor infantry commander | next Polydamas slew a commander
of proud Epeans friend son Phyleus | Meges a one Cyllenian Otus
Meges saw this leapt at Polydamas | however by stooping Polydamas
avoided his attack Apollo not | going to let the son of Panthous rot
in the front line so Meges missing him | caught full in chest with spear Croesmus Jim
who fell with a thud Meges began then | to strip the armour from his shoulders when
he was assaulted by Dolops expert | with lance practised fighter offshoot most pert
son of Lampus son of Laomedon | attacking at close range he came full on
and pierced the centre of Meges' shield | with spear but Meges well served by the shield
of the stout corslet that he was wearing | with its metal plates his father bearing
from Ephyre and River Selleis | where his host there the good King Euphetes
had made him a present of it to wear | for the times when he would go off to war
and so protect him from his enemies | now it did further service it saved his
son from destruction and Meges replied | with a great thrust of spear sharp-pointed plied
struck the plumed crown of Dolops' brazen | helmet and sheared the horsehair crest clean then
off the top and thus the whole ornament | in its fresh purple dye full resplendent
fell down in the dust but did not despair | of winning because he stood his ground there
and still showed fight what he did not notice | the formidable Manos not novice
spear in hand had come to Meges' aid | from behind up on his flank had essayed
struck in the shoulder with such violence | that the eager spear-point forced its bronze thence
right through and came out at his breast Dolops | fell headlong Meges Menelaus tops
rushed in to strip bronze gear from his shoulder | Hector called on kinsmen to be bolder
appealed to all singled out stalwart one | Melanippus son of Hicetaon
for reprimand before the invasion | he'd lived at Percote but when Danaan
host arrived in their rolling ships he left | his shambling cattle grazing came to cleft
of Ilium won honourable place | among the Trojans living in palace
Priam treated like one of own children | Hector shouted at him angry tone then
"Melanippus are we to take things ly | -ing down like this? is it nought to you fi
on't! they've killed your cousin Dolops? not see | help selves to his armour for free?
then follow me we cannot wait any | longer we must grapple now with enemy

'til we've destroyed them utterly or they | bring Ilium tumbling down on the way
to slaughtering all its men" thus Hector | led off Melanippus followed after
like the gallant man he was meanwhile great | Telamonian Aias to a state
stirring up the Argives "My friends be men" | cried "and think of your honour so fear then
nothing in the field except dishonour | comrades' eyes when disgrace dissed by honour
then more are killed than are saved there's neither | honour nor salvation when we do err
in flight" and though they had scarcely needed | this incitement to defend selves heeded
indeed took his words to heart ringed the ships | with a fence of bronze but Zeus the Trojan battleships
still spurred on to attack Menelaus | of the loud war-cry to Antilochus
a deed of daring then chose this moment | to suggest "No-one younger this moment
than you Antilochus no-one quicker | on his feet also in a fight thicker
why not sally out and see if you can | trash a Trojan?" Menelaus from van
withdrew but he had said enough to put | Antilochus on his mettle put foot
out leapt from front line took a quick look round | let fly with his glittering lance a bound
back from his spear-cast the Trojans then took | but he had not thrown for nothing he struck
Melanippus proud son Hicetaon | by the breast nipple as he coming on
to fight Melanippus fell with a crash | night came down on eyes Antilochus brash
pounced on him like a hound leaping on a | stricken fawn that a huntsman's killed with a
lucky shot as it darted from its lair | thus Melanippus did dauntless and fair
Antilochus leap at you to strip you | of your arms but noble Hector had view
of this scene came running through the melee | to confront him for all's gallantry fey
Antilochus not wait blood spilling | like a wild beast whose gross error killing
a dog or he in charge of the cattle | before crowd starts chase takes to heel rattle
-d turned tail and thus son of Nestor fled | deafening cries hail missiles pursu-ed
but directly reached his own company | faced about and stood Trojans now in glee
ships stormed like flesh-eating lions duty | assigned to them by Zeus who their fury
kept heightening and dashing the spirits | of the Argives denying the merits
of any success so high esteeming | oppos made bolder as he was scheming
to give Prince Hector the upper hand there | so could give the ships more than their fair share
of fire and this thought Zeus the Plan-maker | would enable him full in van cater
for Thetis' extravagant demands | waits 'til sees ship ablaze on strand's last s(t)ands
from that moment intended the Trojans | be thrust back from the ships the Danaans
to be victorious all this in mind | as Hector son Priam made more inclined
to attack the beaked ships not that Hector | was lacking in zeal he raged like the War
-god spear in hand or a fire on the mounts | working its destruction in the deep founts
of the woods and on his mouth there was foam | eyes flashed under brows lowering gleam gloam
-ing there menace even in the swaying | of the helm on his temples as slaying
Zeus himself ally in the sky serving | and from that great crowd of men reserving
for signal honour since he had but a | little time to live because Athena
already speeding up the fatal day | that mighty son of Peleus holds sway
Hector's aim to break the enemy line | wherever most best armed busy bee line
but failed break through for all ferocity | of assault stood as firm and close not flee

Achaeans like Stones in a wall cleaving | no more than a giantgantic cliff heaving
that faces there the grey sea unshaken | by the onslaught of the god-forsaken
howling winds and towering waves that roar | at its foot thus so resolute and sure
did the Danaans resist the Trojans | dismiss all thoughts of flight at last he swans
into their midst aflame from head to foot | picture a wave by a gale raised afoot
sweeping forward under clouds a-scudding | breaks upon a gallant ship her flooding
in foam the angry wind booms in her sail | and whose crew to survive so nearly fail
left trembling aghast that's how Hector fell | on the Achaeans striking panic well
into their hearts and they then stampeded | as kine do when grazing then impeded
by a savage lion who finds hundreds | in some great water-meadow with a herds
-man who has not learnt the art of dealing | with a cattle-killing beast but sealing
only the front or rear so bequeathing | middle section to the lion leaving
devour kill thus whole force was put to flight | by Hector and Father Zeus in own right
a miracle as Hector killed just one | Danaan victim Mycenaean one
Periphetes son of Copreus who | had been employed as the go-between to
carry King Eurystheus' orders | to mighty Herakles but by orders
of magnitude Periphetes was an | improvement on worthless father and an
excellent in all respects fast runner | a good soldier and one of the abler
men in Mycenae and the man's value | enhanced his conqueror's great glory too
he'd just turned to fly when he tripped against | the rim of the shield he carried against
missiles and which came right down to his feet | thrown off balance he was knocked off his feet
fell backwards and as he came to the ground | his helmet on his temples loud did sound
at once thus attracting Hector's notice | Hector ran up served votive lance notice
into his chest killing him right in front | of his friends could counter not this affront
for all their horror at their comrade's death | as noble Hector had scared them to death
very soon the Argives were in among | the ships protected by works upper rung
of the first row but Trojans poured in too | and the Achaeans were then forced back to
the adjoining huts and came to a halt | not scatter all over camp at a fault
kept together by sense of fear and shame | and by mutual playing of blame-game
no-one did more by way them exhorting | than noble Nestor role not aborting
Warden of the race who appealed to each | and every man with the means of outreach
the parents' name "Be men my friends and think | of what the people of the world will think
of you and remember your children too | your wives your property your parents who
may be alive or dead so for the sake | of your absent dear ones this plea I make
to stand firm here and not to turn and fly" | and Nestor's appeal put fresh heart in nigh
everyone and Athene cleared from their eyes | the unnatural mist that had made sties
and befogged them and there was daylight now | in both directions behind where the prow
of the rest of the fleet lay and in front | where still in the balance the battle-front
Hector of the loud war-cry and his men | visible to all including those then
standing idle in the rear as well as | those too engaged beside black ships' hausers
idea join part host Argives himself | that had from the fighting detached itself
did not commend itself to the proud heart | Aias kept moving made strides of great part

up and down the decks of the ships swinging | huge pole 22 cubits it winging
was made pieces spliced together designed | for sea-battles and he was then aligned
with a trick-rider with a team of four | picked horses he gallops in from a more
rural spot to a big city and down | a busy road where there are many town
-folk to admire the great skill which he needs | be jumping on and off his several steeds
as they fly along Aias dance-breaking | from one ship's deck to another making
enormous strides voice went up to the sky | exhorted Danaans terrific cry
to defend their ships and huts there Hector | equally unwilling to stay sector
with the crowd remain among his many | men-at-arms exactly as a tawny
Celtic eagle swoops on a flock of birds | geese say or cranes or long-necked swans that girds
self by a river Hector dashed to front | made straight for a blue-prowed ship Zeus up front
pushed him from behind with hand tremendous | and spurred on his men to follow him thus
by the ships again fierce was the struggle | you'd have thought through tussle would just muggle
but were fresh and unfatigued so eager | they to come to grips save in their temper
as they were fighting there was this difference | felt in for disaster Achaeans since
saw themselves destroyed but every Trojan | filled with hope of killing lords Achaean
burning up the ships such were their feelings | as they closed Hector at last the feeling's
of gripping the stern of sea-going ship | was the fast salt-water craft of the trip
Protesilaus brought to Troy though never | carried home to his own country ever
round this the Trojans and the Achaeans | fighting hand-to-hand for the Achaeans
was not a matter now of standing off | and standing up there to a volley of
arrows or javelins united in their | resolution stood man-to-man and there
they fought with sharp axes and strong hatchets | with long swords and double-pointed bayonets
and many a fine black-hilted sword fell | to the ground from the warriors' hands fell
and many another ripped from shoulder | earth ran black with blood Hector so bolder
once he had laid hold of the ship never | let go kept hands on the mascot ever
at the stern and shouted to the Trojans | "Bring fire and raise the war-cry you Trojans
all as one Zeus for all does repay us | thus the ships the things that today play us
onside came here against will of the gods | started all these troubles for us the sods
though through the cowardice of our Elders | though wishing fight to the ships they held us
withheld the troops but as surely an all | -seeing almighty Zeus blinded us all
then now he's backing us sweeping us on" | this stirring address then made them fall on
the Achaeans with an even greater | ferocity Aias could no longer
keep his post overwhelmed by hail missile | and in fear of death gave way little while
retired from afterdeck of the trim ship | to the seven-foot bridge amid the ship
there he stood on the alert when any | Trojan came up with a torch fiery
fended him off from the ships with his pole | all the time in that voice terrible toll
of his was calling to the Danaans | to fight on "Friends you gallant Danaans
servants of Ares be men and recall | your former prowess where's a stronger wall
that might keep disaster off or do you | believe we have allies in the rear too?
but there is no walled city hereabouts | would save the day with reinforcement bouts
we are in the Trojan plain and all Troy | is up in arms we cannot now deploy

the sea at our backs and our own country | a long way off so do not go gently
into that good night if to save our skin" | as he spoke kept furiously thrustin'
with his pointed pole and when a Trojan | came near the black ships with a petrol can
in the hope of gratifying Hector | who hounding them on Aias in sector
ready and struck with his enormous spear | in this way he wounded full twelve men clear
before ships without parting from weapon | it seemed that he could just go on and on

ἑκκαίδεκα

Book 16

# PATROCLUS FIGHTS AND DIES

*how Patroklos in armour Achilles*
*fought so gave the Trojans the real willies*
*and thus drove them back from the hollow ships*
*but slain at last Hector cashed in his chips*

while this battle was raging round the (b/r)ill | -found ship Patroclus reached his lord Achill
-'es hot tears great runners down his face like | water trickling from a spring dark streak
-like fashion down a precipice highborn | Achilles of nimble feet was now torn
when he saw his friend's condition at (n)once | asked what did ail him "Patroclus you ponce
why are you in tears like a little girl | trots at mother's side all the while a-(s)whirl
begging be carried plucking at her skirt | to make her stop looking up at her hurt
with streaming eyes 'til at last she takes her | in her arms? that's how you look as the blur
of tears rolls down your cheeks have you something | to tell the Myrmidons or anything
for myself? or some news from Phthia | that has reached you privately? for If a
father of us two were now indeed dead | we should have mighty cause for grief instead
but I understand yours Menoetius son | of Actor is today a living one
and Peleus son of Aeacus is | certainly alive and well among his
Myrmidons or maybe you are weeping | for the Achaeans now suffer sweeping
bloody slaughter by black ships in payment | own iniquities in which made no dent
still? out with it now don't keep secret great | to yourself but share it with me now straight"
Patroclus the knight by reply words these | after a great sigh "My lord Achilles
noblest of the Argives do not grudge me | these tears terrible distress the army
is in because each former champion | is lying by his ship bearing wounds on
himself from arrows or spears almighty | Diomedes son Tydeus mighty
hit Odysseus great spearman been wounded | Agamemnon also ship a wound did
Eurypylus took an arrow in thigh | and our surgeons are attending them nigh
with all the remedies at their command | and while they try to heal the wounds to hand
you Achilles remain intractable | heaven preserve me from this bile evil
you cherish warping a noble nature | to ignoble ends and what will future
generations thank you for in their ire | if you won't help us in our need most dire?

pitiless man you're no son of Thetis | and the gallant Peleus thus it is
only the grey sea and the frowning crag | that could have made such a hard-hearted hag
is it possible that you're secretly | deterred by word from Zeus some prophecy
your lady Mother has disclosed to you? | then at least allow ME to replace you
at once with the Myrmidon force behind | and I might yet bring some salvation kind
to the Danaans and lend me your own | armour so the Trojans valour disown
as take me for you and break off the fight | let our weary troops recuperate light
as even a short breathing-space makes all | the difference in war the Trojans are all
at the point of exhaustion too and we | new fresh might drive them back to the city
from the ships and the huts" so Patroclus | made his appeal yet how simple was thus!
had he but known it was praying for there | his own doom an evil death however
he had certainly aroused Achilles | the great runner crying out "Prophecies
my lord Patroculs? what are you saying? | if I know any it's not swaying
my conduct nor is it true privately | I've had word from Zeus via my lady
Mother what's cut me to the quick's that a | chap no better than me should plunder a
prize I won just 'cos he's got more power | after all I've gone through in my full flower
of power more than can bear awarding | me that girl the host made point rewarding
special for I'd sacked a walled town I'd won | her with my own spear but Agamemnon
King son of Atreus has then her snatched | out of my arms it is me who is despatched
like some miserable tramp now yet what | is done cannot be undone to think that
a man could nurse a grudge forever I | was wrong in supposing however I
did think of keeping up the feud until | reached my own ships the fight and tumult still
dress yourself in my armour glorious | lead my Myrmidons battle-amorous
into the field now that all-conquering | Trojans black cloud flies round ships hovering
the Argives hanging on to a narrow | strip ground behind beach breadth of an arrow
the whole of Troy seems to have taken heart | turned out against us no doubt in large part
as don't see MY helmet's trip ad-visor | flash in foreground fear would grip hard fly for
their lives soon fill gullies with their dead | if the King had only me befriended
but now they're fighting round the very camp | spear Diomedes no more safety ramp
-art with which maybe save the Achaeans | from destruction heard not Agamemnon's
hateful voice even it's the murderous | Hector's shouts ringing in my ears chorus
as he's hounding on his yelling Trojans | who've swamped the plain trouncing the Achaeans
and yet Patroclus you must save the ships | attack with all your force before the chips
are down and the fleet is sent up in flames | preventing return to our home domains
but listen while I tell you exactly | how far to go to get the whole army
Danaan to value and respect me | as they should and send the lovely lady
back to me with ample compensation | directly you have swept the host Trojan
from the ships return to me even though | Zeus the Thunderer should let you know
of a chance of yourself winning glory | you must not seize it because without ME
you must not fight this warlike host Trojan | because you would then only me cheapen
so don't lead men to Ilium in flush | of winning killing Trojans in the rush
or an eternal god from Olympus | may cross your path and so oppose you plus

the Archer-King Apollo loves dearly | the Trojans turn back when you have clearly
saved situation at the ships leave the rest | to do the fighting on the plain as best
can ah Father Zeus Athene Apollo | how happy I'd be any Trojan no
way gets away alive and no Argive | either and if we two should then survive
the massacre to pull down Troy's holy | tower diadem single-handedly!"
while Achilles and Patroclus talking | the moment came Aias no more walking
the plank deck unable to keep post conquered | by the will of Zeus and also zonkered
by missiles from the Trojans triumphant | his shining helm being their mark constant
rang terribly now upon his temples | as darts dented the stout plates with dimples
on either side exhausted left shoulder | by swinging his shield effort still bolder
even though volley impact failed bringing | it crashing in on him he was wringing
sweat streamed panting from all limbs had not had | instant to relax wherever looked had
each new moment added to his troubles | tell me now you Muses in your bubbles
self-Olympusing how Achaean ships | first set on fire Hector cashed in his chips
went right up to Aias struck ashen spear | with great sword below point socket clean shear
the head off leaving the truncated shaft | foolishly dangle asternly haft aft
in Telamonian Aias' hand | while the bronze head sped away fell to land
with a clang and deep in his noble heart | Aias realised with shudder the part
that the gods now taking in the matter | and then also that Zeus the Thunderer
intent on a Trojan win was rendering all | his luttes futiles back out of range did fall
so the Trojans were throwing blazing brands | into the ship in a moment all hands
wrapt up in inextinguishable flames | round her stern fire swirled its deadly game gains
Achilles slapped his thighs to Patroclus | turned cries "Up my royal lord Patroclus
Commander of the Horse! I see a blaze | at the ships they're going up in a haze
of flames if only they don't capture them | and cut off our retreat! quickly now then
arm yourself I'll go assemble the men" | so Patroclus the shimmering bronze then
put on began by tying round his legs | splendid greaves fitted with silver clip-pegs
for the ankles on breast Achilles' | lovely cuirass scintillating star is
on shoulders slung bronze sword with its studded | -silver hilt next then the great thick shield girded
on sturdy head set the well-made helmet's | sporting too a mighty long horsehair crest's
great plume nodded grimly from the top tip | at last picked two strong spears suited his grip
of peerless Achilles only weapon | that he did not take along with him then
his long heavy spear most formidable | and no other Achaean was able
wield this save Achilles who knew the way | to handle it was made from an ash way
up on the high top of Mount Pelion | it had been given by the great Cheiron
to his father Peleus to bring death | to his noble foes to drive to his death
Patroclus picked Automedon told him | to harness the horses quickly for him
thought more highly of this man than any | save Achilles the breaker of any
battle-line having found that in action | most reliable of any faction
keeping always within call Automedon | yoked for him Achilles' horses one
Xanthus other Balius wind-swift pair | Podarge the Storm-Filly had foaled for their
sire the Western Gale when she was grazing | beside Ocean Stream he then was phasing

in as an outrigger the thoroughbred | Pedasus Achilles brought captured led
from Eetion's gaffe but Pedasus's | one of the now ordinary horses
but he kept up with the immortal pair | meanwhile Achilles had gone around their
huts got all his Myrmidons under arms | fell in like flesh-eating wolves all fell charms
of natural savagery that have killed | high in mountains great antlered stag selves filled
as rent him 'til their jowls are red with blood | then go off in a pack to lap the good
water from surface of a dusky well | dark with their slender tongues and gore were bel
-ching still indomitably fierce their | bellies distended though each commander
captain of the Myrmidons rushed to post | round squire swift son of Peleus formed host
Achilles like the War-god Mars-halling | charioteers troops shield-walling calling
each of the fifty fast ships Achilles | had brought fifty crew on its benches he's
himself of course the supreme commander | but installed five lieutenants under
him and the first company was led by | Menesthius of the flashing helm high
son of the divine River Spercheus | Polydora a daughter Peleus
he was the love-child of a woman plus | a god of the Tireless Stream Spercheus
but one Borus son of Perieres | had come forward with a dowry those days
handsome and married his mother known as | the son of Borus and the second was
commanded by the warlike Eudorus | mother Polymele daughter Phylas plus
was also an unmarried girl and she's | a lovely dancer the great god Hermes
the Giant-killer fell in love with her | when caught his eye as she was playing her
part there in the choir of Artemis of | the Golden Distaff goddess also of
chase gracious Hermes took her straight up her | bedroom unseen lay in her arms made her
the mother of a splendid child destined | Eudorus great runner fast as the wind
plus man of war when in due course baby | had been duly brought into the world he
by Eileithyia goddess travail | had eyes opened to sun became avail
-able mighty a powerful chieftain Echecles son | of Astor married the mother paid one
ample dowry and took her home with him | while Eudorus the one who cared for him
and brought him up was his old grandfather | Phylas who could have shown him no greater
devotion than had been his own son bred | and the third company was commanded
by gallant Peisander son Maemalus | who's the best spearman next to Patroclus
of all the Myrmidons charioteer | old Phoenix led fourth next commander here
Alcimedon Laerces' noble | son the fifth when Achilles had all full
drawn up officers men in their proper | places made them a speech of great power
"You Myrmidons let none of you forget | what you have been threatening to do yet
to Trojans all the time I kept you here | by your ships while I indulged anger dear
there's not one of you who did not abuse | your prince a vile brute the term did use
for keeping idle here against your will | so I was a sort of monster evil
brought up on bile and not mother's milk | 'Achilles evil sulk of such an ilk"
you said 'we might as well take to the ships | sail home' I know you oft met with such quips
discussed me in this style well now a bit | of real work has come your way such a fight fit
as you have longed for so go to it then | and fall now on the Trojans like brave men"
his words filled every one then with daring | ranks dressed closer on hearing well faring

their prince and their helmets and their shields bossed | as the blocks of stone were as tightly tossed
as mason fits together when he is | building wall of a high house and wishes
to make sure that he will keep out the wind | stood soclosetogetherendtoendwind
-proofshieldtoshieldhelmtohelmmantoman | glitteringpeaksplumedhelmsmetasoneman
whenmovedtheirheads and in front of them all | Patroclus Automedon set up stall
for battle one desire between two men | fight in the van of the Myrmidons then
but Achilles went to his hut lifted | lid of a lovely inlaid chest gifted
by Thetis Silver Feet mum for son packed | with tunics wind-proof cloaks thick rugs and stacked
on board for him to take on his journey | in this chest he kept a cup most comely
and from which no other man was allowed | to drink the sparkling wine to Zeus avowed
he took it from the chest after sulphur | fumigating rinsed in rill fresh water
washed hands drew some sparkling wine went into | the middle of the forecourt so as to
pray as poured the wine looked up into sky | and all the time he was watched over by
thunder-loving Zeus he began "Lord Zeus | ye Dodonian Pelasgian Zeus
you who live far away and rule over | the whole wide realm of the wintry Dodona
surrounded by your prophets the Helli | who leave their feet unwashed and when sleepy
lie on the ground you listened when I prayed | to you before and for me then displayed
your regard by striking a blow mighty | for me the whole Achaean army
grant me another wish I myself am | going to stay among the ships but am
sending my friend with the Myrmidon host | into the field pray bless him with the toast
of victory mighty all-seeing Zeus | fill his heart with a daring make most use
so that Hector himself may learn whether | my squire can fight on his own or whether
his hands are invincible only when | "I" throw myself into the equation
directly he's swept tumult and fighting | from ships and himself back to me plighting
here at my own ships safe and sound with all | his armour and his men-at-arms withal"
Zeus the Counsellor heard Achilles' | prayer granted him half of it but he is
not granted the rest the Father agreed | that lord Patroclus should at need indeed
chase the Trojans from the hollow peaked ships | but no way get back safely to the ships
when Achilles had made his libation | and prayer to Father Zeus to location
in the chest the cup did return upfront | and then he came back out and stood in front
of his hut interest was not played out | wanted to see Trojan-Achaean bout
meanwhile the armed companies entrusted | to the heroic Patroclus thrusted
on 'til in their fury they could fall on | the Trojans picture a horde of wasps on
the side of a road pouring out as used | by young fool boys to being teased abused
provoke them every time pass nest wayside | the result a public menace beside
no sooner does a traveller come by | unwittingly disturb them and fly high
up in arms and then fly out all for one | fight for their every single little one
that the spirit in which host Myrmidon | poured out from behind the ships and on
went with an indescribable din did | through which the loud voice of Patroclus dinned
aloud the message of exhortation | to his warriors "Soldiers Myrmidon
of Prince Achilles my friends now men be | and so display your old audacity
win glory for the son of Peleus | the best man in the Achaean camp plus

all the best companies in his command | teach Agamemnon what a foolish stand
made when trifled with greatest Achaean | of them all" Patroclus put every man
on mettle fell on Trojans in body | the Argive war-cry re-echoed G(r)imli
by the ships all round but when host Trojan | saw then Menoetius' stalwart son
and beside him his squire Automedon | all their brilliant bronze equipment on
their hearts sank fine lines began to waver | thought Achilles great runner saviour
must have given up feud that had kept him | beside his ships and had reconciled him
-self with Agamemnon now every man | looked around anxiously in hope find an
escape way from sudden death Patroclus | the first to cast a glittering lance thus
he hurled it straight into the mass of men | who were all swarming around the stern then
of the great Protesilaus' ship | and he struck Pyraechmes full amidship
he who'd brought his Paeonians in their | plumed helms from banks broad River over there
Axius at Amydon with a groan | Pyraechmes fell down in the dust lay prone
his Paeonian troops panic-stricken | one and all when saw best fighter captain
killed took to their heels Patroclus swishing | them thus from the ships and extinguishing
fire in Protesilaus' ship blazing | leaving it in a state of half-razing
time being had taken fright host Trojan | had fallen back in utter confusion
the Danaans with a deafening roar | through the gaps between the beaked ships did pour
out upon them and so the Argive host | saved the fleet then from going up in toast
for a while thus they could breathe more freely | akin to moment when touchy-feely
Lightning-maker Great Zeus shifts a dense cloud | from the top of a high mount and each shroud
-'eadland peak ravine starts springs into sight | as the infinite depths of the sky('s)-light
torn open to the very firmament | not done with war gallant Argive ferment
the Trojans from the ships been forced out | but they were not as yet in headlong rout
still confronted them now that the melee | been broken up Achaean war-play
started picking off the Trojan leaders | singly by striking first Areilycus
thus began the valiant Patroclus | a sharp spear in the thigh as he had jus
-turned the bronze point drove through and broke the bone | man fell headlong into dread red dead zone
and meanwhile Menelaus of Ares | favourite clouted Thoas in the knees
which he'd exposed below his shield bringing | him down and next Amphiclus was pinging
at Meges but Meges eye on him then | got in first with a spear-thrust to the stem
of the thigh where man's thickest muscle found | spear-point tore through sinews ground down to ground
descended darkness on eyes Amphiclus | then one of Nestor's sons Antilochus
struck Atymnius with his sharp spear drove | bronze head through flank and thus it did behove
Atymnius to fall with a great crash | before him pained brother's death Maris flash
-charged at Antilochus with spear in hand | before body self planted made his stand
but before he could do any damage | another son of Nestor godlike sage
Thrasymedes made a swift lunge at him | and just as had aimed on shoulder caught him
the point of his spear striking base of arm | severed the ligaments with extra harm
wrenched the bone right out Maris fell with thud | darkness down on eyes these two conquered good
by two brothers sent down to Erebus | they had done good service as spearmen thus
in Sarpedon's company were the sons | of Amisodarus who'd kept the mons

-ter Chimaera brought lots of men to grief | Aias son of Oileus much relief
dashed into the rabble Cleobolus | in trouble took alive save quietus
gave him soon enough a stroke on the neck | from hilted blade blood warmed down to the deck
Fate was tipped set her seal on him purple | Death descended then upon each pupil
Peneleos and Lycon came to grips | each had made a bad cast with their spear-tips
and missed so now they ran at each other | with their swords Lycon struck cone of other
on plumed helmet sword broke off at the hilt | but Peneleos delivered full tilt
on Lycon's neck behind the ear sword-blade | went right through nothing held there then still stayed
save a piece of skin and from that the head | hanging down as then sank to the ground bed
Meriones running hard caught up with | Acamas wounded in right shoulder with
his spear as he mounted his chariot | and descended on his eyes a riot
of mist and meanwhile Idomeneus | with relentless bronze struck Erymas thus
on the mouth the metal point of the spear | passed right through lower part skull under here
the brain smashed the white bones his teeth shattered | chattered both eyes splattered blood be-smattered
blood through nostrils and gaping mouth spurted | the black cloud of Death himself re-asserted
then each of these Achaean chieftains killed | his man like predatory wolves in-filled
the Trojans as if they were lambs or kids | and snatching them from under their dams' lids
when they're lost on the mountains through shepherd's | carelessness like wolves the timid herds
seize their chance to pick off the Trojans no | stomach fight retreat disorderly so
the one desire great Telamonian | Aias now to have a cast at Trojan
Hector no fighter inexperienced | protection broad sweep of shoulders eVinced
with his bull's hide shield and had a cocked ear | for the whistling arrow or hurtling spear
well aware enemy's reinforcement | won day yet tried save men resilient
so kept the field but by now withdrawal | from the ships become noisy rout withal
wild as onrush through sky of a storm-cloud | from Olympus theatens heavenly shroud
clear above it when tempest unleash-ed | by Zeus across Argive works Trojans fled
tails between their legs then Hector's turn fall | carried off at a gallop arms and all
abandoning to fate such of his men | hazards of the trench did there detain then
perforce for many a pair of fast war | -horses snapped off the end of shaft of car
in the trench left their masters far behind | and Patroclus chased them up close behind
slaughter in heart hounding the Danaans | relentlessly on now while the Trojans
whose formations had by now been broken | filled all roadways riot rout outspoken
dust went rolling up to the layer cloud | as strong horses for town made full speed shroud
leaving the ships and the huts behind them | and now wherever Patroclus saw them
in their greatest numbers flying before | gave a wild halloo followed up the more
many men from their cars tumbled headlong | beneath their axle-trees chariots long
overturned with a crash but he himself | driving immortal pair off-heaven-shelf
present splendid that the gods had given | Peleus they pressed on without even
a check cleared the trench with a single bound | in their eagerness to swiftly gain ground
bring Hector within range for was Hector | who he yearned to kill however Hector
had fast horses too carried him away | now in autumn there is many a day
whole countryside lies in darkness distressed | under a stormy sky heavy oppressed

Zeus sends down torrential rain punishment | to men his anger is in full ferment
because regardless of the eye jealous | of Heaven have misused their powers thus
delivered crooked judgements in session | public and justice far away driven
in consequence their streams all run in spate | and hillsides are scarred by torrents of fate
the rivers rush down headlong from the mounts | wrecking the farmlands with their mighty founts
soar with great roar into the sea turbid | such the din Troy's horse fled field perturb did
Patroclus had now cut up companies | nearest heading off their trajectories
towards the ships defeated all efforts | take refuge in city forts last resorts
and there between the ships river high wall | he kept charging in busy killing all
he could in compensation for the dead | Danaan Pronous was the first he dead
-ed with shining spear hit him on the breast | which he had exposed above his shield crest
brought him down with a crash next he attacked | Thestor son of Enops who was sat stacked
up in his polished chariot this man | had lost the plot completely as in pan
-ic reins slipped from hands Patroclus came up | beside him struck him on the right side up
on the jaw drove his spear between the teeth | using the spear as a lever hoisteeth
him over the chariot-rail as a | fisherman on a jutting rock pulls a
monster fish out of the sea with his line | and burnished hook thus with bright javelin fine
he hauled his gaping catch out of the car | dropped on face to die where fell on the bar
next Eyrlaus rushed at him did him o'erwhelm | with a rock on the head inside the helm
heavy the man's skull was then split in two | and straight away he fell face downward too
the ground soul-devouring Death engulfed him | then in swift succession dealt with Erym
-as Amphoterus and Tlepolemus | son Damastor Epaltes Echius
Polymelus son Argeas Pyris | along with Euippus and Ipheus
and in the process then bringing them all | nearest ever been down kindly soil fall
but when Sarpedon saw how his beltless | Lycians were falling to Patroclus
son of Menoetius told his gallants | what thought of them "For shame Lycian ants!
where off to with such speed admirable? | that chap over there wait 'til I'm able
to meet him I will find out who he is | carrying all before him and who is
out of us already such grief wringing | so many of our best men down w(r)inging"
and as he spoke he leapt down from his car | with all his arms and on other side far
Patroclus when he saw him did the same | and then the two men uttering the same
defiant cries made straight for each other | as with crooked claws a couple vulture
with curved beaks clashing on a rocky height | and all the while screaming as dashing fight
the Son of Cronos of the Ways Crooked | saw what went down well-hook-ed fell fuck-ed
by distress sighed to Here Sister and Wife | "Fate's unkind to me here Here Sister Wife
Sarpedon who I love dearly destined | by Patroclus son Menoetius be binned
soon to be or not to be I wonder | I'm in two minds shall I from asunder
this doom snatch him up set him down alive | then in the fair fertile lands of the live
Lycia far from war and all its tears? | or let fall this very day as one fears
now to the son there of Menoetius?" | "How you amaze me Dread Son of Cronos"
said the ox-eyed Queen of Heaven "are you | proposing let a mortal continue
reprieve whose doom long settled from the pains | of death? do as you please to ease those pains

but don't expect the other immortals | to applaud there's this point too re mortals
that you should bear in mind if Sarpedon | is sent home alive what kind restraint on
god Cummings and goings trying rescue | his own son from the fight? for not a few
of the fighters at Troy are sons of gods | who'd soon be calling out bad lockdown odds
of bitter resentment no if you love | and pity Sarpedon let to the (g)love
of Patroclus' sword hand fall when breath | has then departed from his lips send Death
and the sweet god of Sleep to take him up | and bring him to the broad realm the last cup
Lycia where kinsmen retainers will | give him the appropriate burial
barrow and monument dead man's right rite(')s" | the Father of men and gods saw the light's
rite('s) right made no demur sent a shower | bloody raindrops down to the earth mother
as a tribute to his beloved son | who Patroclus in deep-soiled land Trojan
was about to kill far from his own land | and when two had come within range band hand
Patroclus cast struck the celebrated | Thrasymelus noble squire King Sarped
-on lower part of belly brought him down | with shining spear Sarpedon cast sent down
missed Patroclus struck his horse Pedasus | on the right shoulder and in the throes thus
of death whinnied and fell down on Earth's Crust | and with a great sigh did then bite the dust
the other two horses apart now sprang | the yoke creaked and their reins became entang
-led with those of their comrade on the ground | but great spearman Automedon soon found
the remedy for this drew his long sword | from sturdy thigh jumped down deftly on sward
severed reins trace-horse clear pair righted | selves once more at their harness delighted
while the two men resumed their deadly duel | Sarpedon's lance glittered like a jewel
but missed its mark point passing harmlessly | over Patroclus' left shoulder he
then took his second cast and his weapon | did not leave his hand for no good reason
struck where the diaphragm comes up to meet | the busy heart like towering pine meet
or oak great or poplar felled in the hills | men with whetted axes make ships' infills
Sarpedon crashed down groaning ran aground | clutching at dust blood'd stained with abound
captain of the Lycian men-of-war | lay stretched in front of his horses and car
yet even as his life did then up spike | to Patroclus he breathed defiance like
some proud tawny bull who has been brought down | among shambling cows by lion king crown
that has attacked the herd and bellows thus | as the lion's jaws destroy him "Glaucus!"
he cried naming his dearest friend "My dear | Glaucus man among men! the time is here
to fall in love with evil war if there | be any prowess in you everywhere
now run to whip our captains to rally | round Sarpedon and then fight over me
with your own bronze every day of your life | the thought of me will instil in you strife
make you hang your head in shame if you let | the Achaeans spoil me of my arms yet
here where I fell beside their ships hold on | then with all your strength throw every man on
forward into the fight" Sarpedon said | no more dark had descended he was dead
Patroclus then put his foot on his chest | he pulled and withdrew the spear mangle-fleshed
midriff which came with it he'd drawn the spear | -point out man's soul both altogether clear
nearby the Myrmidons held Sarpedon's | panting horses showing inclinations
to panic now their chariot bereft | of its masters and Glaucus distraught left
when he had first heard Sarpedon's call his | impotence to help wrung his heart gripped his

damaged arm with other hand tormented | as was by arrow-wound implemented
by Teucer fighting for his comrades when | he was charging at the wall Achaean
and so then he prayed to the Archer-god | Apollo "Pray listen to me O god
whether in the rich land of Lycia | or in Troy itself as you can hear a
man anywhere when he is in distress | as I now look at wound grievous no less
I have my arm is wracked with pain the blood | refuses dry shoulder paralysed good
I can't hold my spear steady nor go out | and fight the foe and now our best man's out
of the game dead Sarpedon son of Zeus | but he will not now lift a finger Zeus
even for his son and it's you Phoebus | Apollo I ask heal this cruel wound thus
lull the pain giving me strength to rally | my comrades and fight over the body
of our King myself" Phoebus Apollo | heard his prayer and his response not hollow
at once relieved the pain dried the dark blood | from his cruel wound and his heart did then flood
with strength Glaucus was conscious of his aid | rejoiced great god had lent so ready-made
an ear to his prayer so went at once to | all the Lycian captains urged them to
rally round Sarpedon then approaching | some allies Trojan also thus broaching
Polydamas son Panthous Agenor | the noble Aeneas too and Hector
in arms of bronze went up reflected | "Hector you have completely neglected
your allies who're giving their lives for you | far from their dear ones and land and yet you
show no eagerness to help Sarpedon | leader of the men-at-arms Lycian
lies dead was the just and strong defender | of the mighty kingdom of Lycia
and now the brazen War-god's cut him down | with Patroclus' spear make a stand down
there by him what shame if a Myrmidon | in revenge for many an Achaean
who fell to our spears by the gallant ships | with the arms of Sarpedon then off skips
and they desecrate his corpse" each Trojan | heart-broken unbearable Sarpedon
though a foreigner had been a buttress | their city soldier of finest finesse
in the great army that he had brought them | boundless sorrow knew keen to avenge then
made straight for the Argives Hector in van | infuriated death such a key man
meanwhile the Achaeans spurred on by he | son Menoetius Patroclus shaggy
-breasted with the Aiantes he began | pair in little need of exhortation
"My lords let this news whet your appetite | fight make you the men you once were of right
or even better Sarpedon lies dead | was the first who Achaean wall storm led
let's see if we can capture and besmirch | corpse strip armour leave oppos in the lurch
us enrich at same time cut to pieces | some of the friends whose wish for him peace is"
even before he spoke they'd been spoiling | for fight now both sides more selves embroiling
on the one side Trojans and Lycians | the other Myrmidons and Achaeans
joined battle over fallen Sarpedon | with a terrific roar the armour on
men's bodies rang aloud Zeus eclipse did | battlefield in dread night form ellipse did
over beloved son so make struggle | all the more chaotic and terrible
at first the Trojans able to repel | the Achaeans of the flashing eyes well
lost a leader latter of Myrmidon | army the noble Epeigeus son
of the great-hearted Agacles had been | ruler of Budeion a fine town scene
but having there killed a highborn kinsman | with Thetis of the Silver Feet took san

-ctuary plus Peleus who thus sent him | off to the great city of Ilium
land of noble horses with Achilles | man-breaker fight for their allies pleas please
against Trojans and this man had just laid | hands on the corpse when with rock on head played
illustrious Hector hit him inside | the heavy helmet his skull split each side
and he fell face down across the body | soul-devouring Death engulfed him shoddy
now Patroclus grieved at his comrade's loss | sped through the front line and not at a loss
swift as a falcon when he does scatter | jackdaws and starlings so the Horse Master
Rohan Patroclus at the Lycians | and Trojans flew in fury at his man's
death he hit Sthenelaus on the neck | with a boulder and his sinews did wreck
sad son of Ithaemenes the Trojan | front line Hector too before his come-on
fell back but they withdrew under Argive | pressure only as far as one can drive
a long javelin when he's doing his best | in a match or even tight fight contest
with the enemy thirsting for his blood | and Glaucus captain a shield-bearing hood
Lycian was the first to halt facing | about gallant Bathycles effacing
the son of Chalcon had house in Hellas | and he was one of the most prosperous
of Myrmidons Bathycles about | to catch him up when Glaucus just about
then turned suddenly on his pursuer | struck in middle of chest with spear-skewer
bringing him down with a crash and to lose | this fine man heavy and harrowing news
to the Argives but Trojans delighted | round his body now rally ignited
but Argives' impetus not extinguished | bore down on oppos in strength distinguished
now the turn of Meriones to kill | Trojan soldier Laogonus vigil
-ant son Onetor priest Zeus Idaean | worshipped by the local population
Meriones struck under jaw and ear | death for him did no longer linger here
he was engulfed by the unlovely dark | Aeneas fired back with a spear bright spark
hoping to catch him as he strode forward | under cover of his shield but on guard
was Meriones avoided bronze's | tip quickly ducking long shaft to ground is
behind him and sticks there with the butt-end | quivering 'til War-god's heavy hand end
stilled but Aeneas so enraged shouted | "You may well be a fine dancer but outed
you forever would my spear have if on | -ly I'd hit you" great spearman Merion
-'es replied "Aeneas as powerful | as you are you can hardly expect full
compliance from everyone who meets you | of mortal stuff like the rest of us you
are made I too might say if I caught you | in the belly now with a sharp spear you
would soon yield your life Hades of Fabled | Horse then to me the glory enabled
for all your strength and your belief in brawn" | the great Patroclus overheard used his brain
to reprove "Meriones you're too fine | a soldier for such silly talk when time
is against us believe me the Trojans | aren't going to be pushed from Sarpedon's
body by a few rude remarks there'll be | some dead men on the ground before they flee
because battles indeed are won by deeds | the council-chamber is place one word heeds
let's have some fighting and no more speeches" | he led the way Meriones speechless
went with him looking like a god from their | bronze and leather equipment tough shields there
as they met the thrust of sword or double | -pointed spear the trodden earth a trouble
of noise sent up like the clatter that's heard | far hills when bardcutters in glade tree word

(s)(t)(r)eam are working and the sharpest eye would fail | now to recognise the admirable
Sarpedon covered as was completely | head to foot weapons blood dust busily
they swarmed round the body as flies in a | cow-yard buzz round the brimming pails on a
spring day when vessels full selves disarming | excess milk and all the time while were swarming
thus round the body of Sarpedon Zeus | lift bright eyes from sight of site had no use
kept them fixed on the struggling mass of men | and paused to take counsel with himself then
regarding the killing of Patroclus | for a long time he was in two minds thus
whether let him fall to spear Prince Hector | body of godlike Sarpedon over
in this very fight and so let Hector | from his shoulders strip the gleaming armour
or whether allow Patroclus to bring | still more of his enemies to end bling
in the end Zeus decided the gallant | squire of highborn Achilles he would grant
a driving of the Trojans and bronze-clad | Hector back towards Troy left lots dead bad
starts with Hector made a coward of him | leapt into car trim not at a whim grim
wheeled around for flight shouting to others | to take to their heels the Trojan brothers
knew that Zeus now had tipped the Sacred Scales | against him so no Lycian prevails
even fled one and all had they not seen | their own mighty King in heart stricken keen?
and lying where the dead were heaped because | in that battle-royal the Son of Cronos
staged many fell dead upon Sarpedon | and henceforth the men-at-arms Achaean
were enabled to strip the gleaming bronze | from his shoulders Menoetius' son's
handed it to his men to deliver | to beaked ships but Zeus the Cloud-gatherer
had not yet done turning to Apollo | he said "Quick my dear Phoebus Apollo
go and take Sarpedon out of their range | when dark blood wiped off made spotless exchange
carry him to some distant spot where you'll | wash him in running water with jewel
of ambrosia anoint wrap him up | in imperishable robe him put up
into hands of Sleep and his twin-brother | Death who'll make all speed to rediscover
the broad and fertile far realm Lycian | and there then each retainer and kinsman
to give burial with a monument | barrow proper tribute to fallen meant"
Apollo not with a deaf ear stricken | to his father's words from the Idaean
Mountains descended into the rumble | of the jungle at once picked up noble
Sarpedon clearing him of each fell dart | carried him away to a distant part
where he then washed him in running water | and anointed him with ambrosia
wrapped him in an imperishable robe | entrusted him to Sleep twin-brother probe
of Death swiftly set him down in the broad | and fertile realm of Lycia abroad
meanwhile Patroclus to Automedon | and his horses shouts in pursuit Trojan
and Lycian went but he was a fool | now making an error fatal flaw tool
had he kept to Achilles' orders | would have saved himself the grave disorders
of doom and the black night of Death the thoughts | of Zeus however far outstrip the thoughts
of men in a moment the god can make | a brave man run away battle forsake
and the next day will spur him on to fight | now made Patroclus over-keen to fight
who was the first man who the last to fall | to you Patroclus as the gods did call
you to death? Adrestus first Autonous | Perimus son of Megas Echeclus
Epistor Melanippus Elasus | and after Pylatres and Mulius

all these Patroclus killed although the rest | flew and so all-devouring was the quest
vehement of spear Troy of the High Gates | would now have fallen to great fate pet hates
and the Achaean arms if Apollo | had not then taken his position so
on the well-built wall in his eagerness | to help the Trojans and bring his high press
to an evil end three times Patroclus | scaled an angle of the lofty wall thus
thrice Apollo hurled him off by thrusting | with his immortal hands the shield trusting
but when fo(u)rth he came on like a devil | the god checked him with a shout terrible
cried "Back my lord Patroclus! the city | of the lordly Trojans not destined be
taken by your spear and nor even by | Achilles a better man than you by
a long chalk the bees' knees" when he heard this | Patroclus fell a good way back give miss
to the anger of the great god-Archer | his galloping horses halted Hector
at the Scaean Gate debate whether to | drive into the rout again fight or to
order all his men to withdraw into | the city and he was still in minds two
when Phoebus Apollo appeared by him | borrowing stalwart upstanding form trim
of Asius an uncle of Hector | the horse-tamer of Hecabe brother
a son of Dymas dweller Phrygia | on banks of the Sangarius river
in this guise Apollo son of Zeus spoke | "Hector why have you let the fight go broke
and neglected your duty? I wish I | were as much your better as you're mine! I
would soon teach you to your sorrow not pay | to shirk a fight off with you now and pay
Patroclus a call with your splendid pair | you may catch him yet with Apollo's fair
blessing" the god went back to fight fell in | thus the illustrious Hector tellin'
the doughty Cebriones lash horses | into fight the god with Argives merges
casts into confusion gives upper hand | Hector and Trojans Hector turned his hand
to Patroclus alone rest Danaans | left killing none drove his powerful roans
straight at him and for his part Patroclus | leapt from chariot to ground his spear thus
left hand with right picked up jagged stone | sparkling hand just about covered the stone
standing in no awe Hector threw with all | his force did not make idle cast at all
because the sharp stone caught Hector's driver | Cebriones a bastard whose father
King Priam shattered both of his eyebrows | crushing in the bone then both his eyes browse
fall out and roll in the dust at his feet | and drops from the well-built chariot feat
like a diver and yielded up his life | the knight Patroclus then jeered at his strife
"Ha! quite an acrobat I see judging | by that graceful dive! for man adjudging
so neat a header from a car on land | could dive for oysters from a ship and land
plenty for a feast in any weather | didn't know bros Tro had such a diver"
and so he hurled himself at the noble | Cebriones with the fury total
of a lion been wounded in the breast | while assaulting the pens seeking feast best
to his own audacity falls victim | thus Patroclus you flung yourself at him
Hector had jumped down from the chariot | on other side two not chary riot
fought for Cebriones like two lions | on heights way up in mountains of aeons
both of them as hungry and high-mettled | as with body of a stag co-meddled
thus with Cebriones between them these | two of ways of war artificers' ease
Patroclus and illustrious Hector | strove to tear the flesh of each as vector

with the cruel bronze Hector seized on the head | held on Patroclus in his stead instead
clung to a foot rest of the Danaans | and the Trojans then made a merry dance
of the tussle there was such a scrimmage | then as the East and South winds sometimes stage
with one another in a mountain glen | when they tumble around the high woods' pen
causing the long boughs of the beech and ash | and the smooth-barked cornel-tree too to clash
one with another with a wild tattoo | the noise of the snapping branches that too
thus Trojans and Achaeans leapt at fought | with one another destruction sought wrought
no thought of craven flight on either side | Cebriones lay dead the ground beside
bristled with sharp spears and feathered arrows | that had leapt from the strings of the great bows
and many a huge rock crashed on the shields | of those fighting round him and no-one yields
and there lay in a whirl of a dust mite | great even in his fall of the delight
of a charioteer thinking no more | so long as the Sun still on high did soar
volley and counter-volley found their mark | and men kept falling but when the sun's arc
then began to fall towards the time when | the ploughman thinks to unyoke his oxen
the Argives cheated Fate proved selves more able | dragged Cebriones oppos unable
from among the weapons yelling Trojans | stripped his armour issued the bronze death bans
but Patroclus wished more execution | yet rushed into the enemy action
three times he charged with a terrific cry | like wild-willed god of War his sally by
every time nine men killed but when leapt in | fourth alas Patroclus! like demon in
end end-game into sight as in heart yet | of the battle it was Phoebus he met
Phoebus most terrible but Patroclus | had not seen him coming through the rout plus
the god had wrapped himself in a thick mist | for this unfriendly and terrible tryst
now Phoebus Apollo stood behind him | striking his broad shoulders and trim arc grim
of his back with the flat of his huge hand | made eyes from Patroclus' head out stand
knocked off visored helmet it rolled away | with a clatter under the horses' sway
-ing hooves its plume was smeared with dust and blood | crested helm no man been allowed as hood
ever to tumble in the dust when head | sweet face divine Achilles protected
fell into Hector's hands Zeus let him wear | for a little while as end well near there
not only that but the long-shadowed spear | huge thick and heavy with head of bronze clear
was too shattered in Patroclus' hands | tasselled shield baldric fell from shoulders' band
to ground and King Apollo son of Zeus | undid corslet on his breast now no use
so stunned his shapely legs refused carry | and as there in a daze he did tarry
a Dardanian Euphorbus came near | behind him then struck him with a sharp spear
midway between the shoulders Euphorbus | being not just a son of Panthous plus
spearman runner and horseman the best one | of his years and in this fight the first one
he had fought in as a charioteer | while learning about art of war dear here
he'd brought twenty from cars down onto land | and so he was then the first to wound land
on knight Patroclus but did not despatch | after the ashen spear from flesh did snatch
ran back again and mingled with the crowd | not for stay fight Patroclus naked cowed
though he was and unmanned by the god's blow | and Euphorbus' spear Patroclus so
tried to escape his fate then by slinking | back among Myrmidons welcome thinking
when Hector saw great Patroclus creeping | wounded from the field his way made leaping

towards him through the ranks coming up struck | with a spear clear out of luck the poor fuck
now in the lower part of the belly | driving the bronze clean through Patroclus he
fell with a thud whole Argive host appalled | like an indomitable wild-boar mauled
by a lion after a battle fought | up in the mountains in high fury fraught
over little stream where both wish to drink | lion's strength prevails enemy does shrink
panting overcome so after stalling | so many men himself the son falling
valiant Menoetius to short-spear | cast Hector son Priam conqueror here
addressed him "Patroclus you thought you would | sack my town make Troy's women slaves if could
ship them off to your own country fool you | in their defence hasting to battle too
were Hector's fast horses and so Hector | too Hasting's victor vector I Hector
finest spearman war-loving Trojan thains | who stand between them and day iron chains
of slavery so now couple vulture | going to eat you up you poor creature
and even the strong arm of Achilles | did not save you I can now hear all he's
told you when sent you out and stayed behind | 'Patroclus Master of the Horse don't find
yourself back at the hollow ships before | tearing the tunic on breast of Hector
man-killing and with his blood it soaking' | for that must have been what he invoking
like a lunatic took him at his word" | and how has knight Patroclus replied? word
in failing voice "Hector boast while you may | for it is yours the victory today
it's a gift from Zeus the Son of Cronos | and Apollo *they* beat me onerous
task not they took the armour from my back | if twenty Hectors had been on my back
they would all have fallen then to my spear | no hateful Destiny Leto's Son here
did for me then came a man Euphorbus | you were only the third but listen thus
to this and ponder it well as you too | I swear it do not have very long to
live already sov'reign Destiny Death | are now coming very close to you death
at the hands of Achilles peerless son | of Peleus" Death now him called time on
his disembodied soul took wing sailing | for the House of Hades now bewailing
its lot and the youth and manhood now wrecked | and yet the illustrious Hector hect
-ored him again although dead "Patroclus | why be so sure of my early end thus?
who knows? as Achilles son of Thetis | of Lovely Locks may well yet me in this
pre-decease by ending *his* life by spear | -blow from me" on Patroclus Hector dear
put his foot so as to withdraw his spear | from wound thrust at the corpse 'til came off clear
fell face upwards on the ground with same spear | and without a pause he set off to sheer
Automedon the noble squire of swift | son of Peleus keen to give a lift
to Hades but Automedon carried | from harm gift splendid harried not tarried
the swift immortal horses Peleus | from Heaven been graciously granted thus

έπτακαίδεκα

*Book 17*

# THE STRUGGLE OVER PATROCLUS

*fierce battle round Patroklos' body*
*who'll for a little while hold still body?*

now Menelaus son of Atreus | who a clear favourite of Ares plus
Patroclus quick now sees has been vanquished | resplendent in bronze equipment anguished
hastened through front ranks bestrode his body | like a fretful mother-cow standing she
over her first calf brought into the world | thus red-haired Menelaus self unfurled
Patroclus covered with spear round buckler's | ready able to kill all attackers
however Panthous' son Euphorbus | in the body of peerless Patroclus
was also interested and making | close up to it ventured forth "My lord King
Menelaus son of Atreus go | leave this dead man and his blood-stained arms so
for I was the first among the Trojans | and their famous allies to play spearman's
role against Patroclus in this battle | let me enjoy my victory or that'll
be the day for you take your precious life" | red-haired Menelaus fury thus strife
cried "Father Zeus have you ever seen such | o'erweening arrogance? we know so much
of the courage of panther and lion | and the fierce wild-boar most self-relian
-t' high-spirited beast of all but are't | it seems as nothing to the mighty art
of these sons of Panthous with their famous | ash spears! yet Hyperenor horses sus
did as tamer not long survive savour | the delights of youth gave me no waiver
confronting and insulting me he said | I was the most contemptible instead
of the Danaan men-at-arms yet meet | to recall it was not on his own feet
that he went home to delight his loving wife | fond parents and I'll be cutting the life
for you as did for him YOU coxcomb | if you'ld dare up against me to box come
pox get back now join rabble don't stand up | to me or you'll come to grief straight up
the height of folly's to be wise too late" | but Euphorbus not cowed "This very date
King Menelaus you are going to | pay the full price for my brother who you
killed and boast about and whose wife you left | widow in new bridal chamber bereft
and forlorn you caused his parents untold | tears and misery yet could be consoled
still unhappy pair by bringing back head | and armour of yours and put them instead
in the hands of Panthous and the lady | Phrontis but our business brooks no delay see

a quick contest will decide life or death" | then struck Menelaus with all his breath
on his round shield but the bronze did not break | through as stout shield bent back no progress make
then Menelaus son Atreus use | made of spear with a prayer to Father Zeus
and as Euphorbus fell back he struck him | in the base of the throat thrusting at him
with his full weight keeping grip of the spear | through the soft flesh of the neck point went clear
came down with a thud and his armour rang | upon him hair had been in same top rank
as the Graces' lovely locks used to bind | the little curls with twine gold silver kind
now all was drenched with blood and he lay there | fallen sapling as gardener new fare
takes an olive shoot and plants in a place | of its own where can suck up at own pace
plenty of moisture grows into a fine | young tree and every breeze does it entwine
bursts into white blossom but wind unkind | gusty blows up one day and does unwind
it from its trench stretches it on the earth | Euphorbus son Panthous ashen spear worth
-less lay prostrate as Menelaus son | of Atreus his killer thereupon
stripped him of his arms and not one Trojan | dared to come near the illustrious son
of Atreus like a mountain lion | who believes in own strength so pounces on
the finest heifer in a herd grazing | with powerful jaws her neck re-ph(r)asing
tears her to pieces devours blood curd | and entrails while all around him the herd
-smen and their dogs create a din but keep | their distance for their fear of him so deep
nothing would induce them come closer see | Atreides would have found it easy
thus to despoil Euphorbus if Phoebus | Apollo had not grudged his fine truss
sent Hector attack him like the rabid | War-god went to Hector self disguise did
as Mentes a leader of Cicones | said "Hector why so full of cojones
heart bent catching Achilles' horses | so hard to master and drive their courses
at least for a mere man or anyone | save Mother goddess Peleus' son?
while you are chasing this will-o'-the-wisp | redoubtable Menelaus stands crisp
of will over corpse Patroclus has killed | the best man in all Troy the multi-skilled
Euphorbus son of Panthous will never | fight again" with that the god did sever
contact back into the heart of battle | grief wrung very soul did hollow rattle
but presently he peered across the ranks | sure enough he saw them a pair of tanks
Menelaus splendid arms removing | spiked tanked Euphorbus on ground not moving
with the blood pouring from his wound gaping | with loud cry Hector starts like hound scaping
front line resplendent bronze dreaming gleaming | like flames inextinguishable te(e/a)ming
beaming fierce fiery furnace Master-smith | Menelaus recognised him forthwith
from his war-cry dismayed and took counsel | his indomitable soul 'What the hell
shall I do?' asked himself in his distress | 'if I abandon these fine arms no less
the body of Patroclus who fell here | fighting to exact a repayment clear
for my wrongs I shall then be an object | to any Argive sees contempt abject
but if for honour's sake fight with Hector | and the Trojans single-handed I'm more
than likely to be cut off overwhelmed | for fell Hector of the bright plume well helmed
has all the Trojans at his dogged heels | but why debate the point? when a man feels
without the goodwill of the gods he needs | to fight another who the godhead heeds
then he has disaster coming to him | surely no Danaan will think it crim

-inal when he sees me now giving way | to Hector with the gods backing his sway
if only I knew where the great Aias | is even Heaven against us alas
the pair of us might make another stand | and try to save the body for the grand
Achilles it would at all events be | something gained' in this inward debate he
still engaged with the Trojan companies | bearing down upon him in their van is
Hector thus Menelaus now ceding | the body turning and then receding
lots backward looks like a lion bearded | feels chill of fear in stout heart when bearded
from the fold with spears and shouts of shepherds | and dogs and much against his will farmyard's
abandoned thus red-haired Menelaus | withdrew now from body of Patroclus
but when he had reached his own company | he faced about and stood looking every
-where for great Telamonian Aias | he saw him presently on the left as
he was exhorting hounding on his men | who Phoebus Apollo had then stricken
with supernatural fears he began | to run soon by the Telamonian
"Come with me over there let's strike a blow | for the dead Patroclus as we might so
at least save the body for Achilles | naked though it is though not the bees'-knees
armour for Hector has now taken that" | the valiant Aias was stirred at that
appeal he and red-haired Menelaus | went off through fine front line many layers
Hector tugging at corpse of Patroclus | having stripped him of noble armour plus
now wanting behead him with his sharp sword | drag off trunk sherd dogs of war Troy feed horde
but when Aias came with tower-like shield | Hector to rejoin company did yield
leapt into his car beautiful armour | gave to some Trojans take back to tower
-town where he hoped the trophy would redound | to his honour Aias rebound refound
Patroclus with his broad shield stood at bay | lion confronted by huntsmen on way
through forest with cubs plants himself in front | of the helpless creatures defiant front
put on lowering brows to veil his eyes | Aias plants self where Patroclus lies
thus on his other side Menelaus | favourite Ares son of Atreus
took stand each moment added to his grief | Glaucus son of Hippolochus the chief
of the Lycian forces was displeased | with Hector gave him black look he not teased
but took him to task "Hector a fine show | on parade but in battle a no-show
useless as your splendid reputation | after all just hides a coward craven
ask yourself how you are going to save | town and citadel with none to help save
native Trojans none of the Lycians | will be off out to fight the Danaans
for Troy now they've learnt they get no credit | for struggling with the enemy dread (f)it
day in day out so what hope has a one | in the ranks of rescue by such a one
as you when he is in a tight corner | when callously left Sarpedon a loner
your guest comrade-in-arms like carrion | in Argive hands? a sorry carry-on!
you and your city owed a lot to him | while alive but pluck from the dogs save him
you have not even had that and so I | if I have any influence with my
Lycians will take them home that will mean | the end of Troy why if the Trojans mean
business had some real courage the dauntless | spirit that the soldiery then express
in excess when defending their country | makes them tooth and nail fight the enemy
we should soon drag Patroclus into Troy | and if his body could be brought o joy!

in from the field lodged in the great city | of King Priam the Argives would quickly
then return Sarpedon's splendid armour | and we could bring *his* body into our
citadel it is a question of rank | he was squire to greatest soldier camp rank
Argive the best soldiers in his command | but you have failed us you did not dare stand
enemy war-cry ringing in your ears | up against lion-hearted Aias fears
look him in the eye not gung-ho go in | because he's the better man gunga din"
but now Hector of the glittering helm | "Glaucus" ugly look underwhelming helm
"amazed at such effrontery in one | like you always thought you the wisest one
in the whole of deep-soiled Lycia yet | you've destroyed my faith in your judgement set
by talking like this even suggesting | against huge Aias dare not self testing
believe me fighting and the noise of cars | don't frighten me but we're all puppet tzars
in the hands of great aegis-bearing Zeus | in a moment a brave man can by Zeus
be made to run away lose a battle | next day same god spurs him into battle
bear with me now my friend stand by my side | and see what I can do see if your side
of it is true and I prove a coward | all day long or whether I can now ward
off some of these Danaans ferocious | as they are stop their fighting atrocious
for Patroclus' corpse" in a voice loud | gave an order to his warrior crowd
"Trojans host Dardanian fight intends | hand to hand be men my friends
now put forth all your strength I'll gird myself | in gear of peerless Achilles himself
the splendid armour I took from the great | Patroclus when I made him late of late"
with that Hector of the helmet burnished | left battlefield chased his men who'd vanished
carrying the famous armour of son | Peleus away towards town soon on
their tail as they'd not yet gone far from here | and he ran fast in a blur changed his gear
spot lamentable fighting not yet reached | told his Trojans who the love of war preached
take his own arms to sacred Ilium | put on the imperishable well plum(b)
armour Achilles the gods of Heaven | to Peleus his father had given
Peleus when grew old had passed it on | to his son but not destined was the son
grow much older in his father's armour | and then when Zeus the great Cloud-compeller
saw Hector from afar equipping self | in arms of divine Achilles himself
shook head said to himself "Unhappy man! | little knowing how close to also-ran
you are putting on imperishable | armour of a man in war most able
and before whom all others simply quail | and you who his friend speared killed like a quail
Patroclus the brave and most loveable | stripped arms head shoulders with hands culpable
well for a trice great power shall be yours | but you'll have to pay for it you and yours
no home-coming from battle you be will | and Andromache from your hands never will
take the splendid armour of Achilles" | Son of Cronos bowing brow(s)e sable he's
confirming by that his thoughts and so caused | armour to sit easily on not-paused
Hector the savage spirit of the dread | War-god into Hector's heart was now fed
and power and fresh vigour filled his limbs | uttering piercing war-cry battle hymns
he went in search of his allies renowned | to all himself presented newly-gowned
resplendent in the armour of lion | -hearted Achilles and to spur them on
went up and in his turn spoke to each one | first to Mesthles and Glaucus then Medon

Thersilochus and Asteropaeus | and next Deisenor and then Hippothous
to Phorcys Chromius and Ennomus | the augur to give them an enormous
boost made a speech "Attend to me in your | multitudes both ally also neighbour
I neither sought nor wanted numbers when | every one of you here I did summon
from your own cities for what I needed | was men who'd fight with good grace indeed did
against the fierce Achaeans to defend | each Troy woman small child Argives offend
it is for that end I impoverish | my own people who all of you furnish
with free provisions so keep courage high | each of you straight at the enemy nigh
to live or die! that is the soldier's tryst | to one who forces Aias back by fist
or thrust and brings Patroclus dead though is | into the Trojan lines I will make his
half the spoils keeping half for myself he | will share the glory equally with me"
in response they lifted their spears and charged | Argives with all their power fully charged
high hopes had of retrieving the body | from Telamonian Aias sadly
were ill-advised as Aias hovering | to take many a life in covering
corpse Patroclus but for now toward turned | loud-war-cry Menelaus "My well learned
friend Menelaus nursling Zeus starting | think you and I never be departing
home safe from this fight let alone the corpse | I am not so much concerned for the corpse
of Patroclus which will soon be glutting | Trojan bird dogs but ourselves now putting
in danger Hector near to engulf us | like a black cloud Death is now staring us
in the face quick! try a call to Argive | chieftains somebody may hear cry alive"
the loud-war-cry Menelaus complied | gave Danaans piercing call "Friends" he cried
"Captains and Counsellors of the Argives | drink your wine at cost of public lives
by the side of the great Atreidae | Agamemnon Menelaus who high
command share and derive your majesty | and titles from Zeus it is now for me
impossible in the wild confusion | of this fight pick out each chief one call on
come forward each one without being named | and think it infamy we would be shamed
dogs of Troy have Patroclus as a toy" | Aias the Runner of Oileus boy
heard every word first to come running up | to Menelaus through melee next up
Idomeneus and Meriones | squire of the man-killing War-god peer he's
as for the rest who came behind where now | one who could recall all their names and how!?
and led by Hector the Trojans came on | in a mass with a loud roar going on
like that of a great wave when meets current | mouth heaven-fed river clash does foment
and the headlands on either side throw back | the thunder of invading host sea black
but united in their resolution | faced up to them did party Achaean
made fence of bronze shields around Patroclus | and in addition the Son of Cronos
spread a thick mist round each burnished helmet | had no quarrel with Patroclus when yet
alive and squire to Achilles and loathed | thought being carrion carried uncloathed
cursed dogs hostile Troy so now emboldened | comrades in defence make stand 'em bold end
at first the Trojans flung back the bright-eyed | Argives who at first left corpse high and dried
gave ground to them even so the haughty | Trojans not able kill one of party
with their spears for all the pains they'd taken | but start drag off corpse did party Trojan
however Achaeans were not going | leave in their hands long rally got going

soon round Aias who next to the peerless | son Peleus Argives finest finesse
of all in looks in action the noblest | he dashed through the front line as if were blessed
fierce as a wild-boar that then turns at bay | in the mountains with one charge sweeps away
the hounds and stalwart huntsmen sends flying | down the glades proud Telamon's son plying
thus into Trojan ranks Aias mighty | illustrious then scattered the party
that had gathered round Patroclus made up | their minds that *they* would win the glory cup
drag his body into Troy Hippothous | the noble son Pelasgian Lethus
had tied his baldric around the tendons | of the ankle what he then intend-on's
hauling him by foot through battling throng | hoped do Hector and Trojans turn not wrong
but did self bad one soon into trouble | save him could not of friends all the goodwill
as Telamon's son rushed up through the crowd | and straight through the bronze-cheeked helm the spear ploughed
the plumed helmet hit by the heavy spear | and great hand behind wielded that sharp gear
was rent open by the point the man's blood | brains gushing through the visor in a flood
from wound Hippothous collapsed let foot girt | of great Patroclus drop from hand to dirt
following it up came down face forward | on the corpse a long way from deep-soiled ward
Larissa when cut down by spear Aias | life too short now never repay alas
parents for their care at that point Hector | took a turn hurled glittering spear vector
(b)at Aias but Aias was looking out | and avoided the bronze lance just about
which hit one Schedius son valiant | of Iphitus best Phocian gallant
powerful prince whose home in the famous | town Panopeus and Hector struck thus
this man under middle of collar bone | right through bronze spear-point did then moan and groan
stuck out below his shoulder fell with a | thud and his armour rang upon him A
-ias in turn struck Phorcys the doughty son | of Phaenops right in the belly full on
as he bestrode Hippothous broke the plate | of his corslet spear let bowels vacate
falling in the dust he clutched at the ground | Trojan front and glorious Hector found
themselves falling right back while the Argives | with cries of triumph dragged away the lives
of Phorcys and Hippothous and removed | the armour from their shoulders sorely moved
disheartened the Trojans might now have been | forced back into Troy by Achaeans seen
as conquerors who'd by their own valour | exertions have won an even greater
victory than Zeus planned if Apollo | had not roused Aeneas he did follow
precedent taking form of a herald | Periphas son of Epytus who held
kindly disposition to Aeneas | serving his old father beforehand as
a herald until he himself was old | thus in this disguise Apollo the bold
son of Zeus accosted him "Aeneas | if of all of Heaven Zeus e'en 'e 'as
taken against us what hope citadel | save Ilium? I've known men who've done well
in saving their country notwithstanding | Zeus by own strong arms withal withstanding
plus their bravery and numbers but Zeus | is on our side! and thus wishes us use
goodwill to beat Argives and yet you're scared | out of your senses and to fight not dared"
Aeneas looked him in the face and knew | him for the Archer-King Apollo who
gave a great shout "Hector all you Trojan | and allied commanders a great shame on
you to let the conquering Achaeans | drive us into Troy in cowardly scenes
besides one of the gods came up to me | just now told me that Zeus Counsellor he

Supreme is still our ally in this war | and therefore let us now then go straight for
the Danaans see they don't find it yet | too easy the dead Patroclus to get
to their ships" he sallied out took his stand | well in front of foremost fighting brand band
Trojan turn-around faced host Achaean | then he cast spear struck Leiocritus an
heir Arisbas and this man a gallant | aide of Lycomedes the valiant
Lycomedes distressed to see him fall | he ran up and stood beside him with-all
his might let fly with his shining javelin | result then the striking of a chieftain
Apisaon the son of Hippasus | in the liver under the midriff thus
bringing him to the ground Apisaon | was one who had come from fertile Paeon
-ia in fact was their best soldier here | next to Asteropaeus War-god peer
Asteropaeus distressed at his fall | now made a fierce charge by himself at all
the Argives but too late to accomplish | any good as body surrounded swish
curtain certain shields levelled spears bevelled | Aias had gone round strict orders levelled
at all no-one to back from the body | nor break away to fight in front body
stick close to each other and Patroclus | by these tactics of Aias the earth thus
empurpled with blood and men fell in heaps | Trojans and haughty allies in the deeps
mingling their corpses with the Danaan dead | for the Danaans did not fight a red
-bloodless battle either and yet lost far | fewer men as they recalled from afar
duty each other in hurly-burly | friend saved friend from fate unruly surly
end sticky battle raged lewd rude you'd | have thought sun and moon no more shrewd crude viewed
not still in commission for fog had spread | particular part of field not widespread
where the pick of the men were disputing | corpse Patroclus but elsewhere free-booting
in comfort under a clear sky Trojans | and the soldiery of the Achaeans
there was brilliant sunshine over all | no cloud in sight above plain hill no pall
fall fighting desultory as kept their | distance avoided troublesome spear there
it was just the centre that with the fog | and oppos burden of bronze armour bog
-ging them down and so the army Trojan | suffer great distress like host Achaean
two of them famous pair Thrasymedes | Antilochus knew not leading one he's
dead as thought peerless Patroclus was still | alive and fighting the Trojans until
the cows come home at where the two lines met | and so therefore stayed in their own part yet
of the field looking out for casualties | or signs of panic in own companies
as Nestor had told them to do when he | saw them off from the beaked black ships to see
battle but the grim struggle that ensued | death noble squire Achilles continued
unabated all day long while the knees | shins feet hands eyes down to the very lees
of the contending forces with sweat streamed | from their exertions tugged sweet live-dead-streamed
body to and fro between them in such | a restricted space a group of men much
like a tanner gives job to of stretching | a great bull's hide soaked in fat and fetching
it forth stand round in a ring tug at it | with many hands 'til in every part it
is taut and moisture comes out while the fat | sinks in each party had high hopes in that
Trojans of drag Patroclus into Troy | Argives of bring him back to the ship's b(u)oy
the result was such a scrimmage over | the corpse as even Ares warmonger
or Athene would not have displeased in their | most pugnacious mood such was the toil there

and agony that that day dispensed Zeus | to man horse alike over body use
of Patroclus but high-born Achilles | as yet no Inklings Patroclus his squeeze
dead they were fighting far from ships gallant | under the walls of Troy it never Ent
-ered his head that Patroclus had been killed | he thought of him pressing on so strong-willed
to the very gates return safe and sound | never expected him be sack town bound
without him or with him either he'd oft | been told that this was not to be as off't
table by his own Mother who gave use | to him of private info of plans Zeus
not that she had told him now of the thing | terrible that had then been happening
leading to loss of his dearest friend there | over him meanwhile those others with their
pointed spears locked in unending struggle | killing each other life and death juggle
the bronze-clad Achaeans felt it would be | disgrace to their name fall back ever flee
to black ships "Friends" they said among themselves | "if horse-taming Trojan us overwhelms
drag this corpse off in triumph to their town | then the very best thing that could go down
would be that the black earth should swallow us | where we stand" on Trojan side mirror thus
felt the same "Comrades" said one of them too | "even if all of us are destined to
be killed beside this corpse let none retire" | so they felt urged each other on mood dire
so the fight continued metallic din | rose through empty spaces of the air thin
struck the copper sky far from the conflict | the horses of Achilles in conflict
had been weeping ever since they learnt their | charioteer by Hector murd'rous there
been brought down in the dust Automedon | did whatever could Diores' son
with whip whistling lashed them repeatedly | in turn coaxing and cursing them freely
but the pair refused either to back turn | towards black ships broad Hellespont return
or into battle after the Argives | firm as a barrow's gravestone on which lives'
dead wo(e)man speak of memory's token | simply stood there without any motion
in front of their beautiful chariot | with their heads bowed down to the earth and hot
tears ran from their eyes to the ground as mourned | driver luxuriant manes muck-adorned
as they came tumbling down from the yoke-pad | each side of the yoke Son of Cronos sad
sorry for them when saw their grief himself | and then he shook his head and said to self
"Poor beasts! why did we give you ageless thus | not of mortal plain to King Peleus
who's doomed to die? did we mean you feature | in sorrows of unhappy man? creature
most miserable of all creep and breath have | on Mother Earth one thing that I'll *Not* have
Prince Hector shan't drive you and your splendid | chariot are the arms and the brief bid
for fame and stardom not enough for him? | no I'll fill your legs with Vigour and Vim
-to your hearts with courage thus may abound | Automedon bring back from the fight sound
and safe to the hollow beaked ships I mean | the Trojans to recover Achaean
host smite until they reach the well-found ships | sun sets and the blessed darkness in ships"
Zeus breathed fresh power into the horses | thus they shook the dust from their mane courses
galloped away with their fast chariot | join Trojan Achaean chary riot
behind Automedon took fighter's place | although he sorely missed his comrade ace
swept into fight in car without great mate | like a vulture after geese horses' gait
made easy avoid entanglement fate | and as easy to dash into it late
and pursue an enemy through the crowd | and yet kill men he followed not allowed

alone as he was in the sacred car | was finding it not possible by far
to control the fast horses at same time | bring his spear into play in the front line
at last a friend in his own company | Alcimedon son of Laerces he
grandson of Haemon saw difficulty | he was in coming up behind car he
"Which god now has your wits fully nobbled | put silly notion in noddle hobbled
what sense is there taking on the front-line | Trojans one-handed? don't you know your fine
fighter's been killed and Hector himself he's | swaggering round in arms of Achilles?"
"Alcimedon there was no-one like you | for taming also managing these two
immortal horses except Patroclus | while he lived and he"d learnt the Midas-plus
touch from Heaven but now he's dead and gone | so the whip and polished reins take on
yourself while I get down and fight" not crept | fast dismounted while Alcimedon leapt
into the fast-car seized reins and whip | illustrious Hector noticed new trip
turned to Aeneas happened to be near | "Aeneas bronze-clad Counsellor Troy here
I see the horses of lord Achilles | coming into battle feeble pair these
charioteers I think we could take them | if you'd care to join me attacking them
those two would never stand and fight" the brave | son of Anchises was no backward knave
so they went forward protecting shoulders | well-tanned -toughened oxhide shields the bo(u)lders
overlaid with finish bronze Chromius | and along with him god-like Aretus
went with them and had high hopes of killing | the men high-necked horses steal unwilling
they deluded themselves they weren't heading | to disengage from him without shedding
some blood meanwhile Automedon had prayed | to Zeus heart valour impassioned arrayed
there was now no room for weakness or fear | then swung round to Alcimedon his dear
trusted friend "Alcimedon keep me nigh | the horses so can feel their breath on my
back for I'm afraid that if he's not killed | in the front-line Hector's will won't be stilled
death-bat-vector in his fury 'til he | has killed us both and jumped up behind free
the great long-maned horses of Achilles | and given the Argive ranks the willies"
called to Menelaus and Aiantes | "You two Commanders Argives Aiantes
brothers-in arms now and Menelaus | brother to the King come now to help us
leave the best men you can find to bestride | the corpse and hold the enemy beside
*we* are alive but in mortal peril | in the thick this awful battle evil
with Hector and Aeneas Trojan best | bearing down upon us in full-tilt quest
meanwhile and since no-one ever knows what | fate decrees I'm going to try a shot
myself and leave the rest to Zeus" as spoke | swung up hurled his long-shadowed spoke be-spoke
bronze point struck the round shield of Aretus | which failed stop it piercing shield did press thus
on through the belt into his abdomen | he sprang forward fell down on his back then
as a farmyard ox leaps up collapses | when a strong man edge well-whetted axes
it behind the horns cuts through the sinews | sharp spear quivered in his gut not good news
and he was dead and Hector then did cast | at Automedon but glittering past
as he was looking out lance avoided | simple tactic leaning forward voided
long shaft came to earth behind him stuck there | in ground with butt-end trembling in the air
'til War-god stilled it with heavy hand now | they would have been full on at it and how
with their swords if the two Aiantes who'd | come up through press answer comrade call crude

had not there parted them in their fury | find such fair pair far too scary surely
Hector Aeneas noble Chromius | drew back leaving the stricken Aretus
to lie where he fell and Automedon | leaping in like Ares satisfaction
giving vent to after stripping of arms | "That act my sorrow now somewhat disarms
though he better man than the one I killed" | the blood-stained arms into his car he spilled
and mounted it with bloody hands and feet | like a mountain lion bull did eat feat
once more the struggle raged round Patroclus | and now indeed grim and inSidVicious
promoted by ex-Sex Pistol Athene | came down to Anchor and Hope check out scene
rouse Anchoraean punks at whim of Zeus | all-seeing who'd now changed loose mind-set noose
(w)rapping her selfie in a lurid mist | like a sombre rainbow hanging out pissed
in the Loose-id Skies With Diamonds by god | warn of final war of the world the sod
climate crisis destroys all in the field | as lambs to the slaughter at last do yield
she dropped in on soldiery Achaean | and with her will wielded fresh heart in one
and all and the stalwart Menelaus | by fate the nearest son of Atreus
Athene first accosted and exhorted | shape and tireless voice Phoenix imported
"It's you Menelaus who'll bear the blame | if the nimble dogs are allowed to shame
the great friend of proud Achilles under | the walls of Troy hold on don't go under
make all your folk into the fight fire mix" | "My venerable lord ancient friend Phoenix
I only wish Athene would give me strength | and keep the missiles at a good arm's length
then I should gladly take a hand and fight | for Patroclus whose demise has gone right
to my very heart but Hector's fury | burns like a flame and his great bronze flurry
carries all before Zeus wants him to win" | for Goddess Flashing Eyes Athene her win
delighted to note Menelaus use | of prayer first to her before even Zeus
or all other gods she strengthened his knees | shoulders implanted breast bold brazen ease
of a fly that's so fond of blood human | returns to attack however often
and hard one may try brush it from his face | filled by Athene very core with such ace
dauntlessness took his stand beside the corpse | of Patroclus glittering spear did corpse
Trojan called Podes son of Eetion | of great wealth and fine breeding was this one
Hector's favourite of the Trojan folk | they had become friends over the wine-yoke
this man was struck on the belt by red-haired | Menelaus' spear as he then hared
away and the spear went all the way through | fell with a crash to Menelaus who
dragged his body from among Trojan scrum | handed it over to his men welcome
but now Apollo brought his knight Hector | into play approached disguised as vector
Phaenops son Asius from Abydus | Hector's favourite of the foreigners
"Hector Argive will never fear you | again if by Menelaus seems you
are scared he was never a true fighter | though did come into our lines the blighter
just now dragged a dead man out alone one | your good friend Podes son of Eetion
one of our best men he has killed" the news | like a mortal wound but despite his own views
Hector set off through front line resplendent | in his arms of bronze and at this moment
the son of Cronos who'd hidden Ida | under a blanket of clouds discharged a
lightning flash with a great clap of thunder | took up his tasselled glitterring-wonder
aegis shook it out and gave victory | Trojans filled Danaans with misery

in dismay Penelos the Boeotian | in disarray first of host Achaean
turn tail he had then been facing the oppos | firmly when Polydamas a spear blow's
delivered he'd come up cast at short range | on the top of his shoulder found its range
a glancing blow but spear-point grazed the bone | then Hector also in close-quarters zone
wounded Leitus son of Alectryon | great-hearted in wrist put out of action
knowing could no longer handle a spear | gave one look round took to his heels in fear
as Hector chased him Idomeneus | son Deucalion hit on cuirass plus
flush by nipple on his breast but long spear | broke off at the socket so Hector here
retaliated with a javelin cast | at Idomeneus who now had cast
self into car missed him yet by not far | but struck Coeranus squire and driver car
of Meriones who had come with him | from the city Lyctus but outlook grim
now as Idomeneus had set out | that fine morn from trim ships on foot to bout
he would have presented the enemy | with a triumph if this Coeranus he
had not then galloped to the rescue thus | fast horses godsend Idomeneus
saved his life but lost his own to Hector | killer of men whose spear-head struck the jaw
just under left ear knocked all his teeth out | and cut his tongue in half Coeranus out
of the chariot then tumbled drooping | fell reins to earth Meriones stooping
picked them up from the ground with his own hands | to Idomeneus "'Til reach ship stands
lay on now you don't need me to tell you | we've lost the day" Idomeneus blew
the long-maned horses away with his whip | and drove off to mooring his hollow ship
he was a frightened man Menelaus | and also lion-hearted Aias thus
were well aware Zeus had used his powers | give to the Trojans victory prowess
Aias Telamonian turned made thrust | with a loud exclamation of disgust
to Menelaus "Any fool can see | Father Zeus himself helps give victory
to the Trojans each spear they cast goes home | and whether it comes from a bungler's home
or a marksman's Zeus sees it to target | while ours fall gently to the earth's carpet
do no harm at all well we must contrive | without him see how we can manage strive
to bring back the corpse and please our comrades | by getting back to them and not as shades
they must be watching somewhat anxiously | wondering whether anything can be
done to stop the invincible Hector | in his murd'rous rage swooping bat vector
on our ships if but one of our soldiers | could run with message Achilles for us
I don't believe he's even heard the dread | -ful news his dearest friend of all is dead
full but I can't see the man for the task | men horses all lost in fog a big ask
ah Father Zeus save us from this fog pray | give us a sky with it all cleared away
so that we can use our eyes and kill us | in daylight if you must" and so moved thus
by this tearful protest Father soon cleared | the darkness away the fog disappeared
the sun shone out on them brought whole field well | into plain view Aias said "King Menel
aus "look now and see whether you can | find Antilochus Nestor's son the man
we need if still alive tell him run fast | to Achilles say that his best friend's passed
on" Menelaus of loud war-cry did | not refuse but most unwillingly did
he go and like a great lion quitting | a farmyard when he gets tired of pitting
himself against the dogs and men who've kept | awake all night in order that be kept

the fattest of their heifers from his maw | in hunger for meat he's led with the jaw
repeatedly without any success | dart showers burning faggots in excess
hurled by many strong hands scared him away | for all his eagerness to have his way
and at dawn he slinks off disappointed | thus Menelaus the one appointed
retired from the body of Patroclus | he did not wish quit the battle scene thus
much afraid that the Argives in a fit | of panic might then make a gift of it
to the enemy but he did his best | to put on their mettle those of the rest
left behind "You Commanders Aiantes | of the Argives and you Meriones
now's the time to recall how lovable | a man Patroclus was to one and all
was the soul of kindness role always played | now Death and Destiny to him claim laid"
red-haired Menelaus went off peering | all round him like an eagle appearing
having the sharpest sight of any bird | in the air and not deceived nor deterred
high though is by hare crouching pants pooping | under a leafy bush but now swooping
down then seizes him and takes his life so | O royal Menelaus did your so
brilliant eyes range everywhere through your men | many detect whether Nestor's son then
Antilochus still alive red-top-fried | Menelaus his man quickly espied
on the far left of the battle urging | his troops fight spurring on go forth surging
he went close and called "Prince Antilochus | come here let me tell you of a thing thus
terrible I wish to God had never | happened you must have seen the disaster
for yourself that Heaven has sent to arms | Achaean and success to Trojan charms
and now Patroclus our best man's been killed | blow with which each Danaan be ill filled
will you run at once to the ships and tell | Achilles ask him to make haste as well
to bring the body safely to his ship? | naught left on it after the victor's strip
Hector of the bright helmet has the arms" | this news Antilochus keenly disarms
for a while he was unable to speak | as his eyes filled with tears his words stuck bleak
in his throat but he took note nonetheless | of the commands of King Menelaus
and set off at a run after handing | his armour to his squire of long-standing
worthy Laodocus who'd been weaving | his horse to and fro beside leaving
the field hotfoot the evil news sweeping | to Achilles Antilochus weeping
Menelaus was not disposed to stay | and help the weary Pylians hold sway
though missed sorely their departed leader | instead made Thrasymedes commander
returned to post by the lord Patroclus | rejoining Aiantes at a run thus
reported immediately "I've sent | our man to the good ships with a comment
for Achilles but I daren't hope he'll come | at once however angry he's become
with Hector he could not fight Trojans nude | must do our best without the Hey Jude dude
see how can Van the Man-age bring out corpse | save our lives from this yelling Trojan corps"
to this Telamonian Aias thus | "Quite right my noble lord Menelaus
will you and Meriones your arms put | under the body carry out hotfoot
from this turmoil just as fast as you can | while the pair of us stay keep the main man
Prince Hector and his Trojan crew engaged? | Aias and I same-named same spirit gaged
not the first time we've waged war side by side | in a tight corner" the two men then tried
to raise Patroclus from the ground hoisted | him above their heads power-play foisted

on pursuing Trojans gave a shout when | saw the Achaeans carrying off then
body charging like hounds launching themselves | at a wounded boar before young hunt-elves
race along for a while as if they meant | tear him to bits only to be rent sent
bolting in all directions boar-attack | strikes back and runs amok among the pack
thus for a time the Trojans followed up | en masse smiting with swords and doubled up
pointed spears but when the two Aiantes | turned about in the way planted themselves
their colour changed and no-one had the heart | to dash in and dispute a body part
Menelaus Meriones labour | and Patroclus' body recover
from the field to the hollow ships to yield | as fierce about them did chaos wield
ferocious as a fire in a moment | blazes up and falls on a settlement
and consumes the houses in a mighty | conflagration as the roaring wind free
flames beats on so thus did din not ceases | coming up from fighting men and horses
beat upon them as they go the struggle's | epic Eric Burden-like Ani-mules
who are then putting out all their strength | drag a log or some huge timber at length
for a ship down from the mountains by a | winding rocky track and they're tugging a
-way 'til they very nearly break their hearts | what with the labour and the sweaty parts
and behind them the two Aiantes held | the enemy like a ridge with a geld
-ing of trees stretched across country withheld | the floods even when the big rivers meld
coming down in spate torrents confronted | unimpaired and the deluge affronted
then the lower ground and so all the time | Aiantes fended off the Trojan line
attacking the rear a hard beset sect | -or by these two in particular Hect
-or illustrious and Aeneas son | of Anchises as when see a falcon
that is death to little birds after them | a flock starling or jackdaw takes wing then
cries out in alarm the Argives with cries | of terror fled fearing there their demise
before Aeneas and Hector losing | all stomach for fight weapons drop abusing
in numbers at the trench and round about | fleeing Danaans no respite from rout

ὀκτωκαίδεκα

*Book 18*

# ARMOUR FOR ACHILLES

*of how Achilles grieved for Patroklos*
*and for him Thetis asked of Hephaistos*
*for a most splendid set new of armour*
*and of the god's making of that armour*

and thus the battle went on like a fire | inextinguishable meanwhile flyer
Antilochus hotfoot to Achilles | found him by his beaked ships now Achilles
had had presentiment of the event | was communing to an anguished extent
with that great heart of his of deep intent | "Why" asked self with a groan "do they relent
once more the long-haired Achaeans bolting | across the plain to the ships re-vaulting?
Heaven forfend I should have to suffer | what my heart forebodes prophecy Mother
she told me once that while I still did live | best of all the Myrmidons would fall give
up the light of day and now I'm sure that | Menoetius' gallant son's done just that
foolhardy man! did I not order him | to come back here when he'd saved the ships trim
from fire not to fight it out with Hector?" | and with these thoughts racing son of Nestor
– yet it was by no means a Marathon | though that thought much later still lingers on –
stopped before him with the hot tears pouring | down his cheeks and to him then outpouring
the lamentable news "Alas my lord | Achilles! I have a most dreadful word
to tell you would to god it were not true | Patroclus has been killed they fight anew
around his naked body and Hector | of flashing helm now wearing your armour"
when Achilles heard this straight away sank | into the black depths of despair most rank
he then picked up the dark dust in each hand | poured it on his head and smeared it with sand
soiled his comely face with the mix filthy | ashes scented tunic poured wilfully
cast himself down on the earth and lay there | like a fallen giant fouling his hair
tearing it out with his own hands the maid | -servants he Patroclus capture had made
caught the alarm ran screaming out of doors | and all beat their breasts with their hands like claws
sank to the ground by their royal master | Antilochus misery disaster
tears shed other side held hands Achilles | as sobbing out a noble heart still he's
for fear he might take a knife cut his throat | suddenly Achilles a piercing note
gave out loud and dreadful shout his lady | Mother heard him from where she sat in sea

depths by the side of her ancient Father | she took up the cry of grief did gather
round her every goddess and Nereid | there that was in the depths of the sea hid
Glauce there along with Thaleia | and Cymodoce Thoe Nesaea
Speio and the ox-eyed Halie | Limnoreia and Cymothoe
Actaee laera also Melite | with Amphithoe also Agaue
Doto Proto Pherusa Dynamene | with Callianeira and Dexamene
Amphinome Doris Panope she's | far-sung Galatea Nemertes
Apseudes Callinanassa Clymene | came too laneira lanassa Hyphen
Oreithuia Amatheia | of the Lovely Locks and lastly Maera
other Nereids of the depths salt-sea | the silvery cave was full of nymphs see
with one accord they beat their breasts Thetis | led them in their lamentations Thetis
"Attend to me my sister Nereids | I wish you all to know how sorrow bids
my heart ah misery me unhappy | mother of the best of men! a mighty
hero and to eclipse his peers I brought | into the world as a flawless child fraught
with a weakness I nursed him as one tends | a little plant in a garden bed ends
shooting up like a sapling I sent him | via Ship Canal Corinth to Irlam
-Ilium fight against Trojans never | again now shall I welcome him ever
to Peleus' house and he has yet | to suffer each day he lives sees the sun set
and I can do nothing good in going | to him nevertheless I AM going
to see my darling child hear what grief | has come to him though he has had relief
from the fighting" with that she left the cave | the rest went with her (s)weeping in a wave
on either side the surging sea fell back | and when they arrived at deep-soiled Troy's track
they came up one by one onto the beach | where the ships of the Myrmidons were each
round swift Achilles clustered within reach | his Mother goes up to him make outreach
he groaning loud lies with a shrill cry took | her son's head in her hands and to him struck
"My child why these tears?" note of compassion | what has caused this grievous lamentation?
tell me don't keep your sorrow to yourself | for some part at least of what you yourself
prayed for when you lifted up your hands to | Zeus he has fulfilled since for want of you
the Achaeans at the ships have been penned | suffered horribly as you did intend"
Achilles nimble-foot gave a great sigh | "Mother the great Olympian on high
made prayer come true but what delight precious | for me now my best friend's dead Patroclus
who was more to me than any other | of my men and I so loved another
as if he my own self? Patroclus lost | to me Hector who inflicted this cost
stripped him my splendid armour now surplus | wonderful arms the gods gave Peleus
as a wedding-present when they bound you | to a mortal man ah how I wish you
had stayed in the deathless salt-sea Nymph life | Peleus taken home a mortal wife!
but you became my mother and now to | multiply *your* sorrows you're going to
lose your son never welcome him at home | again as I've no wish to call earth home
nor linger in the world of men unless | before all else my spear makes Hector mess
and he dies then paying for the slaying | of Menoetius' son" tears displaying
Thetis "If that is so my child surely | you not long to live as once oversee
death of Hector you're doomed to die forthwith" | with passion reply "*Let* me die forthwith

then since I've failed to save from death my friend | he's fallen far from his motherland friend
-ly wanting my help his extremity | and thus now because I shall never see
my home again I am proven a reed | broken Patroclus all comrades in need
Prince Hector has killed and I've just sat near | -by my ships idle burden earth fair here
I the best man in the Achaean force | best in battle beaten war words perforce
only ... ah how I wish now that discord | could be banished fully from world record
of gods and men and with it too anger | seditious as trickling honey anger
that makes the wisest man flare up and spreads | like smoke through his whole being's binding threads
anger such as the King Agamemnon | roused in me that day! however what's done
is done though we resent it still and we | must curb our hearts at need and so for me
I'll go now seek out Hector destroyer | of my dearest friend Zeus and the other
deathless gods can appoint my death as see | fit so bring it on even the mighty
Heracles did not escape his doom dear | as he was to Zeus the royal and peer
-less Son of Cronos but was laid low by | Fate and Here's bitter enmity and I
too shall lie low when I'm dead if the same | lot falls on me and yet for now my aim
is glory I'll make these women Trojan | and the deep-bosomed daughters of Dardan
-us wipe the great tears from their cheeks tender | with both hands as the dirge raise and render
to teach them just how long I've been absent | from the fray and you Mother you're not meant
to keep me from the field you will never | hold me now" "No my child it could never
be an evil thing for you to rescue | your exhausted comrades from this vile hue
and cry of Hector's but your beautiful | burnished armour is held by the vengeful
Hector the flashy helm is swaggering | round in it yet he'll soon be staggering
around for he is very near to death | so don't think to jeopardise your last breatth
in war before you see me here once more | I'll bring splendid set armour to the fore
from Lord Hephaestus tomorrow at dawn" | she turned away then from her son high-born
spoke to her sister Nereids wholesome | withdraw told then into the broad bosom
of the sea make their way to the Old Man | of the Sea back into her Father's man
-sion "Tell him everything as I'm going | to high Olympus ask if fashioning
a most splendid set of arms glittering | for my son Hephaestus re-itering
he the Master-smith" the Nymphs disappeared | into waters later pollutant-seared
of the sea and now the divine Thetis | of Silver Feet made for Olympus his
glorious set of armour to procure | and its fabrication therefore ensure
the Achaean soldiery back spilling | with cries of terror from the man-killing
Hector reached the Hellespont and ships black | it was more than they could do to drag back
body Patroclus Achilles' squire | out of range withering arrow spear fire
again allies overtaken sallies | Trojan Hector as a wildfire rallies
as one let loose in dense forest raging | three times illustrious Hector racing
up behind shouting for his men's support | seized body's feet drag it away sought fought
thrice the Aiantes flung him from the corpse | fighting like men possessed Hector's core corps
though unshaken when not himself hurling | into the press held ground pounds calls sterling
aloud to his men never once fell back | bronze-clad Aiantes could no more force back
Prince Hector from the corpse than a shepherd | in the field can chase away from his herd

lion starved from kill would have hauled away | and covered himself in glory that day
if Iris of the Whirlwind Feet had not | come down from high Olympus in haste hot
to tell Achilles to prepare to fight | Here sent for Zeus other gods not by right
consulted and presenting herself to | Achilles delivered message "Time to
be up my lord Achilles of men most | redoubtable arise now and play host
to Patroclus for whom the host fighting | tooth and nail for his ghost men benighting
men by the ships for the ghost of a chance | Achaeans safety of his corpse enhance
and for Trojans of hauling it away | to windy Ilium Hector holds sway
above all has set his heart on pulling | off Patroclus he is bent on culling
his head then from his tender neck to stick | it on Troy's palisade so up now quick
lie no longer idle the very thought | that Patroclus might be a plaything sought
by dogs of Troy you should find appalling | and it's you who all will be out-calling
if the corpse comes into your hands defiled" | admirable swift Achilles answer filed
with a question "Lady Iris may I | enquire which god it was who sent you nigh
with this message?" "It was Here worshipful | consort of Zeus" said she fleet of Whirl-full
-wind Feet "and the Sublime Son of Cronos | not told nor other Godot For toss loss
Waiting on snowy Olympus" "But how | can I go into action?" questioned now
the great runner Achilles "my armour's | in enemy hands and my own Mother's
forbidden me to dress for battle 'til | I should see her here once more said she will
bring me from Hephaestus a splendid set | I know of no-one else whose armour yet
I could wear except just maybe the shield | that Telamonian Aias does wield
and he I expect is taking his place | front-line and playing his spear as an ace
for the dead Patroclus" "We gods" said wind | -swift Iris "matter well in mind not binned
knowing your glorious armour's taken | yet go to trench as are present token
yourself to Trojans may be afraid | of you break off the fight and give the frayed
Achaeans time to breathe every little | helps a respite in war is valuable"
fleet-foot Iris took her leave Achilles | favourite of Zeus leapt up off heels he's
Athene cast her tasselled aegis round his | sturdy shoulders and lo! great goddess is
shedding a golden mist around his head | body as a blaze of light created
thus from some far-away beleaguered isle | where men have been fighting a desperate trial
all day from their city walls the smoke goes | up to heaven no sooner sun down glows
over Minas Tirith than light from line | fired fire beacons blazes beyond skyline
alert all highlanders neighbouring | bring rescuing elf ships i(s)land-hopping
such was the blaze that arose to heaven | from the head of Achilles he went then
beyond the wall took his stand by the trench | but recalling his Mother's strict entrench
did not join the Achaean soldiery | there he stood cried aloud while in fiery
distance Pallas Athene raised too war-cry | and the Trojans were utterly by cry
confounded Achilles' cry piercing | as the trumpet call that's sent out fierce ring
when a city's beset by murderous | enemies and their hearts turned un-viscous
when heard that brazen voice even the ill | -starred long-maned horses felt something evil
in the wind began to pull their cars round | and their charioteers were full dumbfound
-ed as they watched the fire fed by Athene | blaze with a fierce steady glare corona s(h)een

from head lion-hearted son Peleus | the great Achilles did send his voice thus
ringing over the trench host Trojan thrice | and famed allies into chaos thrown thrice
dozen of their best men perished there then | by their own chariots on spears Trojan
meanwhile with thankful hearts the Argives hauled | Patroclus out of range stretcher appalled
laid his men gathered round him weeping throng | Achilles joined them and the hot tears long
ran down his cheeks when saw his faithful friend | lying in state by the cruel bronze un-friend
-ed mangled sent to fight with horses car | welcome return again ne'er from afar
Here ox-eyed Queen of Heaven tireless Sun | told to sink into the Stream of Ocean
now the Sun had been disposed to linger but | at last set and the brave Achaeans glut
a bit of respite from the grim struggle | to-fro give-take battle huggle-muggle
the Trojans themselves withdrew from contact | Argives unyoked horse from car artefact
before thought supper gathered together | for debate but nobody dared ever
sit down so held the meeting on their feet | as all of them now had very cold feet
appalled Achilles' reappearance | after from the front such a long absence
discussion begun wise Polydamas | son of Panthous only man of whole mass
who could look into the future as past | and he was of Hector a comrade fast
they were born on same night as brilliant | in discussion as Hector triumphant
in battle much concerned for the safety | of fellow-countrymen "Think carefully
my friends it's my opinion that at this | distance from the walls we ought to end this
fight right now withdraw into the city | not wait for daylight here fatally
open by the ships for while Achilles | with Agamemnon was very ill at ease
the Argives easier to deal with I | myself enjoyed the night that we spent by
the fleet and the hopes to which we aspired | of taking their rolling ships terrified
now though am of him that fiery snappy | spirit to stay in the plain be happy
never where we and them used to meet each | other on equal terms at halfway's reach
but will make our town and our womenfolk | his target so let me persuade you folk
to retire on Troy otherwise I know | what'll happen blessed night for now though
has checked the swift knight Achilles but if | tomorrow he comes fully-armed and if
we're here he'll be easy to recognise | any man who gets free to realise
safety in sacred Ilium may thank | his lucky stars the dogs and vultures thank
you for having their fill of flesh *Trojan* | I say Heaven deem false my word spoken!
but if you take my advice distasteful | as it is our strength we'll husband still full
by bivouacking in market-place while | Troy guarded by high gates and wall the while
sealed by the lofty wooden doors that we | hung on them at daybreak fully armed we
will on the battlements take up post | if Achilles sallies forth we'll play host
at the walls so much the worse for him when | he's tired his horses trotting about then
he'll have to drive them home again he will | not have the nerve force his way in he'll still
never sack the town before that can be | the nimble dogs will have feasted on he"
but these ideas were frowned on by Hector | of the helm that did famously glitter
"Polydamas the man who now tells us | to retire and in the town shut up us
no longer with me on eye-to-eye side | are you not sick of being caged inside
those walls? I know that there was a time when | the gold the bronze and the sheer opulen

-ce of Priam's city talk of the town | world but that has passed and it's all gone down
-hill our houses have been emptied of all | their works of art our treasures nearly all
have been sold to Phrygia and lovely | Maeonia as had incurred mighty
anger of Zeus yet the very moment | that mighty god has left me triumphant
at the ships letting me drive Argive-wise | back to the sea you like a fool advise
defence of town now I you forbid dead | put such notions in anybody's head
not that a single Trojan would follow | your lead because that I would not (sw)allow
listen all of you to me instead now | let the whole army have its dinner chow
in its several messes all obeying | social distancing need for all staying
alert and I advise any Trojan | worried for property make collection
hand it over to state for use public | would be better for the general public
to enjoy then Argives at dawn's peep | we'll arm attack them at the mooring deep
-ly fierce and what if the great Achilles | *has* decided to get up off his knees
and leave his camp? as you have said so much | the worse for him if indeed he does such
*I* am not going to avoid a fight | take flight for I'll meet him as of right rite
face-to-face and then we will see who wins | the War-god has no favourites who wins
determined by him been known to kill one | who thought that it was *he* to be the one
to do the killing" Hector his speech closed | Trojans in their folly by shouts disclosed
approval Pallas Athene had destroyed | their judgment Polydamas who'd deployed
a sound strategy awarded nuls points | but they applauded Hector's foolish plan
whole army settled down for last supper | all night long the Achaeans kept up a
weeping and a wailing for Patroclus | their leader there the son of Peleus
in the melancholy dirge he laid his | man-killing hands upon the breast of his
comrade uttered piteous groans like a | lion when his cubs are stolen from a
thicket by a huntsman comes back too late | discovers his loss follows in his fate
the man's trail through glade after glade hoping | in his misery to answer groping
track down thus Achilles groaned among his | Myrmidons thought with a sharp pang of his
idle words let fall one day at home his | attempt to reassure Patroclus'
noble father "I told Menoetius | I would bring him back his son to Opus
from the sack of Troy covered with glory | laden with share of the plunder stor(e)y
but Zeus makes havoc of the schemes of men | and now the pair of us doomed to redden
with our blood one patch of earth in Troyland | because I shall never see *my* homeland
again nor be welcomed by Peleus | old charioteer Thetis goddess plus
my Mother but be swallowed by the earth | I stand on so then Patroclus this earth
too I'm going below but after you | and so I'll put off 'til later for you
your funeral when I've brought back armour | and the head of the flashy-helmed Hector
who slaughtered you my noble-hearted friend | and at your pyre heaven not forfend
I'll cut the throats of a dozen highborn | youths of Ilium to vent my wrath on
them for killing you but 'til then sweet friend | you are and will be 'til the very end
by my beaked ships wailed and wept for by night | day by the Trojan women in shared rite
deep-bosomed daughters Dardanus who we | took with much toil long spears own strokes handy
when we sacked their rich cities full of men" | Prince Achilles told his followers then

to put a giant three-legged cauldron | on fire haste wash away clotted gore on
corpse Patroclus they put a large cauldron | on the glowing fire with water pooled on
until full brought faggots kindled under | and the flames began to lick the under
-side of the cauldron the water grew warm | and when it had come up to boiling form
in the burnished copper they washed the corpse | anointed with olive oil nine-year corps
the age an unguent the wounds did fill | laid on a bier which the body did fill
and with a soft sheet covered it from head | to foot over the sheet a white cloak spread
for the rest of the night host Myrmidon | great runner Achilles wept and wailed on
for Patroclus now Zeus watching with his | Wife and Sister Here turned to her "In this
you've had your way once more my ox-eyed Queen | Achilles swift resurrection scene seen
anyone might think the long-haired Argives | your own children" ox-eyes och-ayes jives
"Dread Son of Cronos how are't offended? | even a mortal man not intended
for such wisdom as ours still intervenes | on behalf of his friends how could I Queen's
position laid claim of Heaven Here here | both by right of birth and because I'm Here
your acknowledged Consort and you are King | of all the gods from all trouble-making
for my enemies in Troy how could I | possibly refrain?" while these two talked nigh
came Thetis of the Silver Feet making | way to palace of Hephaestus making
of it had been by his own hands of bronze | imperishable god Crooked Foot one's
it shines like a star and stands out among | the houses of the gods and in a throng
of tables found hard at work sweat flowing | as he was bustling about bellowing
in his forge for he was making a set | of twenty three-legged tables to set
out around the walls of his well-built hall | and he had affixed golden wheels to all
their legs so that they could run by themselves | to a meeting of the gods those same selves
amaze by running home again when work quit | not quite finished yet as had still to fit
the ornamental handles on putting | these and for them was the rivets cutting
Hephaestus was engaged upon this task | called for all the skill of which could make ask
when Thetis goddess of the Silver Feet | arrived and just then Charis consort fleet
of the illustrious lame god in her | shimmering headdress beautiful left her
house and saw her and in her hand hers draws | "Thetis of the Long Robe! what now you draws
to our house? an honoured and welcome guest | though visits few in past I would have guessed
but follow me indoors let me offer | refreshment" the gracious goddess led her
in seated her in a chair beautiful | with silver decorations and footstool
underneath then called to the Master-smith | "Hephaestus! come in here now as Ms Th
-etis wants ask favour of you" "Thetis | here?" he cried "the very goddess Thee-'tis
I honour and revere for saving me | after my great fall hour of agony
when my very wicked Mother had tried | do away with me cripple certified!
ah how I should have suffered if Thetis | had not clutched me to her breast treat teat is
Thetis and Eurynome the Daughter | of Ocean of the Circling Stream nine-year
stay with them there making ornaments bronze | buckles rosettes necklaces bracelets ones
in-spiral carpets vaulted cave sea thing | lapped never-ending Stream Ocean seething
with foam no-one on earth or in heaven | knew of the secret cave save for Euryn
-ome Thetis who'd rescued me and here | is Thetis in our house she of the clear

-ly Lovely Locks now I must certainly | my kind benefactress repay duly
entertain her well while I put away | my bellows and tools" and he drew away
his monstrous bulk from the anvil he limped | across room slender legs nimble one glimpsed
took bellows from fire and collected | all the tools used put in well-confected
silver chest then he sponged his face and hands | his hairy chest and his sturdy neck-bands
then donned his tunic picked up a thick staff | and came limping up now from his forge gaff
golden maidservants hastened to help their | Master looked like real girls could speak use their
limbs also with intelligence endowed | handwork by immortal gods avowed
then by his toiling escort supported | the Lord Hephaestus approach purported
clumsy to the spot where Thetis tweeted | and on a polished chair himself seated
he took her hand in his and greeted her | "Thetis of the Long Robe! why thee hither
to our house? an honoured and welcome guest | though visits few in the past I'd have guessed
but tell me what you wish of me I'll be | glad to serve you if I can if the key
task is possible" and Thetis burst thus | into tears "Hephaestus on Olympus
of all the goddesses is there a one | who's had to endure such persecution
as I've suffered from the Son of Cronos? | first Sea-Nymph he chose mortal chronic loss
from all me gave in marriage to a man | to Peleus son Aeacus human
much against my will I had to put up | with a mortal husband who now lies up
at home weighed down by his burden of years | but there's more as Zeus seeing future tears
let me bring into the world and then nurse | child destined outshine peers better or worse
I nursed him as one tends a little plant | in a garden bed shot up a giant
sapling I sent to Troy with his brazen | black beaked ships fight against host Trojan then
but now I'll never welcome him again | to Peleus' house yet lives in pain
every day that he wakes and sees the sun | and yet by going to his side no fun
can do no good now King Agamemnon | has from his arms trophy girl taken on
she the Achaean army gave to him | as a prize of honour at the King's whim
not his as he missed her sorely distraught | by grief and from this action result fraught
Trojans been able drive Achaeans back | among their ships whence they'll not let comeback
Argive ambassadors were sent to plead | with Achilles wonderful offer seed
but refused he was not for averting | their imminent collapse by exerting
himself at all but he lent his armour | Patroclus sent out with strong force armour
-ed behind him to battle fought all day | Scaean Gate would have taken Troy by way
of storm before night fell if Apollo | had not given Hector green good-to-go
to kill brave Patroclus in front line ranks | after he'd made havoc of the line tanks
Trojan and so I have come to throw my | -self at your knees and ask you to give my
son who's soon to die a helmet and shield | as well as pair of fine greaves well weld wield
-ed ankle-clasps and also a cuirass his | former set of armour was lost when his
good friend was by the Trojans laid to ground | and Achilles also laid to the ground
in misery" "Distress yourself no more" | illustrious lame god did reassure
"You can leave everything to me indeed | I just wish it were as easy at need
to save him from the pains of death when his | appointed hour of doom to be met is
as make him a splendid set of armour | of all beholders will be the wonder"

Hephaestus left her went back to his forge | where turned bellows on fire ready to gorge
bade them get to work the bellows twenty | blew on crucibles satisfactory
blast varying force increased critical | moments then subsided non-critical
in accordance with Hephaestus' need | and the stage to which the work did proceed
cast imperishable bronze on the fire | and some tin precious gold silver entire
now he put a great anvil on the stand | and then gripped a strong hammer in one hand
a pair of tongs in the other hand horned | began with large powerful shield adorned
all over finished with bright triple rim | gleaming metal fit silver baldric trim
shield of five layers face decorated | with a number of designs created
executed consummate skill firing | first Earth Sky and Sea and the untiring
Sun and the Moon at the full and with all | Constellations which heavens crowned withal
Pleiads the Hyads the great Orion | Bear nicknamed Wain only constellation
that never takes a bathe in Ocean Stream | but always wheels around in the same dream
location looks across at Orion | the Hunter with a wary eye Dog(g)one!
next two beautiful cities full-peopled | showed in one weddings and banquets scheduled
now afoot brides through streets from homes threading | to the loud music of the hymn wedding
and in the light of the blazing torches | youth accompanied each flute lyre clutches
whirling in the dance the women had come | to the doors of their houses to have some
joy in the show but the men had flocked to | meeting-place because case come between two
litigants re payment compensation | for a man who had had his life taken
defendant claimed the right to pay in full | announced his intention to the people
but other contested this intention | would take naught refused all compensation
and so both of the parties insisted | issue by referee be test listed
and both of them there were then cheered aloud | by their supporters gathered in the crowd
and the Elders sat on the bench sacred | a semi-circle of stone poli-shed
and each as he received the speaker's rod | from the clear-voiced heralds bearing god hod
came forward thus each Elder in his turn | give judgement staff in hand see what could earn
for two talents gold displayed in centre | they were the fee for the Elder mentor
who would give the finest exposition | of the law and make the best decision
now the other city see beleaguer | two armies clearly here not in league err
shown arrayed there in their glittering gear | besiegers unable agree clear here
whether they ought to sack the place outright | town a lovely sight on a lovely site
or to divide up all the movable | property it contained between those able
to help themselves and the inhabitants | however these had not yet crapped their pants
were secretly preparing an ambush | left walls defence to wives' wham(Azon) bush
thus sallied forth under the leadership | of Ares and Pallas Athene the hip
who were both shown there depicted in gold | fully armed and were dressed in vestments gold
-en shining big and bright and beautiful | as gods should be and totally awful
and thus they so stood out above their troops | who of much smaller mortal hoop loop gloops
and so when they had found a likely place | for an ambush in a river-bed space
where all the cattle around came to drink | they sat down in their shining bronze to think
after posting two scouts in distance deep | to watch out for coming of long-horned sheep

shambling cattle with their horns too crooked | soon made appearance wandering crooked
in the charge of two bucolic herdsmen | idylly playing on their Pan-pipes then
and so rustics suspecting no evil | the ambushers who then on the swivel
caught sight of them quickly dashed out promptly | head off herd lowing oxen o'er the lea
fine flocks of white sheep the shepherds killing | but the besiegers debate distilling
hearing the commotion of this affair | in the herds mounted at once behind their
high-stepping horses and made for the scene | of the action quickly reached and then seen
a pitched battle on banks of the river | exchange volleying the bronze spear Shearer
Strife and Panic were shown at their work there | was the dreadful Spirit of Death out there
laying hands on each freshly wounded man | and dragging a corpse by foot through the van
the cloak on her shoulders red with blood mulled | human the soldiers met and fought and pulled
each other's dead away just like real men | large field of soft rich fallow Heph showed then
being ploughed for the third time as several | ploughmen across driving their teams on full
to and fro and when they reached the ridge edge | and had to wheel around hard by the hedge
a man would come up and hand them a cup | of mellow wine and then they turned back up
the furrows and toiled along through the deep | fallow soil to reach the other end steep
field though of gold behind with black then filled | as a field does when it is being tilled
the artist had achieved a miracle | showed too a king's estate the sharp sickle
hired reapers wielded many an armful | of corn in rows along furrow fell full
while others were tied up with straw by sheaf | -binders three were standing by the relief
boys who were gleaning behind came leaping | up to them bundles in their arms keeping
them constantly supplied and there among | them was the King himself staff in hand strong
standing by swathe quiet satisfaction | and in background an attendant faction
under an oak a feast was preparing | great ox killed cooking welfare not sparing
and the women were there sprinkling the meat | for workers' meal handfuls white barley meet
next scene vineyard laden with grapes munchies | beautifully wrought in gold in bunches
black but supporting poles showed up throughout | in silver and round it ran moated rout
of blue enamel outside that fence tin | and the vineyard was approached by a sin
-gle pathway for vintage time pickers use | and carried away delicious profuse
fruit in baskets by merry girls and boys | and accompanying them there a boy's
singing out the lovely song of Linus | in treble voice sweet music tuneful thus
lyre and all kept time with him following | the music and words with feet a-flowing
showed too herd of straight-horned cattle shewing | the cows of gold and tin they were mooing
as they from byre to feed hurrying | where rushes swayed beside stream murmurying
four golden herdsmen were herd allotted | with them Kompany of Nine dogs trotted
but the head of the herd calling far far | away savage lion pair from afar
had seized a bellowing bull roared aloud | as they dragged him far from the madding crowd
the young men and dogs ran up to rescue | but the pair had quickly taken their cue
had rent great bull's hide lesson learnt entails | their lapping up his dark blood and entrails
in vain the shepherds incited egged on | their fast dogs but they had no intention
biting the lions careful to avoid | though stood barked close as dared that too a void
to this picture illustrious god lame | large grazing ground white-fleeced sheep added frame

set in a beautiful valley complete | with farm buildings pens well-roofed huts replete
next the god depicted a dancing-floor | just like the one Daedalus designed for
Ariadne she of the lovely locks | in the spacious Cnossus of the bullocks
and the youths and marriageable maidens | dancing on it their hands able made dens
on one another's wrists the girls in fine | linen lovely garlands on heads fine line
men in closely woven tunics showing | faint gleam of oil and gold daggers throwing
hanging from silver belts ran lightly round | circle of old smooth on skilful feet sound
as the wheel of a potter when he sits | and works it with his hands to see if it's
going to spin and there they ran in lines | meet each other large crowd stood ancient lines
all round delightful dance enjoying | a minstrel among them song deploying
divinely to lyre while acrobat leaps | keeping time then with his musical beats
turned cartwheels in and out among the folk | for closing the wonderful shield did yoke
him around the very rim the mighty | Stream of Ocean when finished finally
shield in all its size and strength Achilles | made brighter than blazing fire cuirass he's
then made a huge helm to fit each temple | and the chasing on it was beautiful
and on the top he put a golden crest | also made him greaves of pliant tin best
and when had finished the renowned god lame | each piece gathered up laid the full claim fame
before Achilles' Mother she took | the glittering armour and slung her hook
swooped off with the bundle from Hephaestus | like a falcon from snow-clad Olympus

ἐννεακαίδεκα

*Book 19*

# THE FEUD IS ENDED

*of how Achilles and Agamemnon*
*in front of the Assembly Achaean*
*were at last reconciled and Achilles*
*went forth to battle former enemies*

as Dawn in her saffron mantle arose | from the River of Ocean a-new rose
daylight bring to immortals and to men | Thetis descended on the ships stern then
bearing Danaan god's gifts in hand found | her son Achilles prostrate on the ground
his arms the corpse of Patroclus around | weeping bitterly many of's men round
him wailing stood the gracious goddess up | to them went and took her son's hand in cup
of her own said "My child here lies a man | struck down by the will of Heaven's white van
no grief of ours can alter that so let | it be take the splendid armour brought yet
to you from Hephaestus set armour more | beautiful than any man's worn before
ever" the goddess laid the arms before | elaborate loveliness of labour
they rang aloud and every Myrmidon | was struck with awe did not dare to look on
them backed away the more Achilles looked | the more his passion rose and he was hooked
(shortly before he was to be – well – fucked) | and from underneath their lids his eyes plucked
and they flashed fiercely out like points of flame | picked up the splendid gifts for the great game
fondled them with delight and when he had | taken in all their beauty he turned glad
before mad bad to Thetis "Mother this | armour of the gods for indeed is this
craftsmanship we might expect from Heaven | no mortal could have made it I'll even
now go into battle in it but I | am terribly afraid that a plague fly
may defile my lord Patroclus' corpse | by settling on the open wounds strength corps
and breeding worms in them as life has gone | out of him all his flesh would turn rotten"
"My child have no anxiety that score | I'll arrange to keep the flies off for sure
save him those pests that devour the bodies | of men killed in battle so his body's
able to lie here through all the seasons | of a year and yet still his in season's
preserved might be fresher than now indeed | so go and summon the Argives at need
to Assembly and self reconciling | with your Commander-in-Chief of Men King
and then arm yourself for battle prepare | quickly and put out all of your strength there"

and she breathed valour indomitable | into her son and to save Patrocl
-us from decay she treated his body | with ambrosia red nectar which she
instilled through his nostrils meanwhile still | all along the watchtower beach Prince Achill
-'es gone at the top of his reach bawling | the soldiers of the Argives outcalling
as a result even the men who used | to hang out about the ships helmsmen used
to take charge of the steering-oars left on | board to steward oversee provision
came to the Assembly now Achilles | had at long last reappeared after he's
done sulky abstention from toil of war | those two servants of Ares to the fore
steadfast Tydeides the excellent | Odysseus came limping in though still rent
by their wounds using spears as walking staves | and they sat down in the front row the braves
last of all Agamemnon King of Men | he too suffering from the wound given
by Coon son of Antenor with his bornze | -headed spear in the thick of the fray frenz
-ied all Achaeans gathered together | to speak rose Achilles the great runner
"My lord Atreides we have been at | daggers drawn but not proved a good thing that
either for you or me keep up this feud | desperate about a girl my wish crude
she been killed by Artemis' arrow | on board ship that day when with view narrow
I chose her for myself when I had sacked | Lyrnessus less Achaeans been attacked
stacked the dust of this wide world slaughtered by | Trojans while I sat aloof angry nigh
Hector and the Trojans who profited | from our quarrel which will still be cited
by the Argives for many a long day | but we must let bygones be gone today
for all our resentment curb our hearts now | far be it from me persist anyhow
in my rancour and now as far as I | am concerned our feud is ended and I
suggest you immediately summon | to battle the long-haired host Achaean
so that if the enemy should decide | to bivouac by the ships I may not hide
but pit myself against their strength again | deem a Trojan dodging my spear refrain
and coming out of this battle alive | will think self lucky if got to survive
and rest his legs" the Argive men-at-arms | shouted for joy and waved about their arms
when heard noble-hearted son Peleus | renounce his feud in noble manner thus
it remained though for Agamemnon King | of Men speak so rising but not risking
moving from seat to centre-stage | spoke from where he stood at this precious stage
"Friends Danaans and servants of Ares | when a man stands up to speak courtesy's
only then to give him a fair hearing | not interrupt best orator fearing
speak wrong with such disorder how can one | talk or hear anything when everyone
makes enough din to drown out the loudest? | am addressing myself to the proudest
my lord Achilles but I wish the rest | of you to hear and what I say digest
the Achaeans have often against me | cried out thus making indeed the very
point you sir with speech did initiate | but I was not to blame 'twas Zeus and Fate
also the Fury who walks in the dark | who blinded my judgement on that day dark
of the meeting when I took it upon | myself the prize of Achilles to con
-fiscate what could I do? at such moments | there's a Power that completely cements
command Ate Zeus' daughter eldest | who blinds everyone spirit accursed pest
that she is and never ground alighting | with her insubstantial feet but flighting

through men's heads corrupting them and seeing | this one or other brought down Zeus being
blinded even by her once and he's known | to stand above men gods everyone own
yet Here tricked feminine wiles wielding she's | on the day to the mighty Heracles
Alcmene going to give birth in Thebes | of the Great Walls solemn pronouncement he's
made to the assembled gods there 'Listen | to me you gods and goddesses even
this day the goddess Eileithyia | of travail will soon bring into world a
human child who's born of a stock up top | with my blood in their veins and who shall top
all his neighbours' Lady Here took this up | and for the mighty Zeus then trap set up
'It's a lie as time will show prophecy | you will not fulfil come now you mighty
Olympian give me your word solemn | that today the child from womb of woman
to issue to come of a stock up top | with your blood in their veins shall be on top
of all his neighbours' and Zeus saw no harm | this gesture took oath solemn the disarm
by charm completely blinded but Here sped | down from the top of Olympus did head
to Achaean Argos where as she knew | also had on its way a baby new
the noble wife of Sthenelus the son | of Perseus but just seven months gone
Here brought this child into the light of day | before his proper time postponed the day
when Alcmene to deliver forbidding | goddess travail her usual bidding
then she went to Zeus the Son of Cronos | 'Father Zeus' to him did the news flash toss
Lord of the Lightning Flash I hasten to | inform you there has indeed been born to
-day a noble child who is to be King | of the Argives and him they are calling
Eurystheus his father Sthenelus | so he's from stock Zeus as son Perseus
and so it is a thing very fitting | he should over the Argives be sitting'
Zeus was deeply mortified in rage seized | Ate by her glossy hair and out squeezed
a mighty oath that this arch-destroyer | of the mind should set foot again never
in Olympus and the whole starry sky | whirled her round his head and cast her from high
heaven and its stars and Ate soon found | herself in the world of men down on the ground
Zeus could not think of her without a groan | whenever he saw Heracles his own
beloved son at the tasks grim | that Eurystheus had then set for him
was the same with me when the great Hector | of the flashing helmet was then once more
slaughtering Achaeans at the ships' sterns | I could not forget the Ate and stern's
the thought who had caused me to be blinded | on that day but because I *was* blinded
and Zeus robbed me of my wits I'm willing | to call it quits propose fulfilling
ample compensation claim gird yourself | thus for battle lead whole army yourself
as for the gifts here I am ready to | produce all lord Odysseus promised you
when he went up to your hut yesterday | if you like the fighting you can delay
though I know how eager you are and my | servants shall fetch all your presents from my
ship so you may assure yourself of their | excellence" Achilles stood his ground there
replied "Your majesty Atreides | Agamemnon King of Men can wait these
gifts produce them if you like at your own | convenience or keep with you turn own
thoughts to battle without least further pause | before us such an enterprising cause
ought not to be arguing time wasting | I must be seen in the van so wasting
once again Trojan forces with spear bronze | think of me when one come(s) to grips with one's

man each of you" this brought a remonstrance | from the wise Odysseus "No way this stance
can now hold most worshipful Achilles | the men have not yet had their rice crispies
and gallant as you are yourself you must | not order them to march on Troy on just
meagre fare fling them like this at oppo | the battle won't be but a brief stopo
-ver once the two forces become engaged | and their fighting spirit sees them enraged
urge the men rather to take food and wine | by the ships these their courage will define
and strength for they're in need of nourishment | it's impossible energy be spent
to such an extent man stands up all day | 'til sunset no food to enemy prey
his heart may be very set on fighting | yet exhaustion him unawares b(l)i(gh)ting
he is then attacked by thirst and hunger | and his willing but weak legs give under
him asunder but when a man imbued | with satisfying fill of wine and food
before an all-day fight can carry on | with high heart unflagging strength 'til broken
off be the battle I ask you then to | dismiss the soldiery and tell them to
prepare a meal as for the gifts let King | Agamemnon see to their place making
before the Assembly so all the men | may see them for themselves and you too then
be satisfied further let him stand up | before the whole Assembly and give up
his solemn oath to you that he never | went into the girl's bed and slept with her
in return you too must be offering | spirit forgiving as peace-offering
then him give you a rich in-hut banquet | so your vindication complete acquit
and may I recommend that *you* my lord | Atreides be much more hard-wired board
in your future dealings? it's no disgrace | for king when has given offence with grace
then to come forward and repair the breach" | "My lord Odysseus most welcome your speech
to me" said King Agamemnon "failing | in naught naught missing each point unfailing
you dealt with I am not only ready | but anxious to take the oath you steady
-ly prescribe not be myself forswearing | meanwhile let Achilles here pause (s)wearing
though I know he is eager for action | and let all the rest of you see action
in your places until the gifts are brought | from my hut and we make formal pact ought
you yourself Odysseus are the man who | I entrust with this task go and pick you
some young men the best you can find whole force | and then go to my ship and fetch perforce
all the presents we promised Achilles | last night not forgetting females of these
and let Talthybius make haste prepare | me a boar for sacrifice to Zeus fair
and the Sun in the presence of this vast | Achaean host" but Achilles aghast
rose again to his feet "Your majesty | Atreides Agamemnon King" he
said "of Men you are taking the right steps | but you'd do better still to take these steps
some other time when a lull in the fight | and my blood's not up as well up as it might
be now for our friends who fell to Hector | at time he the most triumphant vector
are lying mangled on the plain and you | and Odysseus now choose this moment to
announce a meal! but my way is different | for I should make the men fight now when spent
and are fasting and hungry and give them | a square meal at sunset because by then
we would have wiped out our shame 'til that's done | I for my part will not let sup or crumb
pass through my lips with my friend lying dead | in my hut by the sharp bronze mangl-ed
his feet toward the door and his comrades | weeping round him with that in mind all fades

can't interest myself in your programme | or in anything at all except dam
-nable blood slaughter groans of dying men" | "Achilles" replied the nimble-wits then
"son Peleus flower of Achaean | chivalry you're for sure a stronger man
than me also not a little better | with the spear but in view of my greater
age and experience I may well claim | to have somewhat more in the judgement game
than you that being so you must constrain | yourself allowing my ruling refrain
nothing exhausts a man as quickly as | a pitched battle where the sword as slick as
a sickle strews the field with straw for each | little grain and when end of reaping reach
Zeus battle-arbiter has tipped the scale | against you wish the troops express the scale
of their grief by starving for Pat's dying | impossible daily men fall lying
in their hundreds there'd never be an end | such austerity now no we must bend
our hearts to steel bury our dead and let | one day's tears suffice for them lament yet
all moreover who survive the carnage | must attend to their food and beverage
if we are to continue under arms | carry on the fight 'til one side disarms
so let none of you hold back await your | second call to action for this *is* your
summons it will go hard with anyone | left behind at the ships we'll rope in one
and all then fling our whole force at these horse | -taming Trojans" so Odysseus now hoarse
picked these men for the duty him assigned | then so King Nestor's sons he first does find
Meges son Phyleus Meriones | Thoas Melanippus Lycomedes
son of Creon and they set out for King | Agamemnon's hut and once there barking
a few sharp orders the work was done then | they had fetched out from the hut the seven
tripods that he had promised Achilles | of gleaming copper cauldrons twenty these
and the twelve horses immediately | after brought out skilled work women stately
seven or rather eight with Briseis | lovely cheeks and Odysseus after this
a sum of ten talents in gold had weighed | out led way back to the army arrayed
young Achaean noblemen displaying | the gifts middle of Assembly laying
them down Agamemnon rose to his feet | Talthybius of the godlike voice meet
stood by the King holding a boar between | his hands Atreides knife teeth between
he always carried beside great scabbard | of his sword then began rite the laggard
haggard cut a little hair from the Boar's Head | raising his hands in prayer to the Zeus-head
the Argives all sitting comfortably | quiet in their places customary
listened with Mother-King and he looked up | into the broad sky and then summoned up
a prayer "I call first on Zeus the highest | and best of gods at his worthy behest
on the Earth and Sun and on the Furies | who make men pay dear for their perjuries
in the world below to bear me witness | never laid hands on girl as such sinless
Briseis either by way of louvring | her into my bed any manoeuvring
whatsoever she was untouched during | stay in my huts a word false enduring
in this may the gods deal out to me all | the penalties that they impose on all
who take their names in vain" and cut boar's throat | merciless bronze relentless old goat smote
Talthybius took the carcass with swing | into bosom of the grey sea did fling
for the fish to eat then Achilles rose | to address the Argive warrior rows
"How utterly a man can be blinded | by Father Zeus! I can't think that what did

my lord King then would have stirred me to such | lasting bitterness or behave in such
an unprincipled way to forcibly | take my girl if Zeus not contriving he
the massacre of the Argives but now go | take your meal and then to battle! not slow"
soldiers pleased to accept this dismissal | scattered every one to vessels several
while haughty Myrmidons took gifts present | quarters of Prince Achilles to present
where they laid them down and left the women | in his hut and the horses were driven
into his own herd by his squires noble | and so Briseis came back beautiful
as golden Aphrodite but when saw | Patroclus lying there mangled by raw
and sharp bronze gave a piercing scream threw her | -self down onto his body and tore her
breast and tender neck and fair cheeks with her | hands as lovely as a goddess in her
grief cried "Poor Patroclus my heart's delight! | woe is me! I left you in this hut (b)right
alive when I went away and now I | come back my prince find you dead such is my
life an endless chain of misery I | saw the husband who my father and my
lady mother gave me lying mangled | before his city by bronze cruel angled
I saw my three brothers my brothers dear | borne as I too by the same mother here
all meet their doom but you when Achilles | swift killed my man sacked city King Mynes
you would not even allow me weep | you said you'd arrange for me to reap keep
title Prince Achilles' lawful wife | take me off in your ships to a new life
in Phthia give me a wedding-feast | among Myrmidons you no beast gentlest
with me always how can I ever cease | to mourn you?" and thus wept on Briseis
the other women took up the lament | ostensibly for Patroclus each meant
though at heart for own unhappy lot grot | as for Achilles the Argive chiefs got
around him and pressed him to take some food | but with almighty groan refuse mode mood
"Kind friends if you have any regard for | my wishes I beg you not to ask for
I'm in terrible distress I can't think | of sating hunger or desire to drink
I'm to hold out at all costs 'til sunset" | this proved enough rid him of most chief set
but the two Atreidae stayed and thus | too did the admirable Odysseus
with Nestor Idomeneus also | Phoenix old charioteer they tried so
hard in his anguish to him give comfort | but could come to his heart no kind comfort
'til he'd flung himself into the bloody | jaws of battle memories came floody
back to his mind and he broke out afresh | "How often have you yourself in the flesh
my most unhappy beloved friend made | dainty meal before me in this hut laid
in your quick and ready way when all set | on the horse-taming Trojans make onset!
and now you lie mangled here and I go | fasting still plenty in the hut but no
way can I bear the thought of it so much | do I miss you could have suffered no much
more cruel blow than this not even the news | of my father's death who via the muse
is shedding giant tears in Phthia | at this time I dare say for me the dear
son he's lost while I am fighting Trojans | in a foreign land for wretched Helen's
sake nor even if they told me that my | son Neoptolemos living in Scy
-ros was dead perhaps he is and yet I | liked to think previously would be I
alone who would perish here in Troyland | far from Argos where horses graze the land
and that you would get home to Phthia | and then fetch my son from Scyros in a

fast black beaked ship and show him everything | all artefacts and servants possessing
and my big house with its high roof because | I have a suspicion that Peleus
if he's not dead and gone by now only | half alive crushed old age burden daily
expectation of the news most dreadful | that I myself am dead" and Jesus Achill
-'es wept as he spoke the chieftains murmured | in sympathy each of them enamoured
in thought of all that he had left at home | the Son of Cronos saw their not-at-home
distress and was sorry for them he turned | at once to Athene "My child have you spurned
your favourite? is there no longer room | in your heart for Achilles sat in gloom
there in front of his high-beaked ships mourning | for his blessed best friend food adjourning
without taste of crumb or sup while the rest | have gone to eat? run and into his breast
nectar and sweet ambrosia invest | so he may some good nourishment ingest"
with this encouragement from Zeus Athene | who'd scarcely needed such an urging scene
swooped down from heaven through the upper air | like a shrieking long-winged bird of prey prayer
while Argives were with arms themselves filling | throughout the camp nectar she distilling
and sweet ambrosia into his breast | so bitter pangs hunger don't him infest
once this done she made her way back to her | great Father's palace as every soldier
pouring forth from among the gallant ships | thick and fast as a host of cold flake chips
that come scudding down from the clouds before | a northerly gale helmets to the fore
resplendent bossed shields plated cuirasses | and ashen spears poured out of the asses
of the ships the glory of arms noble | lit the sky a-glitter bronze did ripple
like laughter over the plain and the earth | resounded to marching feet's bitter mirth
among all Achilles admirable | donned his arms in the intolerable
fury that possessed him he gnashed his teeth | his eyes blazed like a fiery grouse peat heath
as put on the divine gifts Hephaestus | had made for him heart full evil lust thus
for Trojan dead first he tied round his legs | splendid greaves silver angle ankle-pegs
next put the cuirass on his breast over | shoulder slung the bronze sword with its silver
-studded hilt the great thick shield took up soon | it flashed into the distance like the moon
or like the gleam that sailors catch at sea | from a fire on an upland farm lonely
when they're driven away from home alone | down the highways of the fish by winds' moan groan
such was the sheen went up into the sky | from his great ornamented shield held high
he picked up the massive helm located | on his head like a star scintillated
above it danced the golden plumes Hephaest | -us had lavished lovingly on the crest
Achilles tried himself in the armour | to see if it fitted and how it wore
if allowed his splendid limbs free movement | light as a pair of wings in a moment
lifted him up last from his cue-case gear | took heavy long formidable flash spear
no Argive could wield save he who knew way | to handle it was made from an ash way
up Mount Pelion given by Cheiron | to his father Peleus bring death on
his noble foes meanwhile Automedon | and Alcimus saw to the yoking on
of the horses settled breast-straps onto | their chests and inserted the bits into
their mouths drew the reins back into the well | -built car Automedon picked up the well
-shiny whip by its handle and leapt in | behind the pair Achilles followed in
girt for battle resplendent in armour | like the dazzling sun and played reprover

of father's horses in voice terrible | "Xanthus and Balius of line foal full
celebrated Podarge try this time to | do better and bring your driver back to
his friends alive when the fighting is done | instead of leaving him behind dead on
the field as with Patroclus" from under | the yoke he was then given an answer
by one horse Xanthus of the feet glancing | the white-armed goddess Here once enhancing
with human speech Xanthus had head humbled | so that his mane from the yoke-pad tumbled
by the yoke and swept the ground "Indeed my | dreaded master we'll bring you neigh safe nigh
home once more today yet the hour of your | death is drawing near it will not be our
fault but a great god and Destiny's strong | hand and neither did aught to us belong
of indolence or lack of speed that let | soldiers Trojan strip the armour full set
from Patroclus' shoulders was the best | of gods Phoebus Son Leto of the Best
Tresses who killed him then in the front line | let Hector have gory glory run fine
though we may with the West Wind's speed and there | is nothing faster known on earth you there
too are doomed to fall in battle to god | and man" the Furies struck him dumb poor sod
because Achilles of the nimble feet | was angry with him "Xanthus it's not meet
to waste your breath by now prophesying | my end know quite well Fate in wait lying
doomed to perish here far away from my | dear father and Mother but meanwhile I
am not going to stop 'til I've given | a bellyful of war to host Trojan"
with that he raised the mighty battle-cry | drove powerful horses to front on high

εἴκοσι

*Book 20*

# THE GODS GO TO WAR

*of how Achilles made havoc among*
*the Trojans and their allies when on song*

by beaked ships the Argives drew up nigh high | for battle round never-say-give-up-die
tireless dire son Peleus other side | the Trojans too fell in on the high side
of the plain at the same time Zeus ordered | Themis from the summit rugged-bordered
Olympus call the gods to Assembly | equivalent of going Wemberley
for the c(o)up final and she went the rounds | summoned them to his Palace out of bounds
only Ocean all other Rivers came | Nymphs who haunt the delightful woods of fame
sources of streams grassy water-meadows | all came Cloud-compeller's hallo(o)(w)s
in-house sat in the marble gallery | Hephaestus great Architect made for ye
great Father Zeus when all had foregathered | Palace Poseidon ignoring not erred
the call of the goddess but had come out | of the sea to join them had sat devout
down in their midst and enquired what purpose | might have in mind the King of the Porpoise
"Lord of the Lightning Flash why've you convened | Assembly of gods? Is't for what fate's screened
about the hosts Trojan and Achaean | who're about to resume hostile action
this very moment?" "Lord of the Earthquake | you've read my mind aright for god's sake
know why I have summoned this gathering | they concern me even while lathering
each other yet I propose stay here | seat self some Olympian bower near
from which I can enjoy the spectacle | and the rest of you I now enable
to join Trojans and Achaeans give live | aid to the side horse-taming or Argive
for if Achilles is allowed to fight | the Trojans without an opposing blight
won't for moment hold that fiery spirit | even before at sight very limit
of him they just used to tremble and run | and now that he is an embittered one
because of loss of his friend dear I fear | may cheat Destiny the walls of Troy clear"
these words from the Son of Cronos unleashed | s/he-gods-dogs of war immortals released
at once left for the scene of the action | in two hostile groups to fleet Achaean
made their way Here also Pallas Athene | so did Girdler of World Poseidon seen
with Hermes there the great Bringer of Luck | cleverest at the wonder-work of P(l)uck
of them all and Hephaestus followed them | exulting in his enormous strength then

for though he limped he was active enough | on his slender legs and in a great huff
to the Trojan side went Ares in his | flashing helm Phoebus of Flowing Hair sis'
Artemis Archeress Leto after | the River Xanthus also the laughter
-loving Aphrodite 'til the moment | when the gods descended among men meant
Achaeans had carried all before them | because Achilles had reappeared then
after his too-long absence from the front | Troy's knees wobbled an affront back to front
beneath them in their terror at the sight | son Peleus not slight light blight at fight
resplendent in his arms and as deadly | as the War-god but scene changed when medley
Olympians got to the field and Strife | the great Battle-maker then came to life
for though Athene raised the war-cry and how | standing by the trench beyond the wall now
sending her voice down the shore echoing | on other side Ares re-echoing
raging like a black squall and inciting | Trojans giving great cries piercing siting
self at one moment on citadel heights | next from the banks of Simois' flights
as ran along slopes Callicolone | blessed gods threw each ally colony
forces at each other's throats so opened | a grievous breach in their ranks so opined
posterity up on high Father Zeus | of men and gods thunder ominous use
and down below Poseidon caused the wide | world and the lofty mountain-tops to slide
every spur crest of Ida of many | springs so shaken while the Trojan city
Argive ships trembled in the underworld | Hades King of the Dead was frightened hurled
himself from his throne afraid Poseidon | and his earthquakes might indeed split open
the ground overhead expose to mortal | and immortal eyes the Chambers hateful
of Decay with horror fill gods themselves | such turmoil battle Lord of the Ring's elves
began between the gods little wonder | when Poseidon faced Phoebus down under
with his winged arrows and Athene of clear | Flashing Eyes faced Ares and when then Here
was confronted by Apollo's sister | Artemis of Golden Distaff Archer
-ess and was goddess also of the chase | Leto formidable Hermes to face
he the Bringer of Luck and Hephaestus | the mighty swirling river called Xanthus
by the gods and Scamander by mankind | thus they went to war god-to-god un-kind
as for Achilles wished nothing better | than in the swirling throng to meet Hector
son of Priam for Hector's was the blood | with which he yearned to glut the stubborn good
god War but Apollo the Marshaller | of the Host intervened at once after
filling him with daring moved Aeneas | to seek confront the son of Peleus
disguising himself also mimicing | the voice of Lycaon he box ticking
a son Priam "Aeneas Counsellor | of the Trojans what's become of all your
boastful threats? did you not tell the Trojan | princes over the wine-cups man-to-man
you'd face Achilles son of Peleus?" | "Lycaon why do you press us precious
thus to pit ourselves against the haughty | son Peleus? as I hate the naughty
thought behind it for this won't be first time | I've been confronted by the swift sublime
Achilles as once before he chased me | with his spear away from Ida when he
raided our cattle and sacked Lyrenessus | and Pedasus then saved by Zeus' sus
who gave us strength and speed of foot or I | should have fallen to Achilles met my
doom and to Athene for she went ahead | of him make things safe she who did egg-head

him on slaughter Leleges and Trojans | with his spear impossible any man's
chance against him always I did conclude | with him save skin a god did not elude
quite apart from that his spear has a way | flying straight never stopping 'til finds way
to human flesh but if the gods decide | to see fair play he'll have no easy ride
even though likes to think he's made of bronze" | "My lord" the King Apollo then responds
"Son of Zeus why not invoke the deathless | gods yourself? aren't you known to be no less
than the son Aphrodite Daughter | of Zeus whereas Achilles' mother
is of a humbler rank with the Old Man | of the Sea Father in comparison
to Zeus? straight at him then with the hard bronze! | don't let his threats and insults despondenc
-y cause" and so Apollo breathed courage | into Prince Aeneas who now does rage
forward up through the front lines resplendent | in his gleaming shiny bronze equipment
but the white-armed goddess Here not taken | unawares when saw Anchises' son
moving through the press to attack the son | of Peleus her friends she did beckon
to her side "Poseidon and Athene I | look to you to handle this affair I
see Aeneas now coming to attack | Achilles resplendent bronze arms at back
held Phoebus Apollo come let's send him | forthwith to the right-about or from him
and opponents take the cue one of *us* | might stand by Achilles and enhance thus
his powers for his spirit must not be | allowed to fail him must be made to see
the best of the immortals love him those | who up until now have saved the oppos
from defeat of no consequence at all | from Olympus to join battle we all
came down so Achilles should not suffer | harm at Trojan hands today though later
he must endure what Destiny has spun | for him what very first thread of life done
when came from his mother's womb but if all | this is not conveyed to him in a call
from Heaven be by terror affronted | when finds himself by a god confronted
for the gods are difficult for any | man to deal with when face him openly"
Poseidon Earthshaker restrained her here | these words "You must control yourself here Here
not be so outrageously aggressive | I for one prefer a stance more passive
and not set the gods at each other's throats | I suggest that for now we burn our boats
leave it to the men to do the fighting | while we watch on safe spot on alighting
of course if Ares or Apollo starts | the fight of if play the part of upstarts
and lay hands on Achilles to keep him | out of action then we ourselves will imm
-ediately be embroiled but not long | I think our enemies will before long
have to break off the battle and go back | to the other Olympus gods forced back
by our sheer strength" the god of the Sable | Locks with this proposal was then able
to take his companions away with him | to the mighty earthwork lofty trim grim
the Trojans and Pallas Athene had made | for hero Heracles as palisade
against the great sea-beast when it came up | from the beach on dry land put itself up
against him then Poseidon and the rest | of the gods sat selves down spread a mist fest
impenetrable around their shoulders | their divine opponents shrugged their shoulders
on brow of Callicolone sat down | round Lord Phoebus and Ares Sacker-Town
thus both the parties settled down in their | oppo camps took their further counsels there
shrank from plunge first into horrors fiery | of war but Zeus in his on-high eyrie

still in control meanwhile the plain was filled | by in-human(e) combatants and sparkled
with the bronze of infantry and horses | earth shook beneath feet as the two forces
rushed each other intervening space us | seeing two champions intravenous
come together Aeneas Anchises | son and the mighty godlike Achilles
bent on single combat Aeneas first | to step forward enter into list worst
defiant huge helm nodded on his head | held out in front with gallant shield spread led
and bronze spear brandished from the other side | the son of Peleus sprang out beside
to meet him and he was like a lion | whose ravages caused town men rely on
to turn out and destroy him and at first | lion goes his way contempt treat purports
but when one of the bolder young men hits | him with a spear then he gathers his wits
with a snarl the froth collects on his jaws | he growls to himself in pause the ground paws
in noble indignation lashes flanks | and ribs with his tail thus himself uptanks
into a fighting fury then with eyes | aflame he charges and in passion flies
determined spear injury to counter | kill or perish in the first encounter
thus Achilles impelled by pride fury | launch attack Aeneas of majesty
and when they'd come within range great runner | Achilles who did contrive opener
"Aeneas what has led you to desert | ranks spurt so far out meet me purport squirt?
Is your thought in fighting me 'Thus I am | aiming to step into shoes of Priam
become King of the horse-taming Trojans?' | your killing me will not achieve your plans
for Priam to abdicate for you he | has sons of his own his health is sound he
is not half-witted either so perhap | the Trojans have offered you a nice snap
of their best land with plenty of vineyards | and cornfields if you can go the hard yards
against me for your private use if you | succeed in killing me? well I think you
will find it difficult for I seem to | recall once before from my spear fled you
or have you forgotten that time I caught | you alone cut off from your cattle fraught
taught you to scuttle right down Ida's slopes | you ran so fast then you never had hopes
of looking behind in time escaped me | in Lyrnessus you were a refugee
I followed up sacked the place with the help | of Athene and Father Zeus and did help
myself to the women I captured free | carrying them off into slavery
though you yourself eluded me with aid | from Zeus and the other gods but not aid
though you fondly hope I think this time round | my recommendation to you now sound
is to get you back and join the rabble | and not to stand up and with me dabble
or you'll come to grief for it is the height | of folly be wise too late in the fight"
"My lord Achilles do not imagine | that you are going to have your weigh-in
scaring me with words as though I were still | a child in insults and abuse my will
well prepared give you an equal measure | for we know each other's measure treasure
in pedigree and we know each other's | parents for though never seen the other's
their names are familiar to our ear | as household words it's common knowledge here
you are a son of the admirable | Peleus and Thetis of the Sable
Locks Child of Brine while I can claim rather | magnificent Anchises as father
and Aphrodite as my dear Mother | of those two couples one or the other
is to mourn the loss of a son today | for I am sure that you and I no way

will not settle our affair leave the field | with no more than little small-talk wield yield
such as this but if you would care to hear | the story of my house though well-known here
it then starting with Dardanus of Zeus | Lord of Clouds a son and Dardanus
founded Dardania at a time when | the sacred city of Troy had not then
been built to shelter people on the plain | still inhabited well-watered terrain
of Ida and Dardanus had a son | King Erichthonius richest person
on earth he had three thousand mares feed-in | in the marsh small foals re-joice-in-breedin'
and one day as they were out there grazing | North Wind on their beauty stunning gazing
overcome black stallion form taking | in order to them to be love making
and they in due course twelve foals producing | and these on the land frolics inducing
could run across a field of corn brushing | the highest ears yet not a whit crushing
when they made the sea rolling then swimming | their playground and the white foam were skimming
on the crests of the waves and now the King | had a son who was called Tros who was King
of the Trojans Tros himself sons tripod | of splendid Ilus Assaracus god
-like Ganymedes who grew up to be | of all youths the one of the most beauty
in world due to his good looks was kidnapped | by the gods because his pathway was mapped
to be Zeus' cupbearer foregather | with the immortals Ilus was father
to the noble Laomedon whose sons | were Priam Lampus while Hicetaon's
offshoot Ares Tithonus Clytius | but Tros' second son Assaracus
was the father of Capys of whom son | Anchises is my father while the son
of Priam is Prince Hector that chum my | pedigree such the bloodline mine claim I
and as for prowess in war that's a gift | from almighty Zeus who might gift uplift
to a man in greater measure or less | as he sees fit but come let us not mess
about in the heart of battle talking | like two silly little boys not balking
at sling shipload insults at each other | quite enough a merchantman to scupper
the tongue is glib with a wide range of words | at its command it can express our moods
and thoughts in any style and as a rule | one gets the kind of answer as the tool
one has employed and yet what call is there | for you and me to evil banter share
like a pair of nagging women lost their | tempers come out into the street from their
houses to pelt each other with abuse | not caring in their fury what's fake nuis
-ance or true? whatever I want to fight | and no words of yours shall deflect my flight
'til we have stood and had it out with spears | enough now! let's taste each other's bronze fears"
and then Aeneas hurled his heavy spear | at the other's formidable shield clear
point of the weapon rang loud on the shield | unearthly in shock Achilles did wield
forward thrust with his mighty hand thinking | that the javelin long-shadowed blinking
Aeneas the magnanimous bound | to pierce it however foolish he found
his fear for he'd forgotten the splendid | gifts of the gods are not fabricated
to fail and crumple up when hands human | assault them now they served him well even
the heavy spear of doughty Aeneas | didn't break through the shield but was stopped as
it hit the gold Hephaestus had put in | -to his gift and yet it did succeed in
passing through two layers but there were three | more for Lord of the Crooked Foot did see
his way to put on five two of bronze two | tin on the inner side of the shield too

one gold layer where the ashen spear held | Achilles with long-shadowed spear did meld
in turn struck Aeneas' rounded shield | very edge bronze oxhide backing did yield
the ashen shaft from Pelion burst through | resounding crack Aeneas though self threw
back ducked thrust man-covering shield above | himself in terror and lance clove with love
the leather from the bronze passover here | of his back and ended its long career
by sticking in the ground shaft had not touched | Aeneas but he was so deeply touched
by closeness of shot lost wits had shits there | unseeing eyes utter discomfort bare
but now Achilles his sharp sword drawing | at him with terrific shout clawing
Aeneas picked up a lump of rock then | only to lift it was a feat even
beyond the strength of any two men bred | now but alone no effort it hand-led
and as Achilles came on Aeneas | might have struck him on helm or shield whereas
it had already saved his life that shield | Achilles would have closed right in and keeled
Aeneas with his sword if had not been | for the watching eye of Poseidon keen
the Earthshaker turned to the gods beside | with a cry of concern he did not hide
"I cannot help just being sorry for | magnanimous Aeneas as soon for
final fall to Achilles and go down | to Hades' Halls because like a clown
he took Apollo at his word as though | the Archer-King would save his life just so!
why should an innocent man who's always | been liberal with his offering-ways
to the gods of the broad sky need suffer | for no good reason save that in other
people's troubles he's found himself involved? | and so let us on action be resolved
and rescue him from death even the Son | of Cronos might be angry if he's done
to death as after all he is destin | -ed to survive and to save from extin
-ction house of Dardanus house whose founder | Zeus loved more born of a mortal mother
than any other child Priam's line loss | of all favour with the Son of Cronos
and now the great Aeneas shall be King | of Troy and thereon shall be following
his children's children in the time to come" | "Shaker of Earth you must call the outcome"
said Here the oxide Queen "whether rescue | Aeneas or just leave him alone to
his fate because Pallas Athene and I've | repeatedly sworn never leave alive
in presence of all the gods folk Trojan | spare from their doom not even that day when
their whole city is being consumed by | devastating fires will be lit there by
the warrior sons of proud Achaea" | and thus did Poseidon the Earthshaker
here hear Here out then plunged through the melee | and rain of spears making for the levee
where Aeneas and the most famous son | Peleus getting their engagement on
once there his first step was to spread a mist | before Achilles' eyes then de-list
the ashen spear entangled in noble | Aeneas' shield at feet of Achill
-'es laid it swept Aeneas off the ground | high into air with such a great bound round
of the god's hand that he vaulted over | all intervening lines horse-car cover
infantry came down on the very edge | of battlefield where the Caucones wedge
preparing to enter into the fight | Poseidon Earthshaker with him caught right
up there and took him to task "Aeneas | what's the meaning of this you reckless ass?
and which of the gods then told you to fight | proud Achilles not only better wight
than you but favourite by far greater | of the immortals? if you meet ever

that man withdraw at once or find yourself | in the Halls of Hades before your shelf
-life but when he is dead and gone you can | boldly play your part up front as no man
on the Achaean side is then going | to kill you" Poseidon state play showing
left Aeneas there quickly returning | to Achilles from eyes overturning
the mist had baffled Achilles who stared | with all his might decided he had shared
a miracle as his spear was lying | there on the ground the man he'd been trying
to kill with it was nowhere to be seen | gave exclamation of disgust obscene
"The immortal gods" he thought "must indeed | be most fond of Aeneas do such deed
though felt there was but little truth in all | his boastful words well let him go withal
will be so thankful to have saved his skin | this time he'll not be very keen risk in
another fight with me so now I'll put | Argives on mettle see what sort shot putt
I can do against other Trojan tanks" | and so Achilles hurried down the ranks
with a word of exhortation for each | man "Noble Achaeans don't stand there each
one of you waiting for the Trojans but | each one of you pick out your man and put
your heart into the fight I may be strong | but I can scarcely deal alone for long
with such a force and fight them all even | immortal gods like Ares Athene then
couldn't do a lot of damage if threw | themselves at such a mass of men not to
take it easy I propose not at all | what swift foot and strong arm can do at call
shall be done on earth as i'st in Heaven | I'm going straight through their lines and don't en
-vy any Trojan who comes near my spear" | thus he roused his men but on other spear
-side illustrious Hector was hounding | on the Trojans was even propounding
an attack on Achilles thus he cried | "Gallant Trojans no need be terrified
by the son of Peleus I too could | fight the gods with the spoken pen word good
though with a spear it would be far harder | for compared to us they're far hardier
Achilles won't do all he says he may | succeed up to a point but lose his way
there stop short and I'm going to meet him | though his hands are like fire and indeed grim
and although he possesses a great heart | like burnished steel" thus Hector put new heart
into the Trojans who to the ready | brought spears up battle-cry ready steady
two forces fell on go at each other | Phoebus Apollo went up to Hector
told him on no account seek a meeting | Achilles "Stay with the rest leave him fleeting
let find you in the crowd otherwise he'll | fell you with a cast of his spear or he'll
close and strike you with his sword" this warning | Hector back into the massed ranks fawning
his heart misgave when he heard the god's voice | but no room for fear choice in vice invoice
of Achilles' strong heart and he sprang | at the Trojans and his fine armour rang
with his terrible war-cry the first man | he killed Iphition gallant son one
Otrynteus and leader of a large | contingent and his mother had it large
Naiad who'd borne him to Otrynteus | sacker of towns below heights Tmolus
snowy in rich land Hyde Park gate great | Achilles as this man came in full spate
caught him full on the head and thus (s)mashing | his skull split in two and he came crashing
down and Achilles made mock of him thus | "You've fallen low son of Otrynteus
most redoubtable of men *this* is where | you die at Gygaean Lake though there
born on your father's land by the swirling | streams Hermus Hyllus fish-breeding Sterling"

as Achilles triumphed over him night | of death descended extinguished the light
of his eyes he left him where the front lines | met be torn to bits by Argive lions
car tyres demolished then Demoleon | a staunch and veteran fighter and one
of Antenor's sons hit him on temple | through the bronze-sided helmet the metal
of the helm failed to check the eager spear | and thus the point went through awfully clear
pierced the bone and so spattered the inside | helm with brains his zeal quenched betide beside
Demoleon was gone Hippodamas | was next he had leapt from his car alas
flying before him when Achilles struck | with long-shadowed spear in back bad luck stuck
he yielded up his life with a bellow | like a bull when it's dragged around below
the altar of the Lord of Helicon | by the young men in whose ministration
the Earthshaker delights such was the roar | that came from Hippodamas as his core
spirit left his bones but Achilles thus | already then after Polydorus
with his spear this prince a son of Priam | "the fastest runner of them all I am"
his father had forbidden him to fight | as was youngest his favourite bright light
but the foolish boy had seized the moment | to display his speed among the men front
-line dashed about until he met his death | for Achilles could run a man to death
too and as the young man was then darting | by with a lance full in back imparting
just where the golden buckles of the belt | were fastened overlapped by corslet felt
point transfixed him came out by his navel | he fell on his knees with a groan whole fell
world went black before his eyes and as sank | he clasped his bowels to him with a hand shank
when Hector saw brother Polydorus | sink to the ground clutching his entrails thus
his eyes dimmed with tears could no longer bear | to stay aloof like a raging fire there
made at Achilles brandishing his spear | directly Achilles saw him appear
he leapt to meet him to himself saying | in exultation "Here now essaying
one who struck me the cruellest blow of all | when he killed my dearest friend we are all
done now with dodging one another down | the corridors of battle a black frown
greeted Prince Hector with "Come quickly on | and meet your fated end the sooner son"
"My lord Achilles" Hector bright helmet | answered unperturbed "don't think you'll upset
me with words as though I were a small child | because if it comes to insults and wild
abuse I'm well prepared to give you tit | for tat I know you're a good man far bit
better than me but matters like this lie | on the knees of the gods and although I
am not as strong as you they may yet choose | let me kill you with spear-cast choice so use
lance before now as sharp as any has proved" | he poised and hurled his spear cast much improved
but Athene by a miracle that cost | her but a little breath blew so spear tossed
at illustrious Achilles way lost | flew back fell at feet Hector so em-bossed
-Achilles his eagerness to kill fol | -low charged with terrific cry but Apol
-lo hid Prince Hector in a dense mist snatched | away previous Aeneas feat matched
easily thrice noble swift Achilles | dashed in with his bronze spear and three times he's
lunged at empty mist the fourth time charging | like a demon at Hector discharging
in a terrible voice ranted "You cur! | managed to save your poxy skin once more
but only just Phoebus Apollo took | care of you once again no doubt you book
prayer spot with him before get anywhere near | earshot of the battlefield spear fear here

but we'll meet once more and I'll finish you | if I can find a god to help me too
for now I'll try my luck against the rest" | even as he was speaking he addressed
Dryops struck full in the neck with javelin | Dryops with a crash at his feet fell in
ruin Achilles then at Demuchus | cast Philetor's tall handsome son A+
he hit him on the knee right brought him down | took his life bringing his long sword drawn down
attacked Laogonus and Dardanus | sons of Bias hurled both from their car thus
to the ground with a spear-cast first bloke broke | the other at close quarters with a stroke
of his sword Tros son of Alastor next | this man came up close so as to be text
of kin Achilles clasp his knees in hope | would shrink from killing at a stroke the dope
one of his own age just take prisoner | leave him alive doomed fail petitioner
the young fool should have known as Achilles | was not kind or tender-hearted as he's
a man of fierce passions and so when Tros | desperate mercy dire straits' last dice toss
loss put hands on knees and in the liver | with his sword Achilles struck still liver
fell from him and drenched his lap with dark blood | he swooned then and there of black night the hood
fell on his eyes and Achilles then went up | to Mulius and struck him too high up
on the ear so hard the bronze point came out | at the other ear and next for a clout
now was Echeclus son of Agenor | Achilles caught him full square on the fore
-head with a stroke his hilted sword the blood | made the whole blade as warm as heated mud
for Fate had set her seal on Echeclus | the shadow of Death descended no fuss
on his eyes and next was Deucalion | Achilles pierced his forearm with the bron
-ze point of his spear just where the sinews | of the elbow are attached not good news
Deucalion waiting for him arm crooked | down by the spear now Death in the face looked
Achilles struck the man's neck with his sword | sent head and helm flying off down sand sward
together from the vertebrae up welled | the marrow the corpse on ground lay stretched felled
next quarry Achilles the son Rhygmus | royal Peiros deep-soiled Thrace noble plus
cast at him caught him full the bronze javelin | a-(r)rest did lung tumbled from travellin'
chariot then Achilles with no fuss | sharp spear struck Areithous squire Rhygmus wuss
in the back as he turned the horses round | and when he too had been swept to the ground
they bolted Achilles a-mock ran spear | like a driving wind whirls the flames of fear
here and there when conflagration rages | on in sun-baked mount-side's gully pages
and the high forest's consumed he did hound | his prey with fury of a rabid hound
earth dark with blood at their imperious | master's will the horses hooves enormous
of the great Achilles trampled dead men | and shields alike with no more ado then
than when a farmer's yoked a pair of broad | -browed cattle trample white barley aboard
broad threshing-floor lowing bulls tread out grain | his car's axle-tree and rails around splayn
with blood thrown up by horses' hooves and tyres | and the son of Peleus never tires
he presses on thus in-quest for glory | his unconquerable hands full gory

εἴκοσι ἕνα

*Book 21*

# ACHILLES FIGHTS THE RIVER

*of how Achilles fought with the River*
*of Trojans back within Troy the driver*

when reached the ford of eddying Xanthus | noble River's Father immortal Zeus
Achilles cut the Trojan force in two | one party he drove across the fields to
-wards the city where the Argives had been | hurled back the day before in panic scene
when illustrious Hector ran amuck | these spread across the plain in a wild ruck
to hamper escape Here them confronted | dense fog rest chased effronted affronted
into a river bend where great Xanthus | of the Silver Pools ran deep and fell (s)(p)lush
into the water with great resounding | splashes river-bed them resurf-bounding
and as swam around in the eddies whirled | the banks either side their cries back unfurled
'twas as though a swarm of locusts driven | to the river by the outbreak sudden
of a fierce fire huddled in the water | as an escape from the flames however
here it was Achilles the force driving | torrent cluttering with medley diving
men horses Xanthus roar once more making | spear propped by a tamarisk leave-taking
of bank with nothing but his sword his word | leapt in like a demon in his heart murd
-er laid about him right and left and hid | -eous groans went up once ones sword sordid
met the water reddening with their blood | just like small fry in terror flee in flood
before a huge delfin corners crowding | into a small sheltered Cove for shrouding
know to be caught is to be eaten up | the Trojans cowered under either cup
overhanging banks now so harmful kill | -er river when slaughter tired arms Achill
-'es chosen twelve young men did them derive | from river chattels to be toll price live
for lord Patroclus as death drovered them | dazed like fawns onto the bank and tied them
hands behind with stout leather straps fitted | those taken from their own tunics knitted
then he left them there for his retainers | take to ships in eagerness remainers
to slaughter enemy again takes on | his first encounter was with Lycaon
one of Dardanian Priam's sons who | was making escape from the river goo
had met him before soiree sortie night | and had managed to take him captive right
under the nose of his father's vineyard | where Lycaon young fig-tree shoots trimmed (s)hard
with a sharp knife to make chariot rails | when the mighty Achilles him derails

like a bolt from the blue Achilles on | that occasion had put Lycaon on
board ship sold him in city of Lemnos | and was Jason's son there bought him 'n loss
him from Lemnos borne ransomed price heavy | by a man with whom he'd become friendly
Eetion of Imbros who despatched him | to sacred Arisbe but he made him
-self scarce slipped away from his protector | managed to get back to Troy however
he enjoyed the company of his friends | for just eleven days the twelfth it ends
by Fate he once more into the hands falls | of Achilles who now into the Halls
of Hades was going willy-nilly | to send him he'd recognised easily
he was quite unarmed not of helmet bent | shield spear as had thrown down his equipment
limp and exhausted as he was by sweat | and struggle to escape the river's threat
Achilles cried in anger and surprise | said to himself "Marvels ever arise!
I'll have every Trojan I've killed rising | against me from west's gloom if apprising
their cue from this chap here runaway slave | who was sold in sacred Lemnos and gave
folk the slip and now turns up again here | and treating the high seas as if were clear
no Brexit barrier at all would-be | traveller I'll do more for him now he
shall taste the point of my spear for I want | to satisfy self see if he is wont
to come back as easily as before | from the new destination I've in store
or if the fruitful Earth with so many | strong men in her lap will release any"
and as Achilles stood there wondering | Lycaon drawing nigh and blundering
to reach his knees as by fear stupefied | by one single great desire reified
avoid his fate escape a death dreadful | raise his long spear aimed a cast did Achill
-'es ducked Lycaon then ran in and grasped | his knees while the spear over his back lapsed
planted self in the ground still hungering | for human flesh knees man war-mongering
with one hand and with the other gripping | the spear embracing never let slipping
Lycaon then made his supplication | "Achilles show mercy have pity on
me I cast myself at your knees but I | have a kind of claim on your regard my
prince for you were the first Argive whose bread | broke when seized in our lovely vineyard bed
carried me off from my father and friends | sold me in sacred Lemnos which there ends
in a good price however a ransom | for three times as much was indeed handsome
and so Ilium reached twelve days ago | and now some evil Fate has had a go
brought me into your hands again Father | Zeus must hate me so as your prisoner
to have made me twice! son Laothoe | I am short-lived it seems and she is a
daughter of old Altes King of warlike | Leleges Legolas high fortress like
to live of Pedasus set on the banks | of Satniois and Priam gave thanks
and then made her one of his many wives | had two sons and you'll have taken their lives
because the noble Polydorus fell | to you and your sharp spear an evil fell
end awaits me here for I've little hope | of escape now that God has tied a rope
round my neck but there *is* one more reason | ultra-viral you spare my life even
beg you not to overlook it I was | not delivered of the same mother as
Hector who killed your brave and gentle friend" | thus the highborn son of Priam did end
his plea for mercy with Achilles there | but in the voice that replied to him there
was no mercy "You fool don't talk to me | of ransom I don't wish to hear any

speeches before Patroclus end aligned | to spare Trojans was not disinclined
I took many alive sold them abroad | but now not a single man found abroad
God puts in my hands before Ilium | is going to live and will get fulsome
just deserts and that holds good foe every | Trojan there ever in this time may be
and for the sons of Priam above all | yes my friend and you too must die withal
why make such a song and dance about it? | even Patroclus died by not a bit
better man than you by far look at me | am I not big and beautiful to see
mighty son of great man with a goddess | for my mother? and yet Death and chanceless
Destiny sovereign wait for me also | a morning is coming or maybe so
an evening or a noon when somebody | is going to render up my body
in battle with a cast of her breast spear | or an Amazon arrow my love dear"
when he heard this Lycaon's spirit failed | and he quailed collapsed loosing the spear wailed
his hands held out however Achilles | drew out his sharp sword and struck him with ease
right beside the neck on the collar bone | two-edged blade buried burrowed flesh to bone
sinking forward lay stretched out on the ground | and the dark blood ran out of him and drowned
the earth Achilles took him by the foot | hurled him into the river taunt afoot
by way of farewell "Lie among the fish | there where they can lick the blood all they wish
from your wound your mother will not lay you | on a bier and do mourning for you
but swirling Scamander will roll you out | into sea's broad bosom where will dart out
many fish through the water to the dark | ripples upon the top to eat the stark
white flesh of Lycaon and perdition | to you all 'til we finally come on
to sacred Ilium's great citadel | you in rout and I a killing vessel
from behind and nothing shall save you no | not even the most fair Scamander o'
the Silver Eddies to whom for years you | are sacrificing bulls and into who
-se pools you throw living horses and one | by one for all that you shall come as one
to an evil end 'til you've paid me for | the killing of lord Patroclus and for
the beaten Achaeans slaughtered by their | gallant ships without me there" River there
displeased by killing scene instigated | by reference self exasperated
started ponder ways and means curtailing | exploits Prince Achilles tale retailing
disaster sale to Trojans yet meanwhile | Peleus' son slaughter-bent hurled vile
self the while clasping his long-shadowed spear | at one Asteropaeus father dear
was Pelegon himself a love-child of | Periboea eldest daughter of
Acessamenus and the broad River | Axius the Swirling Stream attacker
Achilles when Asteropaeus good | -ly just emerged from the water was stood
facing him with two javelins emboldened | by Xanthus slaughter resented bold end
sought fate of youths Achilles slaughtering | merciless along his stream quartering
the man Asteropaeus challenged him | "And who on earth are you who now dares him
to face Achilles? who are your people? | for the fathers of men are liable
to weep when they meet me in my fury" | " O royal son of Peleus" said he
"why ask you for my pedigree? it's a | far cry from the land of Paeonia
the deep-soiled whence I came to Ilium | eleven days ago the head of some
number of long-speared Paeonian troops | the line of Axius of the Broad Loops

is mine he was father of the spearman | famed Pelegon I'm deemed son of this man
but enough now! let's fight lord Achilles" | he spoke defiantly Prince Achilles
raised then the ashen spear of Pelion | but the brave Asteropaeus was one
ambidextrous and cast both spears at once | he hit the shield of Achilles with one's
not pierced it as the point stopped by the gold | that the god into the gift installed bold
other grazed Achilles' right elbow | and thus then causing the dark blood to flow
though it passed over him stuck in the ground | and still hungering for its flesh full pound
and it was now the turn of Achilles | his straight-grained ashen shaft then hurls with ease
at Asteropaeus intent deadly | but missed his man struck instead harmlessly
high river-bank with such force buried half | the length of his ashen spear in earth's hearth
and drawing sharp sword from side no fuss-wuss | son Peleus charged Asteropaeus
trying in vain drag ashen lance in trice | out of the bank with his great hand and thrice
had managed to shift it but a little | but each time had to give up the wiggle
he tried again this time to bend and break | the ashen shaft but before he could make
any progress Achilles was on him | and killed him with his sharp sword he hit him
in the belly by the navel and all | his entrails poured out on the ground withal
lay there gasping and black night descended | on his eyes and Achilles descended
on his chest trampling on it and removed | fine armour over him triumphed much moved
"Lie there learn how difficult is for son | even River-god's to fight a scion
of almighty Zeus you said you liver | of lineage of a noble River
but I can trace my pedigree to Zeus | himself Aeacus whose son Peleus
King of many Myrmidon's my father | Aeacus was a son of Zeus greater
line thus than the scion of a River | by as much as Zeus himself is greater
than all the Rivers that run murmuring | to the sea look at River purrpurring
past you now he's a mighty one and would | help you if he could and yet it's no good
fighting against the son of Cronos Zeus | not even King of Rivers Achelous
can match Zeus nor can the deep and potent | Stream of Ocean the one great key portent
source of all rivers every sea each cell | that does exist of kind spring and deep well
even he's afraid of mighty Zeus' | bolt and peal terrible thunder of his"
Achilles pulled his bronze spear from the bank | other on the sand dank left lying (b)lank
lapped by the dark water being dibbled | busily by the eels and fish nibbled
at his kidneys and devouring his fat | after Paeonians he went out flat
next in their plumed helmets been left beside | the swirling river in panic beside
selves when they'd seen of their leader the kill | fell to hands and sword of mighty Achill
-es Thersilochus Mydon Mnesus | Thrasius Aenius Astypylus
and Ophelestes he killed and indeed | swift Achilles would more yet death decreed
were it not for the River eddying | human form resentment eddifying
took to check him caused his voice to issue | from one of the deep pools "Achilles you
are more than man both in your strength and your | outrageous deeds the gods themselves at your
side always but if the son of Cronos | really means you all the Trojans off toss
I implore you at least drive them away | from me do your foul work out of the way
on the plain my lovely channels are full | of dead men's bodies and I'm so awful

-ly choked with corpses that I cannot pour | my waters onto the sacred sea shore
and you are wallowing in slaughter still | have done with it lord! you should really chill
stop I'm appalled" "Scamander child of Zeus | your will shall be done but I'm not the use
pure killing going stop impertinent | Trojans until I've penned them penitent
in own town tried conclusions with Hector | to see which of us to be conqueror
which be killed" he fell upon the Trojans | then once more like a fiend but the Trojans'
Scamander of the Deep Eddies appealed | to Phoebus Apollo "For shame" he squealed
"god of the Silver Bow and Son of Zeus! | is this how your Father's will you deduce?
did he not tell you many times that you | were to stand by the Trojans and that you
were to protect us 'til the evening dusk | should throw its shadows over the ripe husk?"
when he heard this great spearman Achilles | leapt from the bank and plunged up to his knees
in the middle of the stream Scamander | rushed on him in spate and no scam and err
did not filled all his channels foam soaring | cataracts and like a bull there roaring
flung up on land the innumerable | bodies victims of bloodily able
Achilles that had choked him and hiding | still living in deep ample pools abiding
that beautified his course there then arose | angry waters round Achilles verbose
beat down on his shield did him overwhelm | unable maintain hold full-grown over elm
but came out by the roots brought whole bank down | and crashed into mid-river did its crown
bridging it from side to side it clogging | tangle branches self flogging once-blogging
Achilles fought his way from the current | in terror made dash for the bank urgent
but great god not done yet with Prince Hot Lips | Achilles his exploits meant to eclipse
and so save the Trojans from destruction | he rose menaced him with an eruption
black wall of water son Peleus fled | gained a spear-throw's start by the great wing-spread
speed of the black eagle that great hunter | who is the strongest and fastest punter
by far on wings bronze on shoulders clanging | grimly as escaped wave overhanging
angry roar Scamander pursuit rolling | great runner Achilles more than strolling
by far but gods so much greater than man | time and again was caught up by the van
of flood like gardener irrigating | his plots channel among plants ungating
for the fresh water from a spring mattock | in hand he clears from the trench all obstruc
-tions and the water starts flowing it sweeps | the pebbles out of its way more than seeps
in a moment runs singing down the slope | outstripping its guide at a pacey stroke
sometimes swift and excellent Achilles | tried to make a stand and see if all these
gods of the broad sky were pursuing him | whenever stopped mighty billow on him
from heaven-fed river came crashing down | on his shoulders (s)peed off at prospect drown
struggled to his feet but water still ripped | madly by and him around the knees gripped
and sweeping the loose earth from beneath him | the son of Peleus groaned aloud grim
and looking up into the broad sky cried | "O Father Zeus will none of you gods hide
me from the River? then I would welcome | any other fate not that I blame some
others of Heavenly Ones so much as | my own Mother whose predictions were as
a chimera fooled me she said I'd fall | to Apollo's fell darts under the wall
of the embattled Trojans ah why could | Hector not have killed me? the man who would
be deemed finest bred in Troy the killer'd | then have been as noble as the one killed

but now it seems that I was doomed to die | a villainous death caught in the storm eye
of a great river like a boy in charge | of the pigs who's swept away by the charge
of mountain stream trying crossing in spate" | in rapid response to his appeal Fate
sent both Poseidon and Athene to stand | by him taking human form took each hand
in theirs and uttered words reassuring | Poseidon "Courage my lord! assuring
no reason for undue alarm when two | allies like me and Pallas come down to
your help with the blessing of Zeus believe | me you're not destined be brought down to grieve
by any River and this one will soon | subside as you'll see yourself it down-tune
and here's some good advice from us you would | do well to take it whatever now could
be a hazard don't stop fighting 'til you | have every Trojan who now escapes you
penned up inside the famous walls of Il | -ium and don't go back to your ships 'til
you've taken Hector's life we're vouchsafing | you this victory" Achilles chafing
much heartened now by this encouragement | from Heaven across the fields onward went
and they were completely inundated | afloat fine armour bodies inflated
but high-stepping Achilles fought his way | upstream and Pallas Athene eased his way
so enhancing his strength that the increasing | deluge could not stop him so unceasing
though Scamander's rage indeed in access | fresh fury son Peleus enmesh mess
flung up a huge billow with crest curling | to Simois curlew call unfurling
"Dear Brother to overpower this one | let us unite or he will soon move on
to sacking Priam's royal city not | a single Trojan to resist one jot
come quickly to my help fill your channels | with water from the springs and the canals
refill withal your mountain streams raising | a great surge and sending it down abra(i)sing
with logs and boulders so that we may check | this savage who is carrying break-neck
all afore him he thinks himself a match | for the gods but I'm determined to catch
him out and not let his strength or beaut | -y save him now nor the splendid suit beaut
-eous armour it shall lie deep | in slime underneath my flooded feet keep
and as for him I'll roll him in the sand | pile high above him the shingle at hand
the Argives won't know where to find his bones | I'll bury him so deep in silt earth moans
his barrow will be ready-made for him | and thus there will be no need to build him
another when they hold his funeral" | heaven-fed River did fun roll lethal
towering up rushing on Achilles | with an angry surge that with corpses seethes
and blood and foam and a dark wave hung high | above the son of Peleus and nigh
on engulfing him when Here in horror | for Achilles as thought River terror
swirling so set on sweeping him away | let out a scream and turned sharply to say
to her Child Hephaestus "To arms my Son | god of the Crooked Foot we rely on
you in this battle to deal with Xanthus | quick to the rescue deploy your flames thus
while I go rouse the West Wind and the South | to now blow in fiercely from the sea mouth
and spread conflagration until army | Trojan bodies armour ceases to be
you must burn the trees on Xanthus' banks | and set the very River on fire thanks
to you he will eat humble pie and beg | for mercy but don't hang you on that peg
nor mitigate your fury 'til you hear | a shout from me then you can lower here
your raging fires die" Hephaestus replied | to his Mother's call as one terrified

with a most terrific conflagration | starts on plain leads devout consummation
wished of bodies of the many victims | of Achilles scattered about by hims
-elf flood shimmer stemmed whole plain parched no rain | like threshing floor newly sprinkled arraign
that the North Wind dries up in the autumn | to the farmer's delight when dealt with some
of his task the plain and consumed dead thus | attacked the River then did Hephaestus
with his dazzling flames elms and tamarisks | willows caught fire and the lotus brisk risks
being consumed along with the rushes | and galingale professes profuse is
by the lovely stream fish and even eels | in their beautiful home each tumbling reels
about being tortured by the hot breath | of the Master Engineer out of breath
scalded the River cried out "Hephaestus | you're more than a match for any god thus
I can't cope with white heat white light of yours | the fight's off let that Achilles of yours
go straight in drive Trojans from their town own | why should I help when others argue moan?"
and yet the fire devoured him as he spoke | his limpid water already bespoke
bubbling as melted fat pig does call | well-fed when doth seethe the whole of the cawl
-dron as the dry logs underneath blaze up | bring to boil thus lovely Xanthus burnt up
and then saw his own waters going up | in steam conquered by the blast he gave up
to the great Artificer ceased to flow | in his distress he called on Here to show
mercy cried "Here why has your Son chosen | my personal stream for persecution?
compared with all the others who're fighting | on the Trojan side I myself citing
little to earn it but if you bid me | I will stop but so must he as for me
I will do more I undertake on oath | to make no attempt and to be most loath
to save the Trojans from their doom even | on day when whole city burns in season
of the witch devastating fires lit there | by the warrior sons of Achaea"
when the white-armed goddess Here heard this cry | from Xanthus at once to her Son did cry
"Enough now my noble child Hephaestus! | we must not treat a god so harshly thus
merely to help out a man" Poseidon | heard her here put out the conflagration
and the stream then began to flow once more | between each beautiful Sandy Shaw shore
there was no more fighting between these two | after the River's setback Here saw to
that though still resentful but now the feud | between the other gods came to head (c)rude
in open violence driven by their | passions opposing sides each other there
fell on with a terrific roar which made | high heaven ring aloud whole world wide made
groan again Zeus sitting on Olympus | heard the racket and laughed to himself thus
in delight when he saw the immortals | come to grips for they wasted no mortal's
time before closing and Ares Breaker | of Shields began it as god Line-Breaker
made for Athene bronze spear in hand shouting | abuse as he came and her call-outing
as meddlesome vixen whose impudence | boundless and high-handed interference
had so set the gods at each other's throats | reminded her of sowing wild war oats
when she had incited Diomedes | Tydeus' son to wound him Ares
cried "You made no secret of it and you | took his spear in your own vile hand and you
drove it at me and cut my flesh now I | -'m going to make you pay for what I
suffered from you then" then he struck Athene | on tasselled aegis so magic cloak seen
to withstand even Zeus' thunderbolt | endured blow from long-shadowed shaft vault volt

of murderous War-god and she drew back | with her great hand picked up a great block black
of stone lying on the ground a big rough | boulder folk past had used to mark a rough
field boundary with this she cast and struck | rabid War-god full on neck out of luck
brought him down his armour rang aloud (c)rude | and there he lay covering length nine-rood
with his locks in the dust Pallas laugh did | made him an insulting speech "You stupid
fool! did it not occur to you before | match think of my strength superior?
you can regard self as working off | Mother Here's curses been telling you off
to ill ever since you angered her by | deserting the Achaeans to stand by
the insolent Trojans" Athene ends play | with him her brilliant eyes turned away
Aphrodite Daughter of Zeus Ares | took by the arm led from field senses he's
scarcely recovered and so was groaning | the while but white-armed goddess Here owning
this move by Aphrodite to Athene | called in her excitement "Look check this scene
unsleeping Child of aegis-bearing Zeus! | there goes Aphrodite again the use
-less hussy escorts butcher Ares through | the melee and off the battlefield to
safety after her quick!" Athene's heart it | leapt up and she sped after Aphrodit
-'e closed with her and struck her on the breast | with her fist Aphrodite not her best
showing no fight at all at once collapsed | both on the bountiful earth lay prolapsed
Athene crowing over them "So may each | who helps the Trojans fight and thus does breach
the order of things against Argive-wise | men-at-arms acquit himself these likewise
show as much daring and resolution | as Aphrodite then when did run on
to Ares and braved me in my fury! | and then we should soon have sacked the lovely
town of Troy and have finished with the war" | white-armed goddess Here smiled at sally raw
saw Athene's Poseidon Earthshaker now | challenged Apollo "Phoebus why are now
we two still standing idle and apart? | is that right when others have made a start?
we should be ashamed not to play a part | in the fighting and go back without heart
to Olympus and Zeus' Bronze Palace | you're younger and my greater age pal ace
and experience make it quite unfair | for me to start but what a fool you there
and what a short memory do you have! | because all the hardships you seem to have
forgotten that you and I both endured | at Troy when from the gods were indentured
and were sent by Zeus to serve the haughty | Laomedon for a year and then he
wages was to pay at his beck and call | we both were and my task was to build a wall
for the Trojans round their town a stable | strong splendid one make place impregnable
while you looked after the shambling cattle | of crooked horns on the wooded wattle
spurs of Ida of the many ridges | Phoebus and the work he then obliges
us to do we did but when happy hour | came the remuneration for all our
work Laomedon unconscionable | refused outright make pay available
packed us off threatening lash foot-and-hand | together send to some distant island
for sale even talked of lopping off ears | we came home out of sorts with angry tears
for him about wages promised withheld | that is the man whose people you're now held
in hock to instead of joining with us | see to it these insolent Trojans thus
shall be utterly wiped out together | their children every wife lover ever"
"Lord of the Earthquake" Archer-King replied | Phoebus "with very little sense applied

you'd credit me if for sake of men | I fought you such a wretched specimen
that like leaves flourishes a little while | on the bounty of the earth flaunt their style
fleeting in a moment droop fade away | no let us now from battle shy away
before it's too late leave these men to do | their own fighting" with that Phoebus made to
turn and go thought it an improper thing | with his Uncle be have a come-to-blows fling
but now he had to listen to biting | comments Sister Artemis words fighting
Mistress of Beasts and Lady of the Wild | to him did not at all mince words wild child
"So the great Archer runs away handing | Poseidon a victory and landing
a cheap one-two too! what's the sense numbskull | of ever carrying a bow dumb's cull
that you'll never use? I've oft heard you boast | to the immortals when Father played host
that you would stand up to Poseidon then | never let me hear you say that again"
Archer-King Apollo had no retort | for his Sister but Here of Zeus Consort
was infuriated with Mistress plus | of the Bow said tartly "Impudent huss
-y are daring to stand up to me? | yet I know your bow and arrows twee she
-lion you are to many women who | Zeus lets you destroy at will but if you
match yourself with me you will regret it | find much better sport limp wrist fist of it
to slaughter the wild deer in the high hills | than fight against your superiors' wills
but since you test me and would like to try | conclusions just how much the stronger I
am let this teach you" Here broke off with twist | of left hand seized Artemis by each wrist
while with her right swept bow and arrows | from her shoulders and then she gave her blows
on the ears with her own weapons grinning | as the victim writhed arrows came dinning
out of her quiver Artemis then burst | into tears and fled from her in a burst
of speed as a pigeon before a hawk | has the luck to get clear in a tight squeak squawk
into rock cleft or hollow thus goddess | fled off in tears leaving her bow hapless
arrows on the ground but Mother Leto | by Hermes the Guide was reassured so
Giant-Killer called across to her here | "Do not be afraid Leto that *I* here
am going to fight you people who come | to blows with the Consorts of Zeus have some
uphill work it seems no you can boast to | your heart's content and tell the gods that you
got the better of me just by brute strength" | and so Leto then gathered up at length
crooked bow and arrows that had tumbled | here and there in the swirling dust humbled
retired with her Daughter's weapons in arms | meanwhile the Maid herself had reached the (ch)arms
of Olympus to the Palace of Zeus | sat on Father's lap sobbed loose at such use
divine robe on her bosom a-quivering | Son of Cronos took Daughter shivering
in his arms asked her with laughter merry | "Which of the Heavenly Ones so very
ill-used you my darling Child?" Huntress | Lovely Crown "Father to my distress stress
was your Wife Here who beat me quarrelling | among the gods at her bedevilling"
while these two talking Phoebus Apollo | went into sacred Ilium was so
concerned about the walls afraid Argives | might well forestall the day Destiny's lives
end Troy decreed sack splendid town forthwith | the rest of the everlasting gods with
some dejected while others in great glee | returned to Olympus sat down with thee
Father the Lord of the Black Cloud meanwhile | Achilles went on destroying in style
men and strong horses fell to him alike | dealt tribulation and disaster like

do angry gods when balloon smoke goes up | to the broad sky from a town they've lit up
making all its people toil many mourn | so old King Priam climbed bastion torn
Poseidon had built saw the gigantic | Achilles the Trojans driven panic
-stricken before him impotence utter | and a great cry of alarm did utter
came down from bastion gave fresh orders | to tried watchmen posted by wall borders
to manage the gates "Hold the gates open | 'til all our routed forces reach town pen
have Achilles at their Achilles' heels | fear massacre once through walls host in steals
they are sheltered and can breathe once more close | the wooden doors I'm appalled at the close
prospect of having that savage penned up | in the city" and the men then decoup
-led the doors and thrust back the bars the door | swung open there was now such a lot more
hope of saving the troops and Apollo | moreover rushed out to meet them and so
avert a massacre they were flying | straight for the city and high wall dying
of thirst and covered with dust from their flight | across plain Achilles heels on their right
rite with great spear still intent on glory | still in grip of the gory high fury
that had seized him Troy of the Lofty Gates | would indeed now have fallen to the fates
stirred by the sons of Argos if Phoebus | Apollo had not intervened and thus
inspired so Antenor's son Agenor | an excellent and mighty man of war
and the god into his heart breathed daring | stood by him against an oak well-faring
as hidden by a thick mist to save him | from heavy hand Death dilemma for him
when Agenor saw Achilles sacker | of towns approaching stood waiting attacker
though with many dark misgivings in his | noble heart ruefully considered his
position he thought "If I fly before | the great Achilles join as just one more
in the general stampede he will catch me | nonetheless slit coward's throat easily
on other hand might just leave the rabble | to be chased by him slip from wall scrabble
on foot by that other way to the Plain | Ileian and reaching the mountain
foothills of Ida could hide in the wood | and after bathing in the river's flood
and then washing the sweat off my body | in eve get back Troy's sheltering body
but why do I contemplate such a course? | as Achilles is bound to see the course
I take away from town into country | open then he'll come full tilt after me
catch me up for me will be death certain | and all others would see fall earth's curtain
as far too good a man left one meet thing | here in front of town be fate one meeting
he too's vulnerable after all and he | has but one life and no-one believes he
is immortal even if Zeus the Son | of Cronos lets him carry everyone
before him" that settled it Agenor | braced himself and Achilles waited for
without a tremor once he had made up | his mind in single combat to stand up
to him and thus a leopardess steps out | from her jungle lair the hunt to face out
and neither feels nor shows a sign of fear | when baying of hounds does her here hear
even if the man gets in first with lunge | or cast pierced by spear courage does not plunge
does not fail her and she grapples with him | or dies in the attempt and so with him
excellent Antenor's son Agenor | the admirable refused fly before
the son of Peleus without trying | conclusions his circular shield plying
before his body and his spear aiming | at Achilles boldly called out naming

"My lord Achilles" he shouted "no doubt | you thought that you were going to rout out
the proud city of Troy this very day | that was a foolish mistake let us say
Troy'll survive yet to see much hard fighting | she has plenty of stalwart sons plighting
their Troyth to her while we're under the eyes | our parents children wives no lies surprise
it is you who to your doom are haring | redoubtable as you are all-daring"
he launched the sharp spear from his hand heavy | struck Achilles' shin below the knee
sure enough making the tin of his new | shin-guard greave ring grimly on leg sinew
but the god's work stood up well to the blow | bronze point rebounded it had had a go
but not wounded him son of Peleus | in turn attacked godlike Agenor fuss
of Phoebus did not let him win this fight | hid Agenor in a thick mist of might
swept him off dismissed him unmolested | from the field the Archer-King infested
a ruse on Peleus' son to steer | him away from all other soldiers here
made self look exactly like Agenor | and in Achilles' path did show for
Achilles set off eagerly pursued | a chase across the wheatfields then ensued
heading him off now towards Scamander | of the Deep Pools a little meander
ahead Apollo all the time fooling | the mighty Achilles into drooling
could overtake by running still harder | but meanwhile every Trojan survivor
reached the town in a mass with grateful hearts | and filled it as crowded in spirit parts
so low that they had not even waited | for one another outside the gated
city-walls in order to find out who | might have managed to get away and who
had fallen in battle so hasty way | did they come pouring in all that's to say
those whose o'erhasty legs had saved their lives | to run from Achilles back to their wives

εἴκοσι δύο

Book 22

# THE DEATH OF HECTOR

*how Achilles fought Hector and slew him*
*brought body back black hollow ships trim grim*
*swept into their own city like a flock*
*of frightened sheep rabble Trojan in shock*

first dried sweat off bodies rank drank quenched thirst | as leant against the enormous fist burst
of the battlement whilst the Achaeans | advanced towards the wall with Everyman's
shield on the slope Fate for her own evil | schemes kept Hector where he was the devil
outside the town before the Scaean Gate | meanwhile Apollo revealed his true state
to the son of Peleus "My lord why | are you chasing me? you're a man and I
an immortal god as you might have known | if not been so immersed in affairs own
and are you not now business neglecting | Trojans to dead dizzy mess (s)electing?
do you not see that they've shut themselves up | in the town while you've been running amuck
out here? you'll never kill *me* I'm immune | from death" the nimble-footed did near swoon
with anger rounded on the Archer-King | called him the chief god of Mickey-taKing
"You've made a fool of me by here luring | from real job man-of-war-wall life curing
to think of all the Trojans who might yet | have bitten the dust not got themselves set
inside Ilium! so have you robbed me | of a most spectacular victory
by saving their lives easy task for you | who'd no penalty to fear much as you
I should like to pay out if only I | had the power" turned thoughts to do or die
dashed away thence towards the town running | with the easy speed of the horse gunning
a chariot race when puts on sprint spurts | finishes course first King Priam purports
see him as he is rushing towards them | over the fields and as he approached then
the bronze on his breast flashed out like the star | comes to us autumn from afar by far
outshines all rest evening sky easily | it's called Orion's Dog Siriusly
though the brightest of all stars bodes no good | brings much fever aftermath dogged flood
as it does to us poor wretches the old | man gave a groan lifted up his hands tolled
with them on his head and in a voice full | of fear and loathing very terrible
cries entreaties to his son beloved | in fixed resolve there he's done resolv-ed
to battle with Achilles had taken | stand before the gates "Hector!" old man then

called stretching out his arms in piteous | appeal "I beg you not do this to us
my dear son don't stand up to him alone | unsupported you will only be prone
to defeat and death at his hands he is | by far stronger than you are and he is
savage the dogs and vultures would soon be | feeding on his corpse what a load would be
lifted from my heart! if the gods loved him | as little as I do that foul man grim
who's robbed me of so many sons splendid | killed or as slaves to distant isles vended
even today there are two I can't find | among the troops who in town refuge find
Lycaon and Polydorus children | by Princess Laothoe love token
if the Argive has taken them alive | we'll ransom them presently with a hive
of bronze and gold of which she has plenty | for Altes the honourable ensured she
as daughter got his fortune but if dead | now in the Halls of Hades enough said
a-new sorrow me and their mother | who brought them into the world no other
in Ilium will mourn for them so long | unless you also fall and join the throng
of Achilles dead come inside my child | to be the saviour of Troy and the child
-ren of Troy and don't throw away your own | dear life give a triumph to scion own
of Peleus have pity on me too | your poor father who is still able to
feel deeply think of the hideous fate | Father Zeus has kept in store for my date
sell-by the horrors I'll have before me | before I die my sons massacred see
my daughters mauled tidy bedrooms pillaged | their babies by brutal Argives spillaged
on the ground and my sons' wives hauled away | by foul Achaean hands in the last play
my turn will come to fall to the sharp bronze | and when with sword or javelin someone's
laid me dead to pieces I shall be torn | by rabid dogs at own street door all shorn
the very dogs I have fed at table | and have trained to keep watch on my gate'll
loll round it maddened by their master's blood | ah it looks well enough for a youngblood
killed in battle lie there his wounds he shows | because death can find nothing to expose
in him that is not beautiful but when | an old man's killed the dogs on him batten
defile his grey head grey beard parts privy | we are plumbing the very depths prithee
of human degradation" Priam plucked | at his grey locks and hair from his head looked
to tear but failed to shake resolve Hector | then his lady mother it's her turn for
wailing and weeping and her dress aside | thrusting and in the other hand one side
of her breast exposing him imploring | and with the tears down her cheeks now pouring
cried "Hector my child have regard for this | pity me how oft did I give you this
breast and soothed you with its milk! bear in mind | those days dear child and determine to find
a way to countermand your enemy | from within the walls don't go to meet ye
savage in single combat and you need | not think that if he kills you I'll pay heed
to laying you on a bier and bawling | my eyes out for very own boy darling
nor will your richly dowered wife but far | away from both of us beside the Ar
-give ships you'll be eaten by dogs nimble" | in tears dear son appeal symbol simple
but cymbal-voiced entreaties met deaf ears | for Hector held his ground despite dread fears
let monstrous Achilles his knees approach | knocking like mountain snake who by rash poach
pouch poisonous herbs that he has swallowed | maddened lets one to where form out hollowed
coiled in his lair approaching watches him | with baleful glitter Hector stood firm grim

unflinching glittering shield supported | by outwork wall but by dread transported
transfixed groaning at his plight took counsel | with his own great soul indomitable
"If I retire behind the gate and wall | Polydamas will be the first to call
me out that in this last night's disaster | when Achilles came back to life after
us I did not take his advice order | withdrawal to Troy I was out of order
but as it is now to have sacrificed | host my perverted whims surfaced sufficed
so could not face my compatriots nor | trailing-gown ladies would not care bear for
to hear some commoner say 'That Hector | trusted in his own right arm and therefore
lost an army' and yet it *will* be said | and then I would have known would have been dead
sure would have been far better for me to | stand up to Achilles and either to
kill him and come home alive or myself | die gloriously still thinking of self
of course or I could put down my bossed shield | and heavy helm my spear to the wall yield
on own authority make overtures | to Prince Achilles promise make ventures
deliver Helen all her property | to the Atreidae all the poxy
things that Paris brought back with him to Troy | in not-hollow ships when seeds did deploy
of this Achaean war I could beside | swear share the rest of the goods on our side
with the enemy and then try induce | my guys on oath in Council not traduce
the bargain vow that they would hide nothing | divide of the movables everything
in our dear city into equal parts | but why do I think playing such a part's
for me when I've every reason to fear | if approach Achilles try self endear
he'll show no pity or any regard | for me kill me out of hand with heart hard
just like a woman naked and unarmed | as I should be? no harmed's the hour not charmed
to see Achilles and me as a pair | of trysting lovers to each other fair
billing and cooing like lad and his lass | waste no time come to Thermopylae pass
and then we should know to which of us ye | Olympian means to hand victory"
while Hector stood engrossed in this debate | inward came Achilles nemesis fate
looking like the war god in helmet-skirt | flashing flashy flirty for fight well girt
right rite shoulder brandished spear ashen pen | -insula formidable Pelion
the bronze armour on body all glowing | like a fire blazing sun overflowing
Hector looked up and saw him and trembled | with the fear within his heart dissembled
left the gate and ran away in terror | but the son of Peleus no error
counting on in his speed after in flash | light as the mountain hawk who's the most dash
-ing thing on wings when swoops chase timid dove | and shrieking close behind his quarry-love
lunges at her time and again in his | ardour keen get 'arder make out with his
kiss-kill off Achilles in hot pursuit | and like the dove flying before her suit
-or Hector then fled before him under | the walls of Troy tearing earth as-under
past the lookout post old fig tree windswept | yet some way away from the walls they kept
sped along the cart track until they reach | the two sweet springs of the eddying reach
of Scamander sources in one of these | water comes up hot rising as steam breeze
hangs round like smoke above bush fire blazing | two even summer flow-'erself-raising
in full spate cold as hail or snow freezing | or water that's turned to ice when seizing
up where are standing still just close beside | the troughs of stone both beautiful and wide

where the lovely Trojan wives and daughters | fleshy flashy glossy Polly garters
once washed in peaceful days before Argives | came here then went on the chase of their lives
Hector before and Achilles after | a good man however one far better
at his heel(')s furious thus then the pace | because it was not a spurious race
sacrificial beast or leather shield prize | they were competing in man-ner life-size
horse-taming Hector's very existence | at stake the pair went three times the distance
round King Priam's city with feet flying | two powerful racehorses swift-plying
round the turning-post up for the splendid | prize tripod or indeed woman offer did
normal at warrior's games funeral | the contest being watched by gods feral
silence total then until the Father | of men and gods then turned to the other
immortals with a sigh "I've a warm place | in my heart for he being chased apace
before my eyes around the walls of Troy | I grieve for Hector as if my own boy
he has burnt the thighs of many oxen | in my honour rugged heights Ida then
up in the lofty citadel of Troy | but great Achilles seeks him to destroy
pursuing him at full speed round the town | of Priam intent on hunting him down
consider thus ye gods and now help me | to make a decision on whether we
shall save his life or let a good man fall | here and now to greatest runner of all
Achilles son Peleus?" "Dad!" exclaimed | Athene "what are you saying? is the famed
Lord of the Bright Lightning and the Black Cloud | seeking save one of the mere mortal crowd
whose doom has long been settled from the pains | of death? do as you please but see no g(r)ains
of praise from the rest of us" "Rest assured" | Zeus the Cloud-compeller her reassured
"Lady of Trito sweet Child of mine I | did not really mean to spare him on my
goodwill you can count act as you see fit | act now" with this encouraging big hit
Athene who'd been itching to be showy | play part sped straight down from high peaks snowy
of Olympus meanwhile nimble-footed | Achilles relentless chase hot-footed
of Hector as a hound who has started | fawn from its mountain lair after darted
through the cwms and glades even when it takes | cover in thicket runs on through the brakes
picks up the scent finds his quarry the swift | Achilles was not to be by a nift
-y trick of Hector's then thrown off the scent | because more than once dashing Hector went
towards the Dardanian Gates hoping | as he was under the high walls sloping
along to be saved from his pursuer | by the skill of one above wall archer
but Achilles kept always inner course | intercepted him every time off course
of course heads off towards country open | however him could never gain on then
Hector there could not shake off Achilles | as chase in a nightmare deep knees unease
when nobody pursuer or pursued | can move a limb as if to the ground glued
you may ask how could Hector have escaped | when Death so near it so closely him sc(r)aped?
he did so only via final hol | -low intervention great Phoebus Apol
-lo came to him for the very last time | renewed strength speed for a time chimes still rhyme
at midnight Achilles been mooting | so through head moves to men not try shooting
at quarry that his fame might be forestalled | one of them might have his renown installed
by striking his Hector with an arrow | but when they reached the Springs margins narrow
for the fourth time the Father now held out | his golden scales see what may be fallout

putting sentence of death in either pan | one Achilles other Hector horseman
raised balance by the middle of the beam | Hector's side doom deem no redeem end dream
dead man Phoebus Apollo deserted | Athene the Flashing-Eyed goddess skirted
girt Achilles spoke these momentous words | "Illustrious Achilles now the word's
been given darling of Zeus our chance come | return to the ships with a most handsome
victory for Achaean arms Hector | will fight it out to end bitter vector
but you and I are going to kill him | no escape however much Phoebus him
-self exerts grovels at the feet of his | Father Zeus the bearer of the aegis
stay still a while and recover your breath | while I persuade him to fight to the death"
Achilles well pleased did what she had said | on his bronze-bladed spear leaning his head
while Athene left him to go to Hector | accosts bearing aegis final vector
deceit conceit appearance voice tireless | Deiphobus "My dear brother" address
"the swift Achilles must have worn you out | chasing you at that speed city about
let's make a stand face him here together" | "Deiphobus always loved you better
have I than all the brothers Hecabe | and Priam gave me and I shall only
from now on think even better of you | since only you had the courage when view
did my plight to exit the walls of town | while all the rest of them stay hunkered down"
Flashing-Eyed Athene replied "Dear brother | I can assure you our lady mother
and father begged and implored me to stay | within one after other did then say
my men were there and did the same they're all | weak at the knees as in mighty awe all
Achilles but by worry on behalf | of you I was tormented not by half
let's attack him and be not niggardly | with spears and we'll discover rapidly
whether Achilles is to kill the pair | of us off with our bloodstained armour fair
fare to the black ships or he be conquered | by your spear" 'twas Athene's ruse that conquered
led him up to Hector Achilles met | Hector of the flashy flashing helmet
spoke first "My lord Achilles been chaste chased | by you thrice round the great town and not faced
up to you and so letting you come near | as I'm running no more but staying here
I've made up my mind to fight man to man | kill or be killed let's make a bargain man
you with your gods I with mine no compact | could have better guarantors than that fact
if Zeus allows me to endure and I | kill you no outrage do to your corpse I
undertake that custom does not sanction | all I'll do Achilles of your golden
armour strip you then give up your body | to your men will you do the same for me?"
Achilles looked at him grimly "Hector | you must be totally off your rocker
to talk to me of a pact a lion | does not make any bargain with a man
nor the wolf see eye to eye with the lamb | they are enemies to the end I am
the same now with you friendship between us | impossible be no truce between us
of any kind until one has fallen | so glutted the god of battles stubborn
with blood what courage you may have summon | now's the time to show your daring spearman
-ship not that anything can now save you | when Pallas Athene's waiting to fell you
with my spear for this moment you will pay | the full price for the grief you put my way
when your lance mowed down my friends" Achilles | poised his long-shadowed spear on back heel 'es
hurls illustrious Hector on lookout | manages to avoid its heavy clout

so n'er cast 'til may's out he crouched his eye | on the weapon over his head did fly
stuck in the ground but Pallas Athene snatched | it up and back to Achilles despatched
Hector the great captain had not vision | this move called across to peerless scion
of Peleus "A miss for the godlike | Achilles! it seems Zeus gave you fake-like
news of the date of my death! too cocksure | you were but so glib so clever for sure
with your tongue and trying to frighten me | and of all my usual strength drain me
nevertheless you will not make me run | catch me in the back javelin fun stun gun
or drive through my breast as I charge if you | get the chance however before that you
will have to dodge this one of mine Heaven | grant all its bronze be buried full on then
in your flesh! this war would be easier | for us if you our greatest prick-teaser
scourge were dead" swung up his long-shadowed spear | cast the middle of the shield bull hit sheer
enough but spear clear from it rebounded | Hector angry at having propounded
so fine a throw for nought discomforted | no maximum second dart comforted
he shouted aloud to Deiphobus | asked for a long spear but Deiphobus
White-shield-bottle lees knees dregs nowhere near | realising what had just happened here
cried "Alas! so the gods did beckon me | to my death! I thought that right beside me
stood the good Deiphobus but now he's | in town I've been fooled by Athene with ease
Death's no longer far away he's staring | me in the face no haring off faring
Zeus and his Archer Son must long have been | resolved on this despite mean goodwill mien
and the help they gave me so now I meet | my doom but let me sell my life full meet
dearly at least not inglorious end | after some feat of arms that will well bend
the ears of generations still unborn | and thus in death one shall not be forlorn"
Hector had a sharp long and weighty sword | hanging down by his side in a scabbard
and he now drew this braced himself and swooped | high-flying eagle through black clouds earth stooped
peregrine pounce tender lamb hare crouching | thus Hector charged his sharp sword uncouching
Achilles sprang to meet him with passion | inflamed savage and as was his fashion
kept front covered with shield decorated | four-plate glittering helm oscillated
as moved head made the golden plumes splendid | that Hephaestus on the crest lavish did
dance round top and bright as the loveliest | jewel in sky Evening Star against rest
when comes out at nightfall scintillated | the sharp point on spear articulated
in right rite hand bent on Hector breaching | looks for the likeliest place him reaching
touch-teaching flesh Achilles saw Hector's | body completely covered by armour's
fine bronze taken from the great Patroclus | when killed him opening own gear did sus
spotted at gullet where the collar bones | lead over from the shoulders to neck zones
easiest place to kill a man is this | as Hector charged Prince Achilles with his
lance drove at this spot the point went right through | the tender flesh of Hector's neck although
heavy bronze head did not cut his windpipe | left him able pipe up a final gripe
at his conqueror as Hector came down | in the dust the great Achilles came down
hard on him in triumph "Hector no doubt | you fancied as you stripped Patroclus out
you would be safe you never thought of me | I was too far away you fool you see
down by the hollow ships there was a man | being held in reserve far better than
Patroclus the man who has brought you low | so dogs birds of prey won't be slow are so

going to maul and mangle you while we | Achaeans the funeral rites o'ersee
of Patroclus "I beseech you" Hector | said failing voice once helm glitter vector
"by your knees your own life and your parents | don't throw my body to Achaean rents
canine by the ships take ransom for me | because my father and my fair lady
mother will pay bronze and gold aplenty | to be taken home give up my body
so the Trojans and their wives may honour | in death ritual fire-flower-power"
the swift Achilles scowled at him "You cur | don't bring me to knees or in your prayer sur
-ly sully name parents I just wish could | summon the appetite to chew your cud
having myself carved and eaten you raw | pay back all that you've made me suffer for
but this at least is sure that nobody | at all is going to keep you dog-free
not even if the Trojans should bring here | weigh out a ransom some ten or a clear
twenty times your worth promise more besides | not if Dardanian Priam decides
to pay your weight in gold not even so | shall your mother lay you on a bier so
she can mourn the son she bore but the dogs | birds of prey will eat you 'til your flesh clogs
their gullets" Hector of the flashing helm | -et spoke thus once more to him at the helm
of death "How well I know you and can read | your mind! for your heart is an iron reed
unbending in the wind I've been wasting | my time and yet pause before me wasting
in case the angry gods recall how you | treated me when your turn comes round and you
are brought down at the Scaean Gate in all | your glory by Paris Phoebus withal"
but death then cut Hector short and his soul | disembodied took wing lacking console
House AtreHades its lot bewailing | and the youth and manhood flailing failing
but Prince Achilles spoke to him again | although he was already well gone then
"Die! as for my own death let it come when | Zeus and rest of deathless gods call it zen"
he withdrew his bronze spear from the body | laid down as removed bloodstained armoury
from Hector's shoulders then Ach-Danaan | soldiers running up when Ach-Dan-aan
entourage formed around gazed in wonder | at size and marvellous good looks Hector
not a man of all who'd there collected | without wound bleach ingested injected
infected left each went in struck body | eyed friends jest boldly took form bodily
"Hector is now easier to handle | than his setting-the-ships-on-fire scandal"
from stripping Hector excellent and swift | Achilles stood up made speech gave short shrift
to Hector "Friends Captains and Counsellors | of the Danaans now that the actors
in Heaven have let us be so bettered | of this man who inflicted unfettered
more damage than all the rest together | let's round town reconnoitre together
armed learn what the Trojans mean to do next | if they'll abandon their fort now is ex
-champion their there or decide hold it | without Hector's help and yet what is it
I say? how can I think of anything | at this moment but the dead man lying
by my beaked ships unburied and unwept | Patroclus whose memory will be kept
forever by me while I'm still living | can walk this good earth my own life-giving
darling comrade I'll remember even | though the dead forget their own dead even
in Hades' Halls? so come now soldiers | of Achaea let's go back the bolder's
the better to the black ships carrying | this corpse a song of triumph marrying
'We've killed noble Hector won great glory | he treated like a god in Troy story'"

next subject fallen prince outrage shameful | slit the tendons back of both feet ankle
to heel inserted leather straps made fast | to chariot leaving head to drag last
lifted famous armour into his car | got in and with a touch of his whip star
-ted the horses who flew off with a will | dragging behind Hector raised a pall ill
of dust black locks on either side streaming | and the dust on his head thickly teeming
so comely one once Zeus now let defile | by enemies own native soil profile
Hector's head humbled tumbled in the dust | his lady mother then when she saw just
what they were doing to her son she tore | her hair and then plucking the bright veil sore
from her head cast it away with a cry | loud bitter his father anguish to die
for groaned deeply the people around them | took up the cry of grief the whole town then
gave itself up to despair they could not | have lamented louder if Troy red hot
going up in flames from its towering | citadel to street lowest-lowering
in his horror the old king headed for | the Dardanian Gate great longing for
to be outside but when his folk impelled | him with difficulty halt he grovelled
in the dung was all of them imploring | by his name every man was deploring
"Friends let me be you overdo your care | for me please let me go alone out there
to the Achaean ships I want to plead | with this monster may-be perhaps indeed
shamed by Hector's youth pity my old age | he too has a father of the same age
after all Peleus who gave him life | brought him up to be a curse on the life
of all Trojans though none has suffered so | at his cruel hands as the father of so
many sons who by him have been slaughtered | in the heyday of their youth then butchered
and yet though I bewail them all there's one | for whom I am even more grieving on
and that's Hector ah if he could only | have died in my arms! to hearts' content we
could have wept and wailed for him the mother | who had brought him into the world to her
sorrow and I" thus Priam through his tears | and Troy's folk added their own moans and tears
Hecabe-led the Trojan women bent | went into a deeply poignant lament
she cried "My child! ah misery me woe! | why should I live thus suffer like this so
now that you are dead? night and day in Troy | you were all my pride my light and my joy
and to every man and woman in town | a saviour greeted with a god's renown
while alive you were their greatest glory | but now Destiny cruel and Death gory
have taken you away" Hecabe wailed | and wept but Hector's wife not yet assailed
by the deadly news because nobody | had gone out to tell her that her hubby
remained outside the gates at work was she | in a tight corner of her house lofty
on a purple web of double width like | Penelope decorating with like
floral pattern and in her innocence | to her ladies-in-waiting she called hence
that they put a big cauldron on the fire | so Hector back home from battle on fire
could have a nice hot bath never dreaming | lay dead beyond all her day-dreaming
by the hands of Achilles and bright-eyed | Athene but now into her ears arrived
the keening moaning at the battlement | she trembled all over at what it meant
and was so disturbed she dropped her shuttle | called on ladies again planned off scuttle
"Come with me two of you as I must see | just what has happened because that surely
cry my husband's noble mother I heard | and for me my heart to my mouth has stirred

I can't move my legs as something dreadful | now threatening House of Priam's thread-rule
Heaven defend me from such news but I | terribly afraid Achilles caught my
gallant husband by himself outside town | chased him out into the open and down
indeed may already have put an end | to headstrong pride passion fate not forfend
Hector would never hang back with the crowd | always sallied out completely uncowed
in front of the rest and let no-one be | as daring as he" and Andromache
with palpitating heart rushed from the house | like a mad woman her ladies in-house
went with her and when they came to the wall | where a crowd had gathered the men withal
she climbed up the battlements searched the plain | saw them drag Hector before town view plain
the powerful horses were him hauling | along at a light and easy mauling
towards the Argive ships the world went black | (like Bilbo Frodo when Ring finger back)
as night before the eyes of Andromach | -'e 'eck then lost her senses and fell back
-wards to the ground dropping the whole of her | gay headdress coronet and cap from her
head and the plaited snood and veil golden | Aphrodite gave her on the day when
Hector of the flashing helm having paid | a princely dowry for his fair bride maid
came to fetch her from house of Eetion | and as she lay there with a dead faint on
her husband's sisters and his brothers' wives | crowded around her and everyone strives
to support her between them when at length | she recovered a modicum of strength
and came to herself she burst out sobbing | to ladies Troy laments grief hearts throbbing
cried "Alas for Hector alas for me! | because we under the same unhappy
star were born you here in Priam's house plus | I in Thebe-Under-Woody-End Placus
the house of Eetion who brought me up | from babyhood of more unlucky pup
the unlucky sire and who wishes she | now had never ever seen the spritely
light of day for you're on your way somehow | to Hades the unknown world below now
leaving me behind in such misery | a widow in your house and a baby
no more than your son is the one we got | between us unhappy parents our lot
and you dear Hector now that you are dead | will bring no joy to him but only dread
nor he be a joy to you even if | escapes the horrors this like Iraq-if
-fy war for naught lies ahead in his state | save strangers hassle into his estate
eating and an orphaned child is cut off | from his playmates goes about joy well off
oft with most downcast looks and tear-stained cheeks | and in his dire necessity he peeks
in at some gathering of father's friends | plucks a cloak here a tunic there 'til ends
when one charitable then upholding | wine cup to his mouth a moment holding
just enough wet his lips leave palate dry | both parents living another boy spry
who beats him with his fists and then drives him | out and away from the feast jeers at him
'Out you go! you've no father here dining" | shouts child tearful running in fear whining
widowed mother little Astyanax | for who the way fate's fallen out the knack's
gone sitting on his father's knees to eat | naught save mutton marrow fat neat not meet
and when he was tired of play and sleepy | slept in a bed cradled softly deeply
in his nurse's arms and full of good cheer | but now with his father far gone from here
on Astyanax will crowd in evil | Protector of Troy called you proud devil
seeing in you the one defence of long | walls and gates you by the ships laid along

far from your parents will be eaten up | by w(r)iggly worms when dogs are full up
lying naked for all the delicate | lovely clothing women did fabricate
that you possess at home all of which I'm | going to burn to ashes now's the time
it is of no use to you will never | lie in it the folk of Troy shall ever
accord you the final mark of honour" | and so then did Andromache through a
tear-filled visage make a piercing lament | the women all joined her in sorrow bent

εἴκοσι τρία

*Book 23*

# THE FUNERAL AND THE GAMES

*of the funeral the great Patroclus*
*and the games that followed Earth'sPat(w)reck-less*

while the town of Troy to lamentation | gave itself up the Argives to station
Hellespont withdrew when reached the mooring | to their several vessels selves restoring
of those who were not then dismissed the ones | only the battle-loving Myrmidons
Achilles kept with him his followers | said "Myrmidons of the fast horse lovers
my trusty band of brothers we will not | unyoke our horses from the chariot
yet mounted as we are we'll drive them past | Patroclus and now mourn him at the last
as a dead hero should be mourned and when | we've wept and found some solace in tears then
we will unharness them and supper here | we will all perhap find then some good cheer"
the Myrmidons fell to lamentation | with one accord Achilles leading on
mourning company drove long-maned horses | three times round the dead while goddess Thetis
stirred them all up to weep without restraint | sands of time a moisture tint taint not faint
their warlike panoply bedewed with tears | fit tribute so great creater past tears
Panic Punic now son of Peleus | as laying his man-killing hands callous
on his comrade's breast led them in the dirge | melancholy "Rejoice Patroclus" urge
did "even in the Halls of Hades I | am fulfilling all the promises I
made you I have dragged Hector's body here | for the nimble dogs to eat at your bier
I am going to cut the throats of twelve | of the highborn youths of Troy as a salve
for my anger at your death" Achilles | thought of one more indignity how he's
to bring lower still Prince Hector flung down | on his face in the dust by pyre son down
Menoetius his soldiers took off their | burnished bronze equipment unyoked there their
neighing steeds sat down many a hundred | by the ships swift black Achilles funded
fare for them delicious funeral feast | thus the fated end of many a beast
white oxen last gasp fell iron's soul knife | sheep and bleating goats soon there lost their life
and fine fat hogs were stretched across the flame | having their bristles shaved did now them tame
cupfuls blood then poured all around corpus | meanwhile Prince Achilles of Peleus
the swift son taken by the Argive kings | dine with the lord Agamemnon as King's
guest though hard to make him come still grieving | for his comrade as they were receiving

welcome croeso King's hut told the clear-voiced | heralds put a big cauldron three-leg-joiced
on the fire in the hope of inducing | the clotted gore from his body sluicing
save he would no way hear of such a thing | he even took a vow did the swear thing
"By Zeus who is the best and the greatest | of gods it shall be sacrilege to test
water on my head 'til I've done the burn | of Patroclus made him mound my hair shorn
for I'll never ever suffer again | as I am suffering now in such pain
however long I live for the moment | though I hate the thought of all nourishment
we must yield to necessity and dine | your majesty Agamemnon at fine
hint glint dawn may order wood collected | and everything can then be selected
that dead man should have with him when travels | into the western gloom's deep dark perils
so Patroclus may be consumed by fire | as soon as possible the men retire
normal service may resume when he's gone" | and this they all readily agreed on
and so did they now set to with a will | prepare their dinner in which they all will
equal share ate with zest when satisfied | that their thirst and hunger they'd put aside
for the night to their huts retired but son | Peleus weary groaning laid down on
the shore of the sundering sea among | his many Myrmidons but in a long
open space where waves on the beach splashing | his splendid limbs exhausted from trashing
Hector right up to very walls windy | Troy no sooner fallen into kindly
loving sleep soothed then engulfed resolving | all his cares than that poor ghost (d)evolving
Patroclus looking talking the homme he | himself exactly like the same comely
eyes and stature and same clothes used to wear | stopped by his head invoked duty of care
(scene's the dead sailors come into the dreams | of Captain Kat where Dylan Thomas schemes
Under Milk Wood deems a play for voices | Tom Stern's Eliot's top bill-in'-voices)
"You are asleep you have forgotten me | Achilles now I'm dead you neglect me
when I was alive you never did so | I cannot pass the Gates of Hades so
bury me instantly as I'm kept out | by the disembodied dead spirits' shout
a rout their clout bars me cross River | join them but left me a limbo-liver
forlorn pace up and down this side Gaping | Gates give me that hand aid my escaping
now for once you have passed me through the flames | I'll never return from those s-Hades games
never again on earth will you and I | seated close out of earshot lay plans I
have been engulfed now by the dreadful fate | that must have been from birth my lot await
it's your destiny too most worshipful | Achilles under rich walls Troy ship-full
of death find and now just one more request | pray do not let them put my bones to rest
apart from yours Achilles together | let them lie like you and I together
raised in your great house when Menoetius | had brought me there as a child from Opus
because I had had there the misfortune | to commit homicide dancing fate's tune
by accident killed Amphidamas' | boy quarrel in a kids' game whose name is
knuckle-bones but the knightly Peleus | welcomed me to his palace and brought us
up with the same loving care appointed | me squire let Grecian urn be appointed
the golden vase say your lady Mother | gave you to hold our bones" Achilles "Dear
heart what need was there for you to come ask | me at all attend to whatever task?
as of course I will see to everything | and that what you ask do the exact thing

but come now nearer to me so that we | may hold each other in our arms only
a moment maybe and draw cold comfort | from our tears" Achilles' spirit fort
fought sought clasp held out his arms but in vain | vanished like a wisp of smoke down the drain
gibbering underground Achilles leapt | up in astonished amazement and clept
hands together in his desolation | cried "Ah then it is true some creation
of us does survive even in the Halls | Hades but no intellect the play all's
the thing capture ghostly semblance of man | for all night long the shade of that poor man
Patroclus (and it looked exactly like | him) has been standing at my side alike
weeping and wailing telling me of all | the things I should do" his outcrying call
wakes Myrmidons further lamentation | Dawn's russet mantle toes clad king crimson
stole up upon them all wailing around | the pitiable dead lost not found sound
King of Mice and Men sent out mules and men | each canny cannery row great camp then
to fetch wood Meriones officer | in charge of the party he was the squire
of the lovable Idomeneus | men in hands carried woodmen's axes plus
stout ropes together with mules walked ahead | up dale and by many zigzag paths head
down and come at last to spurs of Ida | of the many springs set to work with a
will fell the tall oaks with their long-bladed | axis and the trees decapitated
the Achaeans split the logs and roped them | to the mules who in trying to haul them
down to the plain through undergrowth tangled | with the pressure of feet the ground mangled
the woodcutters also all carried logs | by orders of Meriones' blogs
amiable Idomeneus squire | and when at last they'd arrived shore sure-fire
laid them neatly down at spot on the ground | where Achilles planned to build a great mound
for Patroclus and himself having stacked | this huge supply of wood all round off backed
and sat down waited there in a body | Achilles then ordered everybody
of war-loving Myrmidons don their bronze | and for every charioteer at ones
to yoke his horses they hurried off then | got into their armour the fighting men
drivers mounted tanks calvary cavalry | led off and after them mass infantry
too many to count and at the centre | procession Patroclus did there enter
his own men carrying him they'd covered | his body with the locks of hair severed
and cast upon it and behind them Prince | Achilles cushioned the head did eVince
the bearing of chief mourner despatching | high-born comrade to the Halls fire-catching
of Hades and when to place appointed | for them by Achilles they dismounted
Patroclus quickly built him a noble | pile of wood but now occurred to Achill
-'es excellent swift a fresh idea | and therefore now stepping back from the bier
he cut off from his head an auburn lock | that he had let grow ever since that lock
Spercheus dedicated let grow fine | he looked out angrily across the wine
-bar-dark sea dit "Spercheus answer there | yours to my father Peleus' prayer?
he promised you that at my home-coming | from Ilium I would then be combing
off this lock for you and the offering | rich fifty noble rams you proffering
for sacrifice by your very waters | where you have a precinct and the altar's
fragrant that indeed was the old king's vow | but you've denied him what he prayed for now
for as I'll never see my own country | again I propose part with unhappy

lock and give it to my lord Patrocklus" | as he spoke put the lock in the hands thus
beloved comrade gesture gathering | whole moved and would still have been lathering
at sunset if Achilles not sudden | thought he went up to King Agamemnon
"My lord Atreides you're the man then | to whom all the soldiery will listen
of course they can moan as much as they wish | but for now I ask you them to dismiss
from the pyre and then tell them to prepare | their midday meal as those of us who share
role chief mourners will see to everything | here although I would prefer remaining
the Achaean commanders" on hearing | Achilles wish Agamemnon then King
of Men dismissed the troops to their trim ships | but chief mourners stayed piled up the wood chips
made a pyre a hundred feet long and broad | and with sorrowful hearts body a-board
laid on top at the foot flayed pre-cook-ed | many well-fed sheep and of horns crooked
cattle shambling Achilles great-hearted | taking fat from all of them imparted
onto the corpse from head to foot and stashed | the flayed beasts around Patroclus attached
as of rite two-handled jars of honey | and oil leaning them against the bier he
in his zeal high cast onto the pyre four | high-necked horses groaned loud at the labour
as did so the dead lord had kept as pets | nine dogs Achilles slits throat of two vet's
thrown them on the fire but then he went on | to an evil deed twelve brave men each son
of a noble Trojan put to the sword | lit pyre so to pitiless flames afford
fodder them then gave a groan spoke once more | to his beloved friend "All hail for sure
from me Patroclus in the very Halls | of Hades I am now enacting all's
been promised by me so twelve excellent | Trojans sons city's noblemen now sent
to be consumed by the same fire as you | for Hector son of Priam a plan new
not give to flames but to the dogs to eat" | yet despite Achilles' threat dog meat
the dogs did not so meet daily nightly | hounded Zeus' Daughter Aphrodite
anointed roses' oil ambrosial | so not be lacerated by Achill
-'es dragged him there to and fro moreover | Phoebus Apollo dark cloud did over
hover caused it to sink from sky to ground | settle on corpse whole area around
where it lay covered so heat sun getting | at one side or other not be fretting
too soon the skin on his limbs and sinews | but to corpse Patroclus come some bad news
the pyre refused to kindle remedy | though suggested itself to the lordly
swift and excellent Achilles standing | clear of the pyre he prayed then expanding
on splendid offerings two of the winds | Boreas of the North Zephyr who winds
via the Western Gale rich libations | made them from a golden cup their stations
implored them to come from so that the wood | would readily kindle so co(r)pse would
quickly be cremated Iris heard prayer | and sped off to convey his message there
where the Winds had all together sat down | banquet draughty house Gale Western blew down
Iris came running up and when standing | on threshold saw her they all upstanding
each to come and sit beside inviting | but Iris explained an errand citing
"I must get back to Ocean Stream and land | of the Ethiopians where they stand
an entertainment for gods immortal | in form of a banquet sacrificial
anxious not to miss but I've message | Achilles great Western Boreas sage
-'s praying for you makes you offering | now very splendid package proffering

if you will come and do some fire-kindling | for Patroclus for whom sorrow-kindling
whole army Argive" message delivered | Iris off and the two Winds delivered
uproarious lift-off the clouds driving | before them swiftly at sea duck-diving
swiftly with noisy breath billows raising | when at deep-soiled land of Troy hell raising
fell well hard upon the funeral bier | fire blazed up terrific roar air did sear
howling round the fire they helped each other | all night long fan the flames as the mother
of all fires and all night long Achilles | with two-handled cup did replenish these
from a golden mixing bowl libations | poured and drenched the earth with wine in gallons
and called on the spirit of unhappy | Patroclus as a father weeps when he
is burning the bones of a son who's passed | on his wedding day left his well-harassed
folks in despair Jesus Achilles wept | as he burned his ex's bones slowly crept
round the pyre on leaden feet with many | a deep groan and then at the time when ye
Morning Star comes up herald a new day | on earth and following in his wake gay
Dawn spreads her saffron mantle all over | the sea the fire sank down flames gave over
pair of Winds into exit stream pouring | heading home across Thracian Sea roaring
waves ran high and Achilles exhausted | turning from fire to ground last resorted
at once fell fast asleep but the other | chieftains who'd joined Agamemnon bother
the man resolved and now the whole party | approached roused by voices and footsteps he
sat up told them just what he wanted done | said "My lord King of Men Agamemnon
other leaders united Achaeans | the first task gives us this situation's
put out with the sparkling wine whatever | portion of the pyre the flames reached ever
then we must collect lord Patroclus' | bones being most careful distinguish his
from others although that will not be hard | as lay in the centre of the pyre hard
by separated from rest who were burnt | on the verge horses and men centre weren't
we will put the bones in a golden vase | sealant a double layer of fat bars
contamination against the time when | I shall be coming to my own end then
shall have vanished into the world below | myself and considering his barrow
I don't ask you build a very large one | something that is seemly but no more than
later you can build a big and high one | you who are left of the host Achaean
in the well-found black ships when I am gone" | they did the business then as the swift son
of Peleus had directed and first | they extinguished with great sparkling wine spurts
all parts funeral bier in which the fire | had done its work ash piled in a deep pyre
then with tears on their cheeks they collected | the white bones gentle comrade selected
a golden vase with a sealant of fat | double-layered laid it in his hut vat
covered it with a shroud of soft linen | the next step call his barrow design in
laying down a ring of stone revetments | round the pyre fetched the wholesome elements
of earth piled up inside and when the troops | had built the monument the party troops
off rather poops as Achilles stopped them | all to sit down in a wide ring told them
exactly where the sports were to be held | and for these he brought out the prizes held
in the ships cauldrons tripods horses mules | sturdy cattle grey iron gowns girdles
women first event a race chariot | for which he offered the well-drawn great lot
of prizes for the first woman well-skilled | the fine crafts tripod handles ear-shaped filled

capacious four-and-twenty pints would hold | for the runner-up a mare six-year-old
and broken in and there was naturing | in womb a little mule she's nurturing
and for the man in third a fine kettle | four-pint which the flames had yet to fettle
still as bright as ever and for the fourth | two talents of gold and last for the fifth
two-handled pan by fire not touched then he's | stood announced contest Argives Achilles
"My lord Atreides and men-at-arms | Argive these the prizes the wonted charms
that await each winning charioteer | of course if we were holding our sport here
in honour of some other man then I's | the one who would walk off with the first prize
because you do not need me to tell you | my horses the very best of all too
immortal and present from Poseidon | to father Peleus who passed them on
to me but I and my most splendid pair | will not this time be competing as they're
in mourning for their driver glorious | and how kind he was to them Patroclus
always with clean water them down-washing | and then on their manes olive oil lashing!
no wonder they stand there and for him grieve | their manes sad trailing on the ground they leave
and in their sorrow they refuse to move | event open to any who seeks prove
his horses and chariot are the best" | announcement brought out the drivers ablest
first to spring to feet Admetus' son | Eumelus King of Men was a horseman
excellent next mighty Diomedes | son of Tydeus harnessed the breeds he's
of Tros that he had taken earlier | from Aeneas when Apollo saved their
master's life then red-haired Menelaus | son of Atreus scion of great Zeus
who yoked a fast pair Aethe a mare | of Agamemnon's and his own horse fair
Podargus Aethe Agamemnon | been presented by Echepolus son
of Anchises on condition not come | with him on trip to windy Ilium
but could now stay at home in great comfort | not to such a dire place of last resort
he happened to be a very rich man | who lived in the broad-lawns-based Sycion
this was the mare that yoked Menelaus | champing to be off fourth Antilochus
the noble son of the magnanimous | Pylos-sandy Nestor son Neleus
chariot-horses of Pylian breed | father went up to him and gave at need
(as Polonius to son Laertes | "Hamlet" wisdom from here does Shakespeare tease)
some useful tips though he knew his business | well enough himself said "Antilochus
young as you are you still stand well with Zeus | and Poseidon as they've taught you the use
of horses so there's no great need for me | to put you right but expert though may be
at wheeling around the turning-post your | horses are very slow I'm afraid you're
going to find this quite a handicap | but even if others go like the clap
-'ers drivers do not know a single trick | that is not part of your race rhetoric
you must fall back my friend on all the skill | that you are able to summon up still
if you do not yet wish to say good-bye | to the prizes as it is by and by
brains not brawn that make the best lumberman | and skill again enables a steersman
ship keep straight course over sea wine-bar dark | blowin' in the wind yaws in whine-far ar(c/k)
and it is by his skill that one driver | beats another as average driver
leaving too much to chariot and pair | is careless at the turn loses ground there
one side or the other horses wander | off course if does not right they meander

but the cunning driver although behind | a slower pair always has in eye's-mind
the post wheels close in so not caught slacking | when the time comes for oxhide reins cracking
and stretching his horses firmly keeping | them in hand watches the man who's leaping
ahead but now let me tell you something | look out for obvious enough some thing
can't miss it round six feet height up totting | dead tree-stump oak or pine but not rotting
in the rain and by two white stones is flanked | road narrows here but going can be tanked
on either side of the old monument | which either marks a burial ancient
or has been put up as a turning-post | by folk earlier age long past the post
turning world turning-post in any case | that my lord Achilles chose for this race
as you drive around you must hug it close | and you in your light chariot must close
in a little to the left call on your | off-side horse give rein as you touch with your
whip but make sure the near horse hugs the post | so close anyone might think was your host
just scraping it with the nave of your wheel | however you must have a careful feel
not touch the stone or might wreck your horses | smash up car which would delight the forces
but not look well for you so use your wits | my friend beware the manoeuvres of twits
because if you could just overtake them | the turning-point of the turning world then
no-one could catch you or pass with a spurt | not even if came behind with alert
thoroughbred of Adrestus Arion | the great who was himself sired in heaven
or the famous horses Laomedon | the best Troy's bred" thus expounding to son
the whole art of horsemanship King Nestor | went back to his seat and the fifth was Mer
-ion(jon)es get his horses ready | and now they all mounted their rock-steady
cars and cast their lots into a helmet | that the great Achilles shook first lot set
to jump out was that of Antilochus | son of Nestor then that King Eumelus
followed by that of son of Atreus | that great red-haired spearman Menelaus
Meriones drew the fourth place starting | galling last Diomedes departing
best of them all they drew up side by side | Achilles showed them the point-turning-tide
far away on level ground he'd posted | venerable Phoenix squire father's boasted
as umpire there keep eye on the running | report back at same moment all gunning
their horses with whip shook reins on their back | set going with sharp word command attack
horses then started off across the plain | without hitch swift left behind ship terrain
dust that rose from underneath their chests there | like a storm-cloud or fog hung in the air
their manes flew back in the wind one moment | in touch with fruitful earth next ferment
bounding high in the air heart each driver | as was struggling stood on car not to err
but to be first beating hard and they yelled | at horses who flew on cloud of dust swelled
but it was not 'til their teams galloping | rounded mark been given a walloping
head back to grey sea that each showed his form | and each horse itself then stretched its own form
there was a sprint now hundred Demeters | and none as fleet as covered the metres
fast mares Eumelus now shot out of ruck | next stallions Diomedes have pluck
of breed Tros close behind not much in it | it looked very much like that in a bit
they might leap into Eumelus' car | as were flying along behind not far
heads just over him warming bare back there | the sweep of his broad shoulders with breath their
Diomedes would have taken the lead | or at least made it a dead heat indeed

if Phoebus Apollo who angry still | son Tydeus had not had the ill will
to knock the shining whip right out of hand | Diomedes seeing that out of hand
Eumelus' mares the better going | than ever and his own were now slowing
for lack of anything to spur them on | so apoplectic giant tears ran on
down his cheeks but Athene had had eye on | Phoebus when he'd committed the foul on
Diomedes she sped after the man | gave him back his whip spurred horses on man
Apollo had brandished a yellow card | Athene 1 then 2nd harsh hard red card
she was so enraged chased Eumelus too | and used her power as a goddess to
break the yoke of his chariot result | mares ran off on ground shaft crumpled result
while poor Eumelus himself was flung out | came down by wheel chariot carry-out
the skin taken off elbows mouth and nose | his forehead bruised tears welled down cheeks did hose
he was robbed of speech then Diomedes | swept around the wreckage with horses these
powerful having left the others well | behind Athene his pair with strength did swell
let their master triumph next after pair | Diomedes Menelaus red-hair
Atreus' son then Antilochus | who's shouting at his father's horses thus
spurt like Diomedes' pair urging | "Show me your best paces now on surging
not asking you to race that pair ahead | the horses of the gallant Diomed
-es Athene's just speeded up make her fair | favourite win Atreides' pair
though do catch up with don't get left behind | by them and be quick about it too mind
or Aethe be turning up her fair | nose at you and she is merely a mare
why are you now hanging back so my friends? | I tell you straight at King Nestor's hands' ends
what you can expect no more attention | he'll slit your throats without hesitation
for a moment if you take it easy | now and leave us stuck with a prize measly
so after 'em full tilt! trust me to find | a way by slipping up swiftly behind
to get past them where the track is narrow | I shall not miss my chance" his horses so
took threat heart Europa fast remainer | for little while veteran campaigner
for now speeded up very soon saw place | where sunken road shrunk narrow space apace
and ran through a gully there where water | by rains of winter piled up flood brought a
torrent carried good part of it away | deepened whole defile to a hollow-way
Menelaus occupying the track | made it difficult to make a comeback
but Antilochus did not keep to it | deciding to drive a little off it
to one side and pressed Menelaus hard | alarmed Manos shouted aloud car jarred
"You are driving madly Antilochus | track's narrow here hold in your horses plus
it soon gets wider you could pass me there | but that you do not hit my car take care
and wreck us both" Antilochus pretends | that he has not heard him as he intends
to ply his lash and drives more recklessly | than ever both ran on for the carry
-ing distance of a quoit when a man young | casts it after his tender arm has swung
to test his strength Menelaus' pair | straight away gave way so fell behind there
their rivals then he eased pace now fearing | powerful horses collision nearing
in the road upset the light chariots | and if that being so their masters' lots
due to their eagerness to win would find | them rolling in the dust long way behind
but give the other a piece of his mind | red-haired Menelaus managed words find

"Antilochus you're the most appalling | driver in the world" cried "we've been falling
into error thinking you had some sense | well have it your own way but in one sense
you shan't carry off the prize 'til answered | on your oath for this affair" then transferred
to his horses "Don't stop don't stand and mope" | shouted at them "you can easily cope
with that pair ahead of you who'll weaken | in the leg by a long chalk sooner than
you neither of them as young as they were" | his horses by master's reprimand were
frightened and sped on with a will better | soon close second post first-place pace-setter
in the meantime from their seats in the ring | spectators for horses were out looking
saw a dust cloud rapidly approaching | Idomeneus of Crete encroaching
horses first to see as he was sitting | well above rest on high ground outside ring
and when he heard voice driver arising | in the distance that voice recognising
too one of the horses who were leading | who showed up well as a chestnut breeding
all over except for a round white patch | on his forehead making a full moon match
Idomeneus stood the spectators | called to "My friends Captains and Counsellors
of the Argives am I the only one | who can see the horses or anyone
else too? seems to me from old breeding | new pair and a different driver leading
Eumelus' mares who were well ahead | on first leg of race as outward did head
must have come to grief for I certainly | saw were in the lead when reaching nearly
turning-post now can't see them anywhere | though I've searched the Trojan plain everywhere
perhaps Eumelus dropped his reins could not | steer horses around the mark and his lot
fell then an accident while was wheeling | yes that is where he must have been reeling
tossed out and having his chariot smashed | while his mares went wild in panic off dashed
but do get up have a look for yourselves | sure the leader looks like one of our elves
Aetolian to me Argive king | of Tydeus the great son horse-taming
Diomedes himself" but the Runner | Aias son of Oileus no sooner
rudely contradicts Idomeneus | "Why must you be ever showing off thus?
the high-stepping mares have way long to go | and you're not the youngest man here you know
nor do you own the sharpest pair of eyes | yet laying down law you're always all-wise
here among your betters really you must | control your tongue the mares Eumelus t'
ones in front the same pair that led before | and there's Eumelus in his car for sure
with the reins in his hands" the commander | Cretan offended to the offender
"Aias you are a most cantankerous | ill-natured fellow failure courteous
be quite unlike an Argive but come now | let us have a bet about who is now
leading we'll stake a tripod or cauldron | and as referee King Agamemnon
you will soon learn the truth when you pay up" | Aias Ruinner in fury rose up
to give Idomeneus insolent | repartee quarrel to take nasty bent
if had not leapt to his feet Achilles | himself and intervenes between both these
"Aias and Idomeneus stop this | quarrelling interchange of insults is
a breach of good manners you'd be the first | to condemn in others so why not just
sit in the ring fix eyes on the horses? | soon be coming the horses for courses
for victory then each can recognise | them for himself pick out the winner's prize
and the second prize" Diomedes now | very close driving with the whip and how

swinging his arm right back for every lash | as sped on to the finish the whip-crash
making his horses leap into the air | always showers of dust falling on their
driver as fast pair over ground flying | car overlaid gold and tin hard vying
left on the fine dust barely a mark-tyre | Diomedes drew up centre entire
of arena sweat pouring down from his | horses' necks and chests he leapt down from his
glittering car leant whip against the yoke | Sthenelus his gallant squire soon did yoke
the prizes he took possession promptly | giving the tripod with the ear-shapely
handles exultant men he's invoking | them to lead the woman off unyoking
then the horses next up Antilochus | son of Nestor beaten Menelaus
not by a turn of speed but by a trick | even so Manos with his horses quick
came in close behind was no more in it | than the space that separates the wheel-bit
from the horse when he strains in the harness | pulls him along speeding with such closeness
the tip of his tail keeps brushing the tyre | and barely any gap close up nigher
however far he runs more than that not | between Menelaus the Top-Carrot
and the peerless Antilochus it's true | dodgy trick time by as much as threw
a discus been left behind in his rear | Menelaus but soon up behind near
Aethe's mettle had begun to tell | Agamemnon's lovely mare went like hell
longer run Menelaus would have passed | would not have ended level at post last
even Meriones worthy squire here | of Idomeneus came in a spear
-throw behind the famous Menelaus | long-haired horses longest mean delay us
he the poorest at art racing-driver | and the last of them all the arriver
Admetus' son Eumelus dragging | his handsome chariot driving (f)lagging
horses before him and when this he sees | sorry was swift excellent Achilles
for the man so he stood up in the ring | and to all those gathered there suggesting
"The best driver of the lot came in last | only fair give him a prize at the last
the second for of course Diomedes | takes the first" all welcomed and Achilles
encouraged by the men's applause about | give the mare to Eumelus when jumped out
Antilochus King Nestor's son and lodged | formal protest with son Peleus urged
"My lord Achilles I'll resent keenly | your following suggestion unseemly
you're proposing to rob me of my prize | because of Eumelus' car's demise
his horses coming to grief as did he | though he drives so well but the fact is he
ought to have prayed to the gods immortal | then would never have had the place final
but if you're sorry for the man and fond | of him there is plenty of the gold bond
in your hut and copper and sheep women | -servants too and splendid horses so then
choose something later on from these and let | him have a prize that's than mine even bet
-ter or hand it to him now and so hear | troops cheer but I won't give up this mare here
anyone who cares to try can come fight | me for her with his fists and see who's right"
this speech drew a smile from the excellent | swift Achilles always likeable bent
for Antilochus his comrade-in-arms | and delighted now with his wor(l)dly charms
gave a gracious answer "Antilochus | if you really wish this for Eumelus
send to my hut for an extra something | as consolation prize even that thing
I will do for you I'll give the cuirass | that I removed from Asteropaeus

of bronze plated with bright tin all over | gift he'll value forever moreover"
Achilles told his squire Automedon | to fetch cuirass from hut Automedon
went and brought it to him and Achilles | gave to Eumelus who it did much please
but this was not all for Menelaus | by no means forgiven Antilochus
and got up in a mood very ugly | speaker's staff by herald him handed he
called for silence Menelaus looking | like the king he was so began talking
"Antilochus you used to be fellow | sensible but see that ill you've done so!
with your own far slower pair by jiving | in across me you have made my driving
look abysmal robbed my pair of a win | my lords every Counsellor and Captain
of the Achaeans I appeal to you | to judge impartially between the two
of us so that none of our men-at-arms | will then be able to say without qualms
'Twas only by lying Menelaus | walked off with mare beating Antilochus
as his horses so much slower it's his | rank power brought him out on top in this'
no on second thoughts I will hear the case | myself and I am not afraid to face
accusations Danaan injustice | be fairly tried Antilochus in this
my lord come forward here in proper way | in front of your chariot and pair stay
hold the pliant whip you always drive with | touch your horses swear in the name forthwith
Earth-shaker Girdler of World you did not | foul deliberate block my chariot"
"Enough said" the wise Antilochus "I | a much younger man than you and you my
senior and better know well enough how | a young man comes to beak all the rules now
his mind quicker but judgement not so sound | so forgive me then for now I have found
deep within I'll give you the mare I won | something more or better of my own don
-ate you should ask for such as I'd rather | give at once than fall forever farther
out of your majesty's favour perjure | myself before the gods" son great Nestor
led the mare over and handed her to | Menelaus whose heart warmed like the dew
that hangs on corn ears when the fields bristle | crop ripens Menelaus' gristle
heart thus within you warmed formed the answer | you gave "Antilochus me the yielder
in turn I can't be angry with you now | you've never been impulsive until now
or unbalanced though this was certainly | one where the high spirits of youth got thee
then better of discretion another | time careful not overreach one better
no other Achaean would have found me | so easy to placate because for me
you've suffered much and laboured hard and so | have your noble father and brothers so
I therefore accept your apology | but also I'll give you the mare though she
is mine to now show our countrymen here | in me there's no pride or malice to fear"
handed over the mare to Noemon | of the wise Antilochus' men one
and thus himself took the shining kettle | Meriones in fourth had to settle
for the two talents gold the fifth the two | -handled pan unclaimed Achilles gave to
Nestor crossed the ring "My lord venerable | keepsake for you too of the funeral
Patroclus let it remind you for he'll | no longer among us himself reveal
and the prize I am giving you bears no | relation to the sports because I know
that you will not be boxing or wrestling | going javelin-throwing or foot-racing
your years sit too heavily on you for | that" Achilles put prize in hands Nestor

delighted "My dear boy dead right in all | you say I'm infirm of limb not at all
steady on my pins now my friend and my | arms no longer swing out lightly from my
shoulder as they did ah if only I | were still as young and vigorous as I
was when the Epeans buried lord bard | Amarynceus at Buprasion hard
by and his sons then held sports funeral | to honour their noble father royal
and there was no man there who could match me | either among Epeans or (w)holy
free Pylians themselves or mettlesome | Aetolians in boxing gave some
stick to Clytomedes son of Enops | wrestled Ancaeus of Pluron none stops
me in foot-race Iphicus defeated | he was a good man very sweet-feated
and with the javelin I cast farther than | Phyleus Polydorus far out man
to two Moliones lost one event | the car-race they grudged me in the event
and cut across me in the crowd because | a victory for them suited their cause
after all to keep at home the prize chief | they were twins and one the driver-in-chief
start to finish the other plied the whip | before replacement hip was once quite hip
but now I must leave this sort of thing to | the young take painful old-age lessons to
heart but back then in class of my own stood | well you must now get on with your own good
friend's funeral sports I accept meanwhile | with great pleasure your award wonderful
because I'm delighted to think that you | always knew how well disposed I to you
never let a chance go by of paying | the respect our states'-men me displaying
and may the gods reward you graciously | for all the kindnesses you have done me"
when he'd heard all that Nestor had to say | by way of thanks Achilles made his way
through the crowd of spectators and brought out | the pair of prizes for the boxing-bout
and for the victor in this painful sport | blow-for-blow fought retort of last resort
fetched sturdy mule and tethered in the ring | six years old and broken in a hard thing
in the case of mules and for the loser | two-handled mug Achilles announcer
contest to Argives standing up "My lord | Atreides and the Achaean horde
I offer these prizes for which I wish | that our two best men should to the finish
put up their fists and box and Apollo's | favourite winner if each here follows
that decision can take this sturdy mule | to his hut mug of handle double-drool
the loser will receive" there rose at once | one who was a champion boxer once
huge fine-looking fellow Epeius | -emblazened kit son of Panopeus
put his hand on the sturdy mule "Come on | to carry off the mug which is the one?
the mule's mine as no-one will knock me out | take her I'm the best boxer here no doubt
true I'm not so good at fighting no-one | an every-any-event champion
but isn't that enough? at any rate | I will tell you any opponent's fate
I am going to tear the fellow's flesh | to ribbons mash bones mushy peas mess mesh
suggest has all his mourners standing by | when I've done with him and waving bye-bye"
the challenge received in complete silence | only man who dared to take it up thence
heroic Euryalus son of King | Mecisteus son Talaus falling
of Oedipus went to Thebes for the sports | funeral and there him winning reports
from all Cadmeians Euryalus | was got in readiness for the fight plus
warmly encouraged by famous cousin | Diomedes very keen to see win

he helped him on with his shorts bound pair thongs | oxhide excellently cut on hands longs
start two dressed stepped into middle of ring | each other their mighty hands addressing
fell to fist met fist terrible scoring | of jaws and from limbs sweat began pouring
presently Euryalus took his eye | off his man who as excellent did spy
Epeius leaping at chance gave punch | on the jaw which left him in state drunk-punch
knocked out his legs were cut from under him | lifted up upper-cut took it on chin
like a fish leaping from weed-spread sands | flopping back into dark water's handst(r)ands
when the North Wind sends ripples up the beach | his chivalrous opponent did outreach
gave him a hand and set him on his legs | his followers gathered round were his legs
helping across the ring each trailing foot | head lolling on one side and now afoot
the spitting of blood clot's still senseless when | they put him down in his own corner then
they had to go themselves and fetch the mug | losing no time son of Peleus dug
out and displayed fresh prizes event third | for victor two legs big but better third
cauldron to go on the fire it was worth | Argive reckoning not quite costing earth
yet dozen oxen and for the loser | brought forth woman trained for household use her
thoroughly put through paces domestic | four ox on cattle market branding stick
Achilles announced new event Argives | called for couple entries couple high-fives
for the next contest Telamon-Ian | great Aias arose at once e'en Ian
Odysseus at one resourceful who knew | knew all the tricks and both put on shorts new
and stepped into the middle of the ring | each in powerful arms each encircling
looked like a couple of rafters sloping | good builder joining together coping
with the roof of a house wind resisting | with huge hands' pressure backs creak as twisting
as sweat down in great torrents came streaming | and many blood-red weals up were seaming
along their sides and shoulders still tussling | each one for the fine cauldron still muscling
that was not yet won and yet Odysseus | being no more able to bring down sus
his man than Aias baffled by the brawn | of Odysseus in time in brain did dawn
on them that they were in fact just boring | the troops Telamonian point scoring
"Royal son of Laertes Odysseus | of nimble wits either you or I mus
-t'other allow try a throw what happens | afterwards is in Zeus' business plans"
he then lifted Odysseus off the ground | but Odysseus' craft was not unfound
-ed caught Aias with a kick from behind | hollow of knee needy needed hit find
upset his stance and flung him on his back | himself on Aias' chest falling back
the spectators were duly impressed but | admirable Odysseus stalwart hard nut
had now to try a throw Aias shifted | just a bit him off the ground lifted
but could not throw him he crooked a leg round | Aias' knee they both fell to the ground
cheek by jowl lay there were smothered in dust | they jumped up off themselves did selves off dust
and would have then tried for a third-round dust | -up if Achilles himself had not just
risen to his feet then and interposed | said had enough on each other imposed
and that they must not wear each other out | "You have both won of that there is no doubt
so take equal prizes now and withdraw | more events still fill drop jaw claw craw maw"
both readily accepted decision | wiping off the dust their tunics did don
at once went on son of Peleus ace | to offer the prizes for the foot-race

first of chased silver mixing-bowl holding | six pints in the world the loveliest thing
masterpiece craftsmanship Sidonian | across the misty seas by Phoenician
traders shipped presented King Thoas when | into his port they were putting back then
Euneus son of Jason had given | Patroclus in payment for Lycaon
Priam's son and now Achilles offered | up as a prize of honour for friend dead
to the runner who should come in the first | in the foot-race the one after the first
was to have a large and well-fattened ox | the third and last in the finishing box
half a talent of gold Achilles stood | announced the contest invited the good
competitors to come forward Aias | son of Oileus the Runner thus has
jumped up at once as so too Odysseus | of the nimble feet and Antilochus
Nestor's son fastest of the younger men | so the three of them did toe the line then
Achilles pointed out the turning-post | they went all out from scratch Aias did post
soon lead very close behind Odysseus | and as close as a girdled woman thus
does bring the shuttle on up to her breast | draws careful get bobbin past as can best
warp so little in it Odysseus' | feet were falling in the tracks Aias'
before the dust had settled down again | he kept up so well that his breath did fain
fan the head of Aias there did he strain | every nerve in his body to attain
the win all the Argives cheered him shouting | encouragement to one was all-outing
already as it was as they drew near | end Odysseus offered silent prayer here
to Athene "Hear me goddess as I need | your valuable aid so come down and speed
my feet" and Pallas Athene heard his prayer | and so she lightened all his limbs fair there
then the final dash up to the prizes | when there's one of life's so-called surprises
Aias slipped as flat out Athene's doing | where ground dung-littered from the do-doing
cattle slaughtered by the swift Achilles | for Patroclus' funeral so he's
had mouth and nostrils filled with cattle-dung | while the excellent and much-endurung
Odysseus having caught him first finished | carried off the silver bowl well-finished
illustrious Aias took possession | of the farmyard ox and he stood there then
his hands on one of the animal's horns | as spat out dung of dilemma on horns
and did remark to all the spectators | "Damnation! I swear it was Athene's claws
tripped me the one who always attendance | like a mother on Odysseus does dance"
but they just laughed at him delightedly | Antilochus came in belatedly
took the last prize with a smile made a speech | "My friends I will tell you something that each
already knows the gods favour crowd old | for although Aias only a bit old
-er than myself Odysseus over there | product earlier generation fair
relic of the past and yet his old age | they say's green hope for future green ga(u)ge age
hard to beat for any save Achilles" | compliment to great runner Achilles
then drew an answer from the prince himself | "My friend I can't let your tribute unself
-ish go unrewarded you've won a half | gold talent I'll give you a second half
he handed the gold to Antilochus | who was delighted son Peleus plus
brought out and put down in the ring a long | -shadowed spear a helmet and a shield strong
the arms Patroclus took from Sarpedon | then stood up told the Argives what next on
agenda "I want our two best to fight | it out for these prizes before the might

assembled troops must put their armour on | the format will be the naked weapon
to one who first gets through the other's guard | pinks his man so drawing blood on the hard
I will give this venerable Thracian sword | with its fair silver mounting from the lord
Asteropaeus whence I took armour | here to be shared by each competitor
I will also give them a good dinner | in my hut" and the role of challenger
assumed great Aias Telamonian | and the powerful Diomedes son
Tydeus armed selves on own side of ring | and the pair on each other advancing
in the centre in mode mood for fighting | looking so fierce all spectators biting
their nails they came within range and they charged | three times when weapons had three times discharged
Aias succeeded in piercing round shield | Diomedes though burnished bronze did yield
spear failed reach flesh due breast-plate underneath | turn Diomedes repeat thrusts unsheathe
above the rim of large shield of Aias | managed to touch him on the neck clear as
his glittering spear-point the spectators | so terrified for Aias fate factors
called on the combatants to stop and share | the prizes but the prince the major share
awarded to Diomedes handed | to him with its scabbard in well-branded
baldric the next prize offered by the son | of Peleus a lump of pig iron
had already done service as a quoit | in hands of Eetion powerful quite
quota quoted carried off aboard ship | with his other possessions by the hip
groovy Achilles after him killing | Achilles stood up contest fulfilling
invited competitors come forward | "This lump is large enough" advanced forward
"keep winner in iron five years or longer | even if his farm is in the outer
reaches won't be lack of iron that sends | his shepherd or his ploughman to the ends
of town he'll have plenty not tell show it" | in response the dauntless Polypoet
'es risen to throw disc as did highborn | Leonteus Telamonian-born
Aias and the noble Epeius | all stood in a row good Epeius
picked up the weight and hurled it with a swing | but the spectators only guffawing
at his effort Leonteus offspring | of Ares the next be thing send springing
then great Telamonian Aias cast | with his mighty great hand and the marks passed
of all the others but when it came to | dauntless Polypoetes' turn to
throw overshot whole field distance by which | herdsman his boomerang flying can pitch
a crooked course among a herd of cows | great chorus of applause follows allows
the mighty Polypoetes' men | get up and carry off their king's prize then
off to soon less-hollow ship next archery | for this Achilles again the arch he
offered violet-coloured iron prizes | form ten double-head axes arises
and ten single-headed he then put up | the mast of a blue-prowed ship long way up
the sands target fluttering pigeon tied | to it by the foot a light cord applied
"He who hits the pigeon can take whole set | double-headers home and if one should get
the string not the bird won't have done so well | but he can have all axes single-cell"
the great Prince Teucer and Meriones | the worthy squire Idomeneus plays
had risen compete shook lots bronze helmet | to Teucer fell lot though seeming well met
too quickly fired arrow force tremendous | yet had forgotten promise portentous
Archer-King most pleasing sacrifices | firstling lambs failed in his artifices

missed the bird Phoebus grudged him that success | yet he did strike the cord by which the jess
was tethered near its foot sharp arrow cut | the string bird up into sky shot hot foot
leaving the string dangling down the Argives | roared there was a great giving of high-fives
but Meriones who had been gaming | an arrow ready while Teucer aiming
from Teucer's hands snatched the bow hastily | vowed sacrifice of first-born lambs promptly
pleasing to the Archer-King Apollo | saw pigeon fluttering solo not low
overhead beneath the clouds as circled | there hit her below the belt well-Circeled
fell-winged the bolt went flighty through came down | at his feet stuck in earth as she came down
settled for a new mast a blue-prowed craft | head drooped plumage all fast adrift raft aft
tail down soon she was dead dropped to the deck | long way from man who broke her heart and neck
spectators were lost in admiration | Meriones took off to ovation
standing set ten double-headed axis | Teucer singles less-hollow ships access
finally the son of Peleus used | move smart next prize in ring cauldron unused
with a floral pattern and of full girth | a long-shadowed spear an ox the first worth
he put these down and the javelin-throwers | rose to compete the two who the throwers
of hats into the ring Agamemnon | imperial and Atreus' son
Meriones Idomeneus' | worthy squire admirable Achilles is
swift to step in "My lord Atreides | we know by how much you exceed all these
here and that in the throwing of the spear | nobody can approach anywhere near
accept this prize take it to less-hollow ships | but if you're agreeable he who ships
the spear shall be Meriones that is | what I at all events suggest" to his
decision Agamemnon no demur | and thus Achilles then gave the bronze spear
to Meriones King now did apprise | his herald take his own beautiful prize

## ■ εἴκοσι τέσσερα ■

*Book 24*

# PRIAM AND ACHILLES

*of how the body of Hector ransomed*
*informed funeral Achilles transformed*

the game(')s over the soldiers left the ring | then to their several ships men scattering
thinking dinner good night's rest on leaving | but Achilles for his friend still grieving
could not get him out of his mind and all | -conquering sleep simply refused to call
he tossed to one side and then the other | thinking always of lost in-arms-brother
of Patroclus' spirit manliness | of all they'd been through together endless
hardships they'd shared fights with the enemy | adventures high seas most(ly) unfriendly
as crowded in on him memories warm | tears poured down his cheeks took river storm form
sometimes lay on side and sometimes on back | and then again turned on his face went back
at last would get up wander aimlessly | along the salt-sea beach drawn dawn-lit sea
-coast rosy-fingered plight then addressing | as normal his fast horses harnessing
Hector to his chariot would loosely | tie to the back of it and after he
had hauled him thrice round his ex's barrow | sight to harrow the blood to the marrow
he would then return to his hut to rest | left corpse stretched out face down in dust distressed
but dead though Hector was Apollo still | felt pity for him saved his flesh from ill
of pollution also wrapped him in his | golden aegis so that Achilles'
sin skin should not scrape when dragged him along | this was the shameful way in which for long
Achilles in wrath mucked up Prince Hector | the happy gods looked on compassion for
him felt even hint to sharp-eyed Hermes | he might do well to situation ease
by stealing the corpse an expedient | that with the rest of them found agreement
save Here Poseidon Lady Eyes Flashing | sacred Troy Priam folk long for trashing
as much now as when't' Ire troubles at mill | started Paris fell fatal flaw trap ill
two fell goddesses humiliating | sheep hut check matchmaking mating rating
by preference for third who him offered | the pleasures and penalties love proffered
eleven days went by on the morning | of the twelfth Apollo mind opening
to the immortals "You are hard-hearted | sordid monsters of cruelty for did
Hector never burn you thighs of oxen | full-grown goats? yet now you will not even
save his body for his wife and mother | to see but also his child and father

Priam's people who'd burn it instantly | give him funeral honours no it's very
brutal Achilles you choose to support | Achilles who has not a decent thought
or feeling in him and listens never | to the voice of mercy but goes ever
on his own savage way like a lion | who when he wants to get his dinner on
lets his own strength and daring run away | with him and pounces on flocks down his way
lion-like Achilles has killed pity | cares not a jot for public obloquy
would make most folk bend the knee for better | or worse for many lose one of fetter
closer than he brother borne same mother | maybe son father or someone other
he weeps and wails for him and then has done | since fateful Providence has endowed one
with an enduring heart but Achilles | what does he for HIS beloved friend? he's
just killed Prince Hector first and then he ties | him to his car thrice the gig drag applies
round the tomb as if an honourable thing | or indeed could any good be doing!
yet he had better beware our anger | great man though he is what's his angle err
in fury but insulting clay senseless?" | but bridled at this Here white-armed goddess
"There would be force in what you say my Lord | of the Silver Bow if gods were on board
to value Hector as do Achilles | first plain man woman-suckled Achilles
though the son of a goddess who I my | -self brought up and later took under my
wing and gave in marriage to a man to | Peleus most favourite we had too
why all you gods here came to the wedding | and you with lute accompanied wedding
but you're keeping worse company today! | never were a loyal friend anyway"
Zeus the Cloud-compeller remonstrated | "Here you must not lose" to her mandated
"your temper with the gods there's no question | the same footing putting the two men on
but the fact remains the gods loved Hector | also in Troy was top in their favour
never failed give me what I like when fine | banqueting was afoot of fat and wine
its proper share my altar never went | without our due privileges he sent
but we must abandon this idea | of stealing the gallant Hector's corpse here
without the knowledge of great Achilles | not feasible his Mother hugs his knees
night and day but let one of the gods tell | Thetis to come here to me and I'll tell
her a way to a wise resolution | Achilles must accept ransom solution
from King Priam and give Prince Hector up" | Iris of the Whirling Feet started up
at once on this mission half-way between | Samos rugged Imbros left airy screen
dived into dark loving bosom of sea | with a resounding splash sank to very
bottom as quickly as a bit of lead | that an angler has attached to the head
of his ox-horn lure with consequences | fatal to the greedy fish found Thetis
in her vaulted cavern surrounded by | a gathering of other salt-sea high
Nymphs in whose midst there she was bewailing | lot of her peerless son soon be failing
losing plot lot as knew in deep-soiled land | of Ilium far from his own homeland
fleet-foot Iris went up to the goddess | "Zeus calls you to his side Thetis goddess
in his unending wisdom" Silver Feet | to this said "What does a god so complete
want me for? I am now so overwhelmed | sorrow fear so far from any calm held
from mixing with gods but I will come | no doubt he wants to discuss with me some
weighty matter" the gracious goddess took | a dark-blue shawl there was naught more of look

black she could wear set out on her journey | Iris of Whirlwind Feet leading swiftly
the way the waters of the sea made way | for them and they exited the sea-way
onto shore darted up to heaven where | they found mighty all-seeing Zeus in chair
of happy-ever-after lasting gods | in session sat around calling the odds
Thetis sat down by Father Zeus Athene | let her have her chair and here Here the Queen
with a cheerful word of welcome passed her | a lovely golden cup returned to her
when she had drunk from it Father of men | and gods with these words did meeting open
"Lady Thetis you've come to Olympus | despite your troubles you are distraught plus
with fear I know as well as you and yet | I must tell you why I called you it's yet
nine days that the gods have been quarrelling | Achilles Hector's body barrelling
Hermes the Giant-Slayer has even | been urged to steal the body but listen
how I propose to settle the matter | Achilles all due honour days latter
give in a way that will make sure of your | affection for me reverence future
you must go quickly to the camp convey | my wishes to your son and you must say
that the gods are displeased with him I most | of all as in his reckless fury most
senseless refused part with Hector's body | and kept it by his beaked ships I hope he
may be overawed by me give it up | meanwhile I will send Iris to go up
to the noble-hearted Priam suggest | that to ransom his son is the course best
he go to the Achaean ships with gifts | Trojan-bearing 'til will Achilles drifts
heart rifts melts" obeyed Zeus goddess Thetis | Silver Feet whose great neat nifty feat is
speed off at once down from peak Olympus | to son's hut found him moaning piteous
-ly while his comrades bustled round him in | busy preparation for the mo(u)rnin'
meal for which a large woolly sheep being | in-hut slaughtered Lady Mother being
close beside him stroked him with her hand spoke | "My child how much longer going for broke
eating your heart out in lamentation | misery forgetful food bed so on?
is there no comfort in a woman's arms | for you who have so short a time in arms
stand already valley shadow of Death | and inexorable Destiny? Death
sends me to you via Zeus who wants you | to know that the gods are displeased with you
and he himself the angriest of all | as in your senseless fury you lost all
decency refused part with Hector's corpse | but kept it there by your hollow ships' corps
come now give it back accept a ransom | for the dead" "If Olympian in some
great earnest and himself so commands me | let them bring the ransom take the body"
while the two talked down by the ships Mother | and son much to say to one another
Zeus sent Iris to Ilium sacred | "Off with you Iris fast as you can" said
"leave your Olympian home take message | to King Priam tell him he must engage
ransom his son by going to the ships | melt heart Achilles with gifts there he ships
and he has to go alone with the rule | no Trojan escort save one drive the mule
-cart maybe older herald relaying | back to Troy the body man man-slaying
Achilles killed say not to think of death | and have no fears whatever at the death
we'll send the best of escorts in Hermes | Giant-Slayer who'll stay in charge 'til he's
brought him into Achilles' presence | nobody is going to kill him once
inside the hut not Achilles himself | nor anyone else Achilles himself

will see to that he's no fool he knows what | he's doing a godless man he is not
on the contrary will spare suppliant | show him every courtesy compliant"
Iris of the Whirlwind Feet speeding on | her errand Troy where great lamentation
met her at the palace in the courtyard | Priam's sons were sitting around there hard
by their father drenching their clothes with tears | in centre sat old man figure of fears
face rigours cut set stone wrapped up in cloak | head and neck defiled by the dung bespoke
he'd gathered in his hands as he grovelled | on the ground his daughters sons' wives hovelled
the house howled thinking of the many men | splendid who had died at hands Danaan
lying in the field the Angel of Zeus | went up to Priam addressed him with use
of a gentle voice but his limbs began | now to tremble "Courage Dardanian
Priam! compose yourself and have no fears | I come here not to herald evil tears
but on a friendly mission and I'm sent | by Zeus who far off as he is has bent
much thought on your behalf and pities you | and ransom the Olympian bids you
Prince Hector gifts bearing to Achilles | you'll truly melt his heart with ease with these
you must go alone obeying the rule | no Trojan escort save one drive the mule
-cart maybe older herald relaying | back to Troy the body man man-slaying
Achilles killed you're not to think of death | and to have no fears at all at the death
because we'll send the best escort Hermes | Giant-Slayer who'll stay in charge 'til he's
brought you into Achilles' presence | nobody is going to kill you once
inside the hut not Achilles himself | nor anyone else Achilles himself
will see to that he's no fool he knows what | he's doing a godless man he is not
no indeed he will spare his suppliant | show you every courtesy compliant"
job done then and her message delivered | Fleet-footed Iris quickly disappeared
Priam told his sons at once get ready | a smooth-running mule-cart wicker body
lashed on top then he went to his lofty | cedar-wood bedroom of the whole city
full of the most precious ornaments wife | Hecabe called "My dear" said "on my life
an Olympian messenger from Zeus | just told me of ransom I must make use
for Hector's body going to the ships | melt Achilles' heart with gifts one ships
there tell me what you make of that? I feel | to go down to the ships myself a real
need to visit the great camp Achaean" | but when she heard this "Alas!" she began
"where's the wisdom which people from abroad | and own subjects with praise did laud applaud?
how can you think of going by yourself | to the ships into presence of the self
-same man killed so many a gallant son | of yours? you must have a heart of iron
once you are in his power once he sets | eyes on you and the killing-hunger gets
that beast of prey that treacherous brute will | have no mercy or respect just ill will
for your person no all we can do now | is sit at home and in our great sorrow
bewail our son from here *this* is the end | inexorable Destiny intend
did for him as spun first thread of life when | I brought him into the world the end then
glut the nimble dogs far from his parents | in clutches of a monster who patents
evil whose very heart I would devour | if only get my teeth that far power
that would requite him for what he has done | to my son who after all not the one
to play coward when Achilles killed him | but fighting without any thought of him

-self or of flight or cower in defence | of the sons and deep-bosomed daughters hence
Troy lives" "I mean to go" said venerable | godlike Priam "Don't try to disable
my will or go round the house yourself this | bird of ill-omen as you will not diss
-uade me but if any human being | an augur or priest had been decreeing
this course of action I should have doubted | his good faith and sceptic would have shouted
but I heard myself the goddess' voice | I saw her before me not just a voice
so I'm going and I won't act as though | she had never spoken if I'm doomed so
to die by the ships of host Achaean | then I choose death so great Achilles can
just kill me out of hand once I have clasped | my son in my arms wept my fill and gasped
my last" went to his coffers with lidded | ornamentation lovely he lift did
out from twelve beautiful robes twelve single | cloaks as many a sheet and white mantle
and tunic to go with them also weighed | ten talents of gold and then he assayed
two shining tripods four cauldrons lovely | cup the Thracians had given him when he
went to them on an embassy household | treasure old man in high esteem did hold
but so great his desire to recover | his beloved son he did not demur
at parting with it also were townsfolk | in some small number in the house portic
-o Priam gave the rough side of his tongue | send about their business did not take long
cried "Off with you you riffraff gang wastrel! | do you not have causes to be tearful
in your own homes that you come here me vex? | is it a mere trifle to you the hex
Zeus the Son of Cronos has put on me | the loss of my finest son have to see?
if so you'll learn better as the Argives | will find it easier to take your lives
with Hector dead as for me I only | hope be in Hades' Halls before see
the city plundered and laid waste" he fell | upon them with his staff and they fled well
away from the house before the violent | old man next he fell foul of his sons went
at them angrily shouted at Paris | excellent Agathon Helenus his
Pammon warlike Polites and Dius | lordly Antiphonus Deiphobus
Hippothous and all nine of them he trounced | and what they had to do he now announced
cried "Bestir yourselves my good-for-nothing | inglorious sons! I wish more no thing
than you'd all been killed nigh the gallant ships | not Hector how calamity trips strips
me! I had the best sons in the whole realm | broad of Troy but now all have quit the helm
Troilus that happy charioteer he | the godlike Mestor and great Hector he
who walked among us like a god looked more | like the son of a god than of a mor
-tal mere the war's taken them left me these | rascal kings despicable crew with ease
of the dance heroes who win laurels floor | ballroom when you are not engaged in more
robbing of your own folk their sheep and kids | can't you get busy lord-of-the-flies kids?
I want the cart prepared at once and all | these things put in it as I hear the call
and am waiting to be off" Priam's sons | were terrified by his fulminations
quickly fetched a fine new mule-cart with strong | wheels and lashed upon it a wicker long
took down from its peg a yoke of boxwood | for the mules with knob was well centred would
aid the proper guides for the reins with yoke | they then brought out a nine-cubit-long yoke
-band laid yoke carefully on shaft polished | in the notch at the end of it and swished
the ring over the pin carried yoke-band | round the knob with three turns on either hand

then wound it closely round the shaft and tucked | the loose end in then went to bedroom plucked
the princely gifts that were to buy back corpse | Hector packed them in wooden cart-hearse corps
the sturdy mules they yoked who had been trained | to work in harness and freely distrained
to the King with compliments of the folk | Mysian and thereupon they did yoke
last to Priam's chariot the horses | that the old man kept for his own uses
and fed at the polished manger and while | he and herald lost anxious thought the while
the vehicles being prepared for them | under the high roof of the palace then
they were approached by Hecabe in great | distress held golden cup mellow wine state
meant for them to make a drink-offering | before they left came to car proffering
to Priam himself "There make libation | to Father Zeus pray come safe from mission
into enemy's hands since you're set on | going to the ships your going not on
my say-so but if must needs must address | prayer to mighty Son Cronos whose address
'The Lord of the Black Cloud God of Ida' | who surveys the whole of Troyland laid a
-fore him and ask for a bird of omen | swift ambassador from an eyrie on
high this prophetic bird his favourite | strongest thing on wings flying on your rite
so that you can see it with your own eyes | put your trust in it as your ways wend wise
down to the black ships of the horse-rearing | Danaans but if Zeus the all-seer-ing
refuses to send you his messenger | I should advise you then not to venture
down to the Argive ships however much | you may now have set your heart to do such"
"My dear I'll surely do as you suggest | because it is a good thing to attest
to mighty Zeus ask him for his blessing" | old man had his housekeeper addressing
his hands with clean water brought basin thus | and a jug and attended on him when
he'd washed his hands took the cup from his wife | went fore-centre-court from trouble and strife
to pray looked up into the sky as poured | out the wine made his petition to Lord
"Father Zeus you who rule all from Ida | most glorious and great pray grant my prayer
Achilles receive me with compassion | kindness and send me a bird of omen
your swift ambassador the strongest thing | on wings the one you yourself best liking
fly right on the rite so I can see it | with my own eyes and put my trust in it
as I go down now to the horse-loving | Achaeans' ships" Zeus the Thinker loving
Priam's prayer instantly sent an eagle | the best of birds prophecy inveigle
he one of those dusky hunters whose hue | said ripening grape dark wine-barren sea too
when his wings were fully stretched out would Zoom | across stout double doors lofty bedroom
in a rich man's house him flying then spied | on right rite across town they full high-fived
at the site as he warmed the hearts of all | the old man then mounted his car with-all
speed and drove out by the gateway and its | echoing colonnade and with the cart's
lead preceded driver wise Idaeus | then the horses of Priam who made use
of his whip drove them quickly through the town | yet a crowd of friends kept up going down
and wailing incessantly as though he | had been going to his death but when he
had made his way down through the streets and reached | open country his sons sons-in-law leached
back to Troy went home all observant-eyed | Zeus the two strike out across the plain spied
felt sorry for old man turned to Hermes | his son said "Here's a task for you Hermes
escorting men is your prerogative | and pleasure and with those you like you give

warm vibes give off so off go now conduct King | Priam to ships way him one not seeing
recognising 'til meets son Peleus" | Zeus had spoken Hermes the Guide Argus
-Killer immediately him obeyed | and under his feet bound and soon displayed
the lovely sandals untarnishable | gold carried him at speed full capable
of wind over water or boundless earth | he picked up the wand of boundless great worth
which he can wield at will to cast a spell | on our eyes or wake from the deepest well
of sleep Giant-Slayer with wand in hand | made his flight soon reached Hellespont Troyland
went on foot looked like a young prince that most | charming age when the face starts a beard host
meanwhile the two had driven past Ilus | barrow and stopped their mules and horses thus
drink at river full disappearing | into dark now not 'til Hermes nearing
them that the herald looked up and saw him | and at once then turned around to Priam
"Look your majesty we must beware I | can see a man may be butchered fear I
so let's make our escape in the car or | if not that fall at his knees and beg for
his mercy" the old man was dumbfounded | and with a great terror filled ill-founded
the hairs stood up on every supple limb | was rooted to the spot struck dumb dead dim
but the Bringer of Luck did not wait to | be accosted rather went right up to
Priam took him by the hand and started | question "Father where are you driving" said
"at such a time with those mules and horses | through solemn night when everyone else is
asleep? aren't you afraid of the fiery | Argives your bitter enemies very
near at hand? if one should see you coming | through black night with a load so becoming
what could you do? you are not young enough | to deal with the full-on aggressive stuff
and your companion is an old man too | however I do not mean harm to you
indeed I'm going to see that no rogue lone | molests you remind me much of my own
father" "Our plight dear son" said the old king | "is very much as you are describing
but even so some god now must have meant | to protect me when a wayfarer sent
like you to fall in with a real god-send | if I may judge by your bearing my friend
looks distinguished as well as your good sense | which all betoken a gentle birth" hence
"Sir" said the Guide and Slayer of Argus | "you are so very near the mark on us
and now I ask you to confide in me | are you sending to some place of safety
in a foreign land a hoard of treasure? | or has the time now indeed come when you're
quitting sacred Troy in panic at loss | your best man your own son who was the boss
never failed to keep enemy at bay?" | but Priam the old king in his own way
responded to Hermes a-questionin' | "Who are you and what is your origin
noble sir who speaks to me so kindly | of the fate of my son most unfriendly
who are your parents?" Hermes "I suppose | you are testing out to see what one knows
of Prince Hector I've seen him with my own | eyes in the field of honour I do own
seen oft what's more him hurl back Argive ones | on their ships and mow them down with his bronze
while we stood by not let fight and marvelled | as Achilles called it having quarrelled
with King Agamemnon needs must instil | in you the view I squire mighty Achill
-'es come here in the same good ship as me | I'm a Myrmidon and my father he
is Polyctor rich man about as old | as you of seven sons I the least old
and when we drew lots it fell to me to | join the expedition here although to

-night I left the ships came onto the plain | as at dawn bright-eyed host Achaean plain
view planning then an assault on the town | tired sitting eager fight no chieftain down
camp can hold them in" Priam "If you are | of Prince Achilles a squire from afar
I implore you to tell me the whole truth | does my son lie still by the ships of ruth
-less Achilles or been thrown to his dogs | piecemeal already?" "Well neither the dogs
nor birds of prey have eaten him my lord | so far" Slayer of Argus on record
"his body's intact lies there in the hut | by Achilles' ship though had the butt
-end eleven days flesh has not decayed | at all and nor did any worms invade
they that do devour the dead sad bodies | of men killed in battle but true it is
each day's peep of dawn Achilles drags him | mercilessly around the barrow grim
of his beloved comrade does no harm | to him as preserved by some magic charm
and if you went to the hut yourself you | -'d be stunned see him lie there fresh as dew
blood all washed away on him not a stain | and his wounds too have all closed up again
every wound he had and there were many | who struck him with their bronze shows that every
care being taken by the blessed gods | on your behalf and although the poor sod's
naught but a body they love him dearly" | hearing this made old man very happy
"My child what an excellent thing it is | whatever else one may venture on this
earth give the gods their proper offerings! | my son always gave proper offerings
for as surely as he lived elected | gods Olympus be never neglected
in our home for that they give him credit | now though his fated death he has met it
but now I beg you to accept this cup | beautiful with this Heavenly hand-up
protecting me yourself see me safely | to the ships Achilles' Kompany"
"Sir" replied the Guide and Giant-Killer | "you're an old man I young yet thing iller
tempting me to a bribe behind the back | of Achilles no! if were to go back
on loyalty to my master should be | thoroughly ashamed terrified what be
consequences to myself however | I am ready now to serve you ever
as escort right up to Argos the famed | on ship or land your henchman unashamed
as any attack would be pre-empted | none your guard undervalue be tempted"
Luck-Bringer leapt in horse-car seized whip reins | put fresh heart into the horse and mule veins
when they came to the trench's wall around | the dark ships sentries were just coming round
to preparing their supper the Slayer | of Argus sent all into sleep's layer
unfastens gates thrusts back bars and ushers | Priam in with cartload gifts my precious
went on lofty hut Peleus' son | this hut had been built by host Myrmidon
for their prince with deal planks cut by themselves | and had roofed it with range downy thatch shelves
of rushes gathered in the meadows near | the hut stood in a large enclosure sphere
surrounded by a close-set fence the gate | was fastened by a single pine-wood great
would take three men drive home this bolt mighty | three to draw it three men ordinary
Achilles of course could work it himself | and now Hermes Bringer of Luck himself
opened up for the old king and drove in | with the splendid presents and whose destin
-ation swift Achilles said to Priam | "Immortal god visits you pray I am
Hermes my father sent me escort you | but I shall leave you now because I do
not intend go into Achilles' | presence unbecoming god deathless is

accept a mortal's hospitality | but go inside yourself first clasp each knee
of Achilles and as to him you pray | invoke first his father and then his lay
-dy Mother and his son to touch his heart" | Hermes to high Olympus start did dart
and Priam leapt down from his chariot | left Idaeus to the cart lookout lot
horses and mules walked right up to the hut | where Prince Achilles normally set put
found him in most men some way off sitting | but two to and fro busily flitting
wait on him Automedon Alcimus | gallant finished eating drinking had jus
-t' table he'd used had not yet been cleared | big though Priam was unobserved appeared
approached Achilles grasped his knees hands kissed | terrible man-killers had evil blissed
blitzed many of his sons Achilles stunned | when saw King men shock stock astounded fund
they looked at each other in amazement | as one does in rich noble's tenement
when a foreigner who's murdered a one | own land seeks refuge abroad bursts in on
them like one possessed but Priam praying | already to Achilles so saying
"Most worshipful Achilles think of your | own father same age as me naught hope for
so has nothing but miserable old age | ahead of him no doubt his neighbours rage
at him no-one left from depredation | save him yet at least one consolation
as long as he knows that you're still alive | and can look forward day by day to thrive
on seeing his beloved son come back | from Troy whereas my fortunes had their back
completely broken I had the best sons | in the whole of this broad realm now not one's
left I say not one there were fifty then | came the expedition Achaean when
nineteen of them were borne by one mother | the rest in palace by ladies other
and most of them have fallen in action | Hector only one I could still count on
the bulwark of the Trojans and of Troy | has just now been killed by you my dear boy
fighting for his native land it is to | get him back from you that I have come to
the black ships bringing this ransom princely | with me fear the gods Achilles and be
merciful to me while remembering | your own father though I'm more deserving
even of compassion since I have brought | myself to do a deed that no-one ought
to have to do on earth or has so done | raised to my lips the hand man killed my son"
but Priam had set Achilles thinking | of his own dear father blinking brinking
the verge of tears the old man's hand taking | gently then him from him away breaking
and with their memories then encroaching | on them they both broke down Priam crouching
at Achilles' feet keenly weeping | for man-slaying son Achilles weeping
for father then again for Patroclus | sounds of their lamentation filled house plus
presently though when he had had enough | of tears recovered his composure tough
excellent Achilles leapt from his chair | old man's grey head beard compassion not spare
took him by the arm and raised him then spoke | to him from his heart "You're under fate's stroke
of bitter sorrows indeed much suffered | come here by self how courage have mustered
into the presence of a man who's killed | so many of your sons? with iron filled
is your great heart but pray be seated so | on this chair now let us leave our sorrow
bitter though be locked up in our own hearts | because weeping is cold comfort imparts
little good we men are wretched creatures | sorrow woven in our lives most features
for well you know that Zeus the Thunderer | on his palace floor two jars full wonder

standing where he keeps his gifts set blessing | in one evil other first addressing
gets a mixture two fortunes varying | as sometimes well- and sometimes ill-faring
although when Zeus serves a man from the jar | evil only makes outcast therefore far
is he chased by the gadfly of despair | on the face of the earth all over where
-ever goes way damned alike by gods men | take my father Peleus from time when
born Heaven showered its greatest gifts on | fortune wealth unparalleled earth upon
with the kingship of the Myrmidon folk | goddess for wife though man mortal yoke joke
yet like we others knew too misfortune | no children take on royal line fortune
ends in palace only a single son | and doomed to an untimely death this one
and what is more though old is he growing | he gets no care from me as I'm sowing
death here in your land and far from my own | making life awful for you and your own
however I understand that there was | a time lord when fortune smiled on you as
well they say there was no-one to compare | with you in wealth and for splendid sons there
and in all the lands contained by Lesbos | in the sea where the MaKar reigned boundless
Hellespont and Upper Phrygia too | but the Heavenly Ones brought me here to
be a thorn in your side and you've seen naught | around your town save for fighting and slaught
-ering endure be not broken-hearted | lamenting for your great son departed
will do no good at all you will be dead | yourself before you've him resurrected"
"Do not ask me to sit down your highness | while Hector lies neglected in distress
in your hut but now give him back to me | without delay and my eyes on him me
let set and accept the splendid ransom | I bring hope you enjoy safely home come
because you spared me when I first appeared" | "Old man do not drive me pray too hard" speared
the swift Achilles frowning at Priam | and without your help minded now I am
give Hector back to you my own Mother | of the Old Man of the Sea the Daughter
has brought me word from Zeus moreover I | have absolutely seen right through *you* Pri
-am you cannot hide the fact that some god | brought you to the Argive ships as no bod
normal even young man at very best | would our camp by himself essay the test
of entry for one thing he'd never pass | sentry test unchallenged yet if did pass
would find hard shift bar we keep as a keep | -sake across our gate so don't test me keep
patience now sir when I have already | loads on my mind or I may break for thee
the laws of Zeus suppliant though you are | show as little duty of care so far
as e'n showed Hector in my huts" fear unmanned | so did the old man took the reprimand
to heart then like a lion Peleus | son dashed out of doors taking in the rush
two squires lord Automedon Alcimus | his favourites next to late Patroclus
unyoked horses mules brought in the herald | old King Priam's crier inside installed
gave him a stool to sit on took out then | from polished body of the waggon when
princely ransom had won back corpse Hector | but left two white mantles fine tunic for
Achilles to wrap up the body when | he let Priam take it home the prince then
called women-servants out told them to wash | and anoint the body and once awash
to be in different part of the house so | Priam not see his son Achilles so
afraid that Priam if he should see him | might in the bitterness of grief full grim
be unable to restrain his anger | he himself lose temper in fit anger

kill the old man so sinning against Zeus | and when the maid-servants had made good use
of their skills in washing and anointed | the body with olive-oil appointed
corpse wrapping of fine tunic and mantle | Achilles himself did body handle
onto a bier comrades helped him put in | the waggon then from somewhere deep within
a groan came called to his friend beloved | by name "Patroclus pray please don't see red
at me if you learn deep down in the Hall | sHades I allowed his father's recall
of Prince Hector the ransom he paid me | was a worthy one and I will soon see
you get your proper share even of that" | and the excellent Achilles with that
returned to his hut sat on chair inlaid | he'd left the far side of the room speech made
to Priam "Your wishes are now fulfilled | venerable lord your son's tenure (di)stilled
he's lying on a bier and at daybreak | you will see him for yourself as you take
him away but meanwhile let's turn our thoughts | to dinner for to her food did the thoughts
of even the lady Niobe turn | although dozen children vile misfortune
seen done to death in own house six daughters | six sons in prime while Artemis slaughters
role Archeress the daughters Apollo | then shot down the sons with his silver bow
in his fury with Niobe because | in her pride she had given herself cause
to claim to have done as well as his own | Mum Leto Lovely Cheeks and on her own
contrasted the many children she'd brought | into the world with the two Leto wrought
yet that pair although they were only two | killed all of hers and as was no-one to
bury them Son of Cronos ill craving | turned the people to stone they were bathing
for nine days in pools of blood but on tenth | the gods of Heaven buried them her strength
exhausted by tears Niobe had mind | to take some food and now where feet don't find
a way stands among the crags in the hills | of Sisyphus place said the race Nymph fills
after dancing on rills of Achelous | lie down surrender to sleep my precious
there Niobe in marble does brood on | Ozymandias gods' desolation
row so now my royal lord let's two too | think of food and later when to Troy you
take him you can weep once more for your son | will indeed be a much bewept-for one"
the swift Achilles now himself bestirred | killed a white sheep his men flayed chef-mastered
in the usual manner they deftly | chopped it up spitted pieces carefully
roasted them and withdrew them from the fire | Automedon fetched bread butter from byre
set out at table in baskets handsome | Achilles set meat portions grand and some
and they helped themselves to the good things spread | before them their thirst and hunger sorted
Dardanian Priam let his eyes dwell | on Achilles how big beautiful fell
he was he saw with admiration then | the very image a god in Heaven
Achilles noted with admiration | equal noble looks speech Dardanian
Priam pleasure look each other over | however soon King mover moreover
"Your highness I beg leave now bring end on | for the night it's time that my companion
and I went to bed enjoy boon of sleep | my eyelids not managed company keep
across my eyes since moment when my son | lost his life to you and ever since then
I've been ever lamenting and dwelling | on my countless sorrows and grovelling
in the dung in my stable-yard but I | at last have eaten poured sparkling wine dry
down but prior that nothing inducting" | hence Achilles set about instructing

his men and maidservants to put bedsteads | portico furnish fine purple rugs spreads
of sheets over these add some blankets thick | for covering torch in hand women quick
to quit the living-room themselves busied | at this task and two beds were soon readied
now the great runner Achilles spoke to | Priam in a somewhat brusquer tone "You
must sleep out of doors my friend in case some | Achaean general visits often come
discuss their plans with me it's our custom | if saw you here dead of night one of them
at once news Agamemnon be relayed | your recovery body be delayed
another issue will you tell me how | many days you propose to devote now
to Prince Hector's funeral so that I | myself may refrain from fighting and my
army keep idle for that space of time?" | King "If you really wish to give me time
for proper funeral for Prince Hector | I'll commit ourselves taking your word for
you know how cooped up we are in the town | long journey to the mountain up back down
to fetch wood and one my folk fear to make | as for Hector's obsequies we should take
nine days within our own homes mourning him | and on the tenth day we should bury him
hold the funeral feast the eleventh | build him a mound and if need be the twelfth
we'll fight" "My venerable lord everything | shall be as you wish I'll stop the fighting
for the time you need" he gripped the old man | by the wrist of right rite hand so to ban
-ish from his heart any apprehension | Priam and herald settled down fear shun
for the night in the building's fine forecourt | many things their busy minds giving thought
while Achilles slept in a hut corner | beautiful Briseis herself corner
-ed by his side all others men under | arms and gods spent whole night in the wonder
-full soft lap of sleep Hermes god of Luck | wondered just what the pluck-y piece of luck
he may then need pluck King Priam away | from the black ships unchallenged on the way
by trusty gate-watchmen could get no sleep | in the end he went up to the head deep
Priam's couch said "My lord it seems that since | Achilles now spared you do not eVince
Kompany misgivings judge by soundness | of your slumbers in oppo camp recess
he's let you have the body of your son | at a great price and would not any son
left have to pay three times as much for you | if King whole army came to know that you
are here?" the old man's fears aroused he woke | up the herald and Hermes did then yoke
the mules and horses and drove them quickly | through camp passed not recognised by any
the King as Dawn her saffron cloak did spread | over the country lighting way ahead
reached ford Xanthus eddy(fy)ing use | noble river Father's immortal Zeus
Hermes took leave off to high Olympus | two wailing weeping drove the horses thus
towards town while mules came with the body | Cassandra as Golden Aphrodite
as beautiful was first among the men | and of Ilium the girdled women
-folk to recognise them as they came she'd | climbed to the top of Pergamus whence she'd
seen her father stood in the chariot | with his herald town-crier stood out lot
she saw Hector too lying on a bier | in the mule-cart gave a scream piercing clear
and cried aloud for all the town to hear | "Trojans and women of Troy you used here
to welcome Hector when he came home safe | from battle and he was the darling safe
to say of every soul in the city | so go out there now and feel the pity"
Cassandra's cries plunged the whole of the town | in grief soon no man woman left in town

went down meet with Hector's body the King | at no great distance from gateway being
and his loving wife and mother lady | fell upon the well-built waggon to be
first pluck out their hair for him touch his head | by a wailing throng they were surrounded
and the townsfolk would have stayed there indeed | all of them all day by the gates at need
wept for Hector all day long 'til sunset | if the old man still in chariot set
had not commanded them then to make way | for the horses and mules and told them they
could mourn for Hector later hearts' content | when he'd got him home the admonishment
caused the folk to fall back on either side | made passage for cart through ticket to ride
let family bring Hector to palace | there laid him on wooden bed put in place
musicians to lead the laments sing then | the melancholy dirges the women
wailing in chorus and Andromache | white-armed holding the head of Hector he
once killer of men between each fair hand | presented there their first lament "Husband
you were too young to die leave me widowed | in our home with your son who we so sowed
wretched parents to come into the world | is but a little baby be unfurled
into a man I have no hope for Troy | will tumble before he's even a boy
you her guardian ever have perished | her loyal wives little babies cherished
kept all safe they will be carried off soon | far from town dancing to another's tune
and I with them and you my child will too | go with me at a menial task to
labour wherever under a heartless | master's eye or an Argive in excess
of fury will seize you by the arm hurl | you down from the wall to a death most cruel
venting his wrath on you because Hector | killed a brother of his or his father
or a son yes for when he met Hector | many an Achaean bit the dust for
your father by no means a soul kindly | in the heat of battle and that's why we
whole of Troyland for him now is wailing | ah Hector such desolation trailing
utter to your parents and yet who shall | mourn you as I? as mine is overall
the bitterest of regrets as you did | not die in bed as stretched your arms out bid
me love give me some tender word that I might | have treasured in my tears by day and night"
so Andromache's lament the women | joined her Hecabe took up for them then
the impassioned dirge "Ah Hector dearest | of all my sons the gods loved not the least
while you were still with me in the world now | Destiny's called don't forget you anyhow
swift-foot Achilles took more than one son | of mine sent them over the seas barren
to sail for sale in Samos or Imbros | even in far-away smoke-capped Lemnos
and he took your life with his long bronze blade | but though dragged you oft round the barrow made
for friend you killed (though not brought Patroclus | back to life) you have come back home as flush
as fresh morning dew laid in the palace | like one been visited by Phoebus ace
Apollo of the Silver Bow and put | to death with gentle darts" her words sobs put
all the women into grief unbridled | then Helen with a third lament bridled
"Hector I loved you far the best of all | my Trojan brothers Prince Paris withal
brought me here and married me (I wish I | had died first) but in nineteen years since I
came away to Troy from my own country | a single harsh or spiteful word only
from you have I never heard but others | in the house insulted me your brothers
sisters brothers' wealthy wives your mother | even though if he were mine your father

could not be more gentle with me but you | protested every time and stopped them you
did that out of the kindness of your heart | in your own courteous way these tears tart
I shed both for you my self miserable | no-one else left in the wide realm dismal
of Troy to treat me gently befriend me | and as I pass them they shudder at me"
so Helen through her tears and the countless | multitude wailed with her then the dauntless
King Priam told his folk what they must do | "Trojans bring firewood to the town and do
not be afraid of Argive ambuscade | when he let me leave the ships promise made
me Achilles that they would not attack | 'til dawn of twelfth day from then" on that t/rack
on Priam's orders mules and bullocks yoked | to their waggons and speedily convoked
outside town took them nine days to collect | huge amount wood for pyre project select
but when the dawn of the tenth day brought light | to the world they bore out he of the bright
flashing helm with tears on their cheeks and laid | his body on top of barrow they'd made
then set fire to the wood Dawn came once more | lighting the East rosy-fingered saw sore
the folk flocking together pyre Hector | illustrious when all come full sector
vector complete they began by drenching | with sparkling wine and thus the fire quenching
in all parts of the pyre the flames had bleached | Hector's brothers and comrades-in-arms reached
into the charred remains and collected | his white bones as labouring dejected
lamented many large tears cheeks lapping | took the bones in soft purple cloths wrapping
put them in a golden chest they lowered | quickly into hollow grave they flowered
layer large stones closely set together | hasty-built barrow sentinels hover
on perimeter in case host Argive'd | attack them before the time they'd aggrieved
when they'd made the mound went back into Troy | foregathered again did deploy enjoy
a splendid banquet in palace of King | Priam of almighty Zeus a nursling
such were the funeral rites of Hector | horse-tamer nevermore now forever*
(Dawn's ten-year tenure war worlds does resume | Fate's deadly course threats Earth's demos consume
then there came woman of the Amazons | Penthesilea of those she the Queen's
save then in mortal combat Achilles | as kills her sees eyes love of his life she's
gone as with planet we came to(o) late love/ killing her not softly with her the dove
all our beautiful flora fauna love/ love and only love can save us now love

τό τέλος
THE END

Postscriptum/scrappe(n)dum(b)planet

the way that this tall tale tail's now wending/ we all need to write
a happy ending

* For the last line "Such were the funeral rites of Hector, tamer of horses", some authorities substitute "And now there came an Amazon..." This suggests the line was used by poets after Homer as a link to continue story. We know that such continuations were made, and the next episode is the arrival at Troy of the Amazon Queen, Penthesilea.

# GLOSSARY

## 1) – Achaeans/ Argives/ Danaans (not yet Greeks)

**ACHILLES** – Son of Peleus and a Sea-Nymph Thetis; Prince of the Myrmidons of Phthia in Thessaly. The central figure of the book, where his death at hands of Paris and Apollo is foretold.

**AGAMEMNON** – Son of Atreus and Aerope, oft called Atreides; King of Mycenae, overlord of all Achaea. Elder brother of Menelaus – the pair are called the Atreidae – and C-in-C of the forces at Troy.

**AIANTES** – Plural of Aias.

**AIAS** – Son of Oileus, leader of Locrians. Distinguished from greater namesake as the lesser Aias, or the Runner. Also a marked difference in character – insolent and conceited – as seen in the funeral games.

**AIAS** – Son of Telamon, King of Salamis. Distinguished from the lesser Aias as the great or Telamonian Aias.

**ANTILOCHUS** – Son of Nestor. Plays more prominent role in the fighting and the funeral games than brother Thrasymedes. Younger brother is Peistratus.

**ATREIDES** – Son of Atreus; used for Agamemnon and Menelaus, oft called the two Atreidae.

**AUTOMEDON** – Son of Diores; a Myrmidon, squire of Achilles, serves as driver for Patroclus when he fights without Achilles.

**CALCHAS** – Son of Thestor; chief augur/prophet of Argive expedition.

**DIOMEDES** – Son of Tydeus and Deipyle; King of Argos. Homer's very fond of him and his father. His character's a striking contrast to Achilles'.

**EURYPLYUS** – Son of Eumaeon of Ormenion. Wounded by Paris.

**HELEN** – Daughter of Zeus by Lede, wife of Tyndareus. (Unlike later poets Homer doesn't seem to believe that Lede was visited by Zeus as a swan and Helen issued from an egg.) Sister of Castor and Polydeuces, and of Clytaemnestra. Wed to Menelaus of Sparta. Ran off with/abducted by Trojan prince·Paris to Troy, where spent 19 years as his wife.

**IDOMENEUS** – Son of Deucalion; King of Crete. One of the ablest and most amiable of Agamemnon's captains.

**MACHAON** – Son of Asclepius, the famous physician. He and his brother Podaleirius are the chief surgeons with the Argive forces.

**MENELAUS** – Son of Atreus; King of Lacedaemon/Sparta, and younger brother of Agamemnon.

**MENESTHEUS** – Son of Peteos; King of Athens, and leader of the Athenian contingent.

**MERIONES** – Son of Molus; nephew and squire of King Idomeneus, and second-in-charge of the Cretan forces

**NESTOR** – Son of Neleus; King of Pylos. The oldest of the Achaean chieftains.

**ODYSSEUS** – Son of Laertes and Anticleia; King of Ithaca.

**PATRODUS** – Son of Menoetius of Opus; the squire and dose friend of Achilles.

**PHOENIX** – Son of Amyntor; King of the Dolopes. An old friend of Achilles, whose father made him Achilles' tutor.

**STHENELUS** – Son of Capaneus; squire to Diomedes.

**TALTHYBIUS** – chief herald of Agamemnon.

**TEUCER** – Son of Telamon and a mistress, Hesione. Half-brother of the greater Aias. Best bowman in the Achaean force.

**THERSITES** –A rank-and-file critic of the top brass. Killed by Achilles for jeering at him when he became sentimental after killing the Amazon Queen, Penthesilea.

**TLEPOLEMUS** – Son of Herades and Astyocheia; an Argive prince who settled in Rhodes.

## 2) – Trojans and their Allies (Ilium is used as a synonym for Troy, the Trojan capital)

**ANDROMACHE** – Daughter of Eetion, King of Thebe-under-Placus; wife of Hector and mother of Astyanax/Scamandrius.

**AENEAS** – Son of Aphrodite and Anchises; a Trojan noble, second-in-charge after Hector. A third cousin of Hector, but of the younger branch of the line of Dardanus. Homer hints at his disaffection with Priam and the ruling house.

**BRISEIS** – Daughter of Brises of Lymessus, which Achilles sacked and then captured her. Agamemnon later took her from him to compensate for his loss of Chryseis.

**CASSANDRA** – Daughter of Priam and Hecabe; she was a prophetess whose prophetic warnings were ignored because she rejected the advances of Apollo.

**CHRYSEIS** – Daughter of Chryses, the priest of Apollo at Chryse, near Troy. Agamemnon was forced by Apollo to give her back to her father

**DEIPHOBUS** – Son of Priam and Hecabe; a Prince of Troy

**GLAUCUS** – Son of Hippolochus; a Lycian Prince. Second-in-charge of the Lycian allies to Sarpedon, his first cousin.

**HECABE** – consort of King Priam, to whom she bore many sons including Hector, Helenus and Deiphobus.

**HECTOR** – Son of Priam and Hecabe; a Prince of Troy, and C-in-C of the Trojans and allies. We're supposed to regard Hector as Priam's eldest son and heir, but all else in the story points to Paris, who is maybe forty in the book, whereas Hector's a newly-married of 25 at most. Homer's departed from earlier versions where Paris was the eldest, and created Hector as heir as he needed a better foil for Achilles than the character of Paris.

**HELENUS** – Son of Priam and Hecabe; Prince of Troy. Like his sister Cassandra gifted with second sight.

**IDAEUS** – Chief herald of Priam.

**PANDARUS** – Son of Lycaon; a Lycian commander. A treacherous fool.

**PARIS** – Son of Priam and Hecabe; Prince of Troy. Homer refers to his abduction of Helen as the cause of the war, making only one passing reference to the famous Judgement of Paris of the three goddesses Aphrodite, Here and Athene, which as Aphrodite was chosen as the most beautiful – and as offering as prize Helen, the world's most beautiful woman – may explain Here and Athene's relentless hostility to Paris-ian Troy.

**POLYDAMAS** – Son of Panthous; one of the ablest Trojan leaders. Seemingly a commoner, or not one of the ruling house. A cautious, dear-headed strategist who Homer uses as a foil for Hector.

**PRIAM** – Son of Laomedon, and descendent of Dardanus son of Zeus; King of Troy

**SARPEDON** – Son of Zeus and Laodameia, the daughter of Bellerophon; King of Lycia and leader of the Lycian allies.

## 3) – The Gods-esses

**APHRODITE** – Daughter of Zeus and Dione; the goddess of Love. On Trojan side (of course), rescuing her admirer/protege Paris and her son Aeneas, and coming to the aid of her lover, Ares the War-god. Thought to have been Cyprus-born

**APOLLO** – Son of Zeus and Leto, also called Phoebus or Phoebus Apollo; the god of Prophecy, Poetry and Music. Also the Archer-King, patron of bowmen. Sudden deaths by disease, not violence, are attributed to his darts. Also the protector of herds. On the Trojan side, having a shrine in Pergamus, and a bitter critic of Achilles.

**ARES** – Son of Zeus and Here; the god of War. Though he promised Here and Athene to help the Achaeans he fights for Troy, and in the battle of the gods-esses is ignominiously dismissed by Athene. The term "offshoot of Ares" which Homer applies to several warriors is puzzling. It doesn't seem to mean "son", as in some cases the man's father is mentioned.

**ARTEMIS** – Daughter of Zeus and Leto, and Sister of Apollo; the goddess of the Chase, Mistress of the Bow, and Protectress of wild animals. One of her functions was to kill women with her "gentle darts", i.e. sudden death by disease. She fights on the Trojan side, not very effectively, no doubt following her brother.

**ATE** – Daughter of Zeus; a personification of blind folly or infatuation rather than a goddess.

**ATHENE** – Daughter of Zeus (mother not named), also called Pallas Athene or Athena; the goddess of Wisdom and the Patroness of the arts and crafts. She is also the Protectress of cities and a fighting goddess (though not in the same sense as Enyo, the goddess of War), being on occasion entrusted with the magic arms of Zeus, whose thunder she can also wield. Plays a key part in the war for the Argives – though she has a shrine in Troy – no doubt because of her defeat in the Judgement of Paris, the Trojan who gave the win to Aphrodite. (Homer doesn't mention the legend of her springing fully-armed from the head of Zeus.)

**CRONOS** – Father of Zeus, Poseidon, Hades and Here; the ex-King who had been deposed by Son Zeus.

**DEMETER** – Daughter of Cronos; the goddess of Corn and fruitfulness. Mother by Zeus of Persephone, the Queen of Hades. Little mentioned in the Iliad.

**DIONE** – Mother of Aphrodite by Zeus.

**DIONYSUS** – Son of Zeus and Semele; mentioned only twice. Homer doesn't say he is the god of Wine, only that he was born to give "pleasure to mankind"

**EILEITHYIA** – Daughter of Here; goddess of childbirth; often in the plural.

**HADES** – Son of Cronos and Rhea; the god of the Dead, who received the underworld as his domain when he and his brothers Zeus and Poseidon divided the world between them.

**HEBE** – Daughter of Zeus and Here; a cupbearer and handmaiden to the gods-esses.

**HEPHAESTUS** – Son of Zeus and Here; the Master-smith and great Artificer and Architect of Olympus. Seemingly born a cripple. On the Argive side, and as the god of Fire is called on by by Here to save Achilles from the River Xanthus. Wed to Charis.

**HERE** – Daughter of Cronos and Rhea, and so a Sister of Zeus as well as his official Consort and Queen of Olympus. Full support to the Argives, for same reason as Athene. Also the goddess of motherhood and so controls the Eileithyiae, the minor goddesses of childbirth.

**HERMES** – Son of Zeus and Maia; the ambassador of the gods-esses, though in the Iliad Iris is used more often. He is also the Bringer of Luck. Constantly referred to as the Slayer of the monster Argus. For the Argives, but does little to help them.

**IRIS (THE RAINBOW)** –A Messenger of the gods-esses, especially in the Iliad ( far more so than Hermes.) Occasionally obliges mortals of her own accord, e.g. Helen and Achilles.

**LETO** – Daughter of Cronos and Phoebe; mother of Apollo and Artemis by Zeus.

**PALLAS ATHENE** – see under Athene.

**PERSEPHONE** – Queen of the Dead; see under(-world) Hades.

**PHOEBUS APOLLO** – see under Apollo.

**POSEIDON** – Son of Cronos and Rhea, and a younger brother of Zeus, who received the sea as his domain when with other brother Hades divided the world by lot between them. Also the god of Earthquakes. For the Argives, having an old grudge against Troy (see Book 21) but not always as vehement as his Sister Here.

**STRIFE (ERIS)** – Sister of Ares the War-god; a personification rather than a goddess in the ordinary sense.

**THETIS** – Daughter of Nereus, the Old Man of the Sea; a Sea-Nymph who married a mortal, King Peleus, and became mother of Achilles. Keen supporter of Achilles, but not otherwise concerned in the war.

**XANTHUS** – the god of one of the two chief rivers of the Trojan plain (alias Scamander, plus his brother Simois.) A Son of Zeus, who as god of the Sky is the Father of"heaven-fed" rivers. Homer uses the name Xanthus for a river in Lycia, a horse of Hector, and one of Achilles' immortal horses. The word is nearly the same as that for"red-haired" Menelaus, and seems to indicate the colour of ripe corn.

**ZEUS** – Son of Cronos and Rhea; the supreme Olympian deity. As the minister of Destiny, he is neutral in the war, but supports Achilles in his feud with Agamemnon. Shows great sympathy for the Trojans, especially Hector and Priam.